BSA SINGLES RESTORATION

BSA SINGLES RESTORATION

Gold Star and all post-war pre-unit B, M and C series, plus unit four-strokes and Bantams

Roy Bacon

ANDOVER NORTON

Published by Andover Norton International Ltd
Unit 3 Standen Manor Farm, Standen Manor,
HUNGEFORD, Berkshire, RG17 0RB
First published in 1988 by Osprey Publishing

A CIP catalogue record for this book is available from the British Library

Bacon, Roy H

BSA singles restoration: the most comprehensive guide to the renovation, restoration and development history of all post-war pre-unit BSA singles including the Gold Star, B, M and C series, plus unit four-strokes and Bantams.

1. B.S.A. motorcycle – Conservation and restoration

I. Title

629.2′275 TL448.B2

ISBN 978-0-9570665-2-6

Reprinted in China through World Print Ltd.

FRONT JACKET ILLUSTRATION Don't all scream at once - we know it is a bike which BSA never built. It is purely a figment of the imagination of artist Selwyn Hutchinson, who used an origina A7 brochure to produce a jacket in the style of Osprey's other restoration books.

HALF-TITLE ILLUSTRATION A 1947 B31 parked in a village street which reflects the sparse traffic of the early post-war years A typical BSA task of visiting the local shops.

TITLE-PAGE ILLUSTRATION D.T.Powell emerging from Governers Bridge during practice for the 1951 Clubmans on his 348cc Gold Star. He retired that year but won in 1953.

CONTENTS

BSA
BANTAM
TCR386

Acknowledgements

As the fourth title in the series this book should have been easier to write, but in practice the sheer profusion of BSA models gave problems. Despite these, the prime aim of providing parts identification has been followed even at the expense of some of the more standard techniques included in the other titles. The appendices with the basics of dating, colour and specifications remain in full, along with much more.

Again I have to thank my good friend Don Mitchell who supplied most of the basic data from his stock of second-hand motorcycle literature. Other material of this type came from Dick Lewis, long-time BSA specialist at Weybridge although now retired, and some gaps on export models were filled by Bill Litant, President of the BSA Owners Club of New England.

I am especially indebted to Michael Payne who went through the whole manuscript to check on all Gold Star details. His very considerable knowledge of these machines was reflected in the many detail points he raised and corrections or additions made to the book.

The pictures and line drawings came mainly from the EMAP archives which hold the old *Motor Cycle Weekly* files, for which my grateful thanks. Others were from the *Motor Cycle News* files, courtesy of editor Malcolm Gough, and a number from Amal, BSA and Lucas material originally.

A number of pictures carried the imprint of a professional and photos used came from Cecil Bailey, Frank Dann, Keystone Press Agency, Bruce Main-Smith, Donald Page, Planet News, Brian Smith, Studio Cave and W. Wickstone. As usual all the pictures were returned to their files after publication and I have tried to make contact to clear copyright. If my letter failed to reach you or I have used an unmarked print without realizing this, please accept my apologies.

Finally, my thanks to Tim Parker for conceiving the idea of this series and to Tony Thacker, my present editor, for his help and assistance in completing this volume.

Roy Bacon
Niton, Isle of Wight
November 1987

LEFT *A 1957 Bantam D1 being awarded as a prize in a road-safety competition. The winner, Mrs Cooper, had no licence and the Lady Mayoress of Southampton tries the awkwardly-placed horn button*

OVERLEAF *A 1950 shot of Bill Nicholson riding in the Victory Cup Trial. His machine is a B32 fitted with the all-alloy engine*

Our policy

This book began as others in the Osprey restoration series, but it was soon realized that the vast range of models and all the data on BSA singles would far outstrip the space available. Because of this it was not practical to publish it in the same style as the others, and if we had, the sheer bulk would have been a major handful to use in lounge or workshop.

To cope with this, the book has been revised as a parts information guide complete with all the machine data usually included. What have had to go are the sections on techniques, which are general matters common to all the books.

That information is still to be found in the other restoration books, so if guidance is needed a visit to the local library should give you the answer. It could be best to ask for *BSA Twin Restoration*, but the Norton or Triumph titles should be equally helpful.

In addition to this source, Osprey are producing a series of books on motorcycle restoration techniques which will cover all the main areas involved. These go into greater depth as they are designed to do just this and show the why and how along with some of the wrinkles that make the job easier.

This has allowed all the data unique to the BSA singles to be gathered together rather than the more general information. The data relates to production models built from 1945 to 1973 and to standard UK specification. It does not cover, but should help with, the late pre-war models or the export ones which differ from the home-specification models for which data is included where known.

In all cases, and regardless of the final aim, it is hoped that this book will assist and guide the reader to produce the machine of his or her dreams. It is also hoped that the result will be sound in wind and limb and every endeavour has been made to offer advice which is helpful and safe. However, the onus is always on the reader to ensure that any machine he or she works on or rides is in a safe and legal condition. If you decide to carry out a modification, you must make certain that it will work properly.

Neither the author nor the publisher can accept any liability for anything contained in this book which may result in any loss, damage or injury, and the book is only available for purchase or loan on that basis.

Machine year

Chapter 1 gives details of the way in which models are dated, which causes, for example, 1953 models to run from late 1952 to late 1953. Because of this, the text will use the model year without constant repetition that the feature or model was introduced late in the previous calendar year.

Engine and frame numbers take precedence over model year in determining when a change took place and have been noted where necessary. Parts lists, coupled with these numbers, are always the correct way back to original specification.

Your skills

This book is not a workshop manual, nor is it a primer on being a motorcycle mechanic. It has to assume that you know how your machine works and have a good idea as to how to maintain it. Also that you have a degree of mechanical aptitude and have worked on motorcycles to some extent.

Specifications

There are no extensive tables of data in this book, as much of it is in *BSA Gold Star & Other Singles* (Osprey Publishing) and the rest in workshop manuals. Collect as much data and information as possible to cover your model and year before starting, but remember that part of the art of restoration is knowing which items matter. Most books don't tell you. So there are no endless lists of gaps, settings or tolerances, while the figures and data that are provided are there to back up the manual.

Note

To avoid constant detailing, the singles will be referred to as pre-unit, unit or Bantam. The first is any of the C, B and M ranges, including the Gold Star series. The unit models are those built from 1959 onwards, starting with the C15, and the Bantams run from the D1 to the D175 of 1971.

An M21 belonging to the AA doing stalwart duty on Canvey Island during the floods of 1953. The patrolman is in contact with his HQ using a valve radio and seems to be bearing up with the rigid rear end

1 Early stages

The BSA company produced single-cylinder motorcycles from 1910 onwards and most were in the firm's tradition of offering solid, dependable transport backed by good service.

The post-war range began with just four models of 249 and 496 cc sv or 249 and 348 cc ohv engines. From this small revival it soon expanded to add many, many more. For 1959 the first unit-construction four-stroke was introduced and in time grew from 247 to 499 cc. During all this time, the Bantam went from 123 to 172 cc.

History

The post-war singles range really all stemmed from the pre-war 1937 line designed by the brilliant Val Page. In 1936 he had moved to BSA and set to work sorting out their rather complex range of singles.

The result was a line of simple four-stroke engines in sizes from 250 to 600 cc and with side valves or ohv. There were variations in specification of the cycle parts, but all the engines now had dry-sump lubrication, the electrics tucked in behind the cylinder and a very similar form of construction. All now used a simple tubular frame and dispensed with the 'forged steel backbone' much publicized in BSA advertisements during the earlier 1930s. From these basics, an extensive range of models was built up.

In 1938 the famous Gold Star model first appeared in the range, following Wal Handley's win of such an award at Brooklands in June 1937, and for 1939 its Empire Star companion became the Silver Star. Less exciting was the side-valve, 249 cc C10, first seen early in 1938, and its ohv companion, the C11 of 1939.

During the war BSA produced the side-valve M20 in large numbers plus some C10s for training. They thought that something better than the M20 ought to be available to the services so they devised the WB30. This was based on the B29 which was to have been the Silver Sports model of 1940, and although of 348 cc it used the heavier M-range crankcase.

A small batch of WB30 machines were built but then events moved on and just the M20 was produced for the rest of the war. However, from the design work of this period came the B31 of the post-war years which formed the basis of the pre-unit B range. It was announced in August 1945 and with it there were the 249 cc C10 and C11, plus the 496 cc M20.

These four were quickly joined by the 348 cc competition model B32 and the larger 591 cc side-valve M21 early in 1946. For 1947 the 348 cc models were bored out to 499 cc and listed in B33 and competition B34 forms. The year 1948 brought more variation and a brand-new model in the form of the 123 cc Bantam two-stroke. At first, only the engine unit was listed, but in June the complete machine appeared. Others introduced that year were the C11 in de luxe form and the M33, which was an ohv B33 engine fitted into the M-range cycle parts to produce a more spritely sidecar outfit.

The first year really for the Bantam was 1949, and with it came plunger-frame options for the B range plus some more sporting machines. Two of these were listed as scrambles specials and were B32 models in either rigid or plunger frame, while the third machine was much more interesting for it marked the return of the Gold Star but, for the first time, with a 348 cc engine as the B32GS. It had the plunger frame as standard and was in time referred to as the ZB type, this being its engine number prefix.

The scrambles specials were not listed for 1950 but a 499 cc version of the Gold Star was, as the B34GS. In addition, both the B32 and B34 were listed as being available with Gold Star engines which essentially meant the light-alloy head and barrel. Thus for 1950 and 1951, the two years this option was listed, it was possible for a genuine B32 and B34 frame to have a Gold Star engine complete with its GS prefix stamping and for this to be a factory build and not a hybrid. In theory this option also applied to the B31 and B33 for 1950, while the alloy-engine option ran on for the B32 and B34 to the end of 1953.

The year 1950 saw the Bantam available with Lucas ignition as well as Wipac, with plunger frame as well as rigid and in competition form as well as road. Thus the different combinations available gave a total of eight possible models. The C range had to wait another year, to 1951, for its plunger frame but at the same time it also gained a four-speed gearbox option and,

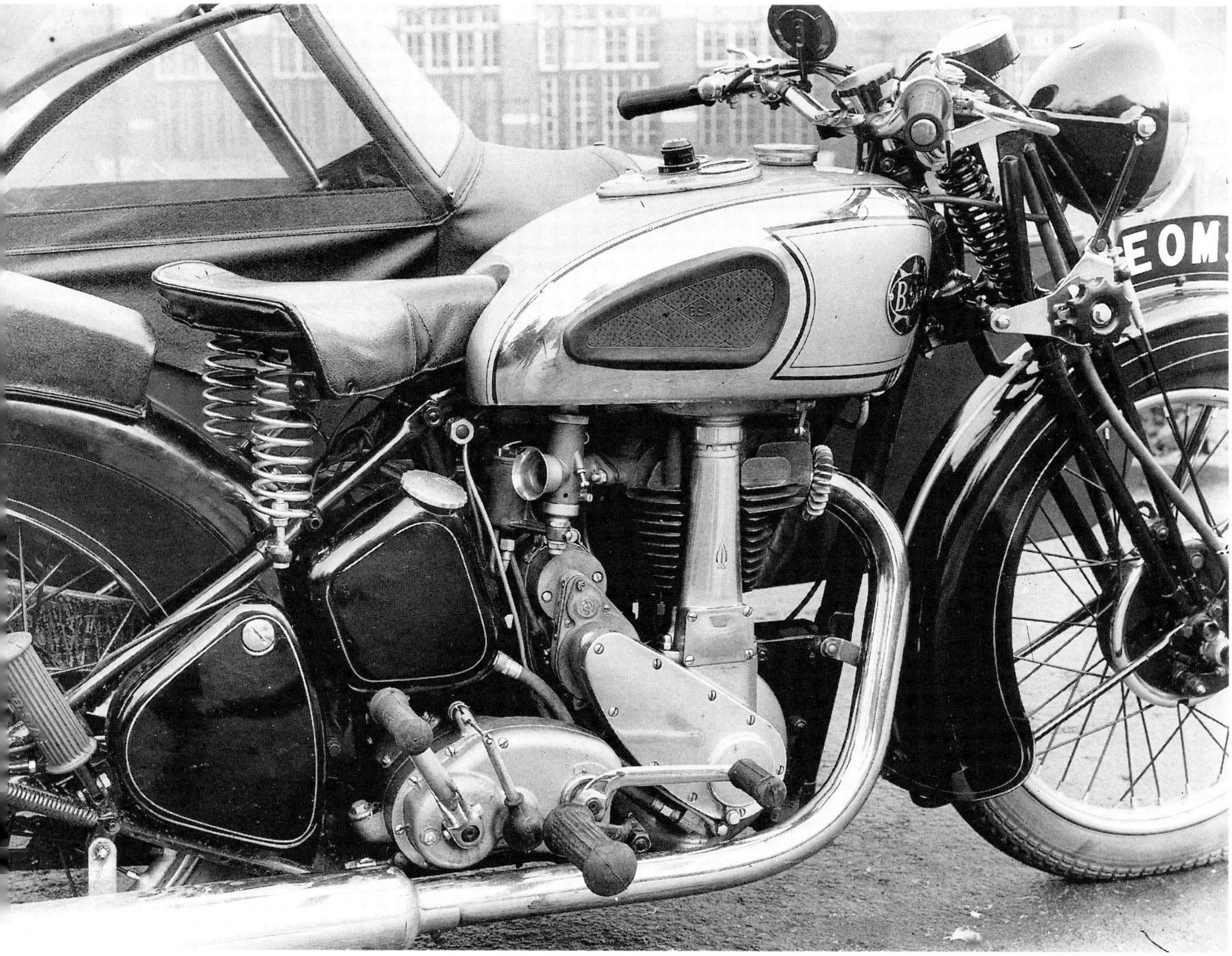
EOM

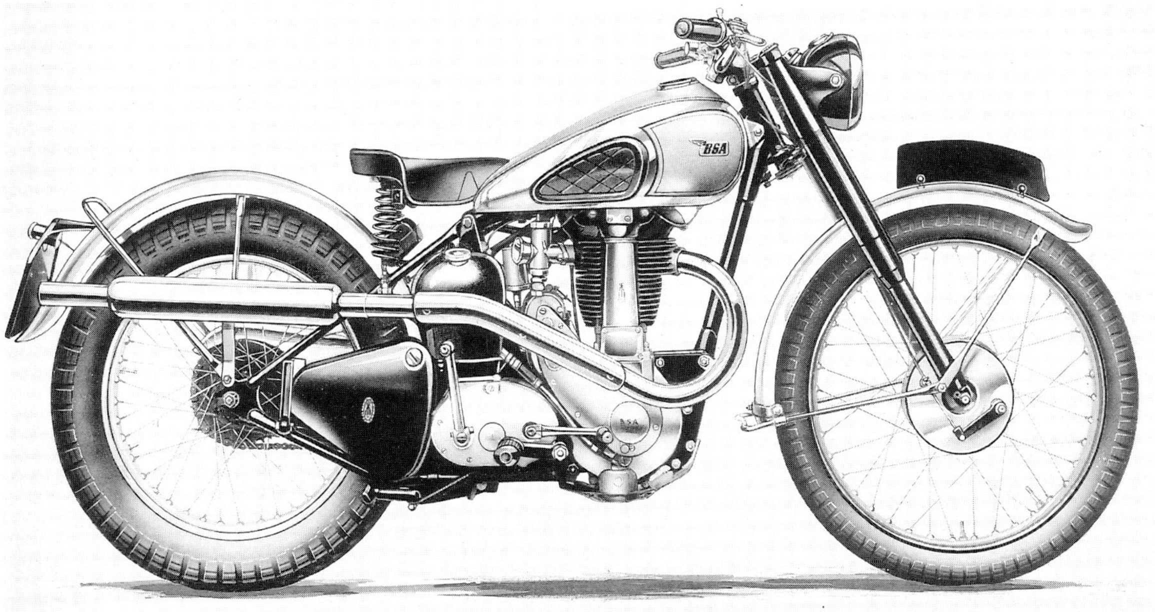
BSA

LEFT *This is a 1939 M23 Silver Star from which the post-war B range was developed; it has the tank top panel common to the time*

BELOW LEFT *The first post-war competition model in the form of the 348 cc B32, with speedometer in petrol tank and little different from the B31*

ABOVE *The prosaic 249 cc C11 from 1946 was offered as a basic ride-to-work machine—still with girder forks at this point*

OVERLEAF *The New York Show of April 1950 with a Gold Star in road trim along with several twins*

along with the de luxe option which continued, this produced four C10 and six C11 variations. That same year the three M models also gained the option of the plunger frame.

The option of the Gold Star engine for the B32 and B34 stopped for 1952 but otherwise the ranges continued as they did for 1953, except that the Gold Star models became the BB series in a pivoted-fork frame.

There was more action for 1954 with the B range changing to a pivoted-fork frame and the big-finned CB series of Gold Star engines appearing while the BB ones continued. At the other end of the scale the Bantam variants with a Lucas generator went, but a 148 cc series came in as the D3 in standard, competition and plunger-framed forms. At the same time the C10 and C11 were replaced by the C10L and C11G with alternators and, in the case of the ohv model, options of plunger or rigid frame and three- or four-speed gearbox.

At the end of 1954 the rigid B-range road models went, as did the plunger ones and the M20 in 1955. For 1955 the BB and CB versions of the Gold Star were joined by the DB but only this last continued for 1956 when the DBD34 also made its appearance. For 1956 the B range was thus down to the four basic machines, all with pivoted-fork frames, plus the three Gold Stars. The M range comprised the plunger-frame M33 and the M21 in rigid or plunger forms, while the C range was reduced to the side-valve C10L and the ohv C12, a C11G engine in a pivoted-fork frame. On the Bantam front the competition models had gone, leaving the D1 and D3 in direct- or battery-lighting forms but in plunger or pivoted-fork frames respectively.

They all stayed as they were for 1957 but for 1958 the road B range changed to alternator electrics and the D3 was dropped in favour of the 172 cc D5, again with a choice of electrics. The D1 and C12 models continued but the C10L, B32, B34 and M33 all went, as did the 348 cc Gold Star and the DB version of the 500. At the same time the M21 went from the lists, although it remained available to special order for a few more years. The last of the rigid-frame M21s went in 1960 but the plunger frame ran on to 1963, mainly for the AA and some armed forces.

However, 1959 brought the first of the unit-construction models in the form of the 247 cc C15, plus the trials C15T and scrambles C15S versions, while the 172 cc D7 Bantam replaced the D5. The C12 was no longer listed but the 348 cc Gold Star reappeared as a DB34 fitted with the smaller engine. The road B range was still there but the B31 went at the end of the year and the B33 during the middle of 1960.

SUNBEAM
BSA
BSA

BSA
BSA

ABOVE *Taken in April 1951, this photo shows how popular the D1 model was from its inception during 1948; still much the same as when launched, but plus plungers*

ABOVE RIGHT *First-place tie in the Tasmanian 421-mile trial of 1951 was shared between these two BSA riders*

Otherwise there were no changes for 1960, but for 1961 the 343 cc B40 appeared as a larger model on the unit-construction theme, and in April it was joined by the SS80 sports version of the C15. In May 1962 came the 343 cc equivalent, the SS90, and about the same time the DB32GS came to a stop, few having been built in that final year.

There was nothing new for 1963 and at the end of the year the last of the links with the early post-war days went with the end of the M21, the DBD34 Gold Star and the little D1 Bantam.

For 1964 there were de luxe versions of the D7 Bantam as well as the two standard ones with direct or battery lighting. All models ran on into 1965 which was a significant year for the four-strokes on two counts. First was a change to timing-cover points for all, and second was the appearance of the B44GP Victor Grand Prix with a 441 cc engine. This model was built solely for scrambles but its engine contained many changes which were to appear in all the other machines in time.

The C15T and C15S were both dropped at the end of 1965 along with the B40 and SS90. The SS80 changed its name to the C15 Sportsman for 1966 and both it and the C15 had their bottom halves revised in July to the B44 design with ball and roller mains. In the larger class the B44VE Victor Enduro appeared in trail bike format and in the 172 cc class the standard Bantams took the name Silver while the de luxe ones ran on.

Most of the range changed for 1967 with a new 247 cc model listed as the C25 and called the Barracuda. This used the Victor crankcase and a new square-fin barrel to enclose a super-sports specification. The Victor Enduro continued and was joined by the B44VS Victor Special and the B44VR Victor Roadster styled on the lines of the C25. On the Bantam front the D7 models were replaced by the D10 series and all these had a much improved alternator and the points set in the primary chaincase on the right. Models were the Silver and Supreme, much as the D7, and the Sports and Bushman with four-speed gearboxes. The latter was built for off-road use.

The 247 cc single changed its name and number in 1968 to the B25 Starfire, while the 441 cc road model became the B44SS Shooting Star. The Grand Prix and Victor Enduro were no longer listed but the Victor Special was still there for export only. The Bantam range became the D14, all with four-speed gearboxes, and listed in standard, Sports and Bushman forms.

For 1969 the Bantams changed their number once more to become the D175 model listed simply in Bantam or Bushman form but with a new head with central plug and many detail changes. The four-strokes were unchanged but were joined by the B25 Fleetstar which was a utility version of the Starfire and aimed at bulk users. It did not continue into 1970 but the remaining models did.

Major changes were made to the four-strokes for 1971 with the oil carried in the frame tubes and the larger models stretched out to a full 499 cc. There were three of them listed as the B50SS Gold Star 500 Street Scrambler, B50T Victor 500 Trail and B50MX Victor 500 Motocross. The smaller models were the B25SS Gold Star 250 Street Scrambler and the B25T Victor 250 Trail.

Due to their financial troubles, BSA only listed the standard Bantam for 1971 and dropped it early in the year, while the 247 cc singles went later. The 499 cc ones lasted a little longer with the B50MX continuing into 1973 but not the other two.

The B25 was also built using the Triumph label in 1968 as the TR25W Trophy in a trail format. Changes

ABOVE *Bernard Codd in the 1956 Senior Clubmans, which he won along with the Junior to complete the double on Gold Stars*

LEFT *A 1952 M21 with AA sidecar on duty in Madras in southern India. Smart salute!*

were cosmetic or to suit the off-road use and this model continued up to 1970. For 1971 there were two more copies of the final BSA 250 listed as the road T25SS Blazer and the T25T Trail. The final outcome of this badge engineering was the TR5MX Avenger which was simply the B50MX. These machines are described and illustrated more fully in *Triumph Singles* (Osprey Publishing).

This was the end of the BSA singles line, but the B50 did live on to power the CCM machines built by Alan Clews.

Restoration work

This begins with the machine and collecting spares and data for it. The spares situation varies from day to day so you just have to keep hunting and accept that some parts will be harder to locate than others. Basket jobs are much more difficult because they may include spares, but for another machine.

Early on you have to assess what you want to do and how well equipped you are to do it. This means being realistic as to your abilities and accepting that in some areas they are lower than others. Plan around this and your facilities in workshop and tools.

Most of us have to use the garage or shed for restoration and this should be clean, dry and well lit. Equip it with a good, solid work bench and only quality hand tools. Be ruthless with all the others you have accumulated over the years. In addition to spanners you will need tools for making or altering parts and may extend this to the luxury of a lathe and welding gear. These last items will totally change what you can accomplish, so learn to use them well.

Keep all receipts to avoid trouble when you register the machine. Collect data you need in the shape of books, manuals, parts lists and service sheets. Check that engine and frame numbers match for the year as BSA hybrids are common.

Work to a plan and make plenty of notes at each stage as you go along. No one remembers it all, so notes and labels for parts are essential and lists of parts will become part of your life.

Security must be remembered now that classic machines have value so keep things locked up. The small, expensive assemblies such as the magneto, dynamo or carburettor can be kept away from the rest and will benefit from the warmth of your home.

Model choice and dating

The choice of which machine to restore is yours and there is a wide range of model types and engine sizes to select from.

ABOVE *The 247 cc C25 Barracuda on show late in 1966, being inspected as a possible learner model under the 250 cc limit then in force*

ABOVE RIGHT *The factory in 1971 with a line producing unit singles in the new oil-carrying frame*

Dating is complicated by the English industry tradition of starting its model year in August or September. Like most confusion it arose from good intentions and came about because the works switched to making the new models when they returned from their annual holiday. Production was thus well under way with stocks in the warehouse or at the dealers when the new models were announced in the press in the run-up to the Earls Court Show held in November.

Thus the maker's year was out of step with the calendar, so it is quite possible to find a machine first registered in October of the year *before* its style. Further complication for the restorer lies in the change-over of parts which may not coincide with the start of a new model year.

The only answer is to work from the engine and frame numbers using the relevant parts book. This list is a most useful publication and is really an essential for the restorer along with a workshop or maintenance manual. Other helpful items are the rider's handbook and a sales brochure, often the only indication of the colours of the machine and its component parts.

A marque history is well worth having as it will fill out the background and I am biased in recommending *BSA Gold Star & Other Singles* as I wrote it. You should also be reading the specialist magazines, *Classic Bike, Classic Mechanics* and *The Classic Motor Cycle*, to note addresses and articles that could be useful to you. *Classic Bike* now publishes a supplier list in the autumn, usually the October issue, and this is something well worth keeping to hand.

It will also be most useful to join the BSA Owners Club as they offer a unique combined experience. No other body has quite the same outlook and members are in the best position to carry out very real evaluation tests on machines, modifications and their effects. There is also the Vintage Motor Cycle Club in Britain (with others elsewhere) which offers a further source of data, a marque specialist, and from their work has come a transfer scheme now available to all.

Dismantling

Start by thoroughly cleaning the machine and noting exactly where the transfers go. Then remove the parts that are fragile or which impede access to major items. Make plenty of notes before disturbing anything as you will never remember it all.

Be careful that the bars do not swing round and dent the tank as you remove it or that you drop the headlamp rim and break its glass. As soon as you can, get the machine up on a bike bench and make sure it is secure. Aim to remove the engine before the wheels to keep the weight stable.

Work the exhaust system off from the tail and remove seat, tank, controls and wiring. Think about how to store the battery and take off the electrical items. All this will leave the machine looking much cleaner and easier to get at.

From then on follow the normal lines to remove the major parts for attention.

Basket case

In some cases the machine will have come in boxes and this makes the job much harder as seldom will it all be there, despite claims to the contrary. To overcome this, the whole machine has to be built up before restoration to check that it really is all there and that it all fits. It can then be dismantled as above.

36
BSA

2 The engine

Most people like to begin with the engine because it is of the greatest interest to them. It is also likely to be the easiest assembly to restore and the least boring.

Engine types

BSA single-cylinder engines divided into three basic groups which were pre-unit, unit and Bantam. All had variations but the first also subdivided into the B, C and M ranges.

The B range was in essence the 348 cc B31 and 499 cc B33, these being road models, plus the same sizes of competition machine listed as the B32 and B34. It was these that made the picture complex as the series included the Gold Star models along with alloy-engine options. The Gold Star engines all had alloy heads and barrels which in time became the distinctive big-finned types, but the basic competition story was more involved. Both engine sizes began with iron top halves, but an alloy option was listed from 1950 to 1953, while from 1954 onwards the alloy parts were standard. In addition, the model was available fitted with the Gold Star engine for 1950–51, and a B32 scrambles machine existed for 1949 only. The complications of the frames which went with these models are dealt with later.

The B range ran from 1945, when the B31 was introduced, to 1963 when the last DBD34 Gold Star left the factory. The B31 lasted until 1959 with the B33 running on for one more year, while the B32 and B34 both stopped at the end of 1957.

The Gold Star engines at first looked much as the iron engine except that the pushrod tunnel was cast within the head and barrel parts so there was no separate tube; thus the rocker box was cast in one with the head and this design continued up to the end of 1951. From early 1952 for the B34GS, and March 1952 for the B32GS, the design was altered and the major external change was to separate the rocker box from the head. This came in at engine 6001 on the 348 cc and both engines had quite a number of internal changes incorporated at the same time. They continued to be known as the ZB type from the engine number prefix and this remained for 1952. For 1953 they went into a pivoted-rear-fork frame and the type became the BB, but the engine was basically the same and continued with its rather sparse fins up to 1955.

Graham Beamish working on his scrambles Gold Star in 1950 when it had an integral head and rocker box

Alongside it for 1954 came the CB series with big-finned head and barrel in both capacities, and these were built for 1955 as well. In addition, for 1955 the DB type was introduced looking much the same as the CB, so for that one year there were three versions of each size of Gold Star in the lists. For 1956 there were only the DB types and they were joined by the DBD34 which had a larger Amal GP carburettor. In 1958 both the DB32 and DB34 were dropped, but the smaller one came back the next year in the form of a 499 cc model fitted with the 348 cc engine as an option. The DBD34 continued through this and both models then ran on in small numbers until the 348 cc was dropped in late 1962 and the 499 cc a year later.

In comparison the C range was simple. Its design differed in that it had coil ignition and chain drive to the dynamo, but in most other ways the models were simply smaller editions of the basic BSA design. Models were the 249 cc side-valve C10 and ohv C11, which ran to 1953 with some changes to the transmission and cycle parts.

For 1954 they were replaced by the C10L and C11G which differed, engine-wise, only in the adoption of an alternator and points in the timing cover. The side-valve ran to the end of 1957 but from 1956 the ohv engine went into a new frame to create the C12. This then ran on to late 1958.

The M range was just three models with one, the M33, built from 1948 to 1957, using the B33 engine as it was for each year. The others had side valves and were the 496 cc M20 and 591 cc M21. Both were pre-war designs very similar to the B range, but more heavily constructed for long life. The M20 was built up to 1955, while the M21 became available by special order only from 1958 onwards, but continued in this way and for the AA up to 1963.

The unit-construction range included four different

LEFT *The original 1938 499 cc Gold Star engine, which differed in a number of details from the post-war type, fitted with a TT carb*

RIGHT *The engine of the 1947 B33 of 499 cc which was simply an enlarged B31*

BELOW *The 499 cc competition B34 engine with its high-level exhaust system and plated mudguards*

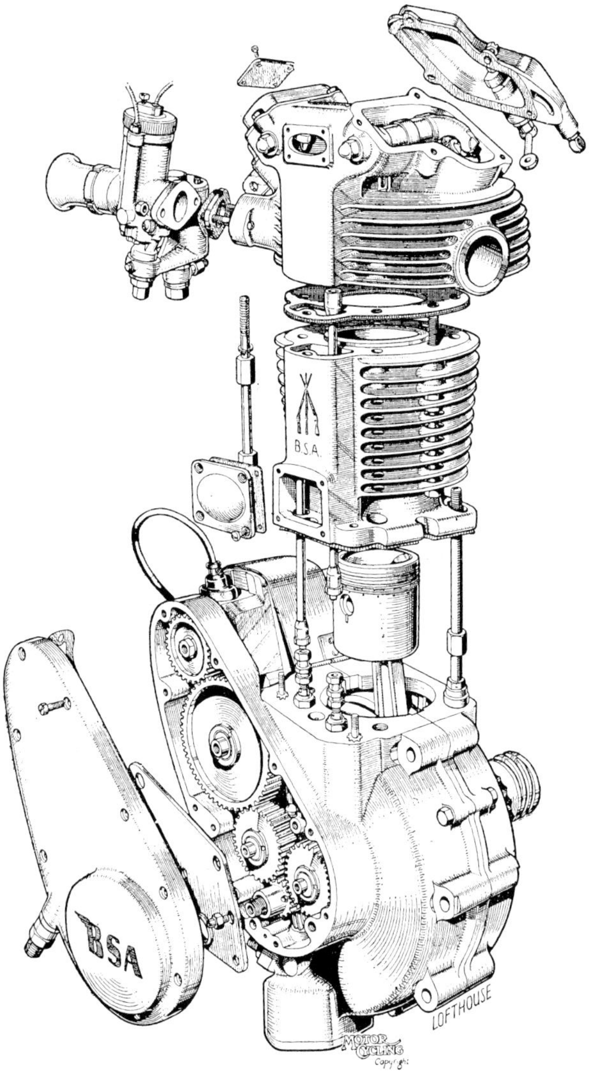

LEFT *The ZB Gold Star engine based firmly on the touring B range*

capacities but really only two basic states of design, both of these having a great deal in common. The start of the range was the 247 cc C15 launched in September 1958 and joined early in 1959 by the C15T trials and C15S scrambles versions.

The year 1961 brought the enlarged 343 cc B40 very much in the same form as the C15 and, during the year, the sports version of the C15 as the SS80. In 1962 it was joined by a matching 343 cc SS90, and these six models continued in this form for the next two years.

For 1965 they all moved their contact-breakers into the timing chest to lose the distributor-type unit from behind the barrel. In addition, the 441 cc Victor Grand Prix appeared in the lists and was important as it represented the second stage of the unit-construction design with a stronger bottom half. The off-road B40 Enduro was built that year as well.

The C15T and C15S models did not continue into 1966 and neither did the B40 or SS90. The C15 did, while the SS80 became the C15 Sportsman, and both were fitted with the Victor bottom half from July. In the larger 441 cc size the B44GP continued and was joined by the Victor Enduro B44VE.

The year 1967 saw the end of the C15 which was replaced by the C25 Barracuda with Victor crankcase, square-finned barrel and one-piece crankshaft. The Victor Enduro was joined by the B44VS Victor Special and the road-going B44VR Victor Roadster with very similar engine unit.

The models changed some names for 1968, to the B25 Starfire for the 250 and B44SS Shooting Star for the road 440, but otherwise they all ran on with little alteration except for the B44VE. The year 1971 brought the big revamp to the range and some changes to the engines, with the larger stretching out to 499 cc. Basically, however, they still followed the lines set down by the Grand Prix of 1965.

The Bantam began just as an engine but soon

ABOVE *The 1950 M33 with its 499 cc B33 engine with iron head and barrel*

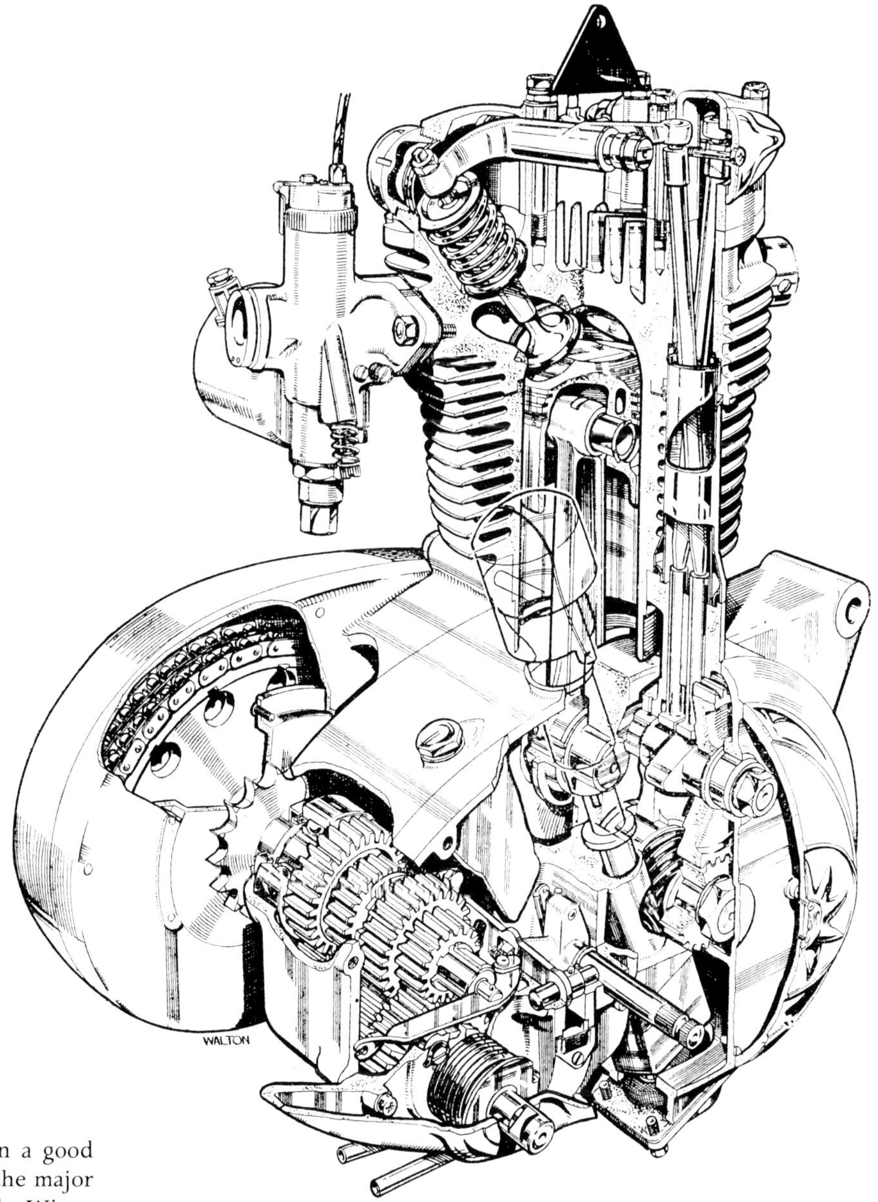

became a 123 cc machine. There were soon a good number of alternatives, but for the engine the major option was that of Lucas electrics in place of the Wipac ones. The competition engine had very few alterations from standard.

For 1954 the Lucas option was dropped and the D3 148 cc engine introduced, this simply having a larger bore than the 123 cc type. The same move brought the 172 cc D5 for 1958 and this became the D7 for 1959. It ran on with direct or battery lighting electrics up to 1966 and was accompanied by the D1 up to late 1963.

The year 1967 brought the D10, still of 172 cc, but with the points in the primary chaincase and a four-speed gearbox for some versions. For the next year all models had four speeds and were known as D14, but again only for a year. The model number altered yet again for 1969, to D175, although the capacity remained at 172 cc, and the detail parts received many changes. This model ran on to early 1971.

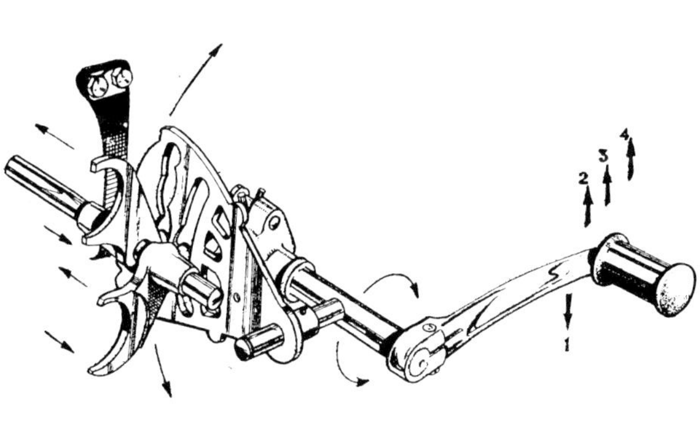

Based on the Triumph Cub design, this is the 247 cc C15 engine in its early form, with points housing aft of the cylinder

ABOVE *The 1961 343 cc B40 engine with pushrods in a tunnel in the barrel, rather than a separate tube as on C15*

LEFT *Engine of the 1966 C15, with Victor bottom half indicated by the C15G engine number prefix*

ABOVE RIGHT *The final 247 cc unit single in the form of the 1971 B25SS model, with 8 in. tls front brake*

RIGHT *The original 123 cc Bantam engine of 1948 with early-type Wipac flywheel magneto, sparse fins and gear indicator*

BSA
GOLD STAR 250SS

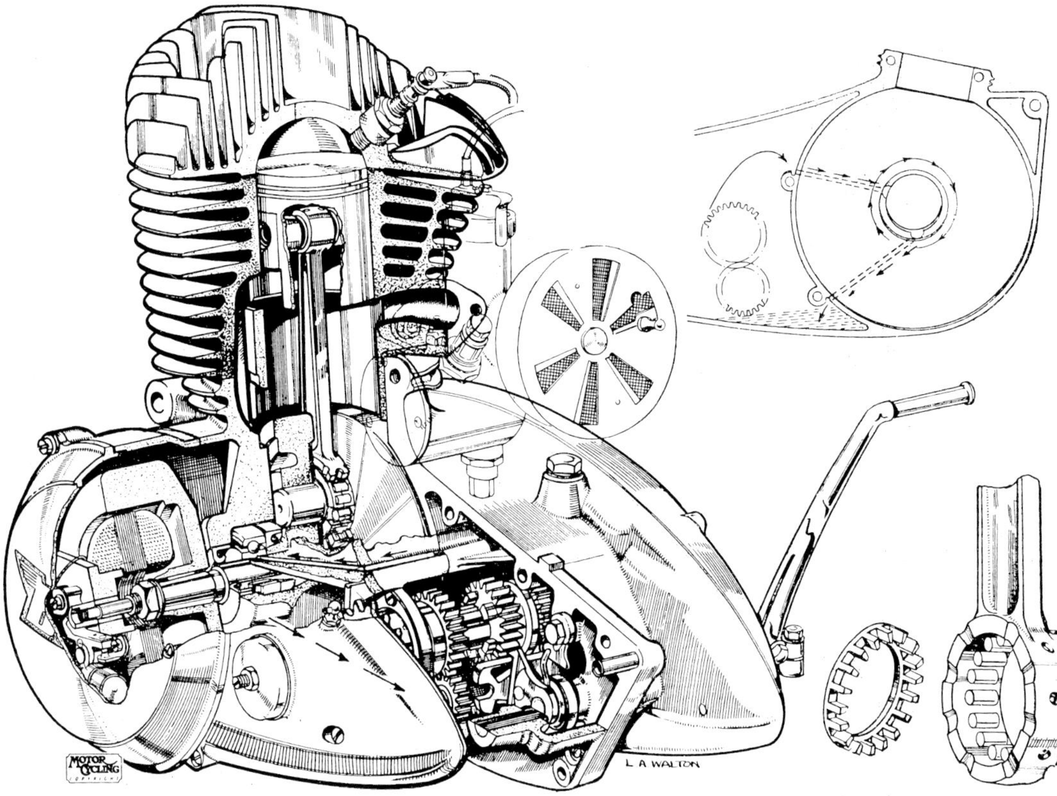

LEFT *Details of the 1958 172 cc D5 Bantam, with caged big-end and gearbox oiling of mains*

RIGHT *B-range model being serviced in Denis Parkinson's garage in 1952. It seems to be in need of a clean and a gasket or two*

BELOW *The final D175 Bantam in 1969 with central plug and four speeds, but still much as in 1948*

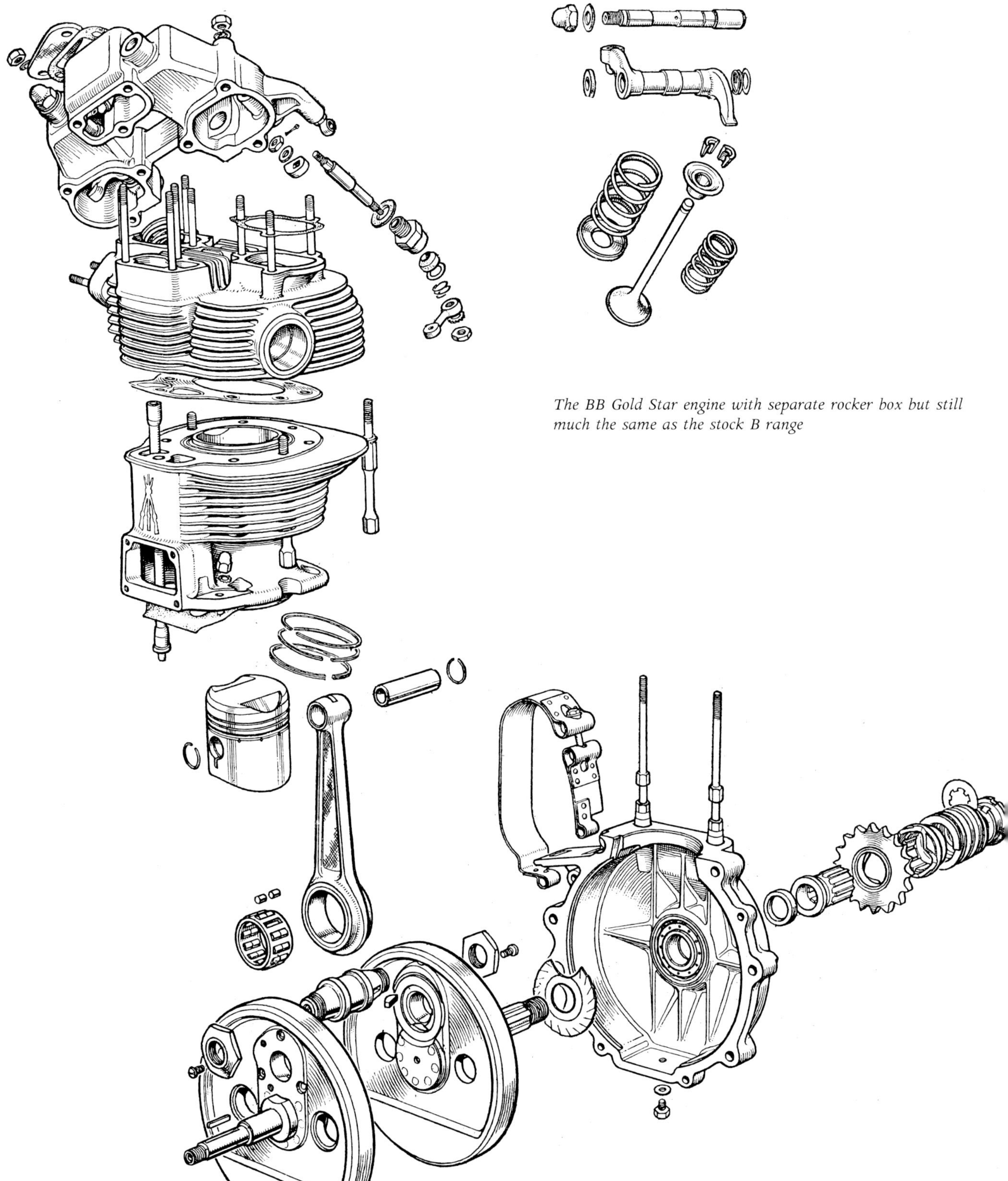

The BB Gold Star engine with separate rocker box but still much the same as the stock B range

All Bantam engines have the same 58 mm stroke and the same fixing centres so any frame can accommodate any engine. Thus they often get swapped around.

Removing and dismantling the engine

The exact procedure depends on the engine type, the model and your strength. All Bantam engine units can be removed in one piece without much trouble, but the others can be too much for one person to manage on their own. If you have to struggle to get it out there will be damage when it is assembled, so seek help.

A solution is to dismantle some of the engine in the frame to reduce its weight, and although this is not so tidy, it is more practical. Do this if it helps, but an M21 crankcase with those big flywheels is still quite a weight on its own.

Bearing all this in mind, drain the oils and follow the manual instructions for your engine. Undo the lockwashers before leaning on the nuts and think first if something is stuck. Be careful of fragile parts and use special tools and pullers where necessary.

Remember that the cost of a puller is always less than the part you will break if you don't use it. Proceed with caution but confidence, and at the end you will have all the detail parts ready for your attention.

Crankshaft

All but one BSA single had a built-up crankshaft and the majority had a roller big-end with either one or two rows of rollers with these caged or crowded. The exceptions were the early unit-construction engines with plain big-ends, and the 247 cc models built from 1967 to 1971 under various names, which had a one-piece crankshaft with two bolted-on flywheels, a split big-end connecting rod and a pair of shell bearings.

All other models were built up with the mainshafts pressed into the wheels and retained, on the four-strokes, by rivets. The two-strokes were simply pressed into place. The crankshafts without a roller big-end had a bush instead which was pressed into the connecting-rod eye and then finished to size. It ran directly on the crankpin. Models with this arrangement were the C15 up to 1963, and thus with a C15 engine number prefix rather than the C15D of 1964, the C15T up to engine C15T-1319 from mid-1961, the C15S up to engine C15S-3000 from late 1961, and the B40 up to engine number B40-3600 built at the end of the 1961 season.

The pre-unit engines all had the crankpin held in the wheels on a taper with a big nut on each end. Unit crankshafts began in a pressed-up form and many stayed that way whether fitted with a plain or roller bearing. With the appearance of the B44 in 1965, a change was made on that series only to crankpins retained by nuts once more, and this design also went into the B50 model although it had a caged needle-roller big-end.

The plain big-end bearing of the early C15 and B40 is a known weak spot so is best changed to the later roller type which will fit straight in. Note that the rods differ between the two engine sizes.

The crankshaft should be inspected for damage and big-end wear before it is dismantled, and notes taken as to the exact position of each item. On all crankshafts remove any plugs or oilway screws so that you can clean out any sludge and check that all oilways are unimpeded from entry to exit. Repeat this after assembly and alignment.

All crankshafts should be primed with oil once assembled to make sure there is no obstruction in its flow to the big-end.

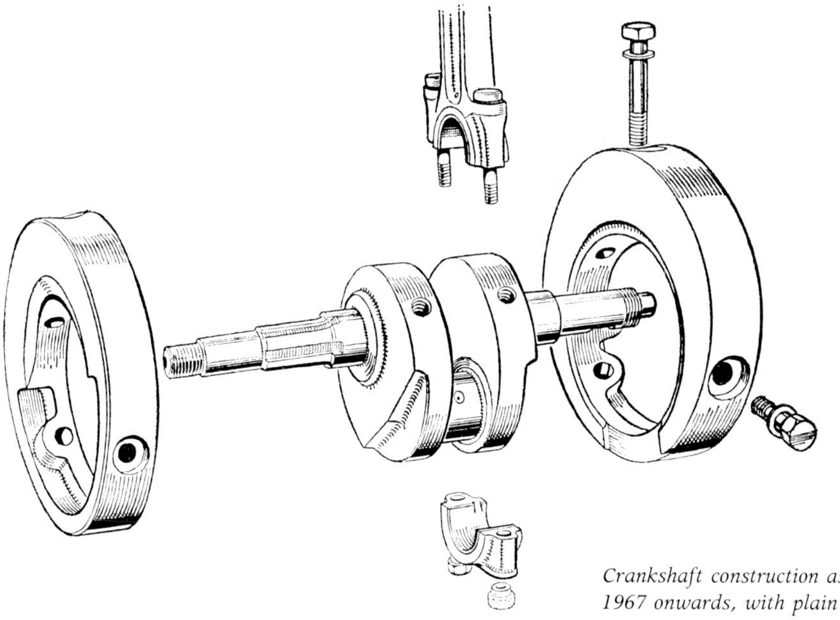

Crankshaft construction as used by the 247 cc engines from 1967 onwards, with plain big-end and bolted-on flywheels

ABOVE *Not a Gold Star, but a 1957 B34 with all-alloy engine, duplex frame and bolt-through alloy petrol tank*

LEFT *Top half of the 1949 ZB 348 cc Gold Star engine with TT carburettor and all-alloy engine*

RIGHT *The 1945 M20 with its girder forks was little altered from the wartime model other than in finish*

Crankshaft types

Some care is needed when identifying BSA flywheels as the same stroke was used for more than one model. Fortunately they often carry the forging number and this may well be one digit away from the part number of the wheel itself. A check on the diameters and lengths of the shaft itself will help.

Starting with the B range, all these models had an 88 mm stroke. The standard models had few alterations, with one gear side serving all years of the B31 and B32. The drive side to match it did not change until 1958 when an alternator was hung on it, and this type has a parallel shaft length outboard of the sprocket spline.

The B33 and B34 had their own pair of wheels but

otherwise copied the smaller engine down to the use of the same shafts. The only variation to this affected the B33 only, which fitted a different set of wheels for 1953–55 but then reverted to the original which stayed in use in the B34 for all years.

It was less simple for the Gold Star engines. The 350 began with a choice of wheels with one pair being fitted to the trials engines and another to the rest. The trials engines took the stock Gold Star wheels for 1953 but then changed to B31 wheels for 1954–55. The stock wheels otherwise went into all ZB and BB engines up to 1955. The CB wheels differed in diameter and were without the crankpin keyway, while the DB had the timing side extended to mate with an oil seal in the case. CB and DB engines had a larger ($1\frac{1}{8}$ in.) diameter for the drive-side roller bearing, earlier engines being 25 mm at this point.

The 500 Gold Star used one pair of wheels for all ZB and BB engines, other than trials models of 1954–55 which fitted the standard B34 parts, but all had the $1\frac{1}{8}$ in. drive-side roller bearing. The CB series had oval wheels to suit the short connecting rod fitted, and again lacked the crankpin keyway. The DB and DBD had smaller, round wheels with the oil-feed extension on the timing side, and of these the DBD had the smallest while the DB32 and DB34 wheels differed.

The M33 used the B33 engine complete with the crankshaft it came with, while the M20 fitted one set of wheels up to the end of 1949 and another from then onwards. The M21 varied a little more with cast-iron wheels being fitted for most, but not all, years. Exceptions when steel ones were used were 1947–49, and these two continued on the AA version of this model. From 1957 a second drive side was listed for the AA when an alternator was fitted in addition to the dynamo. The M20 wheels had a 94 mm stroke while that of the M21 was a massive 112 mm.

The C range had a choice of steel or cast-iron wheels for 1946–48, but after that only the iron ones were used. For 1954 the drive side gained a parallel section outboard of the spocket splines for the alternator, but the timing side remained unaltered. All models had an 80 mm stroke.

The unit engines began with a 70 mm stroke which was used by all 247 and 343 cc models. The 441 and 499 cc engines had a 90 mm stroke. The C15 had its first change of wheels for 1962 when it was fitted with a new alternator, and a second change for 1964 when the roller big-end went in. It had one final change for those engines built from July 1966 and into 1967. These run from number C15G-101 and have the B44-type bottom half with the larger model's main bearings and crankshaft parts to suit. Note that the stroke remained at 70 mm and that this change also went into the C15 Sportsman up to its end in August 1966 at engine C15GS-793. The C15 ran to June 1967 and number C15G-2406. The C15T and C15S both began life with the C15 timing wheel but shared another one on the drive side. The C15S had new

RIGHT *The 172 cc D10 Bantam engine of 1967 with points on the right, but seen here in three-speed form*

BELOW *The 1946 249 cc C11 engine with its points housing angled into the timing case*

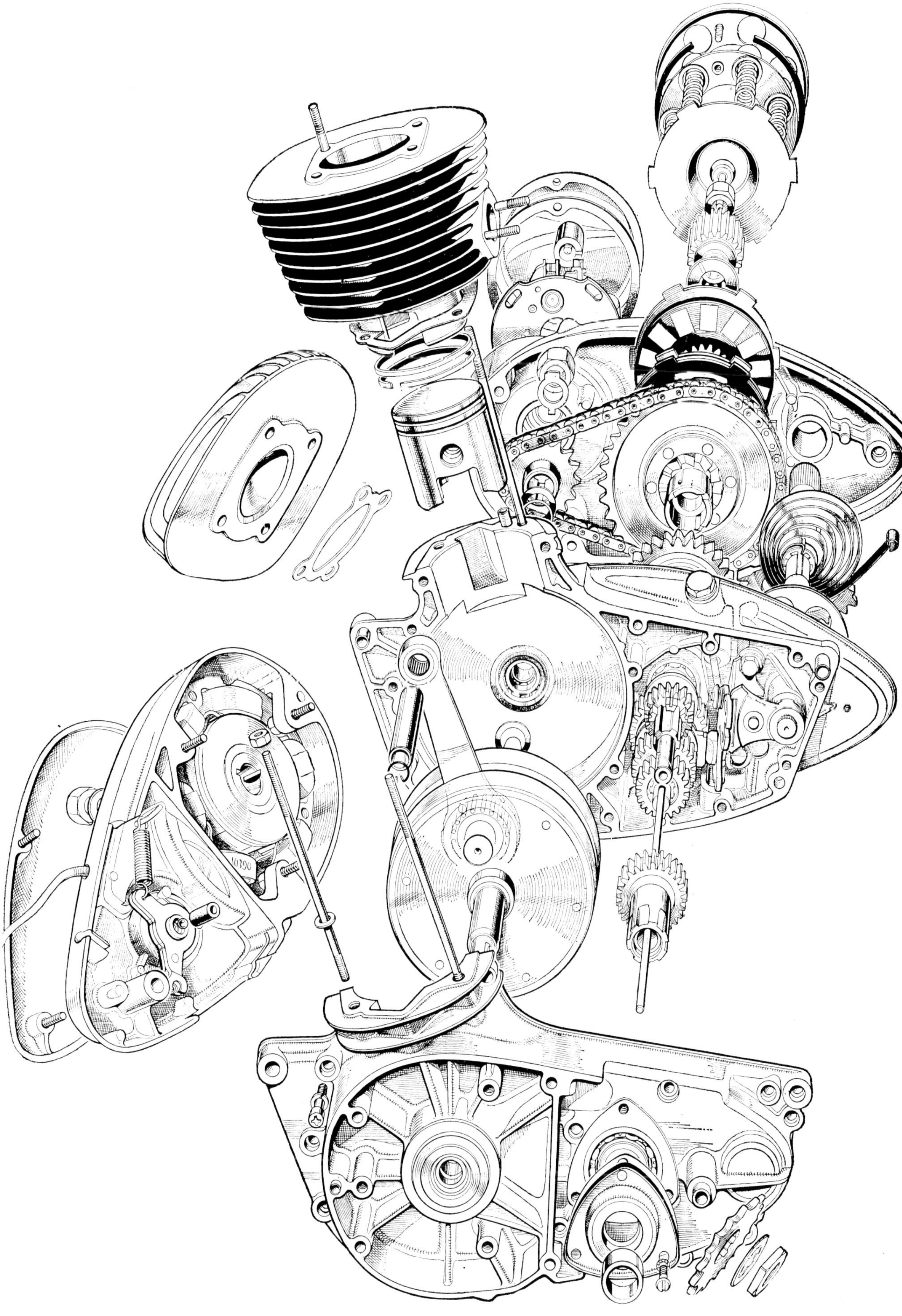

wheels for 1961 and both competition models changed to a new pair for 1962 when they adopted the roller big-end. They shared the same parts until 1965.

The SS80 had the roller big-end from the start and used the same timing-side wheel as the competition models, while fitting its own drive-side one to suit its alternator. For 1965 it changed and followed the same pattern with the competition timing side and its own drive. It took the B44 bottom half for the last few models as detailed above. The B40 may have had the same stroke but it had its own wheels for its one year in 1961, with a plain big-end and a second unique pair for 1962–66. These also went into the SS90.

The B44 had a single timing-side wheel for all years but the drive one changed for 1969. The B50 with the same stroke had a single pair of wheels for all years.

The Bantam had a 58 mm stroke for all engines but despite this managed to have a good variety of shafts and wheels. The first, with a rather thin outer rim, went into the models with Wipac ignition for 1949–52. The inner face of the wheel was flat and the magneto side had a lengthy shaft to support the rotor and the cam on its far end. The shaft used with the Lucas electrics was much shorter and the wheels had much thicker rims.

Both types changed for 1953 when the big-end rollers were made longer and the wheel recessed to compensate. This was the last year the Lucas option was offered. The D3 used the D1 parts and for 1955 both were changed when the drive-side seal was moved inboard of the bearings and a rubbing diameter provided for it on the wheel. The magneto side followed suit for 1958 when the D5, the first 172 cc, was introduced. A seal was added inboard of the main so again a rubbing diameter was added on the wheel to suit it.

The 125 continued in this form, as did the D5 and D7 which superseded it in 1959. The magneto wheel of the larger model differed from the smaller. For 1967 and the D10 the wheels had new shafts with the left becoming a parallel one to suit a six-coil alternator rotor. The drive side was extended to pass out through the primary chaincase to take the ignition cam. The wheels were revised for 1968 with a change to their compression plates, and again for 1969 when the plates lost the hole for the crankpin which had made their fitment rather pointless. At the same time the method of fixing them to the wheels changed from rivets to a system of rolled-in rim lock, and the crankpin holes were increased in diameter.

There was one further set of wheels for the 1967 GPO D7 which were without plates like the D7, but fitted with D10 shafts.

Big-ends

The attention these need is mainly a case of replacement if worn. The roller assemblies are all basically the same but not all have cages, and some are pressed together while others are held by nuts. The four-strokes, other than the early C range, had a bush pressed into the connecting rod whether the bearing was a roller or a bush, while the two strokes ran the rollers direct in the rod eye.

Each series of models tended to keep to one set of parts until the unit engines, which had more variation. Thus all B and M models other than Gold Stars had the same crankpin, rollers, roller cage, nuts, lockwashers, thrust washers and oil-feed plug in the crankpin for all versions and years. The rollers were 24 in number, run in two rows, and of $\frac{1}{4}$ in. diameter and $\frac{5}{16}$ in. length. The crankpin thread was $\frac{3}{4}$ in. diameter.

For the Gold Star a larger thread of $\frac{7}{8}$ in. diameter was used so its nuts were special, as was the pin. That of the CB differed from the earlier ones as it did not have the keyway, while the DB pin was further amended. The DB models also had their own cage which had modified dimensions, but all the earlier Gold Stars used the standard part. All, however, fitted the same 24 rollers as the rest of the B range and, up to the BB model, the same key. The Gold Stars did not have the lockwasher and just fitted a screw in the wheel to lock the crankpin nut, but they used the same thrust washers and oil-feed plug as the B range.

The C range had its own parts with a single row of 15 rollers, $\frac{1}{4}$ in. diameter and $\frac{1}{2}$ in. long, running uncaged on a crankpin with guide shoulders. No thrust washers were fitted and the rollers ran directly in the rod eye. The crankpin nuts differed from the B range but the same key and oil-feed plug were used.

The unit engines had changes to the crankpin in

BELOW LEFT *Bantam 123 cc D1 of 1949 in its simple loop frame and with concentric foot pedals*

BELOW *The drive side of the 1951 C11, showing the location of several electric parts as well as the primary chaincase*

1959, 1961 and 1962. The C15 changed to the roller big-end for 1964 from engine C15D-101, while the competition ones changed around 1961. The changes were from engine C15T-1320 and C15S-3001. The B40 altered for engine B40-3601 and 1962, and its crankpin went into the other engines in time. There were 24 rollers in the bearing, and the cage they ran in was amended for 1965 and carried the $\frac{1}{4} \times \frac{1}{4}$ in. rollers in two rows.

For the B44 a change was made to a pin held by a taper and two nuts, but the cage and rollers remained as they were up to 1970. The pin nuts stayed in use to the end in 1973, and one pin served all B44 models and another all B50 models. The pin diameter of the first was 1.270 in. and the second 1.496 in. The B44 fitted the B40 cage and rollers while the B50 had 20 caged needles, each 4 mm in diameter and 15 mm long. The plain-bearing C25 of 1967 had shell bearings and the one pair served the 247 cc models through to 1971.

The Bantam began with 12 rollers, each 7 × 7 mm, and a pair of thrust washers on its crankpin. For 1953 all the parts changed and the rollers became 14 of $\frac{1}{4}$ in. diameter and $\frac{3}{8}$ in. length. With the introduction of the D5 in 1958, the detail parts were no longer listed as separate items and just an assembly of connecting rod with big-end bearing became available. In this the big-end bearing had 18 rollers, each 4 mm in diameter and 8 mm long, run in a single row in a split cage, this being done for ease of manufacture. This design continued in use for the Bantam up to 1971, although the crankpin itself changed for 1969 when its ends had their diameter increased.

ABOVE *The 1969 441 cc B44SS with humped seat and sculptured side panel and fuel-tank knee recess*

RIGHT *The 1956 148 cc D3 Bantam in its pivoted-fork frame and with lengthy silencer*

Connecting rods

Most BSA rods were steel forgings, but that of the C25 was in light alloy and should be treated with even more care than the others to avoid knocks or bruises. It should also be closely examined for any signs of cracks or other damage and if in doubt should be replaced.

Repair is normally just a case of renewing the big- and small-end bushes when wear dictates this, and grinding or reaming, respectively, to size. In the case of the 247 cc engines from 1967 onwards, the shells may need replacing to suit the crankshaft grind, and the nuts and bolts are best renewed on each occasion. They should be tightened evenly, and in steps.

Rod types

Many BSA models used just one connecting rod throughout their life, which makes identification and replacement easier. All the B range began with a common rod of 7.375 in. centres, and this stayed in use in the B31 and B34 to their demise. The B33 changed to a shorter rod of 6.875 in. centres in 1953, and this rod went into the B32 for 1956–57 after it had fitted another type for 1954–55.

The Gold Stars began with a common rod of

7.375 in. centres but not that fitted to the B range. For 1952, and from engine ZB32GS-6001, the 348 cc model changed to the same rod as used by the later B32 and B33 engines. For both the CB models in 1954 there was another shorter rod with 6.469 in. centres which went into the DB and DBD engines as well.

The M20 and M21 used one rod for all years and this had 8.25 in. centres. The M33 used the B33 engine with its standard rod. Among the C range, all the side-valves had one rod and all the ohv engines another.

The unit engines had rods with 5.563 in. centres for the C15 and B40. The first went into the C15, C15T and C15S but the last two had a change for 1961 and went over to the roller big-end for 1962. They had a further rod change for 1965. The B40 had its own rod with a small-end boss both wider and with a larger pin. It changed for 1962 and the roller big-end.

The 247 cc engine had an alloy rod with split big-end from 1967; this was changed for 1969 when it lost its replaceable small-end bush, and in 1971, with the nuts and bolts altering for this last year only. The rod centres were 5.312 in. Those of the B44 and B50 were 6.00 in., but the first was bored for the big-end to 1.770 in. diameter and the second to 1.811 in.

All Bantam rods had 4.921 in. centres and the first change came in 1953 when the wider big-end was fitted. It changed again for 1955, and in 1958 was altered for the caged big-end. The small-end was amended for 1962 when a needle race replaced the earlier bronze bush. For 1967 and the D10 there was an oval section rod, and the final change came in 1969 when the pin end diameter was increased.

Small-end bush

If worn this will need to be changed and may be pressed out using the new bush, providing the oil holes are lined up first. Otherwise they will need to be drilled after fitting but before reaming. This last operation should be done to give a nice slide-fit on the pin. Avoid hand reaming if possible as a guided machine reamer will do a much better job. Check the oil holes again after reaming.

The B, M and C ranges each had their own bush to which they kept to for all models and years. The first two were reamed for a $\frac{3}{4}$ in. pin and the third for a pin of $\frac{5}{8}$ in. diameter. The C15 series pin was of $\frac{11}{16}$ in. diameter and the rods had one bush for the C15 and another for the C15S from 1961 onwards. The C25 fitted a third type for 1967–68, but from 1969 the pin ran direct in the rod without any bush.

The B40, B44 and B50 all used the bush from the old B range, while the Bantams had a smaller bush and a pin of $\frac{15}{32}$ in. diameter. The original served the 123 cc model to the end and was joined by another for the 172 cc engine with a $\frac{9}{16}$ in. bore. This was used up to 1961 but from 1962 a needle race was fitted to this engine.

Piston

First check the cylinder to see if this needs boring, as if it does, you will need a new piston anyway. Otherwise inspect the existing one carefully. A great many pistons were used by BSA over the years and are included in an appendix, along with the compression ratio they gave. There were usually 0.5 mm and 1 mm oversizes for each engine. If in any doubt, both the piston and compression ratio should be checked.

Keep to the standard compression ratio for your model as any attempt to raise this could bring a major disaster in its train as the middle-aged or old engine objects to the added loads. Should you find yourself with a sports engine fitted with another head in iron, use the iron-head ratio or the engine will overheat.

If you keep the existing piston expect to renew the rings, in which case you may need to remove the glaze from the bores with a specialist tool, or medium-to-coarse emery cloth. Check the gaps on the new rings and note the effect the piston pegs have on the Bantam ones. Make sure that taper rings on four-strokes are the correct way up or you will have a plug oiling problem.

Gudgeon pins should be checked for ridges and changed if not in really good condition, while the clips should be renewed as a matter of course.

One pin and pair of clips served the C range for 1946–58. The B range had two pins, one for the 348 cc engines and another for the 499 cc ones, but the latter also served the M range. One pair of clips did for both B and M models. The early Bantams had different pins for the D1 and D3 but a common wire clip. The D5 had its own items which were revised for the D7 to D14 for 1959–68 and altered again for 1969–71.

The unit engines had a pin in the 247 cc size which was changed for 1967 and the C25, and again for 1971 with a clip change to match in each case. The B40 had its own pin and clip which also served the B44 up to 1970, the clip being that used by the B and M ranges from 1946 onwards. The B50 had its own pin and clips.

Cylinder types

The first check in determining which cylinder you

BELOW LEFT *Final big unit single in the form of the 1971 499 cc B50SS, with its convoluted exhaust pipe and well-warmed electrical box*

RIGHT *The Victor Grand Prix engine unit with its many features which then went into the road models to improve them*

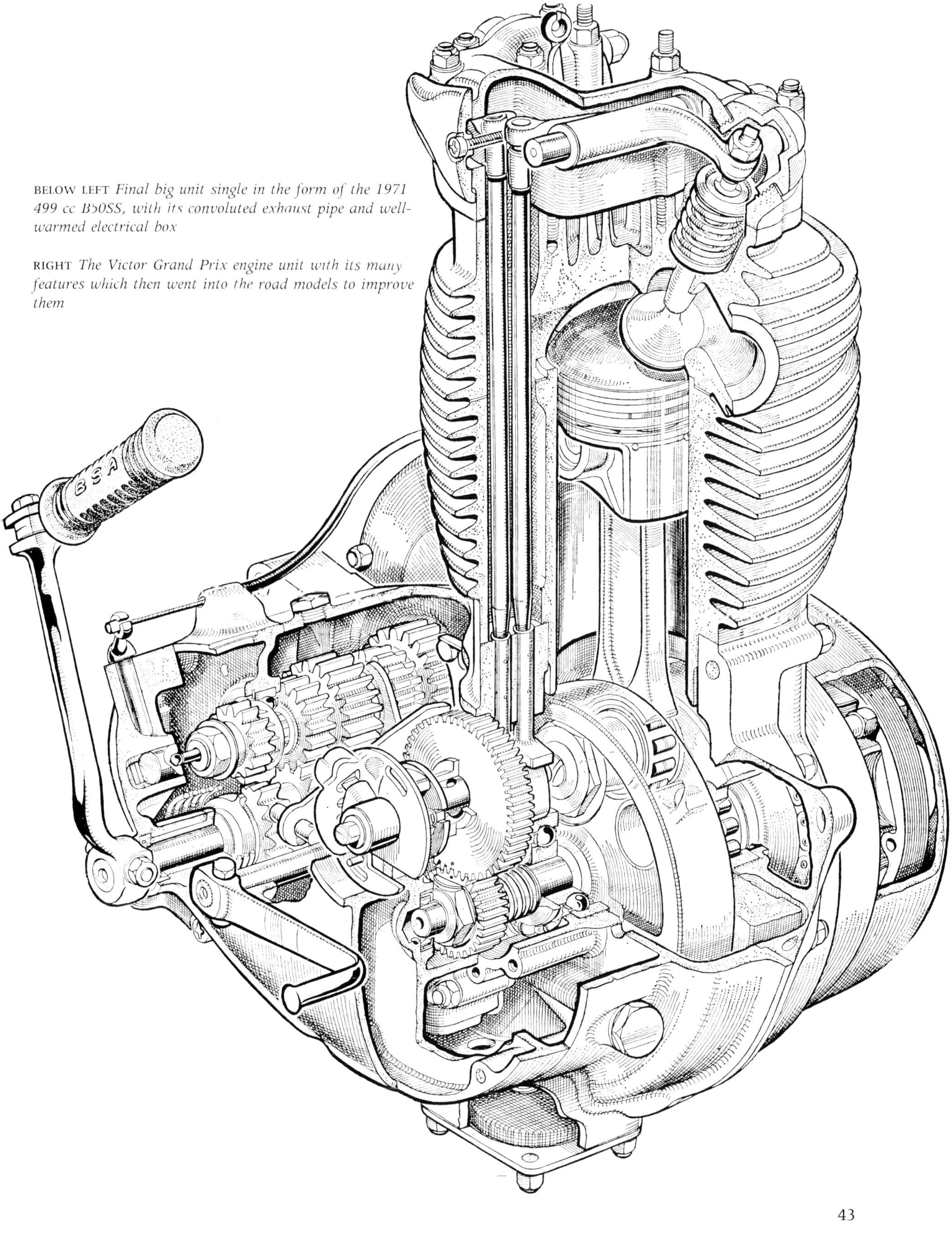

hold is the bore size followed by whether it is a side-valve, two-stroke or ohv. Standard sizes for the B range were 71 mm for the 348 cc engine and 85 mm for the 499 cc one. The M range were 82 mm, except for the M33 which had the B33 engine, while the C range were 63 mm. This rose to 67 mm for the unit 247 cc engines and to 79 mm for the B40 and B44 series. The B50 was on 84 mm. The D1 Bantam was 52 mm, the D3 was 57 mm and all the 172 cc engines were 61.5 mm.

The road B31 and B33 only had one change which came for 1953 when the fin area was increased. The B32 and B34 began with the iron barrels from the road models and used these as standard up to late 1953. For the period of 1950–53 the option of an alloy barrel was listed, and the one used was that from the ZB Gold Star series. For the 1954–57 period, when an alloy barrel was standard, the die-cast late ZB and BB Gold Star item was used. In 1950 only, the B31 and B33 could also have the ZB alloy barrel fitted in theory, although it is unlikely that this happened in practice.

The Gold Star models always had alloy barrels and at first these were sand-cast. From early 1952 for the 500, and March 1952 for the 350, a change was made to die-cast parts and these went on the last of the ZB and all BB series engines. Thus the two versions of the ZB engines differed in many ways. The CB series of 1954 introduced much more finning and that of the 500 CB also went on to the 1955 and later DB and DBD models. For the 350 DB a much thicker $\frac{1}{4}$ in. liner replaced the earlier 3 mm one and became the mounting to the crankcase and for the cylinder head so that the alloy fins were simply a muff. Note that base shims were

ABOVE *The sports unit 247 cc model in the form of the 1961 SS80 with chrome mudguards and decorated toolbox*

FAR LEFT *The power unit of the 1972 B50T with breather from chaincase and rear-pivot chain adjustment*

listed for the Gold Stars from 1952 onwards and were available in thicknesses of 0.01, 0.02, 0.03 and 0.064 in. They could also be used on the B32 and B34 in 1954–57.

The side-valve C model only had one cylinder change which came for 1956 when the fin area was increased. The same thing happened to the C11 for 1951 but it had a more radical change for 1954 and the C11G. For that machine the fins were cleaned up by extending the head studs down through them so the fixing nuts lay below the fins.

The M range was alone in the early post-war days in having a cylinder liner. The same barrel went on both M20 and M21 but was replaced in 1950 by one in which the piston ran direct. This could later be fitted with a liner, but machines built for the AA stayed with the original until a change was made for 1957.

The C15 barrel stayed the same over the years but the linered alloy one of the C25 was changed for 1969. That of the B40 changed for 1965 when an extra stud was added either side of the pushrod hole and this style remained in use from then onwards. The cylinder of the 1966–67 Victor Enduro was unusual in having a compression plate under it. The B44GP barrel was hard-chromed and so had no liner, but the VR, VS and SS versions of the B44 did and all used the same part for 1967–70. The B50 had a new barrel and its liner was listed separately. For 1973 a compression plate was fitted to the B50.

The D1 Bantam began with a barrel with sparse finning, a small crankcase spigot, and stud centres which matched its bore at 52 mm. For 1954 a barrel with a much bigger fin area was used but with the same spigot diameter and stud centres. For 1955 and the remainder of its years, the spigot was enlarged and the stud centres increased to 55 mm. The D3 used a barrel made from the same casting as the last D1 so all models had the larger fin area, spigot and stud centres.

The 172 cc engines all had a flange-fitting carburettor which bolted to the cylinder, so the casting differed from the smaller sizes which had stub-fitting instruments. The same part served the D5 and D7 versions and was modified for the D10 by the addition of a dowel hole in the crankcase face on the right. The D14 varied from that in having an exhaust-port adaptor, while the final D175 had Unified threads for the carburettor studs.

ABOVE *The first 172 cc Bantam was this 1958 D5 which was only built for that year. It had a bolt-on carb rather than the clip-on of smaller engines*

RIGHT *Removing the head and valve gear of an early C15. On assembly, the pushrods must contact the correct tappets*

BELOW *The last of the C15 models in 1967, with few cycle changes from the first*

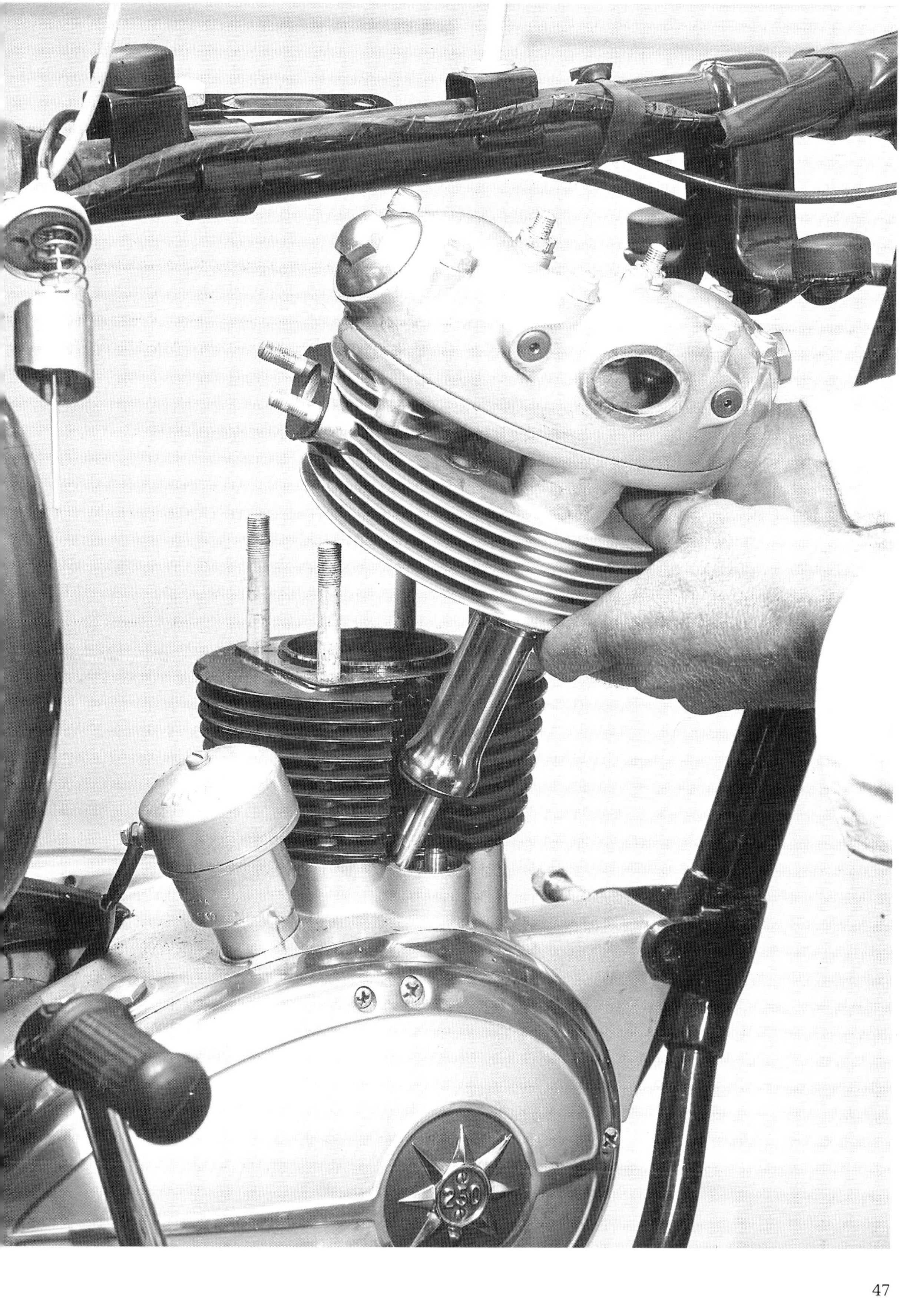

Cylinder head

You may find this a victim of misguided enthusiasm with valve seats cut back due to years of keen, but unnecessary, valve grinding. Each owner may have done this 'to put the sparkle back' with the result that the valve heads are now well masked. The only answer will be an insert—a job for a specialist.

The side-valve and Bantam heads are essentially much easier to deal with as each is a simple casting with plug and fixing holes.

Cylinder-head types

In some cases enough heads were used to cause confusion, so care is needed when checking them. The basic road B31 and B33 were not too much of a problem as they always had iron heads and each had one change only. This came for 1953 when the fin area was increased to match the barrel.

The B32 and B34 both used the iron road-model head up to the end of 1953. From 1950 to this time an alloy option was available and it copied the road model in having the rocker box integral with the head. The B32 used the head from the ZB Gold Star trials model, while the B34 had a new part but one that was very similar to the Gold Star component.

From 1954 onwards both models had an alloy head as standard and the B32 fitted that of the BB Gold Star trials model with the separate rocker box. The B34 copied this action from engine BB34A-264, but up to number 263 a similar but different part was used.

The Gold Stars began in 1949 with the ZB series and while the 499 cc engine managed with one head for all versions, the 348 cc one had a choice. There was one with a 1 in. inlet port for the trials machines and another with $1\frac{1}{16}$ in. for the others.

The year 1952 brought the last of the ZB series with separate rocker box and two types for each engine size. The first of each went on to the Clubmans model and was joined in 1953 by another for trials use on the 348 cc engine, and trials and scrambles for the 499 cc one. It was these last two that were also used on the B32 and B34 alloy-engined models. The ZB became the BB series in 1953 and this remained in the lists into 1955, but during 1952 the part became die-cast in place of the earlier sand-cast production method. This occurred at engines ZB32GS-6001 and ZB34GS-5001.

The CB series with big fins was built for 1954–55 and only one head was used for each engine size. This changed when the DB models were introduced, and for the 348 cc model there were different heads for Clubmans, scrambles and, up to 1956, road touring use, the first with 65 mm carburettor stud centres. For the 499 cc engine there was one head for the Clubmans model, again with 65 mm stud centres, and another for both scrambles and road use. In 1956 the DBD head appeared with 65 mm carburettor stud centres in Clubmans form, but reverted to the common 2 in. for the scrambles DBD head introduced in 1958. These two continued up to 1963, but the DB34 lapsed at the end of 1957.

Of the other pre-unit engines, all began their post-war days with iron heads. The C10 changed to light alloy during 1949 at engine ZC10-1378 and this was modified for 1956 with deeper fins, some of them offset, by which time the model was listed as the C10L. The C11 remained in iron and its only change came for 1954 when it gained some fin area and became the C11G. Both M side-valve models fitted the same head and this was changed to light alloy for 1951. Note that the alloy heads have long-reach plugs while the earlier iron ones take short-reach plugs.

All unit engines had alloy heads and the C15 kept to one type which was also used by the C15T. The C15S began with this but changed for 1960, and again for 1961 and 1965. Along with these there was yet another head with 1 in. bore inlet which existed from 1960 onwards. The SS80 ignored the lot and had its own part. The 1967 247 cc model had a new head with square finning to match the barrel and this was not altered until 1971 when threads were Unified.

The B40 had one head up to 1964, after which it was modified to add a stud either side of the pushrod hole. Another version went on to the SS90. The head listed for the B44GP also went on to the B44VE for 1966–67 and the B44VS in 1967, but from 1968 the latter fitted a head which also served the B44VR and B44SS road models. For the B50 there was a new part.

Early Bantams had both standard and competition heads with the first just having a spark plug and the second a compression release as well. There were three versions of each for the D1 and the changes were to match the cylinder. The first pair had limited fins and stud holes at 52 mm, with the fin area increased for 1954 while the stud centres stayed as they were. For

ABOVE RIGHT *The B40 as built for the Home Office with panniers and handlebar muffs. The latter may not be tidy but can be a real help in winter*

BELOW *The C11 cylinder head with its angled rockers and mounting trunnion. The C12 had an oil feed into this and deeper fins*

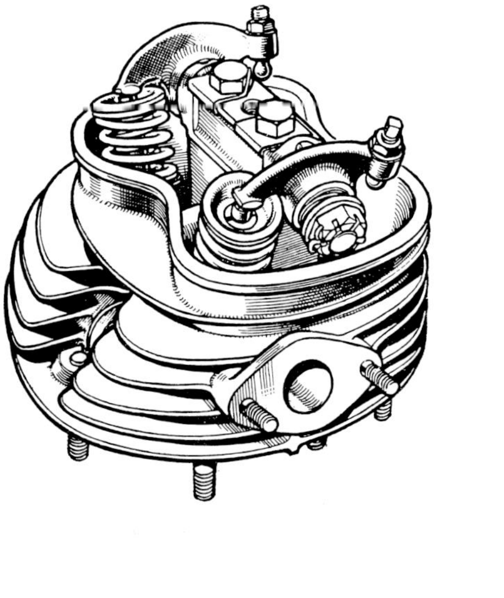

1955 the centres were increased to 55 mm while the fin area remained constant. The competition head was listed up to the end of 1956, although the model had been removed from the lists a year earlier.

The D3 engines all had the larger fin area and 55 mm stud centres, but four heads were listed in all: two standard and two competition. One pair was for 1954 only and the other for 1955 onwards, these being the D1 parts as it was found that the D3 engine would run happily with them.

The D5 and D7 used a common head which continued on to the GPO D7 in 1967, while the D10 took a new part. This last had the combustion chamber diameter reduced and thus an increased squish band. It was changed again for the D14 in 1968 when the compression ratio was raised, and finally for the D175 in 1969 when a central plug was finally provided.

Note that, in addition to the standard Bantam heads, there are a good number of special racing ones about with central plug and more fins.

Gaskets

Paper gaskets may be replaced by a silicone jointing compound, but only if it is used sparingly and kept out of holes in general and oilways in particular. Otherwise head gaskets should be renewed, and other ones are more easily replaced than renovated.

On the road B31 and B33 there was no head gasket but a common base gasket. This was amended for 1958, and that of the B33 differed from the others for 1956–57. The other gaskets for rocker box, tappet cover, rocker access and sump plate were all common to both models and all years. The sump one also went on the M and C pre-unit ranges.

The Gold Star engines fitted a copper and asbestos gasket to the ZB and BB engines, and these differed to suit the changes in cylinder head. From the end of

Racing Bantam cylinder head produced by tuner George Todd and used by most competitors for many years

ABOVE *A 1960 D7 having a new head gasket fitted. Note the cover over the magneto adopted for this model*

RIGHT *Timing side of the BB Gold Star engine with flap valve breather and rev-counter drive taken from the magneto nut*

1952, and thus for BB and CB engines, the peel-off type was adopted in order that no recess remained above the top of the cylinder liner to trap gases and cause head burning. The 499 cc gasket continued right through to the DBD engines but the 348 cc one had a change of gasket for the DB series. The alloy B32 and B34 used the appropriate Gold Star gasket but the iron engines were, as for the road models, without one.

The Gold Star engines had one base gasket for both sizes from 1949 with a change for 1952, and again these items went on to the alloy B32 and B34. The early ZB models used the B-range rocker-box gaskets, but from 1952 a trio of items served the engines with separate rocker box. Otherwise the Gold Star fitted B-range gaskets. The two M-range side-valve engines shared common gaskets for head, base and tappet cover for all years.

The C10 head gasket was altered for 1950 and again for the C10L in 1954, but the same base gasket was used for all years. The tappet-cover gasket changed for 1956 when the barrel was given more fin area. The C11 head gasket was modified for 1947 and then remained in use to the end of the C12. One base gasket and one rocker-cover gasket served all years. The remaining gaskets were common to the C10 and C11 models, with one outer timing-cover gasket used to the end of 1953 and the inner changing for 1954 when it was joined by the points-cover one.

The C15 head, base, rocker box, rocker-box side plate and sump gaskets were common to all years. For the C25 and subsequent 247 cc models there were new items, but only the head gasket ran through to 1971 without change. The base and rocker-box gaskets changed for 1968 and 1971, while the side-cover one altered for 1971.

The B40 head gasket changed for 1965 when it gained stud holes either side of the pushrod one, but the base one stayed as it was and the others were as for the C15. The B44 series had one head gasket for all years but the base and rocker-box ones changed for 1968. The side-cover one remained as on the C15. For the B50 there were new head, base, rocker-box and side-cover gaskets. For all models the sump gasket changed for 1967 and 1971.

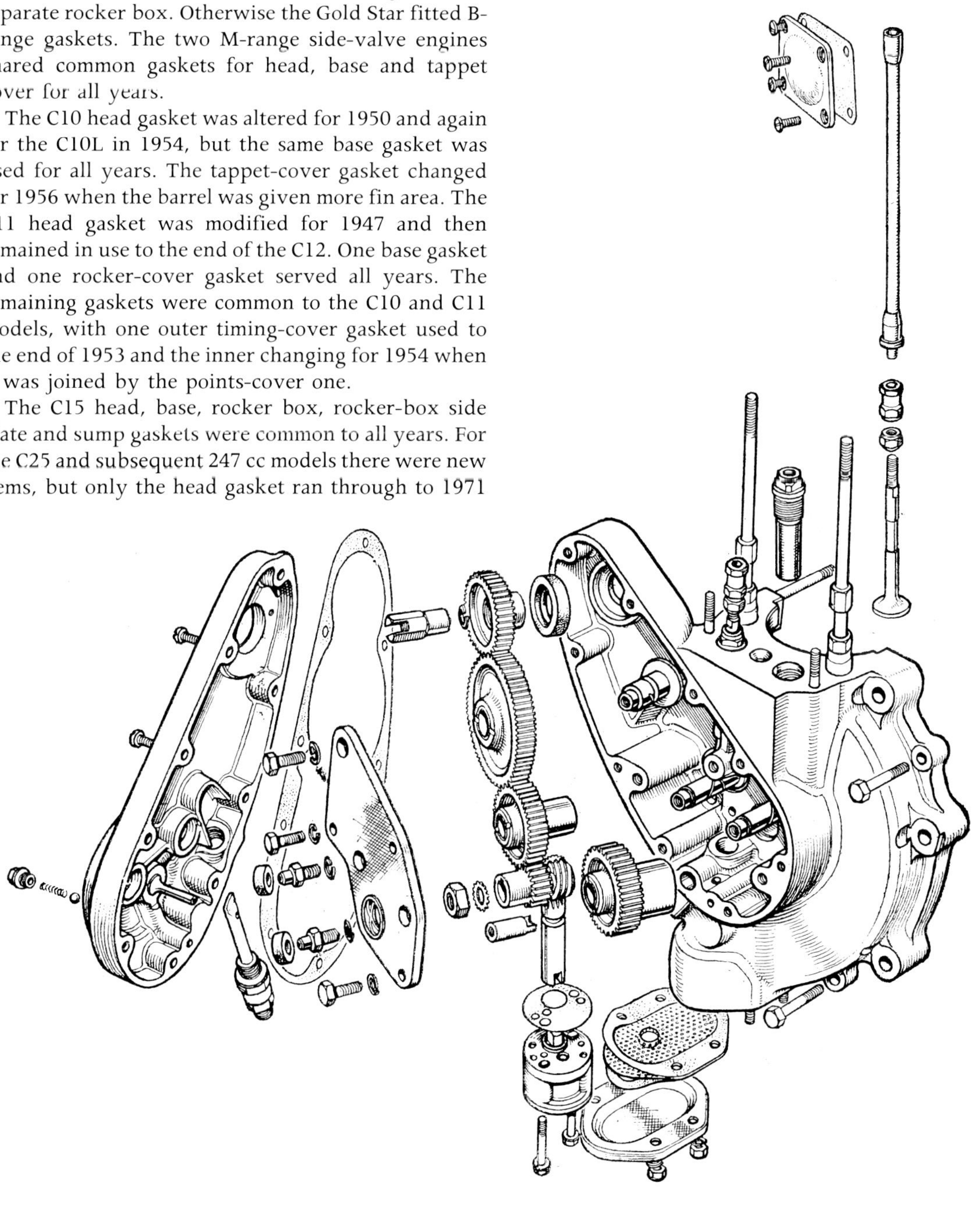

The 1970 Victor Special B44VS in off-road form with small headlight, raised exhaust but close-fitting front mudguard

Bantams went without a head gasket at first but one with 52 mm centres was introduced for the D1 in 1954 and changed to 55 mm centres the following year. This continued in use to 1963 while the D3 had its own head gasket. The original base gasket of the D1 was replaced with one used by both D1 and D3 in 1954, which was superseded by another from 1955 onwards.

The D5 and D7 shared both head and base gaskets while the D10 head gasket also went on the D14 and D175. The Sports and Bushman versions of the D14 had their own head gasket. The D10 base gasket differed from the D7 and another was used by the D14 and D175 models.

Other Bantam gaskets were for the primary chaincase and gearbox sprocket seal. The first changed for 1967 and the D10 when it gained another hole but still fitted the earlier models. The second used two gaskets which were common to all engines for 1949–67.

Valves

Unless they are in very good condition, valves should be replaced, especially the exhaust valve which has a hard time. Grind new valves in lightly without taking too much from the valve seat.

While there was a good variety of valves used by BSA singles, many models did keep to one pair for all years. Machines that did this were the B31, B33, C10 and C10L, C11 and C11G which includes the C12, M20 and M21 which shared, C15 and variants, SS80, B40, SS90 and B50.

The Gold Star was less simple but the 348 cc engine had one pair for each of the ZB (other than 1952), CB and DB versions. The late ZB and BB engines had one pair for trials, scrambles and road use from 1953, and only the inlet of the last two was common. For 1952 one pair served all models and it was this that continued for road use. For the 499 cc engine one pair served the ZB engine, and the exhaust from that was used by the road BB for 1954. As with the smaller engine, the 1952 ZB models had a common pair of valves that went into the road engine from 1953. A second pair served both scrambles and trials engines. The CB had its own valve pair and the DB yet another which changed its inlet for the DBD.

The B32 and B34 both used the road-model valves from the B31 and B33 up to the end of 1953. They then went over to alloy heads patterned on the ZB Gold Star, and the B32 used the valves from the 1953 trials BB engine. The B34 began with the 1952 ZB inlet and another exhaust, but from engine ZB34A-264 changed to the 1953 scrambles and trials pair. The alloy options for the B32 of 1950–53 used the standard valves as also fitted to the B31, but the B34 option fitted the 499 cc Gold Star valves as used in the ZB engine.

Among the unit engines one pair served the C15 and C15T, but while the same exhaust also went into the C15S and SS80, these two shared a different inlet. The same applied to the 343 cc engine with the B40 and

SS90 having a common exhaust and different inlets.

The C25 had one inlet up to 1971 but the exhaust was altered for 1968 onwards. The B44GP and the VE and VS models for the 1965–67 period used the SS90 valves, but another pair went into the VR and SS models and two more into the B50.

Valve guides

These should be removed or replaced with the head hot where it is of alloy, but may be drifted cold from an iron head or barrel. Guides are seldom common to both valves so it is important not to mix them up. Only the C15 had guides located on a circlip, all others having a shoulder or being set to a dimension. This last applied to the side-valve engines, but again take care as the dimension differed from inlet to exhaust.

The measurement was taken from the top face of the cylinder down to the top of the guide. The settings for the C10 and C10L were $1\frac{1}{16}$ in. for the inlet and $\frac{13}{16}$ in. for the exhaust. For the M20 and M21 they became inlet $1\frac{1}{8}$ in. and exhaust $\frac{15}{16}$ in., and while these figures are also correct for 1939, the earlier M range differed and had double guides for each valve. For them the dimensions were inlet $1\frac{1}{16}$ in. and exhaust $\frac{7}{8}$ in., with the bottom of the lower guides set $2\frac{7}{8}$ in. above the crankcase face level. Pre-war C10 engines had settings of inlet 1 in. and exhaust $\frac{11}{16}$ in., and so differed from later models.

Side-valve guides are driven up to remove and are fitted from the top. The inlet and exhaust were different lengths and one pair was used by all C10s while another served all M20 and M21 engines.

The B range all had differing inlet and exhaust guides and only in some Gold Stars was a guide common to both engine sizes. Thus there was a pair for the B31 and another for the B33, both of which changed for 1950 onwards. The B32 used the B31 guides up to 1950 and the 1950 B31 type for 1951–53. Another pair went into the alloy option for 1950–53 and two more served the standard alloy engine for 1954–57. The B34 did the same except that its first change came in 1950 to match the B33.

The Gold Stars had their own special guides for both engines for 1949 but changed for 1950 to the parts also fitted to the B32 and B34 alloy-option engines. For the 348 cc engine this pair continued on to the BB engines, while the CB series fitted the pair also used by the 1954-onwards B32. For the DB engines there was another pair, not interchangeable with those of the CB.

The 499 cc engine only fitted the B34 alloy-option pair for 1950–51 and for 1952–55, and the BB engines used those which were to serve the B34 from 1954 onwards. The 499 cc CB and DB engines up to 1957 fitted the same guide pair as the CB and DB 348 cc machines, so again did not interchange. From 1956 the DBD had yet another pair of guides.

The unit engines began with one guide for both

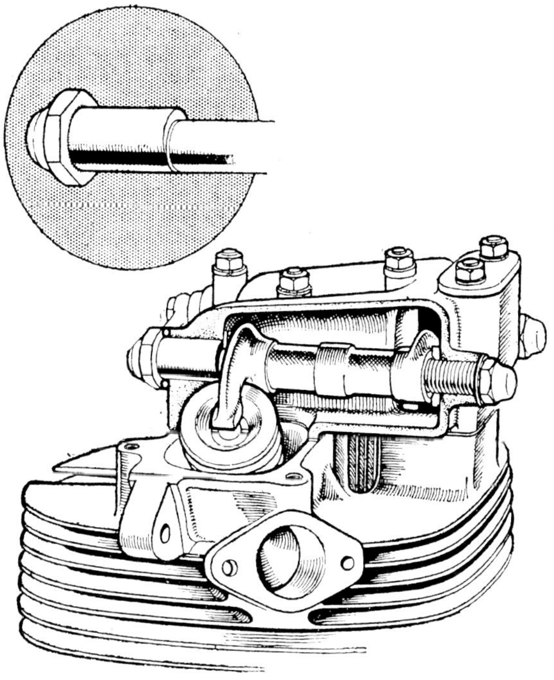

Eccentric rocker spindles adopted by the CB and later Gold Star engines for valve-gap adjustment

valves in the C15, these being circlip located, and another for the B40. By 1965 the exhaust guide had changed for both series of engines but the location method remained for the 247 cc. New guides went into the C25 and B44 series and served all models except a few early 1967 B44VR engines which had guides incorporating the valve-spring seating or cup. A further two pairs appeared in 1971, one for the B25 and the other for the B50.

Valve springs

These should be replaced as a matter of course. All the ohv engines had dual springs while the side-valve ones made do with one. In fact, this was the same one as in the C10, M20 and M21; all used a common part which also did duty as the outer of the C11.

The B range had one pair of springs used as standard for all B31 and B33 machines, plus the B32 and B34 to the end of 1953. There was also a pair of 'special order only' springs listed for 1948–50 for all these engines, and the alloy options, and it was the outer of these that served the B32 and B34 from 1954, together with a new inner.

The Gold Stars began with the special-order springs, except for the 348 cc trials model which fitted the standard pair. For the last ZB and BB models a change was made to those which served the B32 and B34 from 1954 and there were further pairs for the CB alone and DB plus DBD engines.

The unit engines had one pair for the C15, C15T and

B40 up to 1964, after which the outer was changed. A new pair served the C25, the outer of these changing for 1969 and again for 1971. The C15S, SS80 and SS90 all fitted the springs from the DB Gold Star and these also served all B44 and B50 engines.

Valve detail parts

These comprise caps, cups, collets and collars, plus spring insulation washers for some Gold Stars. All these small details need to be cleaned and inspected for any signs of damage or cracking. Replacement is the only answer if any damage is found. Be sure there is no sign of collar collapse or collet pull-through. Check that the taper of the collets and collars match as both 15 and 20 degrees were used in general, plus 25 degrees on the exhausts of the CB Gold Star.

Caps were fitted to all B31 engines and the B32, including its alloy option up to the end of 1953. They were listed in the 1947 and 1954 parts books for the B33 but this would seem to be an error. Cups fitted under the valve springs and were used on ohv engines where they located round the valve guide.

The C11 series used one cup for all years while the B31 and B33 had one each for the early years, both changing to a common part for 1950 onwards. The B32 and B34 used the road-model parts and changed with them, as did the Gold Stars which fitted the B31 and B33 parts for 1949 only, and then used the common part up to the CB series. For the DB and DBD the cup became a washer, but again one part served both engine sizes.

For the unit engines there was one cup for all C15 models and another for the B40, SS90 and B44 up to 1967. For the B44 from 1968 and the B50 another cup was used, and a further one went into the C25 to be changed for 1971.

Valve collets should be kept in pairs and checked for their fit to the valve stem. One pair served all C10 and C11 engines and another looked after the two M side-valve models. The B31 and B33 had one pair for the inlet and another for the exhaust, and these parts also went into the B32 and B34 up to the end of 1953. For 1954 onwards a new pair went into both engines, and the exhaust collet of the B32 and inlet of the B34 were the same parts.

The 348 cc Gold Star began with the B31 parts but the 499 cc version fitted the exhaust parts to the inlet valve as well. For the 1952 ZB and the BB series the parts used were as in the 1954-onwards B32, but in the 499 cc engine the inlet collet was changed for 1954 to the same part used on the 348 cc inlet. New collets went into the CB engines and the inlet had a 20-degree taper angle while the exhaust was of a 25-degree taper. The inlet remained common for the DB and DBD engines but the exhaust of these altered to match the inlet 20-degree taper angle.

Unit engines had one pair of collets for the C15, B40 and B44. The C25 had its own for 1967 but these were changed for 1970 onwards, the same parts being fitted to the B50 from 1971.

The spring collars hold the springs and are locked in place by the collets which must fit snugly. On the side-valve engines one part served both valves on the M range and the C10, while the C11 had its own part.

A single part was used by all B31 and B33 engines, the B32 and B34 up to the end of 1953 plus the alloy-option version, and the ZB-type Gold Star. From 1954 the B32 had a new pair of collars and the exhaust was also fitted to the B34 inlet. This arrangement and the same parts went into the BB Gold Stars, but for the CB series there were new items in light alloy and with 20- and 25-degree tapers in the holes. Both engines used the same pair of parts, but for the DB series a new part served both valves in both engines.

In the unit engines there was one collar for the C15, B40 and B44. Another went into the C25 for 1967 but was changed for 1970; this part then went into the B50 for 1971 onwards.

Spring insulation washers were only fitted to Gold Stars and only on the exhaust side where the part went between the head and the spring cup or washer. One part served both sizes of CB engine and another the DB series.

Valve lifter

This mechanism was fitted to many of the single-cylinder engines and needs to be dismantled, inspected, repaired and assembled as any other.

The only change for the B and M models was to the cable arm which altered for 1955 and 1956, respectively. The same parts served the B32 and B34 including the Gold Stars, and in their case the lever changed on the CB for 1955. On the DB the parts were omitted from the road-racing engines.

There was no valve lifter provided on the C10, C11 or C15, but one was fitted to the C15T and C15S as these were competition models. The lever arm was as used on the late pre-units, but another was listed and became the normal fit from about 1963. It was modified for 1971 onwards.

The B40, B44 and B50 all had valve lifters, but the C25 only had one for 1967–68, having its own lifting spindle which differed from that of the larger engines. For the D1 and D3 competition model Bantams during the 1949–56 period, the same function was provided by a decompressor.

Rocker-box details

Most engines had a very similar design with fixed spindles for the rocker with an oil-feed drilling. The CB, DB and DBD Gold Stars, and the 247 cc engines from 1967 onwards, had the valve gaps set by turning the rocker spindle, which was made eccentric to do this job. All the others had either conventional screws with locknuts in the rocker ends or the adjustment built into the tappets in the crankcase.

ABOVE *The SS90 sports model of 1964, much the same as the smaller and standard machines in most respects*

BELOW *Fine detail of the rocker-box cap from a 1966 C15*

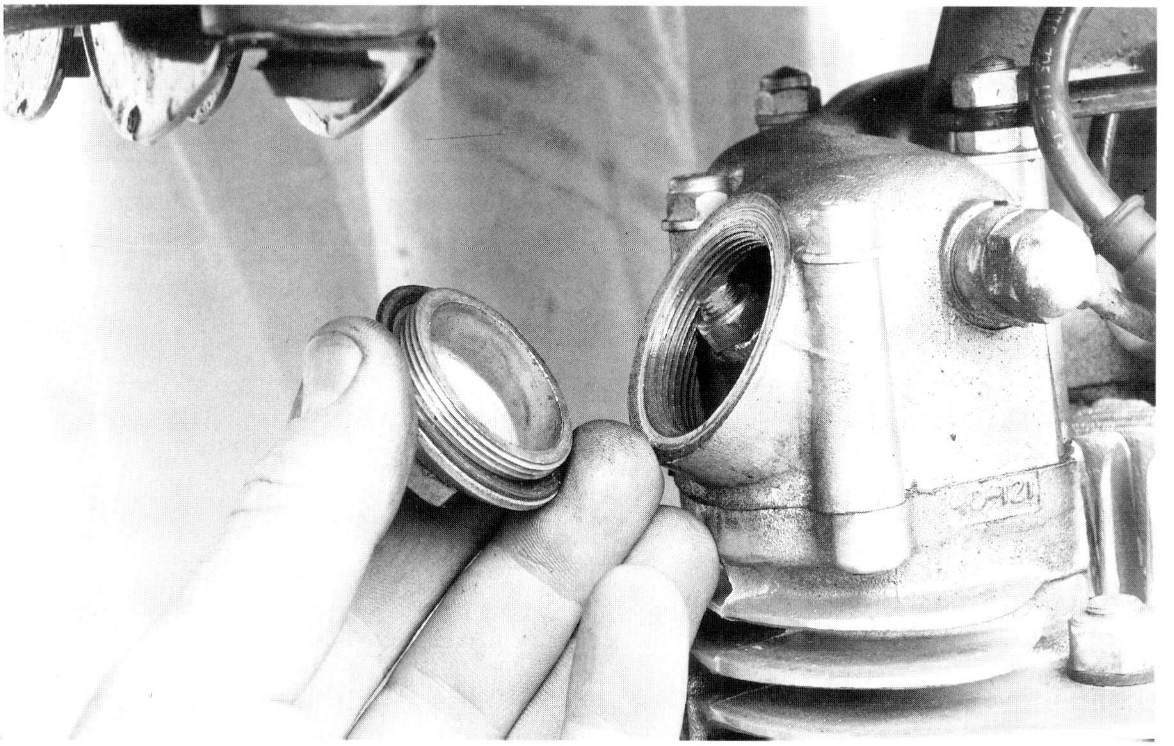

The C11 differed in that the rockers lay across the head and were mounted at a suitable angle on a trunnion bolted to the head. A spring and thrust washer reduced noise and an oil feed was added for 1956.

Parts tended to remain in use for many years and for more than one engine. Thus one pair of rockers served most B-range models from 1946 to 1960. Exceptions were the Gold Stars with one pair for 1949–53, another for BB engines of 1954–55, and a third for CB, DB and DBD engines with the eccentric spindle adjusters. The spindles to match were one for the B models, one for ZB and BB Gold Stars, and the eccentric one for the CB, DB and DBD.

The C11 simply had two identical rockers and the trunnion they pivoted on, which only changed for the oiling modification. The unit singles had one pair of rockers and a common spindle for all models except the 247 cc from 1967. For that machine there were new rockers and eccentric spindles, both of which were modified for 1968 onwards. Otherwise, just the adjuster screws altered for the B44 in 1965.

Rocker box

On most of the B range this is part of the cylinder head, and the C range does not have a rocker box. However, all unit engines, Gold Stars from 1952, and the B32 and B34 from 1954 do have one.

The rocker box used on the late ZB and BB Gold Stars for 1952–55 was also fitted to the B32 and B34 for 1954–57. A revised part went on the CB and DB engines to suit the eccentric rocker spindles.

Rather more rocker boxes were used by the unit engines, with that of the C15 lacking the valve-lifter hole of the competition models. The latter was also fitted to the B40 and B44 engines, but the B50 had its own which changed for 1973 when the side-cover fixing screw was altered from 2BA to $\frac{1}{4}$ in. UNC.

The C25 differed in having provision for eccentric rocker spindles and an oil feed in the top of the casting. Four types were listed, with both the 1967 and 1968 having a valve-lifter hole which did not appear on the 1969 or 1971 types.

Covers and lids

Basically, these are simply alloy parts whose sealing surfaces must be in good order. They are often polished by owners and sometimes even by the factory.

The B range had one pair of rocker-box lids, each held by four bolts, which served all models and years, including the Gold Star for 1949–51. Later Gold Stars with separate rocker boxes, and similar B32 and B34 engines for 1954–57, had a small top cover above the pushrod tunnel.

The C11 had one cover held by one central bolt to enclose its valve gear. This contained two breathers up to engine ZC11-29669 built in 1952, but after that number there were no breathers and no holes for them in the cover. For the C11G in 1954 the cover was altered in shape.

The cover of the unit engines was the rocker box, but this carried two caps and a side plate. The caps began as round items with a large slot but were soon altered to have a hexagon for a spanner, this occurring for 1961 and thus on all B40 models. It was used on the C15, B40 and B44 models and their variations, but the C25 introduced a new part and this was used by the B50 except for 1973 when a new item was fitted with an O-ring to seal it. One side plate served all engines except the 247 cc one built in 1967–71 which had a smaller, simple flat plate.

Rocker-box oil pipes

These fed into banjo connections at the left end of the rocker spindles on the B range and the unit engines, except for the 1967 C25 and later 247 cc engines which had the oil fed into a union in the top of the rocker box. The C12 had a feed into the fixing bolt that held the rocker cover and this arrangement could be fitted to any C11.

The B and unit engines, other than the C25, had hollow banjo bolts to connect the pipe to the rocker spindles; these must be clean and unobstructed, so don't use jointing compound as this could easily block the small feed holes. Also, don't use a locking compound or the bolt will snap off rather than come out again. Note that similar banjo bolts were used to connect the drain pipe that ran from head to crankcase on the B range. The important difference is that the cross-holes in the feed bolts are much smaller than those in the drain ones. For the B range up to 1955, and the road models from then onwards, the feed bolts were the same on inlet and exhaust. For the Gold Star from 1953 onwards, and the B32 and B34 for 1956–57, the exhaust bolt was altered to have a $\frac{3}{32}$ in. cross-hole while the inlet remained at $\frac{1}{16}$ in. as on the other engines. In addition, the feed bolts measure $\frac{29}{32}$ in. from under the head while the drains are $1\frac{3}{32}$ in.

Pushrods

Only the unit engines had much variation with pushrods. The C range had one only, serving all engines and years, while the B range had two. One went into the CB, DB and DBD Gold Stars, and the other into all the rest, with inlet and exhaust being common in all cases.

The unit engines had one pushrod for the C15 series and a second for the B40. The 1967-onwards 247 cc engines were unusual in having different pushrods for inlet and exhaust, while there was more variety for the B44. One type went into the B44GP and VE of the 1965–67 years. For the 1967 B44VS there was another, and for the rest of the B44 range a third which served for 1967–70. A new pushrod went into the B50 for 1971–72 with yet another for 1973.

Pushrod tubes and covers

The B range with iron engines had an alloy pushrod tunnel, sealed to the cylinder head with a gland held in compression by a large nut. There was also a small access plate in the side of the rocker box.

The B-range engines with alloy barrels did not have this arrangement, but there was an access plate on top of the rocker box. All B engines had a common cover to give access to the lower end of the pushrods. It was fitted to the pushrod tunnel or directly to the cylinder, and was also used by the Gold Star series. Only the C15 series of the unit engines had a pushrod tube and this was a simple, chrome-plated tube with top and bottom seals.

Tappets

These can be found on all four-stroke engines except the C10 and C11 which had cam followers. All the C parts were common to all years, except the follower spindle which changed for the alternator models in 1954. The followers themselves were not common, as the C11 type had a recess for the pushrod while the C10 one was simply curved to work against the tappet end.

The side-valve M models had two cams so each could operate a tappet directly. They worked in guides which screwed into the top of the crankcase, and to remove them both the guides and the cam wheel spindles had to come out first. The spindles need a simple puller to extract them but should not be disturbed unless this is necessary. Note that each has a flat on its back shoulder which must be positioned at the top to clear the tappet foot.

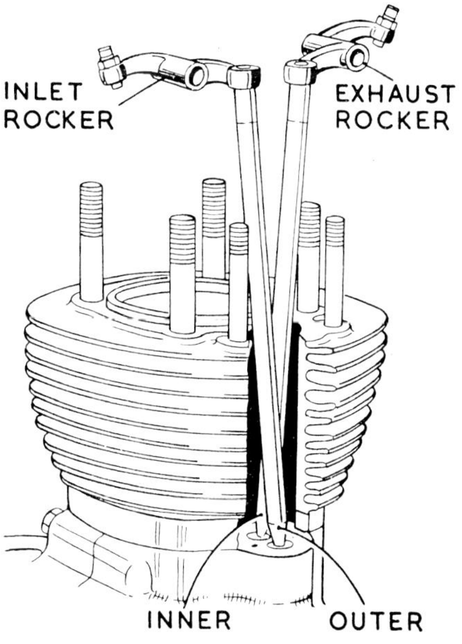

The correct arrangement of the pushrods and tappets on the unit engines

The tappets were not the same, as the exhaust one was given a special treatment by the factory. In addition, the tappet heads differed as the exhaust had a collar machined on it for the valve lifter to bear on. The locknuts and guides were the same for both valves.

The B range used the same design, and some common parts, as the M. Both tappets were the same and as used by the M inlet, as were the tappet heads and guides. The locknuts of the B31 and B32 were as for the M models and so were those of the 499 cc engines for 1951–55. However, for 1950 and from 1956 onwards another type was listed, while prior to 1950 the part is omitted from the parts list. It would seem that the B31 part was fitted up to 1955 and another from then onwards.

The Gold Star began with B-range parts, except for the tappet locknut which was that to be used by the B33 from 1956. With the 1952 engines came revised tappets, and both these and the guides changed again for the CB models of 1954. These had no separate heads as gap adjustment was by eccentric rocker, and while the guides continued unaltered, the tappets were further modified for the DB engines and this type was used in the DBD.

Unit engines had one tappet for the C15 and B40 models. A new part with a 1-degree taper on the foot was introduced for the B44GP in 1965 and went into the C25 for 1967. It was assembled with the thin end pointing to the front. It was modified for 1968 and went into both 247 and 441 cc engines, with a further change for 1971 and the 247 and 499 cc units.

Tappet cover

This was a simple alloy casting used on the side-valve cylinders. One served all M models, and another the C10 for 1946–53. The latter changed for 1954–55 and took an oval shape for 1956.

Camshaft

Unit and C-range engines have a single camshaft carrying both cams, but the B and M ranges have two cams each with a gear to mesh with the crankshaft pinion. Either type needs to be checked for wear on the cam face and the bearing surfaces. Both B and M cams have bushes pressed into them and run on fixed spindles, while the others turn in bushes in the crankcase and timing cover. Check all keyways and threads for damage and a good fit to their mating parts.

Remember that for each engine there were a number of camshafts that would fit physically but only one that was correct for a given year. For the B range there were many cams listed for the Gold Star engines and generally these were stamped with their part number which should aid identification. Be careful in fitting a sports cam to a standard engine as this may not always have the desired effect on the performance. The practical side should not be

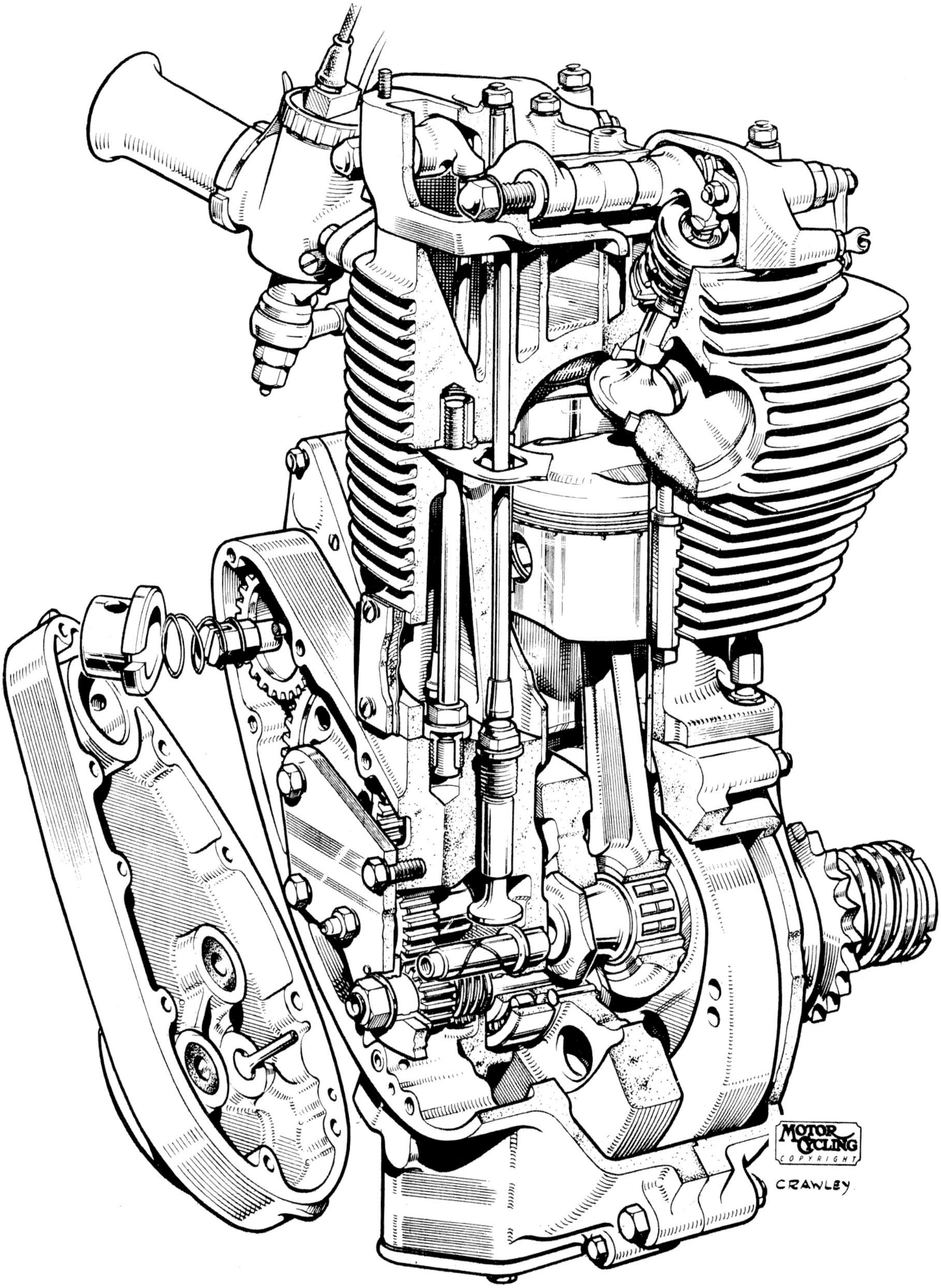

ABOVE *The CB Gold Star engine with big fins, eccentric rockers and timed breather, but still retaining the quill big-end oil feed*

ABOVE RIGHT *A government minister at a late-1966 Earls Court Show inspecting a B40 built for the army*

neglected either, as an alternative cam could give more lift which may result in the springs becoming coil-bound or the valve collar hitting the end of the guide. Thus, on early Gold Star engines, outer valve spring 65-1249 is essential to avoid this problem.

The unit engines should be viewed in the same way, as touring, sports and competition camshafts were all used and the only obvious change was to the timing-side points in 1965. Even the C range presents variations due to the existence of ramp cams. The only way to be certain as to what you have is to check the timing it gives with the gaps set as laid down for this work.

In general it is best to run what is specified for your model and to set it to its correct timing. Exceptions exist but should be used with caution if there is any doubt.

The B and M ranges had one cam gear which served both valves, all basic road models and all years. From this simple start came the complexity of the Gold Star cams which varied to suit touring, trials, scrambles, Clubmans, road racing, grass-track and alcohol fuel. There were a good many of them and the combinations and settings recommended by the factory have been set out in an appendix along with those for the other engines.

The C10 and C11 had the same valve timing but different camshafts. For 1954, and the alternator models, both lost their threaded end which was altered to a hole for the points cam drive. These camshafts had the same timing as before, but late in 1954 ones with ramp cams were adopted and fitted from engines BC10L-3562 and BC11G-10438 onwards. These continued in use up to 1957 and 1958 respectively. For the C10 and C11 these ramp cams were available on camshafts to suit their engine layout and could be fitted to any post-war engines.

The unit-engine camshafts divide into those for the early types and those for 1965 onwards with the points in the timing cover. There were two early camshafts with one fitted to the C15, C15T and B40, while the other, which was more sporting, served the

C15S, early C15T, SS80 and SS90. There were ten of the later 1965-onwards type, so care is needed in checking what is to hand.

Most continued the touring and sports timing of the early camshafts, so to begin with there was one for the C15, C15T and B40 and another for the C15S, SS80, C15 Sportsman and SS90. The B44GP had a special cam and two looked after the late-1960s engines. One served the C25 for 1967–69, and the B44VS and B44SS for 1969. The other, with the same timing, dealt with the B44VE for 1966–67, B44VS for 1967–68, B44VR for 1967 and B44SS for 1968.

The year 1970 brought two new camshaft part numbers as the tapped hole for the points bolt was Unified. One part went into the B44VS and the other into the B25 and B44SS. For 1971 the B25 was given a new part and two cams appeared for the B50. One went into the motocross engine and gave it the timing of the B44GP, but for 1973 this was changed to the other which served the road models for 1971–72.

Camshaft bushes

The B and M cams each had a pair of bushes pressed into them which were then reamed to size. One bush served all.

The C range began with three bushes of which the inner one in the crankcase was common to all models and years. The other two went in the timing cover and were replaced by a single bush for the alternator model of 1954 onwards.

The unit engines had one outer bush in the inner timing cover which was common to all models except the 1973 B50MX. The inner bush was fitted into the crankcase and five different ones were used in all. The first was a plain bush and went in up to 1964. For 1965 there were shouldered parts with one for the 247 cc engine and another for the 441 cc unit. The first was changed for 1967–68 and again for 1969–71, when it was also fitted into the B44 engines, and later went into the B50.

Timing-gear details

The B and M engines had the same layout and detail parts for most years and models. Among those altered, though, were the cam spindles which began as two of the same item. From 1951 the exhaust was altered in detail and this change applied to all B and M engines, including the Gold Star up to the CB series. For the DB a new inlet spindle was fitted but again was very much as the early type.

Higher up in the gear-train, the taper-fit magneto gear was changed for a contact-breaker one for the B31 and B33 for 1958 onwards. The latter fitted a parallel shaft to which it was held by a cross-pin, itself retained by a circlip.

The crankshaft timing pinion of 1946 was still in use in 1963, but from 1952 onwards a special gear was listed for the Gold Star as an alternative to advance the timing by 10 degrees. The other changes also concerned the CB and later Gold Stars and their idler and magneto gears. The first gained some lightening holes and must be fitted correctly with the widest flange, viewed from the end, towards the crankcase. The second was fitted with a pin to drive a timed breather which featured on all these models from 1954 onwards, and this has to be set correctly in relation to the crankshaft as well as for ignition timing.

The C range had fewer changes as all that happened was an alteration in the camshaft gear key part number for 1950, and in the crankshaft pinion during 1947. The latter change went in on engines XC10-4314 and XC11-4423, otherwise all parts were common to both types and all years.

The unit timing side was as simple as the C range but had more variation. Most changes came in with the B44GP in 1965 and then went on to the C25 in 1967. The crankshaft gear was typical of this with one final change for the B50MX in 1973. The key it located on followed exactly the same pattern, but not the nut that held it in place.

There was one for the C15 which went on the B40 for 1965 but prior to that time the larger model had its own part. The B44GP introduced another in 1965 which continued in the 441 cc engines up to late 1969, and this also went into the 247 cc engine in 1967. For the smaller engine in 1970 there was a new nut, but in the larger it went into the B44SS in 1969 and the B44VS in 1970. Another nut served the B50 models. The lockwashers to retain the nuts comprised one for the 1961–64 B40, another for that model for 1965–66, one for the 1973 B50MX, and one for all the other models and years.

The camshaft nut was that used on the B-range crankshaft and it and its lockwasher served all models to 1964, after which the points moved to the timing cover and the nut went. The key was common to all for 1959–70 but changed for the 1971 models.

The worm on the crankshaft drove both the oil pump and the points cam up to late 1964. During 1960 it and its mating gear were modified to improve them and they must only be changed as a pair. The parts continued to be fitted to the 1965–66 C15 models and the 1965 B40 ones, but without the ignition assembly and with the top hole in the crankcase blanked off with a cap. The worm changed for the B44GP in 1965 and the C25 in 1967, with this common part being fitted to 1972. For the B50MX in 1973 there was another one.

ABOVE *Simple timing side of a C11G with two gears and cam followers*

FAR LEFT *A 1961 DBD Gold Star with its timing case off to show how the breather is timed to the magneto gear*

Dynamo drive

For the B and M range the dynamo was mounted on top of the magneto, and for the C models up to late 1953 it was clamped to the back of the crankcase and chain-driven. There were no detail part changes.

Timing and points covers

The cover fitted to B and M models in 1946 lacked the breather valve of later machines but the two will interchange, enabling early engines to be updated. The second cover came in during 1948 and first went on engines YB31-2457, YB32-238, YB33-2011, YB34-224, YM20-424, YM21-603 and YM33-808. It remained in use for these engines from then onwards.

In 1950 it was joined by a version machined to carry a rev-counter gearbox in line with the magneto gear. A coupling connected the two and this cover was listed up to the end of the BB series in 1955 for Gold Star customers who specified a rev-counter. If they did not, the standard cover was fitted.

A new cover was introduced for the CB engine with the rev-counter drive hole opened up to take a rotary timed breather. The DB had a similar cover but revised to mount an oil seal in place of the big-end oil-feed quill. Both had provision to mount a rev-counter gearbox and from 1955 a sealing disc was listed with gasket, screws and locking wire to blank the hole if the gearbox was removed.

Both models in the C range used the same inner and outer covers for 1946–53.

A new arrangement was used on the alternator models introduced for 1954, with one inner cover for

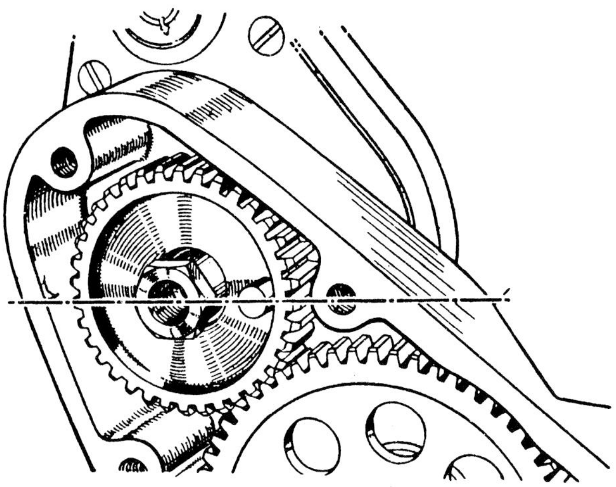

ABOVE *Setting the timed Gold Star breather, which should be as shown at top dead centre*

BELOW *The C15 timing side with the drive to the points housing above and oil pump below. The clamp is for the housing*

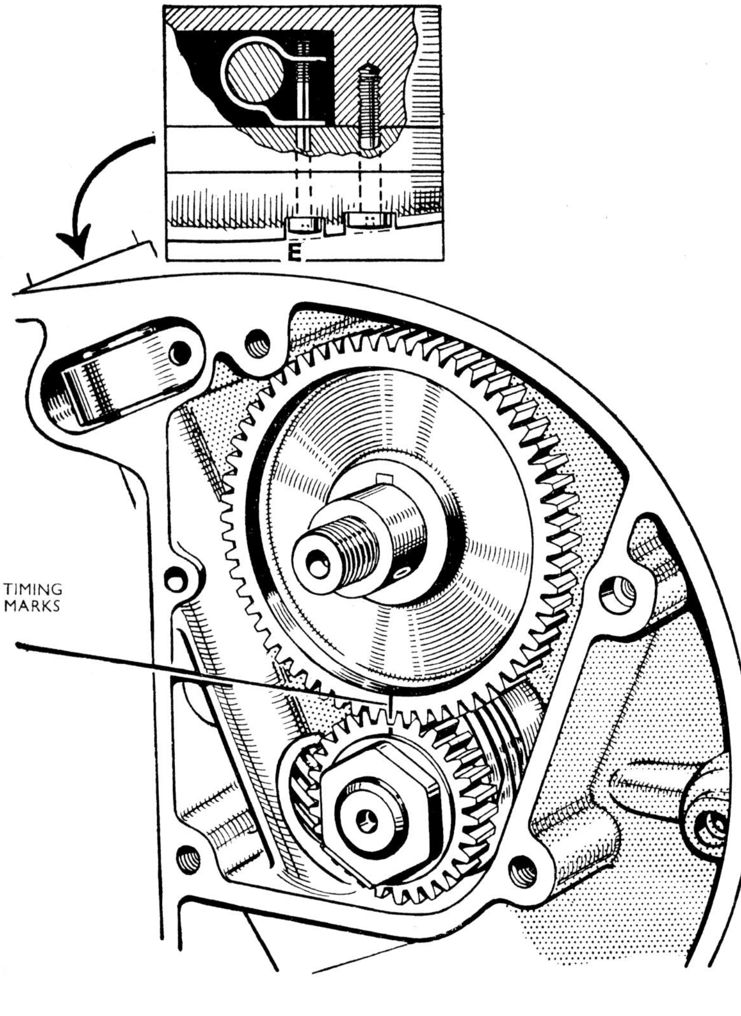

each model and a common points cover. The inner cover included the mounting for the points plate and two of these were listed because the C10L was fitted with Wipac points and the C11G and C12 with Lucas ones.

The unit engines had two styles of cover, with one to suit those made up to 1964 and the other for later ones with timing-chest points. The C15 alone had its outer cover formed with a raised polished rim and this also went on the competition versions. From about 1964 a hole was added in the outer in line with the clutch cable to provide access to this for easier assembly. A rubber bung sealed it once the cable was in place.

The outer cover for the B40, SS80 and SS90 was a common part and differed in appearance to the C15 one as it lacked the polished rim and was buffed all over. In both cases the cover was set off by an eight-pointed star set in a recess which was painted red before the star was assembled. Two stars were listed with the legend '250' or '350' and used as appropriate. The inner cover of the C15 was modified at engine C15-27817 during 1961, but the original remained in use on the B40.

Both inner and outer were revised for 1965 when the points moved and the clutch mechanism became a rack-and-pinion device with an external cable. The outer was common to all models up to late 1967, after which it was revised for 1968 when the points plate type changed, and again for 1969–70 when its screws changed to Unified. For 1971 there were two outer covers listed, one for the B25 with an open slot at the top of the points housing for the wires, and the other with a hole in the same place for this job. This last was amended for the B50MX in 1973 when the kickstart spindle bush that was fitted in it altered.

The 1965 inner covers were two in number with one for the C15 and B40 and another for the 441 cc engine, this having an added oil seal which ran on the end of the crankshaft as part of the oil feed to the crankshaft. A new seal was introduced for 1967, and in the C25 it was located by a circlip which later went into the B50. It and the seal were changed for the B50MX of 1973. The circlip was not used in the 441 cc engine.

There was a new inner cover for the C25 in 1967 and this was modified for 1968 when the oil-system anti-drain valve was moved from the right crankcase to a point just below the points drive. The cover part number did not change until 1969 when the fixing screws became Unified, and it altered again for 1970 and 1971.

The 441 cc engine followed a similar pattern with the anti-drain valve moving for 1968, but the SS model still listed the earlier cover, although the VS one did have a new part. It changed again for 1969 and 1970 with yet another for the B50 models.

One points cover was listed for all for 1965–67 and

ABOVE *A 1967 D10B Bushman Bantam on show*

RIGHT *Early racing Bantam fitted with John Hogan head and modified magneto stator to alter timing*

another for 1968–73. The points oil seal was common to all except the 1973 B50MX but, as with many such part number changes, these arose due to a BSA and Triumph group exercise, as many Triumph numbers also changed for that year.

Bantam covers

These need to be checked in the same way as the four-stroke timing covers for cracks, damage, flatness and thread condition. Many were common or interchangeable but not all, so some care is needed when searching for a part.

The left cover supported the magneto stator and into it went the clutch lift mechanism. One was listed for the Wipac fitted to most Bantams and another for the Lucas generator. Each had its own outer cover. The left cover was modified in 1954 and 1958 for the D1 and D3 engines while another was listed for the D5, but all were very similar and interchange.

For the D7 in 1959 there was a new left cover which was modified from the original type to take an outer cover. This item was cast with the name 'Super' on it. The left cover was further changed for 1967 when the six-coil stator was fitted, and at the same time the outer cover was changed to one with four fixing screws in place of three. For 1968 a hole was added in the cover to give access to the clutch adjuster, and a rubber bung listed to seal this when not in use.

On the right side of the engine went the primary-chain cover and one served all models for 1949–66. A polished version was listed in 1950 only. For the D10 in 1967 the points housing was incorporated into the chaincase and this part also went on to the D14 in 1968. For the D175 in 1969 the case was revised to suit a larger kickstart spindle. In addition, the forward location dowel was changed from a solid pin to the same hollow one fitted at the rear, so the case hole was enlarged. One points cover and oil seal served all models from 1967 onwards.

Crankcase types

The M20 and M21 had their own cases with two mains in each to give more support to their massive crankshafts than the B range. The timing side was common for all years but the drive side changed during 1948 when the oil breather was moved from behind the bearing housing to the timing cover. This went in on engines YM20-424 and YM21-603. A third drive-side case was listed for use on M21 engines supplied to the AA when these had an alternator fitted.

The B range had the same breather change in 1948 so the drive-side case was altered at engines YB31-2457, YB32-237, YB33-2011, YB34-224 and YM33-808. Both sides changed for 1958 when the drive side had the stator fixings added and on the timing side provision was made for the contact-breaker housing. One other alteration was for the B32 and B34 only and concerned the drive-side case which was altered for 1954 onwards.

The 348 cc Gold Star began with standard B-range cases, but these changed for 1952 and the revised type then went on to the BB engines. The 499 cc engine differed from the others in having a bearing plate in the drive-side case which was revised for 1952, while the timing side was special to the model and was used up to 1955 on the ZB and BB engines.

New cases with an additional cylinder-head fixing position were introduced for the CB models in 1954 and were common to both engine sizes. They remained in use from then onwards.

The C-range cases are a confused story from the parts lists as there seem to have been some misprints, but in practice this was not so. One driving side served both models but there was a timing side for each as the top face drillings differed for side or overhead engines. This principle continued on the alternator models of 1954 when new cases were introduced.

For the C15 unit engines there was an early detail change to the timing side with the addition of a grub screw to lock the points drive-shaft bush. The cases were both revised for 1961 and the timing side for 1965 when the points moved. The B40 had its own cases which were changed for 1965.

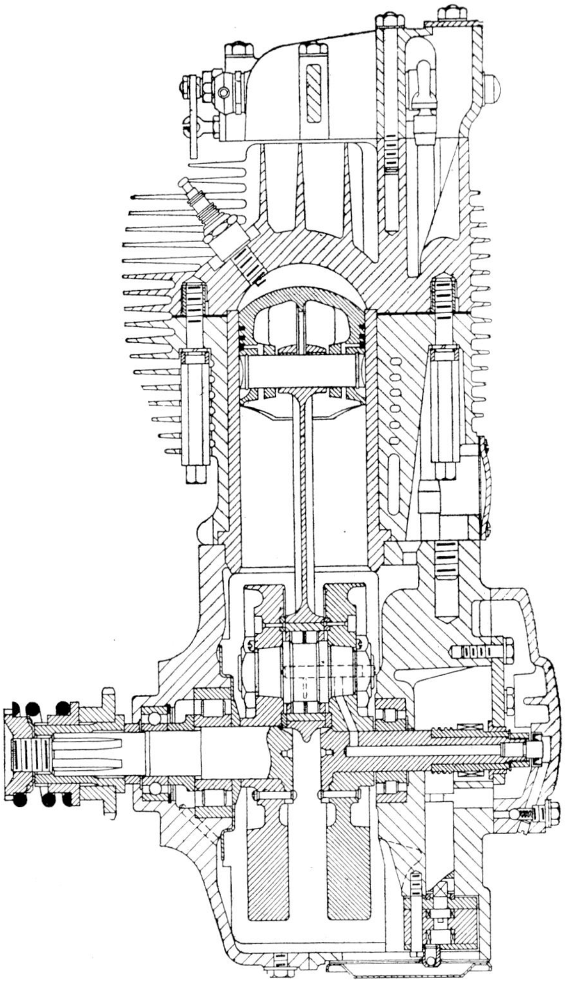

Cross-section through a DB Gold Star engine with sealed oil feed into the crankshaft in place of earlier quill. This is the 348 cc type with the thick barrel sleeve

New cases were introduced for the C25 in 1967 and modified for 1968 when the anti-drain valve moved out of the right one. There were further changes for 1969 when threads were Unified, a rev-counter drive was added in the front of the right case, and a timing plug to the front of the left one, while for 1970 the oil-pressure release became an assembled unit; a final change occurred for 1971. The larger engines went through a similar sequence.

The Bantam began with a pair of cases for the D1 plus a second left case in 1950 to suit engines with the Lucas generator. These had the barrel studs set at 52 mm centres and the top face was bored for a small-diameter spigot. By 1953 the number of fixing screws had risen from 11 to 13, with one fitted from behind the clutch on the right.

The D3 began with its own cases for 1954 but from 1955 shared common parts with the D1. These had 55 mm stud centres, which accommodated the larger spigot and were clamped with 13 screws. For the D1 for 1958 there were revised cases with oilways from the gearbox and primary drive to the mains.

A 1949 D1 Bantam engine and other details including the original flat silencer

The main-bearing lubrication arrangement went on the D5, which had its studs set out at 60 mm, and the same cases were used on the early D7 models. For 1962 they were modified with three extra fixing screws, one under the top rear-mounting bolt hole. The cases were revised in 1967 for the D10 and its new alternator mounting, and at the same time new cases appeared to take the four-speed gearbox. These were revised for the D14 in 1968 and again for the D175 in 1969 when the screw total went up to 17.

Sump plate

As this is what keeps the oil from dripping from the crankcase, a good joint is essential, so the plate needs to be flat and true. Just one served all the B, C and M models, but there was more variation for the unit models.

One plate served the C15 and B40 models, and another the C25 and B44 engines up to 1969. That year a new one was fitted to the B44SS only but went on the others for 1970–71. For the B50 there was a new part with the plate and filter gauze as one.

Main bearings

Many of these were either common to one model for all years or used in more than one range. Thus a roller race used in 1946 is also to be found in the 1973 B50.

The M side-valve and B ranges had two common bearings but differed in that the M had two races on both sides of the crankshaft whereas the B had only one on the timing side. The common ones were the inner drive-side roller which had dimensions of 25 × 62 × 17 mm and the timing-side roller which was $\frac{7}{8}$ × $2\frac{1}{4}$ × $\frac{11}{16}$ in. This was the inner race on the M range and the outer was a ball race of the same size. These two abutted, unlike the drive-side pair which were separated by a spacer. The outer of these was a ball race in the B range and a roller in the M up to late 1955. For 1956 onwards it was changed to a ball race and all were of common 25 × 52 × 15 mm dimensions.

The 348 cc Gold Star used the B-range bearings, but on the 499 cc version the size of the inner drive roller race was increased to $1\frac{1}{8}$ × $2\frac{13}{16}$ × $\frac{13}{16}$ in. In addition it was held in place by a bearing plate. This arrangement was used on all 499 cc engines, while the ZB and BB versions of the 348 cc engine kept to the standard B-range races. The 348 cc CB and DB models were the same as the 499 cc version.

The C range was much simpler. A bush went on the timing side with dimensions of $\frac{63}{64}$ × $1\frac{1}{4}$ × 1 in. and a ball race on the drive side, this measuring 25 × 62 × 17 mm. Both models used this for the years 1946–58.

The unit engines also had a timing-side bush to start with which was 1.306 × 1.442 × 1 in. at first and became 1.313 × 1.442 × 1 in. for 1963 onwards. During 1966 the C15 bottom half was altered to that tried and tested in the Victor Grand Prix, and the bearings changed. The drive side became a roller race and the timing side a ball race, both of 25 × 62 × 17 mm dimensions.

This arrangement was used by all the 247 cc engines from then onwards although the parts list continued to show a drive-side ball race for 1967–69. The same bearings went into all the B44 engines but the arrangement was stiffened further for the B50. These fitted a 25 × 62 × 17 mm roller race on each side plus an outer ball race on the drive side of $\frac{7}{8}$ × 2 × $\frac{9}{16}$ in. dimensions.

Bantams are easy, as although the part numbers changed two or three times, the bearings did not. All were ball races with one of $\frac{3}{4}$ × $1\frac{7}{8}$ × $\frac{9}{16}$ in. on each side and an outer of 17 × 40 × 12 mm on the drive side. The actual positions varied a little over the years as the oil seals were moved from outboard to inboard to suit the changes in main-bearing lubrication.

Stator housing and shield

These parts only appear on a few models. The housing was used on the C range for 1954–58 to support the stator and for the first of those years a shaped shield went between the two parts with a washer to position

Measuring the outer-head-to-barrel gap on a Gold Star. This was then filled with a peel-off gasket of the same thickness as the gap plus a couple of thou

it. For 1955 onwards these were replaced by a simple spinner behind the rotor.

The B range went straight to the same part when the alternator was fitted in 1958 and this was also used for M21 models built for the AA with an alternator. These also had a housing to support the stator.

Assembly

This must be done slow and steady to make sure all is well at every stage. It will be the reverse of the dismantling to suit the problem of installing the engine weight in the frame without damage to either part. Make sure every nut and screw is fully fastened and locked and that none are left loose.

Start by cleaning your tools and bench, lay out all you need and begin with the sub-assemblies. Lubricate parts as you go along and make sure all parts move nicely once assembled. Keep jointing compound to a minimum and out of all oilways. Proceed with thought at each stage and you will not have any trouble. If in doubt, go back and check as the time involved will be small.

Be certain, and the assembled engine will start as soon as you want it to.

3 Transmission

This covers all the mechanical parts from the crankshaft to the rear wheel sprocket, so it takes in two chains, four sprockets, a clutch and a set of gears. Included with the gears are the kickstart and gearchange mechanisms, clutch lift and gearbox shell.

Attention

Articles on the restoration of a machine often state that the owner has not stripped the gearbox but is using it as found. In many cases, it is apparent that the box history is not known and this practice must be condemned.

Unless you check, you cannot be certain that a gear tooth is not about to fail or an errant part about to jam the gears. In the timescale of a restoration the period spent on inspecting the gears is minimal, and even on a straight rebuild the time will be well spent if you thereby make sure the box is not going to lock up on you.

Engine sprocket

The B and M ranges had common sprockets and these ranged in size from 15 to 23 teeth over the years. All interchange with two reservations: first is that the 15-tooth one requires the fitment of a special sliding sleeve, and second is the number of lobes in the shock absorber. Over 1955–56 these changed from four to two and, of course, the parts have to match.

The C range fitted a 16-tooth sprocket for 1946–53 with a 17-tooth one as an option. The parts were changed for 1954 when the alternator was fitted, and from then onwards the C10L kept to 16 teeth while the ohv models had 17 teeth as standard.

All Bantams have a 17-tooth engine sprocket and one part served all up to 1966. For the D10 in 1967 it was modified with a rear counterbore for an O-ring due to the move of the points into the primary chaincase. This second part went into all remaining engines.

The unit engines all had a duplex primary chain and fitted a 23-tooth engine sprocket to most models. Exceptions were first the competition machines of 1962–63 which had 18 teeth, and then the B44 range which had 28. One sprocket served from the Victor Grand Prix of 1965 to 1970, but another was introduced for the B50. This was well recessed at the back to fit around an additional main bearing without altering the original chain line.

Shock absorber—engine and clutch

On the B and M ranges an engine shock absorber was used and the details were unchanged until the two-lobe cam was introduced in 1955 or 1956. Some parts continued as they were. There were no changes on the similar C-range system used up to 1953.

For the pre-unit C range, from 1954, a three-vane clutch absorber with drive and rebound rubbers was used, but the 1958 B range had four vanes. The C15 and other unit engines also had a four-vane clutch hub and at first the rubbers were of two sizes. During 1961–62, and starting on the B40 and C15S, a change was made to the design of the vanes to enable eight identical rubbers to be fitted, and that arrangement was used by all from then on.

Primary chain

Unless this is in perfect condition you can expect to change it, but don't throw the old one away immediately. Check it and the sprockets for any wear pattern that may indicate a lack of alignment. If this exists it must be corrected using the alternative spacers listed, if available, or by making some to suit. These usually fit behind the engine sprocket but other arrangements can be made.

All chain sizes are given in an appendix.

Primary-chain tensioner

This was only fitted to the unit engines and first appeared on the SS80 in 1961. It then went into the C15T, C15S and B40 for 1962 and into the SS90 later that year. Finally, it reached the C15 for 1964. While there was more than one type of distance piece associated with the tensioner, the actual slipper assembly continued in use in the C25, B25, B44 and B50 engines, with the only change coming for 1973.

Clutch hub and centre

This was used in its simplest form in the Bantam as one

DUNLOP
4

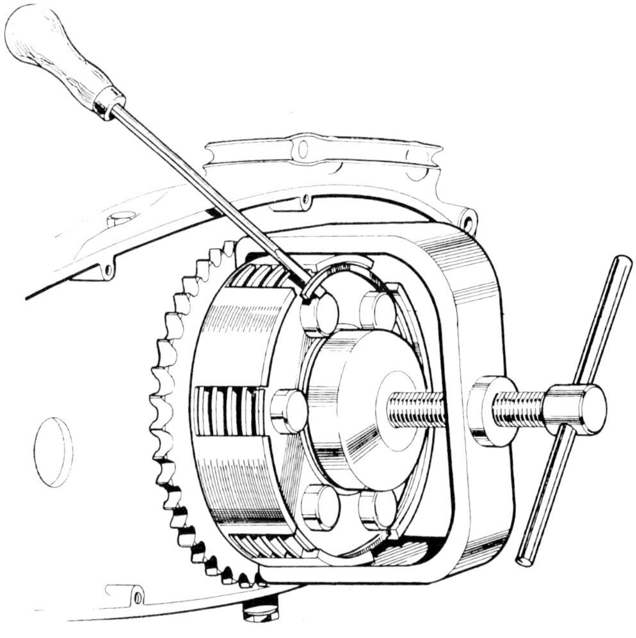

ABOVE *Jarring the engine-sprocket nut tight on a Gold Star before turning the lockwasher over. Note the clutch with adjustment for springs*

LEFT *Not a restoration project but the 1972 Thruxton 500 race. This BSA was leading the 500 cc class until this clutch work was needed*

RIGHT *The Bantam clutch compressor, which is an essential aid. That big circlip must be well home for security*

part splined to the gearbox mainshaft, and was made to take the drive from the clutch plates. In other models it consisted of a hub fixed to the mainshaft with a separate centre splined to it. This carried the studs for the spring nuts and took the clutch plate drive. Where a shock absorber was built into the clutch, the assembly comprised hub, spider vane and centre, except for the early C range which dispensed with the hub.

The C range had a hub change for 1951 and went to spider and centre for 1954. The B changed its hub for 1949 and 1951, and up to 1957 had one centre for the B31 and another for the other models. After 1947 the

RIGHT *The 1967 B44GP Victor Grand Prix*

BELOW *J. L. Kendall in the 1950 Junior Clubmans on his Gold Star, which ran on an open pipe as was allowed in the early races*

M range used the B-range parts, except for models built for the AA which continued with the old single-spring clutch design for some years.

The unit engines had changes to the spider and centre during 1961–62 when the absorber rubbers were altered. Otherwise the hub changed for 1971, the spider for 1973, and two centres without an end flange were introduced for 1971 for the two engine sizes.

On the Bantam one hub served all models up to 1966. For 1967 there were two types, with one for the D10B trail models only; this hub stayed in use for all from then onwards.

Chainwheel and bearing

The chainwheel and clutch drum were either made as one or in two parts riveted together. The whole turned on some form of bearing and the wheel carried a ring of friction inserts in some cases.

The B range all had chainwheels with 43 teeth as standard, while there was a special one with 44 teeth available as an option for the Gold Star. All were fitted with inserts up to late 1957 and this design continued for the Gold Stars to their end. There was variation in the depth of the clutch drum to allow for more or fewer clutch plates and some detail variations to suit model alterations.

The B31 had its own type which served the B32 into 1947, but during the year that model adopted the chainwheel from the 499 cc machines and this served them all in most guises up to 1957. Exceptions were the rigid B32 and B34 of 1954–55 and the Gold Stars for 1954–57 and 1958–63, all of which had their own wheels.

All these B-range chainwheels ran on a double row of caged ball bearings with an outer race pressed into the wheel and an inner with two ball tracks on the clutch hub. Each row of ball bearings had its own cage to form an assembly which clipped into place on the inner. For 1958–60 the B31 and B33 changed their design to a chainwheel without friction inserts, running on a bearing of 20 loose rollers.

The M range began its post-war days with a single-spring clutch with a chainwheel without inserts running on 22 rollers. This design continued in use for machines for the AA, but from 1948 the standard models fitted the parts from the 499 cc B range, including the double-row ball race.

The same ball race also served the C range for 1946–53 when the chainwheel had inserts and 43 teeth, being a thinner edition of the B-range part. For 1954–58 the wheel lost the inserts, retained the 43 teeth and ran on 18 rollers, these being the part also used in the early M clutch.

The unit-engine chainwheel had 52 teeth and always ran on rollers with 24 in use at first, and 25 from 1965 for the B44 series and from 1967 for the C25. The chainwheels varied with the first being used by the C15, B40, 1967 C25 and 1965–67 B44. There was another for the C15T and C15S for 1962–65, one for the B25 and B44 for 1968–70, and two more for the 1971 revamp. One went on the B25 and the 1973 B50 while the other served the B50 models for 1971–72.

The Bantam chainwheel had the drum riveted to it with the kickstart ratchet gear on the rear. All versions had 38 teeth and the original one served up to 1966. It was then modified for the four-plate clutch in 1967 and revised for 1969. The wheel ran on a flanged bush in all three-speed versions which ran to the end of 1967, but the four-speed models introduced that year used a plain bush and separate thrust washer.

Springs, cups and nuts

The M range alone used a single-spring clutch and that only for 1946–47 and some later AA models. The rest used multiple springs with three, four or six of them used to clamp the plates together.

The B range began with six springs which were altered for 1950 and continued on it up to 1957, on the Gold Stars up to 1963 and on the M range for the same period, having been introduced on this for 1948. One set of cups served all these models, and the spring nuts were two standard parts for each spring which allowed the tension to be adjusted so the pressure plate lifted true. With this correct, the setting was locked with the second nut. For the B31 and B33 only, from 1958, there were four new springs, cups and nuts which locked to one another but no longer offered any adjustment.

The C range went the same way with six springs of the type used on the early B models, six cups and 12 stock nuts fitted from 1946. For the revised clutch of 1954 there were new parts and only three of each, with each set locked together to prevent them undoing in use.

The unit engines all had four-spring clutches, with one spring used on the C15, C25 and B40 engines up to 1971. A second went into the B44 and B50 from 1965, and a third was used by the C15S for 1959–64 and the C15T for 1962–64. The spring cups were the same up to 1969, having a change for 1970 and another for 1971. Two types of spring nuts were used, one on the smaller models up to 1970 and the other on the B44, B50 and B25 for 1971.

On the Bantam there were always six springs and cups but never any nuts. Three types of springs were used with the changes coming for 1958 and 1969. The spring cup was common from 1949 to 1971.

Plates

The main plates were the plain and friction ones that took most of the drive, but in many cases there was also a sleeve plate behind the chainwheel and a pressure plate to clamp the clutch together. The numbers of the first two depended on the power to be transmitted and many clutches used more than one type of plain plate. Assembly must allow for this.

The B range began with three plain plates splined to the hub and three friction ones to the drum, plus a sleeve plate. This continued on the B31 but the B32

changed to four of each from engine XB32-317 during 1947, and the same number went into both 499 cc models. For 1951 the sleeve plate on all models was modified, as was one of the plain plates of the B31 which then continued in this form up to 1957. The B33 had the same alteration for 1956–57. These two models changed to a new form of five-plate clutch for 1958 with no sleeve plate but which had a new pressure plate.

The B32 and B34 went to five of the original plates in their rigid-frame form of 1954–55 and at the same time had a change of pressure plate. For 1956–57, when they were in a pivoted-fork frame, they retained the new pressure plate and fitted five new friction plates. The plain ones continued to number five but comprised four of the original plus one of the modified type first seen on the 1951 B31.

The Gold Stars first used the four-plate B33-type clutch but for 1954 went to five plates and the new pressure plate as on the B32. The friction plates were the original type common to the range but were only fitted to the touring, trials and scrambles models. For Clubmans and road-racing use there were new plates of the type the B32 was to adopt in 1956. From 1958 the friction plates were of a revised type and the plain ones became the type first seen in the 1951 B31.

The M range began with a single-spring design with eight Ferodo rings and seven plain plates. Four of these splined to the drum and three to the centre. This design was fitted to the standard machines for 1946–47 and to later AA models. From 1948 the standard models, including the new M33, fitted the four-plate B-range clutch.

The C range used a number of parts from the B range, including both types of sleeve plate, which changed from 1951, until the clutch type changed for 1954. The early clutch fitted the B-range pressure plate but had its own single friction plate. The plain plate began as the original B type but from 1951 became the modified one as used in the B31 that year. From 1954 there were new plain, friction and pressure plates, plus a plain plate for the inner end of the hub.

Unit clutches had fewer changes and all had five plain plates and four friction ones up to 1970, with five being fitted for 1971 onwards when the centre hub was revised. For 1973 both were given new part numbers. One pressure plate served for many years and was revised to improve the spring-cup location for 1970.

The Bantam had three friction plates up to 1966 and four from 1967 onwards. At first they were pierced for cork inserts, but from 1958 bonded-on friction pads were used. The plate was revised for 1967 when the number increased to four. Similarly the plain plate was modified for 1967 when its number rose from two to three.

One pressure plate served all Bantams but the spring-cup plate was altered twice. The first time was in 1950 at engine YD 22001 when three tapped bosses were added to secure the drum cover, and the second was in 1967 for the four-plate clutch.

LEFT *Greasing the ball bearing in the clutch mechanism of a 1963 C15*

BELOW *Elements of the Bantam clutch worm which must be well greased and always seems to be worn out though still able to work well*

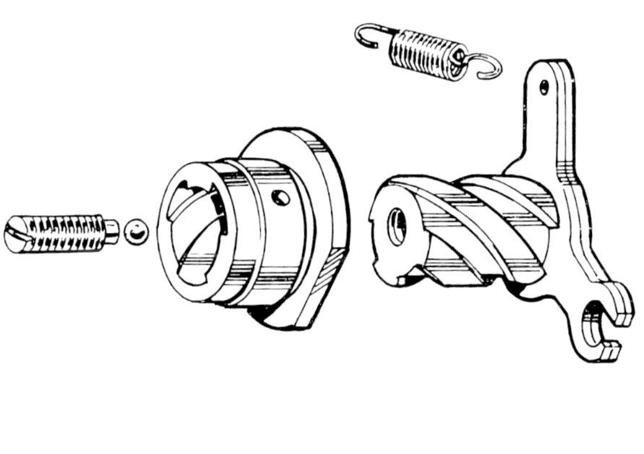

Clutch mechanism

This is the system that connects the clutch cable movement to the pressure plate and all include the clutch pushrod. Various designs were used but all come apart easily for examination. The pushrod must be straight or the clutch will feel very heavy and the load points smooth and oiled so their action is easy.

The M from 1948 and B and C ranges all had a simple lever system to move the pushrod, while the 1946–47 M used a different design as did the 1956-onwards C-range gearbox which had an internal lever.

Unit engines began with a lever under the outer cover, but the design made replacement of the cable awkward unless an access hole was cut in the outer case. For 1965 the design changed to a rack-and-pinion arrangement which was used from then onwards.

All Bantams had a quick-thread mechanism set in the magneto cover on the left. This incorporated an adjuster screw and all parts are common. The quick thread is never a very good fit but will work without trouble if well greased. The two parts must be correctly fitted so the outer aligns with the casting face and the inner with the cable.

Chaincase types

A pressed-steel case was used on all B-range models in rigid or plunger frames, except the 1954–55 B32 and B34, and also went on to the 1949–52 Gold Stars, all the M range and all the C models. The 1954-onwards competition B range, 1953-onwards Gold Stars and pivoted-fork B31 and B33 all had cast-alloy cases, as did the unit engines and the Bantams.

The M range had its own outer for 1946–47 but then fitted the B part which they then shared up to 1954. It was changed for 1955, its last year, on the B31 and B33, and continued in use on the M range. The Gold Stars had their own outer for the 1949–52 period. The inner cases differed with one listed for the rigid B range, one for the M, and one for the M and B plunger models.

For 1953 the Gold Star adopted a cast-light-alloy chaincase and fitted the same two parts from then onwards. Its inner went on to the pivoted-fork road B models for 1954–55 and the competition ones for 1956–57. The latter fitted another inner for 1954–55 when built in a rigid frame, while the road models adopted a third version for 1956–57. During this period the Gold Star outer case was common to the rest of the B range with alloy cases. For 1958 the road B31 and B33 had a new inner and outer case to

ABOVE *A 1954 C11G acting as victim at a Dublin night-school class*

ABOVE RIGHT *Adjusting the clutch on a 1966 D10 Supreme where there must be free-play in the cable-and-worm mechanism*

RIGHT *Primary chaincase of the 1945 B31 shown in model announcement but not continued with, as they were black in production*

accommodate the alternator and continued with these parts to their end.

The C range had one pair of pressed-steel cases for 1946–53. With the adoption of an alternator for 1954 there were two new inners, one to suit the C10L with its Wipac component, and the other for the C11G, and later the C12, which used a Lucas item. The outers also varied, as the C10L part had a boss welded to its underside for a brake pedal stop and different parts were listed for the two ohv models.

The unit engines had one cover for all models for 1959–66 and this had a single access plug for the adjuster in the clutch pressure plate. It changed for 1967–68 when it gained a timing hole at the front, for which a round cover was provided, and a second access plug enabling chain tension to be checked and oil to be poured more easily into the case. It was amended for 1969 when its fixing screws became Unified, and again for 1970 when an oil-level screw was added in its lower rear quarter. This screw changed in 1971 when two new cases were listed, one for the B25 and the other for the B50, the latter having a breather outlet in its top surface.

The Bantam chaincase was common to all models for 1949–66, with a polished one also listed for 1950 only for a model finished in black. The points moved to a housing in the cover on the D10 in 1967, and for 1969 it was revised for the D175. One change was to accommodate a larger-diameter kickstart spindle, and the other changed the front location dowel from solid pin to hollow as fitted at the rear. The points cover was common to all models from 1967 onwards.

Gears

There have been a number of sets of gears used over the years, so if parts are needed it is imperative that they match. It is good practice to replace gears in pairs as an old gear can easily wear out a new one. Consult the parts lists and check the numbers of teeth on the existing gears before shopping.

The B range used several sets of gears just on the road models, with others for competition and the Gold Stars. The first served all for 1946–48 and was then replaced by one derived from the M range which was used by the road rigid and plunger models for 1949–55 and by the competition ones up to 1953. A new set of gears served all the pivoted-fork road models while another went into the B32 and B34 for both rigid and pivoted-fork applications.

A close-ratio gear set was listed for the B range in 1948 only and this was effectively replaced the following year by the Gold Star listings. There were three of these with the standard and trials models using the stock road gears, while the other sets served for scrambles or road racing. These remained in use until a new series of sets was introduced for 1953.

The new sets numbered six overall with the standard as for the road models of 1954, and the trials as for the competition models of 1954. There was also a scrambles set and Clubmans plus road-racing set. Later came a Daytona set, and in 1954 a second racing set, with layshaft needle bearings, appeared. In 1956 the famous RRT2 box appeared with an even closer bottom gear and needle rollers in the sleeve gear as well as for the layshaft.

Component parts of the Bantam four-speed gearbox introduced in 1967

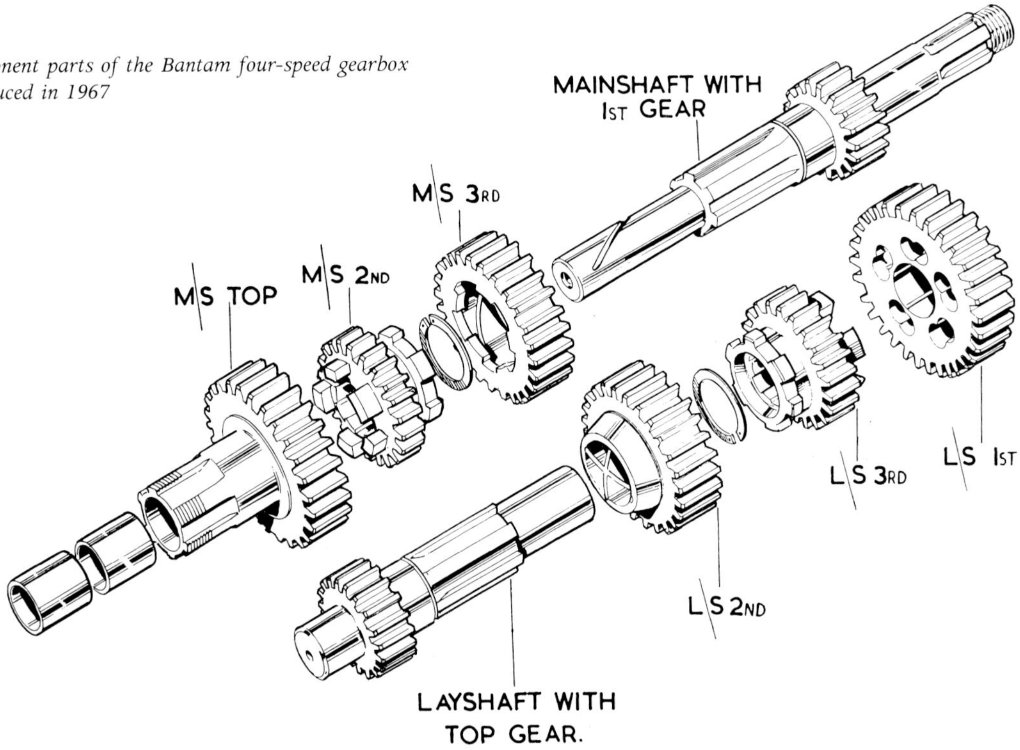

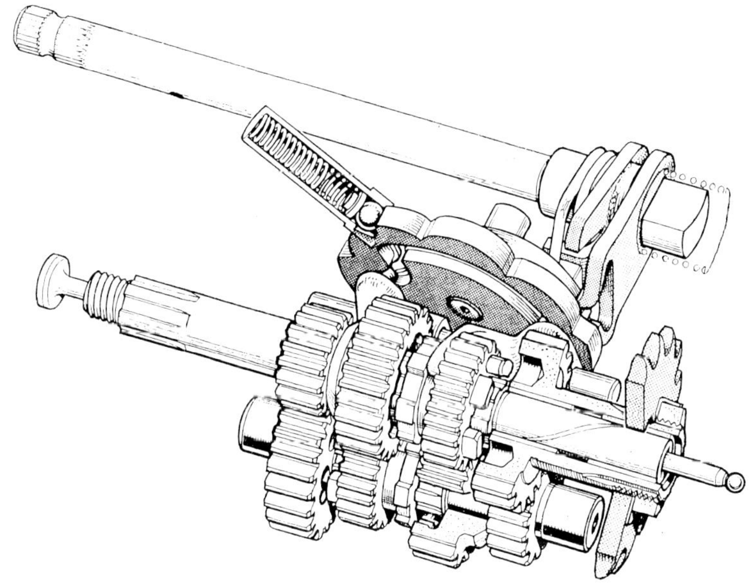

LEFT *The Bantam four-speed cluster and its change mechanism*

BELOW *The B40 of 1964, with pear-shaped tank badges and very much as the C15*

The M range used the same set of gears for all years and this became that fitted by the B range in 1949 when the latter's gearbox was uprated. The C range had a three-speed gearbox, which was used for 1946–55, and two four-speed units. The first was fitted for 1951–55, after which it was fully revised and a new set of gears was fitted.

The unit models varied more and managed to list a total of nine different sets of gears. In some cases the numbers of teeth stayed the same but the tooth form altered, and these must not be mismatched as they would wear rapidly.

The original set soon had the sleeve-gear pair altered to reduce the number of teeth but increase their section. Two other sets were listed for the early days: one for the C15T, and the other for the C15S and the two SS models. All had the tooth form changed for 1965 but kept to the same number of teeth on all gears.

A new set of gears was introduced for the B44GP in 1965 and these went into the last of the C15 and C15S models during 1966 and also the B50MX for 1971–73. A similar set with lower first-gear pair was used by the C25, B25, B44 and B50 road models from 1967–72.

The Bantam began with three speeds and kept the

92
BSA

A Gold Star on the grass. Note the open primary chaincase with clutch shield and the lack of eye protection of both the riders

same set of ratios, with a great jump from second to top, up to 1961 and in all models. Due to the advent of Bantam racing in 1949, the factory was persuaded to make other gear sets with wide and close ratios. Furthermore, by using a selection of parts from these three gear sets it became possible to arrive at three more, although only one was of real value.

The year 1962 brought revised ratios to the D7, with both first and second raised from their former values, and also changes to the gear splines to the shafts. These affected the sliding pair, with other gears remaining as they were. At the same time a further batch of close-ratio gears were produced which kept to the original numbers of teeth but were splined to suit the revised shafts. The same standard gear set served the D10 in 1967 and a completely new four-speed cluster was introduced the same year. This continued in use up to 1971.

Shafts

The B range had its own mainshaft for 1946–48 and then changed to the M-range part which served all years and M models. In the B machines it was used up to 1955 for rigid and plunger models, plus the Gold Stars for 1949–53. A new shaft went into the B31 and B33 for 1954–60 and the same part was used in the Gold Stars for 1953–55. Another took over for 1956–63 in the RRT2 box, while the trials version of the Gold Star for 1954–55 used the mainshaft fitted to the B32 and B34 for 1954–57 which was also fitted to some late USA models. The scrambles Gold Star had yet another shaft for 1954–63.

The B and M ranges had different layshafts for 1946–48 while the B32 had a special one. All changed for 1949 when one served the B models up to 1955 and the last of the rigid and plunger frames, the Gold Star for 1949–53 and all M21 and M33 machines from then onwards. Another went into the B32 and all M20 models, while yet another served the Gold Star for 1953–55 depending on the gearbox fitted, the pivoted-fork B range for 1954–60, plus the rigid B32 and B34 for 1954–55. The final layshaft went into the Clubmans and road-racing Gold Stars from 1954, and the B32 and B34 for 1956–57.

The three-speed C-range gearbox had one layshaft and two mainshafts with the change coming for 1954 when the new clutch was fitted. The four-speed box had a similar change for the same reason but then had a new pair of shafts fitted for 1956 onwards.

In the unit engines the shafts were changed for 1965 when the mainshaft was redesigned and the layshaft altered to run on needle rollers. The mainshaft was given a new number for 1971 onwards. The Bantams had one pair of shafts for 1949–57, a layshaft change for 1962, and the four-speed parts for 1967 onwards.

Bushes and bearings

BSA managed to keep to a small range of ball races for

their gearboxes, along with bushes and one or two needle races. All need to be completely clean before they are checked. If in doubt they should be renewed and any race must turn smoothly without rough spots.

To support the sleeve gear, the B range began with a 130 bearing of 30 × 62 × 16 mm for 1946–48. This same race also served the C range for 1956–58 and all unit gearboxes. For 1949 the B range changed to a 135 bearing of 35 × 72 × 17 mm, and this was fitted to that range from then onwards, into all Gold Star boxes, all M-range boxes and the C-range four-speed box of 1951–55. The three-speed C-range box used for 1946–55 had an LS11 race of $1\frac{1}{8} \times 2\frac{1}{2} \times \frac{5}{8}$ in. and the Bantams had an S9 with $\frac{7}{8} \times 1\frac{7}{8} \times \frac{3}{8}$ in. measurements.

Matters were simpler at the right end of the mainshaft and bushes were used in the B range for 1946–48, the three-speed C range for 1946–55 and the unit engines for 1959–64. The B range fitted an LS8 race of $\frac{3}{4} \times 1\frac{7}{8} \times 1\frac{9}{16}$ in. from 1949 and this also went into all Gold Stars, all M models and the C-range four-speed box for 1951–55. The 1956–58 C-range box had an LS7 of $\frac{5}{8} \times 1\frac{9}{16} \times \frac{7}{16}$ in. and this race also went into all unit gearboxes and all Bantams.

Needle races were used in the Gold Star sleeve gear from 1956 onwards and for the layshaft from 1954, this applying to most that were built. They are also to be found in the C-range box of 1956–58 and the unit models from 1965 onwards. All other applications used bushes, with some being common to more than one range.

Shell and covers

The B and M ranges had different shells for 1946–48, and while both had two mounting lugs on the underside and an inspection plate on the sloping rear surface, the M was alone in having a filler hole at the back of the casting. For 1949 one new shell was used by both ranges and the Gold Star, which was much as the earlier B box but machined to take the 135 sleeve-gear bearing, with 72 mm outside diameter in place of the 62 mm of its predecessor.

This new box was revised for 1950 at frame numbers ZB31-7840, ZB31S-6032, ZB32S-352 and ZM20-4095, and then continued in use on all M models and the rigid- and plunger-frame B ones up to 1955, except for the 1954–55 B32 and B34. The Gold Star had this change but only fitted the revised shell up to 1952. It had a new one for 1953 with a vertical rear face and small inspection panel, and this type could have the reversed camplate fitted to it.

The 1953 Gold Star shell went into the pivoted-fork B31 and B33 from 1954 onwards, but another shell of similar type was used for the Clubmans and road-racing Gold Stars for 1954–63, and was also fitted to the scrambles model from 1958 onwards. This also served the B32 and B34 for 1956–57, but for 1954–55, when in the rigid frame, these machines fitted the 1953 Gold Star shell.

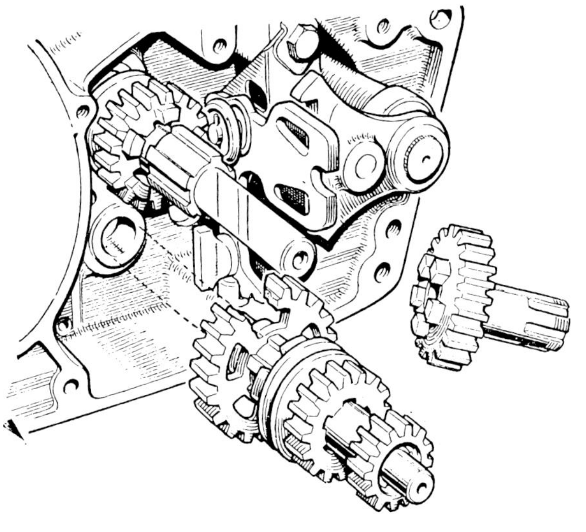

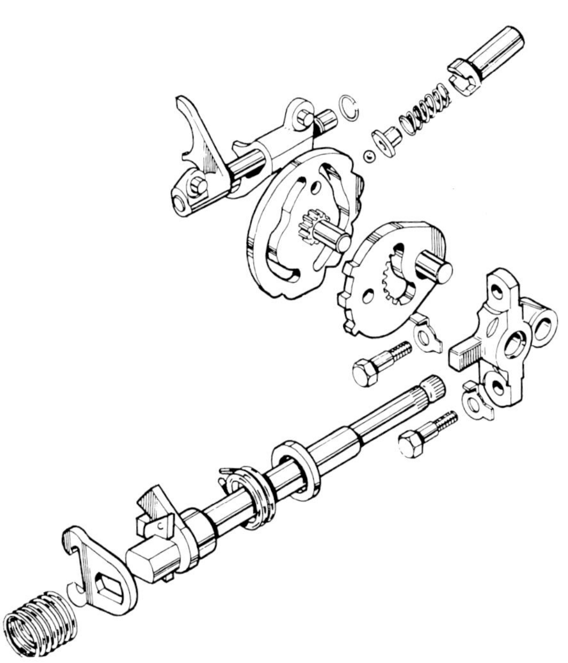

The covers followed the pattern of the shells, so for 1946–48 there was an inner and outer for the B and M ranges. From 1949 one of each served both until the appearance of the pivoted-fork box in 1953. This had one outer for all years and models but two inners. The original went on all B31 and B33 models, the 1954–55 B32 and B34, and the 1953–55 Gold Star. From 1954 the CB, and later DB, Gold Stars had another inner, also fitted to the B32 and B34 for 1956–57.

The C range was simpler with one shell, inner and outer for the three-speed box of 1946–55 and another for the four-speed one of 1956–58. The earlier 1951–55 four-speed box varied in having a change of outer cover for 1954 as well as its own set of parts. None was used for more than one application.

ABOVE *An M21 on duty down on the waterfront in Hong Kong in 1956*

TOP LEFT *The Bantam three-speed cluster. First gear on the layshaft must be that way round in order to engage*

BOTTOM LEFT *Bantam four-speed gearchange mechanism, which has to have the quadrant and camplate gear correctly meshed*

Gearchange mechanism

This begins with the rubber on the gear pedal and runs through to the selector forks which move the gears. There are a number of wear points that need checking and the fork sides are one such. The various springs need to be changed if tired and the whole mechanism must work smoothly.

Each range tended to have its own mechanism which had relatively few changes. The B and M differed for 1946–48, although even then they had many common parts, and from 1949 used the same design with little change. The C range had unique mechanisms for the three-speed and each of the four-speed boxes, while the unit models had a little revision in 1965 and 1969. The Bantam had one mechanism each for the three- and four-speed boxes.

If anything, there was more variety of gear pedals, but also some common usage. The pedal rubber was

often common, with the B-range part going on to the M range from 1948, and also the C range. The early unit models had their own but from 1965 fitted the rubber used by all Bantams.

Speedometer drive—gearbox

This is not found on all models as some take the drive from the rear wheel. It occurs on all B and M machines and C-range ones fitted with the four-speed gearbox. In all cases the drive was taken from a skew gear, pinned to the right-hand end of the layshaft, which meshed with a shaft which turned the cable. The gears must mesh correctly and the shaft seals be in good condition to keep the lubricant within the shell.

Kickstarter

Most models had a quadrant on the kickstart spindle which meshed with a ratchet wheel. This usually went at the end of the mainshaft but on the Bantam was on the back of the clutch. The exceptions were the unit models for 1959–64 which had a pawl and ratchet in the layshaft first gear.

The B and M ranges used the same parts from 1949 onwards and externally there were one-piece and folding cranks to suit the application. Make sure they clear the exhaust pipe in all cases. The C range had different parts for its three gearbox types but all worked on the same principle. The same arrangement went into the unit models from 1965 with different detail parts and the Bantams used common parts with few exceptions for all years. The main spindle was enlarged for 1969.

The kickstart-pedal rubbers varied a good deal on the unit models with no less than seven listed, but for the rest this was not so. One served the M range, another the B and C ranges, and there were two for the Bantams, one for each number of speeds.

Gearbox sprocket, plate and rear chain

One sprocket plate was listed for 1959–68 and another for 1969 onwards, but both were retained by 2BA screws and carried the same seal.

The B and M sprockets differed for 1946–48 but then became common until the B moved on to the pivoted-fork frame and used the Gold Star sprocket. For 1958 the sprocket width was increased except for the M21. The oil seal was added during 1950 at the frame numbers listed under 'shell and covers', and another was used for the pivoted-fork-frame gearboxes.

The B nut and lockwasher were changed for the M type from 1949 and the washer was fitted to all from then onwards. A new nut went on to the new pivoted-fork box in 1953.

The C range fitted one 17-tooth sprocket on the three-speed box and another on the 1951–55 four-speed box. There were also three with 19 teeth to suit the three-speed box and the 1956 four-speed one, for which both wide and narrow sprockets were listed to suit the C12 and C10L respectively. There was also a 17-tooth sprocket for this box when fitted to the C12 in 1956. An oil seal was fitted to the four-speed box for 1952 which was common to the later B range, but it was changed for 1956. The nut and lockwasher of the

LEFT *The use of the Gold Star name on this 1971 B50SS was not a popular choice*

RIGHT *This is a D7, but it is just as hard to get oil into any Bantam gearbox. Removing the chaincase screw helps, but racers fit another filler in the case above the clutch*

three-speed unit were special, as were those of the 1956 box, but the first four-speed box used the same parts as the late B range.

The unit-model sprockets ranged from 14 to 20 teeth over the years with a revision to their form coming over 1965–67. This change was reflected by the oil seal and the lockwasher but the nut remained common to all years and models.

The Bantams had a 15-tooth sprocket for the D1 and D3 while all 175 cc models used 16 teeth. There was also a 14-tooth sprocket listed and this required the fitment of a cutaway seal housing to give the needed chain clearance. One seal served all three-speed models and another the four-speed ones. All used the same left-hand threaded nut and lockwasher.

The rear chain is bound to need renewal on any rebuild and the sizes and lengths are set out in an appendix.

Assembly

This is not hard, but check as you go along. Bearings should be held in place with Loctite as an added security and joint faces can be sealed with the traditional gasket or a silicone-rubber compound, used sparingly.

Work to the manual and check each stage for correct operation. Make certain you have the selector forks in the right position and engaged in the right cam track. Double-check the gear selection as a mistake can be traumatic on the road. Do make sure you have the gears with small shoulders the correct way round so the shoulder is against the adjacent bearing, giving a working clearance between the teeth and the bearing outer race.

Remember to fill the gearbox and primary chaincase with oil before using the machine. A tie-on label on the filler or the gear pedal may help as a reminder.

4 Carburettor and exhaust

These are two areas that can give the restorer considerable problems unless the parts are simply replaced. The difficulties arise because the carburettor wears and the exhaust corrodes all the time the machine is in use, so their condition changes continuously. Both affect the performance of the machine, especially the carburettor, and both are important to the final appearance of the model.

Full details of the carburettors fitted as standard are given in an appendix.

Air filter

For many models and years the filter was an option, but not on the Bantams. From the first, the D1 had a small filter clamped to the carburettor, incorporating the choke. This went on to the D3, D5 and D7 in turn, except for the GPO D7 and the Pastoral model.

The first of these had a smaller-than-standard type 32 carburettor which came with its own mesh filter. The Pastoral used a drum filter mounted high up with its axis vertical and connected by a hose and elbow to the intake. This same design continued on the D175 Bushman and all Pastoral models.

For the rest, a pancake filter was introduced on the D10 models of 1967, but for the D14 of the following year there was another design. This had a replaceable element held in a chamber with lid on the right of the machine. A rubber band held the filter in place and a hose connected it to the engine. The same design went on to the D175 for 1969 onwards.

The C range had the option of a pancake filter for all years and models but was normally sold without one. The same applied to the B and M ranges, and the B models had an elbow as part of their option kit when in rigid- or plunger-frame form. In the pivoted-fork frame the filter went between the oil tank and the toolbox but remained an option to the end.

All the unit models had an air filter as standard which went behind the centre panel on the C15 and B40. The competition C15 had a D-shaped filter until they went to a central oil tank when the filter had to move and took on a wedge shape. The B40 Enduro had a pancake filter, as did the C25 and B25 up to 1970, the B44VR, B44SS and the B44VS for 1968–70.

The 1966 B44VE had an element in a container to the left of the oil tank which also went into the B44VS for 1967. For 1971 all models changed to an air box between the side covers with removable element, and for the 1973 B50MX a completely new design went into the same position.

Exhaust-pipe types

There are a good few variations and it is important to get the correct one or you can have problems in fit and alignment.

The B range began with a low-level pipe for the B31 which went on to the B33 the next year. It served all the rigid and plunger models and was joined by another for the pivoted-fork models in 1954, this being revised for 1958.

The B32 began with an upswept, waist-level pipe which then went on to the B34, but which was amended for 1949 and 1951. For 1954 and the rigid frames there were two new pipes which ran low with tilted ends, but for the pivoted-fork machines of 1956 a new waist-level pipe was used.

The Gold Star variations were more complex. From the start, the 350 and 500 were available with a choice of a pipe for a silencer, an open pipe, an extension for the usual pipe to make up the open pipe length, and a pipe for use with a megaphone. These all existed for 1949–50 and the extension was there because the early regulations for the Clubmans TT races allowed open exhausts; this part was listed to enable owners to make up the pipe to the required length.

For 1951–53 the original basic pipes were listed for the two engine sizes along with the one for the megaphone. For 1953 there was also an extension pipe listed for the 350 and another which went on to both sizes of scrambles engine for 1953–57.

For 1954 there were five pipes and two extensions listed. Two of the pipes were swept back and went on to the CB models for that year and the next. For the BB

The carburettor on the Military B40, which was a good deal different from the stock Amal fitted to civilian models

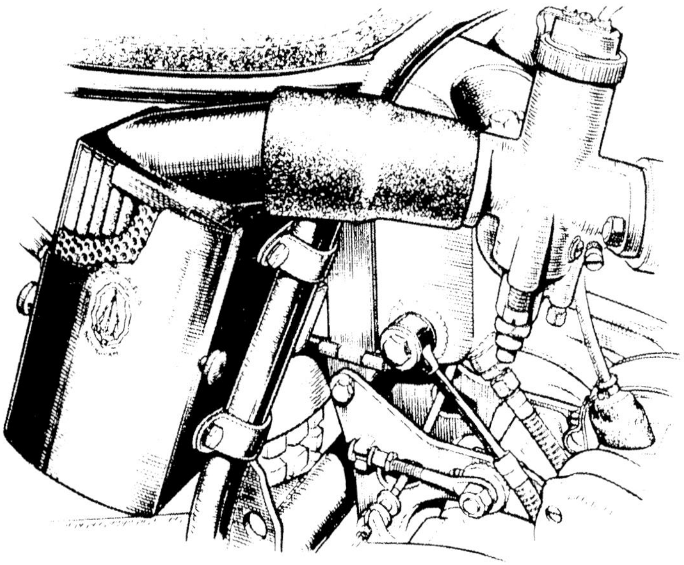

series one served the 350 road, the 500 trials, and both sizes of scrambles engine for the last two years of that engine type. The last two pipes were one each for the 350 trials and the 500 road engines. The scrambles extension pipe was that introduced in 1953 and it was joined by two more which served the 350 and 500 Clubmans models, all three being listed up to 1957.

Four more pipes appeared in 1955 for the DB series with one common to the two sizes of Clubmans machine and another for the two scramblers. These continued in use to the end, with a new extension pipe being listed for the 500 Clubmans in 1957 for both models. The other two pipes were one each for the 350 and 500 road DB models which were built from 1955.

In contrast, the M range was simple. The side-valve models had one pipe for 1946–48 and another for 1949 onwards. The M33 began with one type for 1948 but changed to another for 1949—this remained the fitment from then onwards.

The C range was also straightforward with a pipe

ABOVE *The 1967 B44GP with the air-cleaner cover removed to show the filter*

TOP LEFT *The air cleaner used on the late-type Gold Star scramblers*

LEFT *The 1967 D10 Sports Bantam with its waist-level exhaust system and pipe shield*

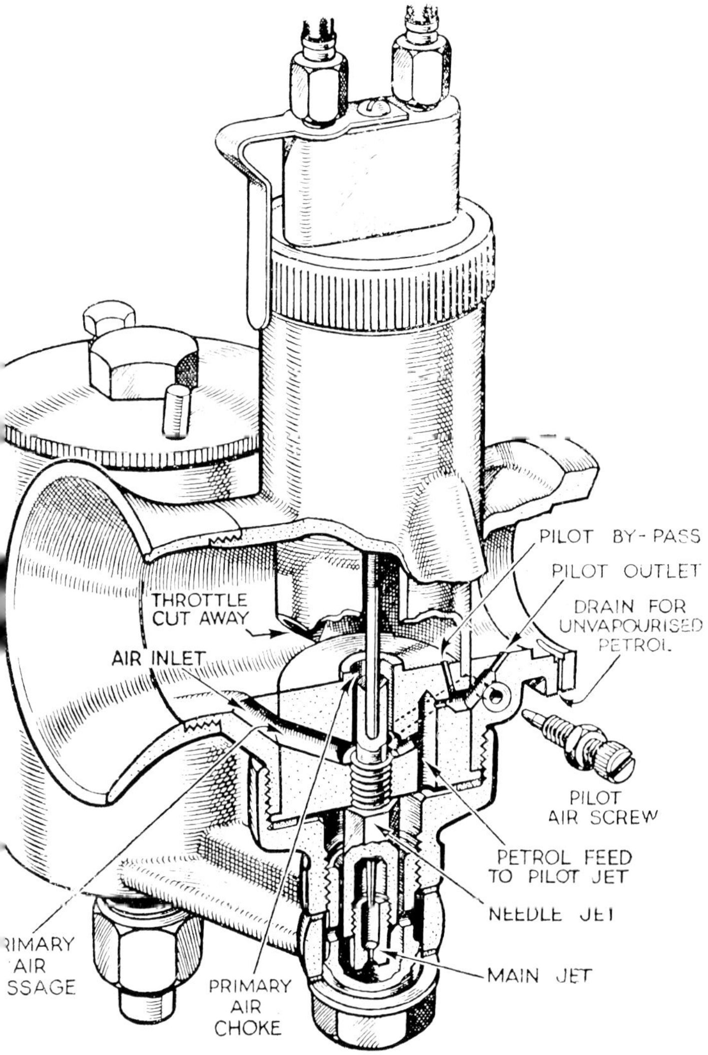

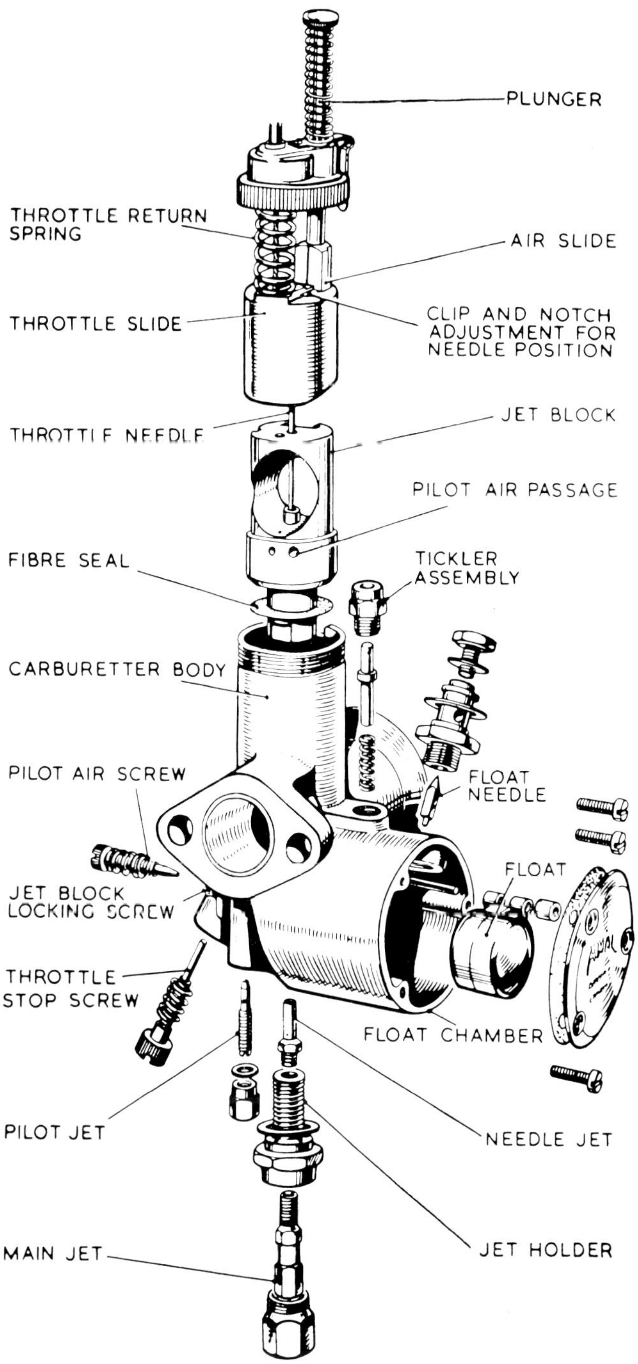

ABOVE *The Amal type 6 carburettor with separate float chamber as used for many makes and years*

LEFT *The big float chamber of the 1961 DBD Gold Star with its flexible mounting which allowed it to be adjusted for height*

RIGHT *Details of the Monobloc carburettor with integral float chamber used from 1955 to 1966*

each for the C10 and C11 rigid-frame models and two more for the plunger versions. A new pipe was introduced for the C10L but the plunger C11G and C12 both used the C11 plunger part.

The unit range of machines had a large array of pipes. There was a pipe for the C15 and another for the B40. In time these went on the SS80 and SS90, and both were altered for 1965. The C15 pipe also went on the C15 Pastoral model.

The competition models began with one pipe for the C15S and another for the C15T and the USA version of the C15. Both ran at waist-level and outside the rear subframe. The scrambles one just ran aft to an open end at first but for 1962 gained a slim, reverse-cone megaphone-cum-expansion chamber. For 1963 the C15T and C15S changed to a common pipe which ran inside the subframe tubing to improve the riding position. The same pipe was used on the B44GP but the B40 Enduro had its own pipe.

The C25 and later B25 had one pipe for 1967–68 and

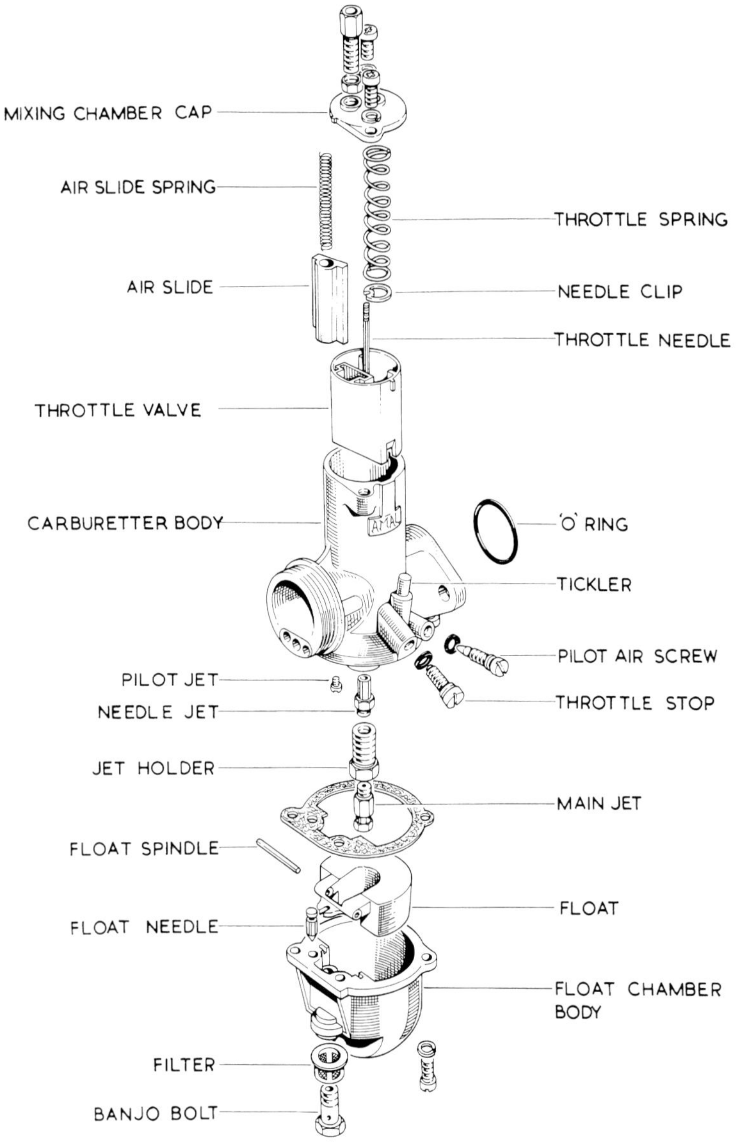

LEFT *The Amal Concentric carburettor used from 1967 onwards*

RIGHT *The 1954 249 cc C11G with plunger rear suspension*

another for 1969–70, while the road B44 copied this with a further change for 1970. The VE and VS versions changed pipes each year, other than for 1966–67, and these were waist-level types to suit the off-road use. Waist-level pipes were also used on the B25 for the USA in 1969 with a change for 1970.

From 1971 all the models had waist-level pipes tucked away behind the frame so that their run was complex. Thanks to this there was one for the two B25 models, one for the B50MX, one for the home B50s and yet one more for the B50T and B50SS. For the 1973 B50MX a further pipe was listed.

The Bantam used one diameter of pipe up to 1967 so the pipe nut was common up to then. For the D14 in 1968 the diameter was increased and an adaptor screwed on to the cylinder exhaust-port thread to allow for this. At the same time the washer was altered to suit.

The original pipe went below the footrest but during 1950, from frame YD 24813, it was amended to run above it. This went on to the D3 and plunger-frame D1 right up to 1963. There was another with tilted end for the competition model in 1950, which was amended for 1951 and then went on to the plunger version and the D3.

A new short pipe was introduced for the pivoted-fork-frame D3 in 1956 and was amended for 1962 and increased in diameter for 1968. A longer edition of the 1962 type went on the GPO machines as these had a short silencer fitted.

For the D7 Trail model there was a special pipe, and both the D10S and D10B had a raised system with the pipe up at crankcase top level. Both had heat shields and the fixings of the front one of these was a pair of tapped holes in the pipe. The D14S, D14B and D175B all had the same arrangement of raised pipe with heat shield but in the larger diameter.

Exhaust-pipe collar

Apart from on the Bantam, BSA exhaust pipes were a push-fit into the cylinder or head, but on many overhead-valve models the appearance was enhanced by a finned collar clamped to the pipe, up against the exhaust port.

One served the B range for the 1946–50 period and also went on the M33. Another was listed for the B31 and B33 for 1953–60 plus the pivoted-fork B34 for 1954–57, while a third went on the B32 for the same period. One more type was listed for the M33 from 1951 onwards. The part was omitted from B models of 1951–52, although owners would often add it themselves, and it is not to be found on CB or DB Gold Stars due to the tight radius of the swept-back pipe.

A collar was only fitted to the smaller of the unit models with one part used by the C15, C15T, SS80, B40 and SS90 in the early years. It continued in use on the C25 and B25 up to 1970, but not on the USA B25 of 1969–70 due to the shape of the pipe.

Silencer types

The B31 and B33 had one silencer for the rigid models and one for the plungers, but three for the pivoted-fork frames with changes for 1956 and 1958. The competition B32 and B34 had different silencers to suit their raised location and changed them for 1949 and 1952. They did use the road-model plunger silencer when in spring-frame form but only up to 1953.

BELOW *Engine and carburettor of the 1966 C15 Sportsman which took over from the SS80*

For 1954, when they were in rigid frames with low-swept pipe, they had a tilted silencer, this arrangement being used for the next year as well. During these two years those which did have a pivoted-fork frame had another silencer, with different ones being used on the two models. For 1956 a new, short silencer went on both, once more at waist-level.

In its first year, 1949, there was no silencer listed for the 350 cc Gold Star, although it plainly had one when exhibited. There was one for the 500 and for 1950–53 one was listed for all Clubmans models. The year 1953 also saw a pair of silencers listed for the road versions of the Gold Star but both were also used on other models. The 350 one was also seen on the 1954–55 B road range while the 500 one was to be seen on the 1954–55 pivoted-fork-frame B34. It continued in use on the 500 and may be found on the later 350.

A further double use came in 1954–55 when the 350 trials Gold Star fitted the silencer from the pivoted-fork-frame B32 of the same years. For the Clubmans models of that period there was an improved tubular silencer which was further improved, for power

12

The 348 cc Gold Star which finished fifth in the 1955 Thruxton 9 Hours race despite, or because of, that well-ground-off silencer

rather than silence, in 1955. This developed into a megaphone shape for 1956 and became famous for its odd twittering noise on the overrun. It was an essential for any self-respecting Goldie owner and remained in use for all Clubmans models.

The M range had one silencer for the rigid side-valve models from 1946–49, another from 1950 onwards, and a third for the rigid M33. The plunger frames all used the same part, except for the M21 plunger used by the AA which had a special part.

On the C range, one silencer served the rigid C10, C11 and C11G, and another the plunger version. The C10L had one item for 1954–55 and another for 1956–57, and the C12 had its own silencer. The C10 sold to the GPO had the stock part finished in dull chrome.

The unit models used tubular silencers up to 1970 with just one serving all years of the C15. This part was also fitted to the 343 cc models for 1965 but before then they had their own part. The SS80 was different again, as was the USA version of the C15 and SS90. For 1965 there was also a silencer with fishtail end to its tailpipe for the 343 cc models.

The C15T began with a short tubular silencer which was modified for 1963 and later went on the B40E. The C15 Pastoral had its own part and from 1963 the C15S fitted a slim megaphone which was also used by the B44GP. The B44VE which was derived from it had a short tubular silencer which went in turn on the B44VS. For 1969 it was modified with welded-on tapped bosses to take a heat shield. A similar arrangement was used for the USA B25 of 1969–70 but with different silencers for each year.

The C25 and later B25 had a silencer common with the B44VR for 1967–68. For 1969 both capacities had a common part without tailpipe, but while this remained on the 247 cc for 1970, that of the 441 cc was modified.

The year 1971 brought completely new silencers of lozenge shape for all models, with one for the B25, one for the B50 home market and a third for the B50T and B50SS. For 1973 the B50MX adopted a rather strange arrangement with twin silencers attached to a junction pipe which was also used by the Triumph TR5MX, itself a copy of the BSA model.

The Bantam began with its own style of silencer, later known as the flat one, and this remained in use up to 1953 on the road models and up to 1955 on the competition ones. More than one existed, as the original on the rigid frame was amended at frame number YD 24813 during 1950, but returned to the first type for 1951. The silencer for the first plunger year of 1950 was also special, but this turned to the first type in 1951 while all competition models used the original flat silencer.

For both D1 and D3 in 1954 there was a new tubular silencer and this continued in use on those models to their end. The pivoted-fork D3 of 1956 differed from

its plunger predecessor in having a much longer, tapered silencer on a short exhaust pipe.

This theme of a long silencer continued on all the road Bantams from then onwards, with new parts for the D5 in 1958 and the D7 in 1959, both with single-bolt brackets. For the D7 in 1962 there was another silencer with a bracket to accommodate two bolt heads for the support plate. In addition there were two more similar silencers, one being for the USA, and two short tubular ones for the GPO version of the D7 and the trail model. This last was as first used in 1954 on the D1.

In 1967 the D10 appeared and continued with a long silencer on the three-speed model, with variations on the others. The D10S had a silencer of the same form with two tapped holes for its heat shield, and the D10B one was similar but with the holes moved. This arrangement continued on the later models with their larger-diameter exhaust pipes, so the D14 and D175 had a plain silencer. That of the D14S, D14B and D175B was the same plus two tapped holes in the side of the body.

ABOVE *The lozenge silencer with guard for itself and tailpipe, as fitted to the 1971 four-stroke singles range*

ABOVE RIGHT *The shielded waist-level exhaust system fitted to the D10B Bushman Bantam for 1967*

Megaphone

A part bearing this name was listed for the C15S of 1963–65 and the B44GP of 1965–67, with another similar one for the B50MX of 1971–72. To most BSA owners they were hardly worthy of the name as they were thin expansion chambers, virtually a bulge in the end of the exhaust pipe. The megaphones that count are those listed for the Gold Star, when such

things were tapered out to a large diameter and allowed the noise of a fast single out for the world to hear. There was one for each engine size in 1949–50 and a second pair was listed for 1953. In 1954 the 500 moved on to a part it kept up to 1963, while the 350 had its own megaphone which was just that for 1954 but had a reverse cone for 1955.

Heat shield

These were fitted to protect the rider and passenger from the heat of the exhaust system and comprised wire grilles or perforated sheets attached to either the exhaust pipe or the silencer and sometimes both.

One was first used on the B32 in 1946 and this part, held by three screws, also went on the B34 until it changed in 1949 for one held by two screws; it was listed up to 1950. The next one was on the early C15T until the exhaust pipe changed, and the one thereafter went on the B44VS silencer for 1969–70.

The USA version of the B25 had a wire grille in 1969, with two types being used, while for 1970 a sheet-metal type was fitted. All these were attached to the silencer. This arrangement continued on both the B25 and B50 in 1971 and for these models there was also a separate tailpipe heat shield.

Certain Bantams also had shields but not until 1967 and the D10. The D10S had two small shields, one on the exhaust pipe and the other on the silencer. The D10B had a single shield held by three screws, one of which went into the exhaust pipe, and this part went on to the D14S, D14B and D175B over the years 1968–71.

Lastly, a final reminder that the whole system must fit the machine without stress or strain to avoid fracture or parts coming adrift.

5 Lubrication

All four-stroke BSA singles had a dry-sump system with a separate oil tank either on the right side of the machine or centrally in a few cases. From 1971, the oil was carried within the frame main tubing, and all Bantams have petroil lubrication.

The four-strokes all had a duplex-gear oil pump with a pressure-release valve and a ball valve on the suction inlet. Filters went in the tank and the sump to protect the pump.

Engine breathing was by flap valve, timed bush or a simple hole.

Oil pump

This runs in oil so seldom wears very much, and even then can usually be reclaimed by lapping the parts so the pump turns smoothly without end-play.

The original 1946 pump went into all the B, M and C ranges and had a circular housing held in a recess in the base of the right crankcase half by two screws. Its presence produced a bulge in the casting and thus the famous kink in the lower right frame rail.

This pump was replaced by another on the CB Gold Star in 1954 with the alteration being a reduction in the number of teeth on the pump gears by one to 12. The same pump was adopted by the rest of the B range and the M and C ones in 1956.

The only other variation of note occurred to the drive spindle of the C models during 1947. The change went in on engines XC10-4314 and XC11-4423.

This simple arrangement was not continued on the unit engines, although one pump did serve the 247 and 343 cc models up to 1966. The pump assembly number altered as the washers under the pump screw heads were deleted, but the rest of the details remained as they were.

The unit pump was rectangular in shape, but still mounted from beneath the engine. Starting with the Victor Grand Prix in 1965, this design was altered for all later machines so that the pump went on to a vertical face in the timing chest.

There was more variety with the later design, eight pumps being listed in all. The original Victor one also went into the B44VE for 1966, but was modified for 1967. It had thrust washers set in the body to limit wear but these were omitted in the pump used by the C25 for 1967–69; it was this latter item that went into the B44VS for 1967.

The B44VR had a pump with thrust washers for 1967–69 and this was also used by the B44VS in 1968–69. It was all change with new internals for 1970, with one pump for the B25 and another with thrust washers for the two 441 cc models. The redesign for 1971 brought two more pumps, both with an extra fixing hole in the drive-shaft casing, so these were held on three studs instead of the two of their predecessors. There were new gears, no thrust washers in either, and different drive spindles for the B25 and B50 pumps.

Oil-system valves and switch

All systems had at least two valves, with one to set the pressure and another below the oil pump. The unit engines also had an anti-drain valve and, right at the end, a pressure switch on the B25.

The pressure-release valve of the C range was fitted into the right crankcase just below the timing case and comprised spring, $\frac{3}{16}$ in. diameter ball and plug. A similar arrangement with a different spring and $\frac{1}{4}$ in. ball went on the B and M ranges in the lower end of the timing cover.

The unit engines had their release valve fitted into the front of the right crankcase half, with one spring used for 1959–66 and another during the years 1965–69; both held a $\frac{5}{16}$ in. ball on its seat. For 1970 all models changed over to an assembly with one for the B25 and another for the B44. More appeared in 1971, again one each for the B25 and B50 with yet another for the B50MX in 1973. Make sure you fit the correct one or your system could be in trouble.

The sump valve was essentially the same for all models, with a ball bearing loose in a short vertical tube just under the scavenge oil pump. It falls under gravity to close, and if it sticks to its seat it will prevent the oil returning to the tank. A prod with stiff wire from below will release it.

The anti-drain valve fitted to the unit engines consists of a $\frac{1}{4}$ in. ball, spring and plug. At first this assembly was located on the inside of the right

ABOVE *The Gold Star raced at Daytona in 1954 was fitted in a rigid frame to suit the combined road-and-beach circuit*

BELOW RIGHT *The improved oil system and bottom half from the Victor as fitted to the C15 during 1966*

crankcase which meant that the engine had to be dismantled to reach it. For 1968 it was moved to the inner timing cover and so became easily accessible by just removing the outer.

An oil-pressure switch was only fitted to the B25, and then only for 1970–71.

Filter

There were two of these, one in the oil tank and the other in the engine sump, with an additional external filter for the 1971 B25 and the military version of the B40. The two main ones protect the intake sides of the oil pump.

The filters are made from a metal gauze or mesh soldered in place and so can be replaced or repaired with two provisos. The first is do not restrict the oil flow and the second is do not decrease the degree of filtration. Thus, do not replace a fine gauze with a wide mesh.

The pre-unit engines all had a sump plate and matching gauze filter through which the scavenge pick-up pipe with its ball valve passed. One sump plate and one filter served all models and years, and it was a well-known oil leak point.

This design continued with new parts on the C15 and B40 models, but a new one-piece item was introduced for the B44GP in 1965. In turn it went on

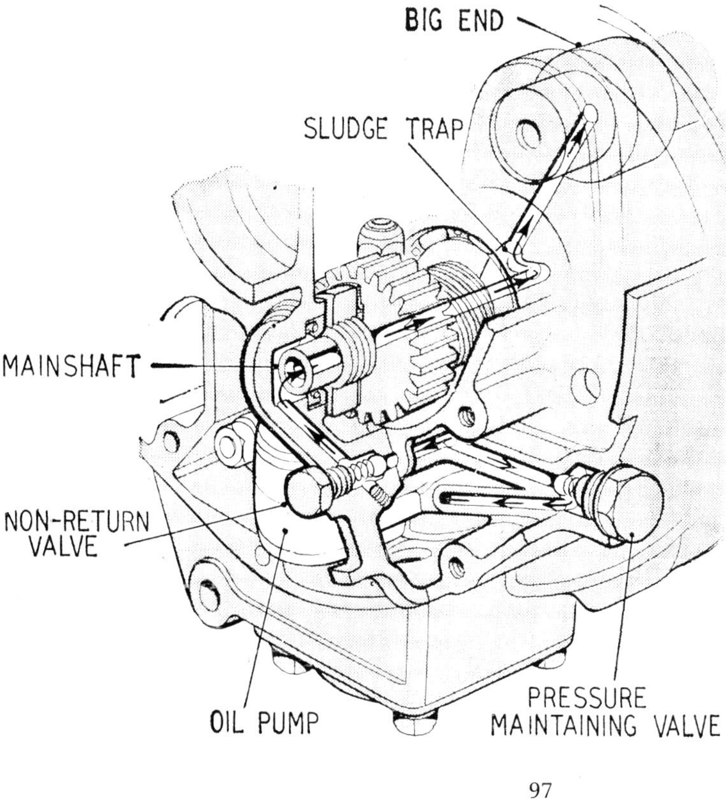

ABOVE *The B44SS Shooting Star of 1969 with twin-leading-shoe front brake and rev-counter drive from the front of the engine*

LEFT *The oil-pressure switch as fitted to a 1970 B25*

ABOVE RIGHT *The 1971 B25SS which carried the revered Gold Star name to the annoyance of enthusiasts*

the C25, B25 and B44VS up to 1969, the B44VE, and B44VR and SS up to 1968. For the B25 of 1970–71, the B44SS of 1969–70 and the 1970 B44VS, the design reverted to two separate parts, both new for the occasion. Finally, for the B50 there was a further one-piece item.

At the tank end of the system, the B and C models began with a common part with the filter attached to a banjo bolt screwed into the base of the oil tank. This went on to all the rigid and plunger-frame machines but not the pivoted-fork ones and the C10L of 1956–57. For these a shorter and fatter filter appeared which screwed into the side of the oil tank to enclose the end of the feed pipe at its inner end. For the B range it was amended for 1958.

The M range differed in having a filter element that dropped into the tank via the filler cap and sat on a mount connected to the return line. It was thus alone in having the filter on the return side and the feed was simply taken from the tank base. The same filter was also used by the Gold Star at first, but for 1953 it adopted a new tank and the short fat filter that was to go into the B range the next year. As for those models, it was amended for 1958.

The unit models fitted a filter in the base of the oil tank with an end connection for the feed line. This was used up to 1966 except on the competition models with central oil tanks, which had a banjo-bolt-type filter but without the banjo. This was done by arranging the tank feed pipe to run into the filter thread in the tank in line with a reduced section and cross-hole.

For 1967 the models reverted to the 1946 part and a banjo connection for all. This changed for 1971 and the new frame when the filter was screwed into the base of the downtube and took an end connection for the pipe. On the B25, and the earlier military version of the B40, an external filter unit was also fitted which went behind the gearbox in the return line of the B25.

Rocker-box oiling

This was done with a small-bore copper pipe connected to a tee in the oil return pipe. It fed to banjo unions on the rocker box where internal drillways took the oil to the bearing surfaces. The oil drained into the valve wells and then via a further pipe to the crankcase.

Note that the banjo bolts differ and that the feed ones have much smaller cross-holes than the drain ones. Don't use locking compound on them on assembly or they will snap the next time you try to remove them.

The C range lacked rocker-box oiling, other than by mist that happened to rise up the pushrod tunnel, until the C12. This had a feed directed into the hollow bolt which held the rocker-box lid in place. A kit was available to enable any C11 or C11G engine to have this feature added.

The unit engines began with the same type of system with a tee from the return pipe taken at the back of the oil tank. This arrangement continued on all the models, but the 247 cc models from 1967 onwards had the feed into the rear of the rocker box rather than the spindle ends.

Pipes

The pipes themselves were usually copper with traditional nuts and unions on the B, C and M ranges, but did include a rubber connection in their length. This not only absorbed vibration but also all the alignment and length tolerances. The B range in the pivoted-fork frame had flexible pipes and these were common to the Gold Star, with the pair becoming one common part for 1958. Do make sure you have all pipes connected correctly with feed to feed and return to return. Double-check to confirm.

The unit engines had a different arrangement with the two pipes at the engine end formed into one block held by a single nut. The first type had a gasket, and alignment of the parts is important. For the competition models of the C15 and the later B40 a second type was introduced with two small O-rings to make the seal. This and their seat faces must be clean

ABOVE *Instructor and pupil with a 1965 D7 Super*

ABOVE LEFT *The engine unit of an early SS90, as built for 1962–64, with the external points housing*

and in good condition if oil leaks are to be avoided.

The first O-ring block also went on the B44VE in 1966, but for 1967 this model, along with the other 441 cc ones and the C25, adopted another similar part. The one used by the B44GP was special to that model.

The fitting was changed for all models for 1968 when the rocker-box take-off was moved from the oil tank and was built into the fitting. This was to improve the oil feed to the box by having the pipe connected nearer to the oil pump. The part was common up to 1970.

For 1971 two separate pipes were used, both screwing into the crankcase where they were locked by nuts. The feed for the B25 was straight but that of the B50 was bent. Both had the same return pipe and this has a side pipe incorporated into it to supply the rocker box. This arrangement continued to the end.

Breather system

This is an area that often gives owners a headache if there are any problems, as much of the system consists simply of holes and these cannot, of course, appear on a parts list. The clack valves, which are often used, can be cleaned, while all air passages must be kept clear.

The C range had a clack valve up to 1953 which was positioned in the left crankcase half just below the cylinder mounting face and to the rear where its exit pointed back. A similar arrangement was used by the B and M models for 1946–47, but in their case the valve was fitted into the rear of the main-bearing boss of the left crankcase.

A timed breather was adopted by the C10L and C11G in 1954 with a hollow mainshaft cross-drilled to release the pressure at the best time, and this system was also used by the C12. On the B and M ranges the breather was moved to the lower edge of the timing cover during 1948 at various engine numbers already recorded. It remained a clack valve with an external drain pipe and internal stand pipe.

The later Gold Stars went to a timed breather for the CB and DB big-fin engines first seen in 1954. This was a ported drum which was driven by a pin inserted in the magneto drive gear and which rotated in the timing cover. At the rear of the cover a banjo connection led the air away.

The Gold Star breather has to be timed relative to the crankshaft and takes its position from the magneto gear; the latter must therefore be correctly set when locked to the magneto shaft.

The unit engines began with a timed breather using the hollow camshaft and a port in the inner timing case. This had an outlet within the outer case which was vented to atmosphere at the rear. This arrangement continued, except that the last stage was amended for 1965. At first a banjo bolt and pipe were fitted to the top of the engine but these were soon

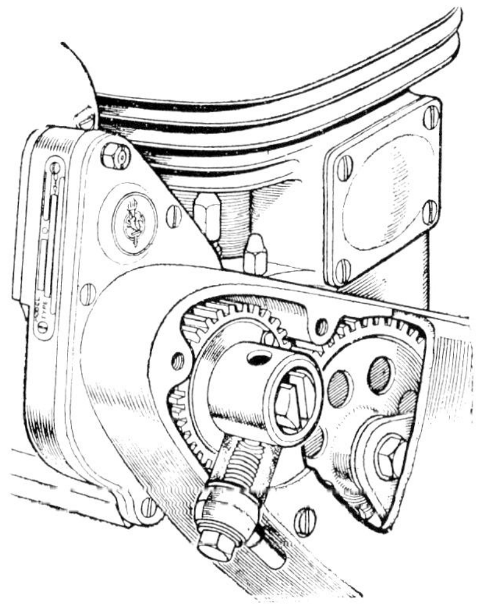

ABOVE *The timed breather, fitted to the CB and later Gold Stars, was driven from the magneto gear*

LEFT *A 1966 B44VE with a non-standard points cover and built in a stark off-road style*

changed. The revised design was a short length of pipe pressed into the inner side of the inner timing cover next to the clutch cable lug. A plastic pipe then ran to beneath the engine. This layout was used from then onwards.

On all engines, good breathing is as important as good joints in cutting out oil leaks, so it is vital that all the parts do their job correctly, including all the holes within the engine that contribute to the system.

Oil-tank types

This container always sat in the same place, other than when the frame was used, and needs to be cleaned and inspected. An unknown tank can be full of horrors as they seem able to harbour more dirt, sludge, spiders and unknown substances than even the underside of mudguards. Whatever it is, you have to get it all out, which may take all the solvents you have. Only then can it be checked properly.

The B range had an alteration to its oil tank and cap in 1946 with the new parts going in at frame XB31-3456 and the new tank continuing to be fitted to all rigid- and plunger-frame road models. The same tank also went on the competition ones for 1946–48 and 1952 plus some Gold Stars of 1949. The filler cap changed again for 1948 and 1951, this last remaining in use to the end of the B range.

The B32 and B34 had a new tank for 1949–51 with the side cut away for the exhaust system and a horizontal hole through the tank in the same area. For 1953 the tank gained a froth tower. All B models in the pivoted-fork frame were fitted with a tank that tucked into the right subframe angle in 1954. This had its filter inserted from the side and was used by the road models up to 1960 and the competition ones up to 1955. These last kept to the second 1946 type while in their rigid frame, but changed to a central tank for 1956–57. The road-model tank had its shape changed to a domed form for 1958, which was matched by the toolbox lid.

The Gold Star began with the standard tank plus another with hinged filler cap. This remained in use up to 1952 although the tank itself was changed for 1950. For 1953 and the pivoted-fork frame, a new tank was adopted that fitted into the subframe angle. This one did not have the filter fitted into the side and its filler cap was special. From 1954 the standard road B-range tank and cap were used with the change to the domed shape for 1958. The scrambles model had the option of a centrally-mounted oil tank from 1959 onwards.

The M range had just one tank for all years and models and this had a hinged filler cap. The cap was that also used by the Gold Star for 1949–52.

The C range had a common tank for the C10 and C11 which was changed in 1947 from frame XC10-6722 along with its cap, both old and new of these being common to the B range. The new tank also went on the C11G in both rigid- and plunger-frame forms. As on the B models, the cap was altered once more for 1948 and yet again for 1950, while in each case the part continued to be common to the other range.

A new tank was used by the C10L in 1954 and this differed in having the oil filter inserted in the front face of the tank. This changed again for 1956 when the filter went in from the side, while the C12 had a similar design to itself. One other tank was listed for the C10 supplied to the GPO in 1948 and this differed from the stock item in having its own cap on a retaining chain.

The unit models began with a conventional tank in its usual location which in turn went on to the C15, SS80, B40 and SS90. The one used by the competition models had a froth tower and the first type was changed during 1960 at frame C15S-2325.

From 1963 a central oil tank was fitted to the competition models and this had its filter screwed into the right side and the filler cap on the right top corner. This tank was fitted to the B40E and the 1966 B44VE without change but was amended for the 1967 B44VE and B44VS. All these tanks had a screw-on filler cap of the type used by the pre-unit models from 1950 onwards.

The year of 1967 saw two tanks listed for the 247 cc model: one for the C25 and the other for the B25, the latter also being fitted for 1968. Both were styled to match the left side cover so were of a complex shape built up from pressings. The tank was supported by bolted-on clips with rubber sleeves and had a bayonet filler cap with dipstick. A similar tank was fitted to the B44VR for 1967 using the same mountings and filler cap, and this became the B44SS for 1968.

OIL LEVEL
B.S.A. MOTOR CYCLES LTD
PROPRIETORS
BIRMINGHAM
ENGLAND
250

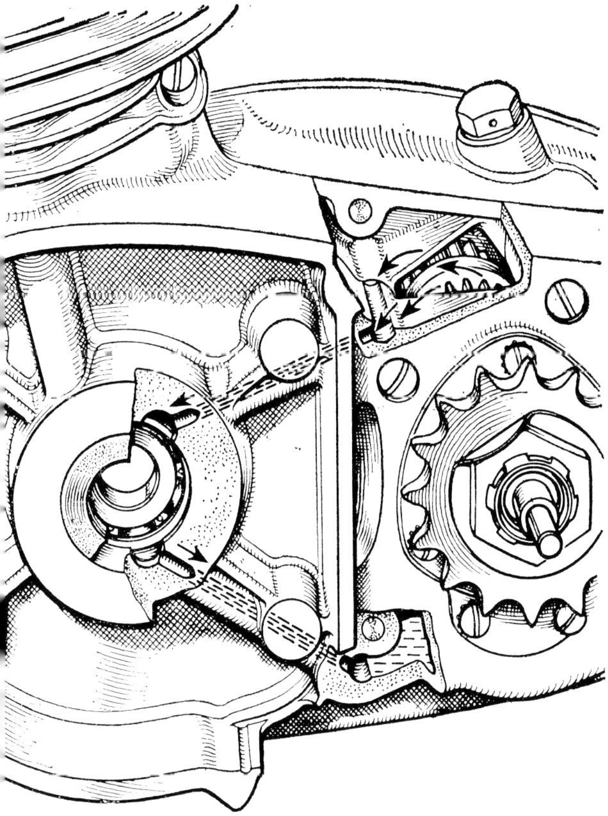

ABOVE *Detail of the main-bearing lubrication from the gearbox, as used on the 172 cc Bantam to avoid bearing corrosion*

ABOVE RIGHT *A D3 ridden from New Zealand being inspected by Brian Martin and Jeff Smith outside Earls Court*

LEFT *A 1964 police C15 with no centre panel and other changes to suit its use by the force*

This rather extravagant design was dropped for 1969 and replaced by a simple tank and side cover. This arrangement was first used by the 1968–69 B44VS which had a tank with welded-on mounting clips. The tank fitted to the B44VS and B25 for 1969 was similar but not identical, as its shape was more rectangular and it had two brackets welded to it for the side-cover fastenings.

These both went for 1970 when the resulting tank was fitted to all three models and equipped with a new filler cap. Only a cap remained in 1971 as the tank became a frame tube and the cap a new screw-in item with dipstick attached. It was amended for 1973 to add an anti-splash disc to the stick.

The oil tanks of the military B40 and the B40 Rough Rider both differed from the items listed above.

Bantam lubrication

All Bantam models avoided the complication of pumps and tanks by running on a petroil mixture. Early tables gave 16:1 for running in and 24:1 thereafter, while later ones specified 20:1 of SAE40. From 1967 the figure became 24:1 of self-mix or 32:1 of SAE40.

This last is a reasonable figure unless a synthetic oil is selected where the ratio may be leaner, but must be to the maker's recommendation. An oil measure was incorporated in the filler cap, with that of early models being about 5 in. long and later ones $6\frac{1}{4}$ in. Two and a half of the first or two of the second per gallon will give a 20:1 ratio, but a check on the actual quantity involved should be made.

Rear-chain lubrication

The unit engines had a bleed from the back of the primary chaincase for this but it is not always adequate. Thus these models, as with all the others, need their chains attended to in the usual way.

Engine-oil grade

This is an area of myths and folklore over which owners may argue well into the night. BSA recommended SAE50 in summer and SAE30 in winter for the pre-units, and SAE40 in summer for the units up to 1967. From then onwards the listing was SAE20W/50 for all seasons. Many owners keep to a monograde for their singles even where a plain big-

LEFT *The dipstick added to the filler cap on the 1969 B25. Note the tank cover and its transfer which replaced the styled tank*

RIGHT *Brenda Collins in New York at the end of a 10,000-mile tour of the USA, Canada and Mexico on her 123 cc D1*

end is fitted, and in all cases a clean filter and regular oil changes are a good idea. A good SAE20W/50 multigrade is better than a poor monograde, but the additives don't last too long in a high-temperature, high-specific-output engine, so the oil-change intervals must not be extended.

Gold Stars and the Victor Grand Prix were often run on castor base oil and this must not be mixed with normal mineral oil. If a change is made from one to the other, the whole system must be fully cleaned out, even if this means a full engine strip.

Many readers may disagree with the above and, as always, the choice is theirs, but it does seem that a good monograde is to be preferred.

Transmission-oil grades

Monogrades are more usual in these areas, which are not subject to the same temperature range as the engine. The primary-chaincase oil is not specified for many BSA singles but engine oil or an SAE20 can be used. The Victor Grand Prix model is one of the few to specifically call for SAE20 and to state that the castor base type used in the engine must not be used in the chaincase.

The gearbox used engine oil for many years but changed to EP90 for 1968. This has a similar viscosity to the earlier engine grade but is better able to cope with the stresses involved in the gearbox and is thus recommended for all models. It was used in the B44GP from its start.

CANADA
Oregon
NEW MEXICO
ARIZONA
BSA

6 Electrics

This is an area that gives many owners considerable difficulties, and even some very skilled engine fitters will admit that it is all a big mystery to them. The problem arises, in part, from the fact that you never see the substance, only its effects. Also, like an oil leak, it can so easily spread all over the place without any obvious evidence as to where it came from.

If you intend to do a restoration, you have to accept that you must wrestle with the subject or it could defeat you. Fortunately, real electrical faults are rare, despite what you may think, as nearly all the troubles are caused by mechanical failures of one form or another. Most can be cured by correct assembly and settings. Remember the need to comply with current local legislation.

Helpful points to remember are as follows. The system has two sides, one dealing with charging and the other with use. Although they may connect in operation and control, they can be thought of as two distinct areas and dealt with accordingly. The most common fault is a poor earth, which is simply a poor connection for the return of the current rather than its supply. Also very common is a poor connection in the supply leads. Finally, buy the tools for the job, which means lighter spanners or wrenches, smaller screwdrivers, pliers, cutters, an electrician's soldering iron and a small meter. The last does not have to be anything special as continuity checks will be its main job, but it will help a great deal. An old ammeter, preferably with centre zero, and reading 15 amps or so, is also worth having to check current flow in and out of the battery. Even if the machine has one, it is not always convenient to use, so a meter with leads can be better.

BSA electrical systems

The BSA pre-unit singles began with the traditional magneto and dynamo in the larger sizes, but the C range always had coil ignition even if its battery was topped up by a dynamo. From 1954 the C range went over to an alternator, which went on to the B range for 1958 and all unit engines. Only the Gold Star and the M models kept to their original fittings and the last often fitted both charging systems for the AA.

The Bantams began with a flywheel generator made by Wipac which continued in use up to 1966, but this was joined by a Lucas generator and coil ignition in 1950. The latter continued to be offered up to late 1953. With the advent of the D10 in 1967, a six-coil Wipac alternator was fitted and powered a system which included coil ignition except on the Bushman model. This had no battery and relied on energy-transfer ignition and direct lighting. From 1967 the points were moved to a chamber on the primary chaincase.

The electric system was 6 volts for many years but went to 12 volts for the four-strokes for 1967, although the Bantams stayed with 6 volts.

Magneto types

These were only fitted to the B and M ranges, and for road use had the dynamo clamped on to the top of the magneto with the assembly held down on its platform by a strap. This must be kept tight to achieve the best mesh of its drive gear. The location dowels in its base keep it in line.

All magnetos used in these ranges rotated anti-clockwise as viewed from the driven end. The road machines had the normal Lucas mag-dyno fitted but magnetos alone were also listed. These were often fitted to the competiton models and to some Gold Stars, and for both there was a choice of Lucas or BTH magnetos up to 1957.

The arrangements for the Gold Star models were sometimes affected by the rules of the Clubmans races they were so successful in. Thus, in the early years when there was no requirement for the machine to have charging equipment fitted, the dynamo was removed and a circular piece of wood or a steel sleeve put in its place for the strap to hold to.

Magneto service

This concerns the points gap, which is 0.012 in., and the brushes. There are several of the latter, for in addition to the high-tension-lead pick-up in the side of the body, there is a brush in the rear of the points plate on face-cam magnetos and an earth brush. There may also be one in the cap for the earthing lead.

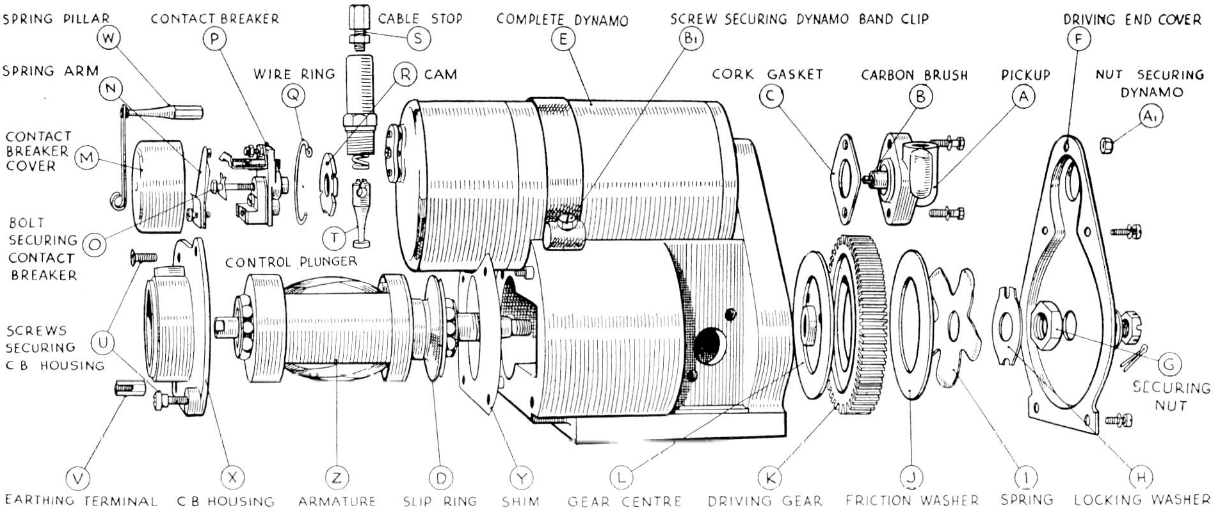

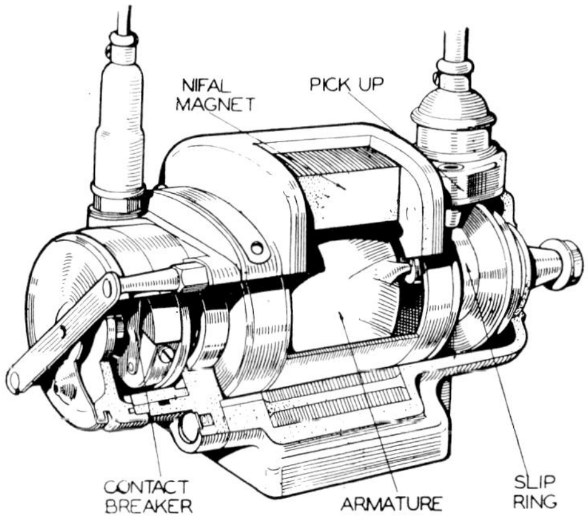

ABOVE *The single-cylinder mag-dyno as used by the B and M ranges*

LEFT *The competition version of the magneto as used by the B32 and B34 in standard and Gold Star forms*

Lucas and BTH magnetos have safety gap screws and these *must* be removed before any real dismantling is done, otherwise the slip ring will be damaged. All brushes need to be examined for cracks and checked for free movement in their holders and their general good condition. If worn, they should be replaced. Note that on occasion a brush or gap screw may be masked by a label, so care must always be exercised.

Magneto renovation

Further work on the magneto is more difficult and concerns bearings, condenser replacement and armature rewinds. All are specialist jobs but the actual dismantling is straightforward. Mark parts first as they can often be reversed; once apart, the details can be cleaned and inspected, especially for any cracks that could leak the high-tension current to earth.

It is a fairly skilled job to replace and set up magneto bearings, and even more tricky to change a condenser or rewind an armature. Unless you are really competent in this work it should be sent to a specialist. This is especially true if the magneto has lost some of its magnetism and is therefore sparking poorly, if at all. Magnetizing equipment is complex and expensive, so it is not really a practical proposition for anyone other than the professional.

Grease the bearings on assembly, which should give no problems. Do make sure all the little insulating washers and bushes are in the right place. More ignition systems fail to work after a rebuild for this reason than any other. Fit the lead, clamp the magneto in the vice, earth the plug to it and give it a spin—anti-clockwise, of course. Check that the earthing connection does its job.

Bantam magneto

Up to the end of 1966 most Bantams had a Wipac flywheel magneto fitted on the left side of the engine. This incorporated both ignition and lighting systems, with a massive rotor flywheel and an internal stator mounted outboard of it, carrying the ignition points and condenser. The ignition cam went on the extreme left end of the crankshaft and both it and the rotor were keyed to the shaft. Timing variation was achieved with slots for the stator clamp screws.

The components of a BTH magneto with flange mounting but also built for platform fitting

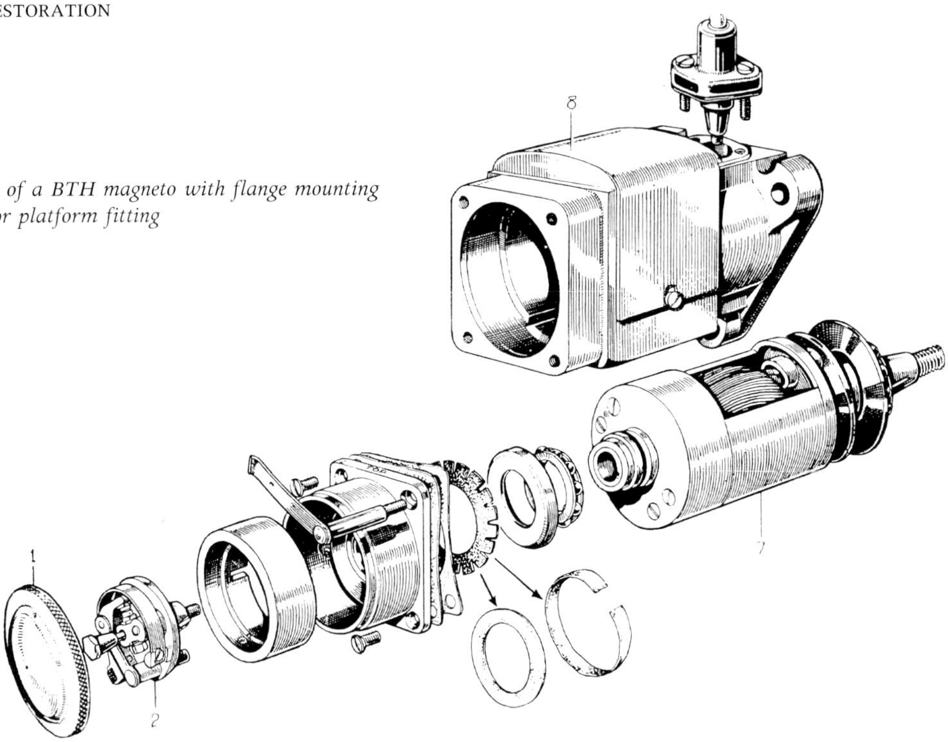

In place of this Wipac unit, some engines were fitted with a Lucas generator during the 1950–53 period. Both were preceded by an earlier version of the Wipac which was only used for 1949. It was called the Geni-Mag, while the later one had the prosaic title of S55/Mk8. The latter had 'Wipac AC/DC' cast on the rotor rim and the parts should not be switched or the output will be too high in volts or too low in amps. The first type was distinguished by a small points cover and a high-tension take-off block set on its centre line. By 1950 it had been superseded by the better-known one, with a large cover held by two screws and a high-tension lead sweeping out from its rear quarter via a simple sleeve moulding.

The first Wipac system gave direct lighting, and the Lucas generator was used to provide a battery system up to late 1953. From then on, the Wipac one was used in either fashion, at first with a negative-earth system but later with a positive one. There was a further change for 1964 when an external ignition coil was used on the de luxe D7 models, and this introduced a second switch in the headlamp with normal and emergency ignition positions.

The whole system was uprated for the D10 in 1967 when a six-pole Wipac alternator replaced the older type and the points cam moved to the right end of the crankshaft. Two stator types were used and the standard one had the six coils joined in pairs, with two pairs also linked. It thus had three connections and used the light switch to regulate the output to demand. This system went on to the D14 and D175 in turn.

The second type had five output wires and went on the Bushman and Pastoral models. Individual coils supplied the ignition system and the stop light, while pairs of coils looked after the lights and horn. The type was revised for the D14 and then continued in use to the end.

The Lucas type IA45 generator was fitted to a modified crankshaft and case, therefore having its own procedures. It is emphasized by the BSA manual that the rotor must *not* be withdrawn from the stator or magnetism will be lost. It is for a positive-earth system only, and later examples had a roller steady bearing at the outer end of the rotor.

There is not a great deal that can be done to the magnetos other than to check them for physical damage, change the points and make sure all the coils are connected electrically as they should be. One fault often found on Wipac stators is for the points pin to be loose in the casting. As it is cast in place, it has to be replaced by one that is best screwed in and locked with a nut at the rear. This was standard practice on racing Bantams in their early days.

Do not run a Wipac rotor above 6500 rpm as they have been known to burst and then exit the engine castings at speed! Note that there existed a special cam to give a retarded timing. If you have one and do not know it, there could be confusion in trying to set the ignition timing correctly and for this to stay compatible with the magneto internal timing for the best spark.

Dynamo type and drive

Lucas dynamos were fitted to the B range up to 1957, Gold Stars, all M models and the C range to 1953. The early models had the E3 type but this was changed to the E3L with higher output for 1949. Two types were

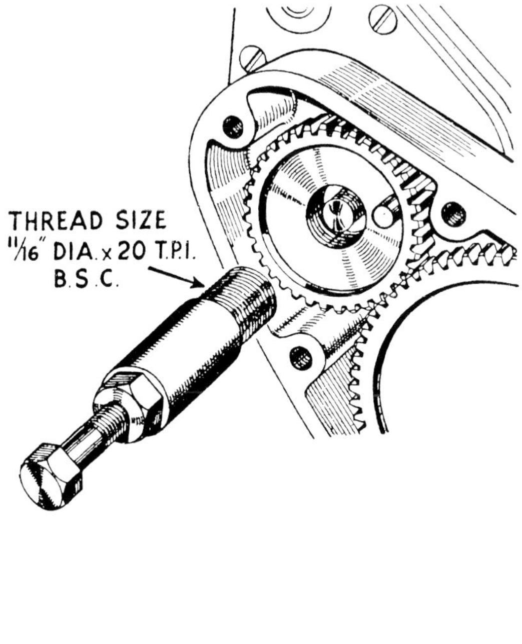

ABOVE *The Wipac Geni-Mag as fitted for 1948–49, with small points cover and top HT lead outlet*

LEFT *The essential extractor needed to pull the magneto gear on B- and M-range engines. Don't even think of not using it!*

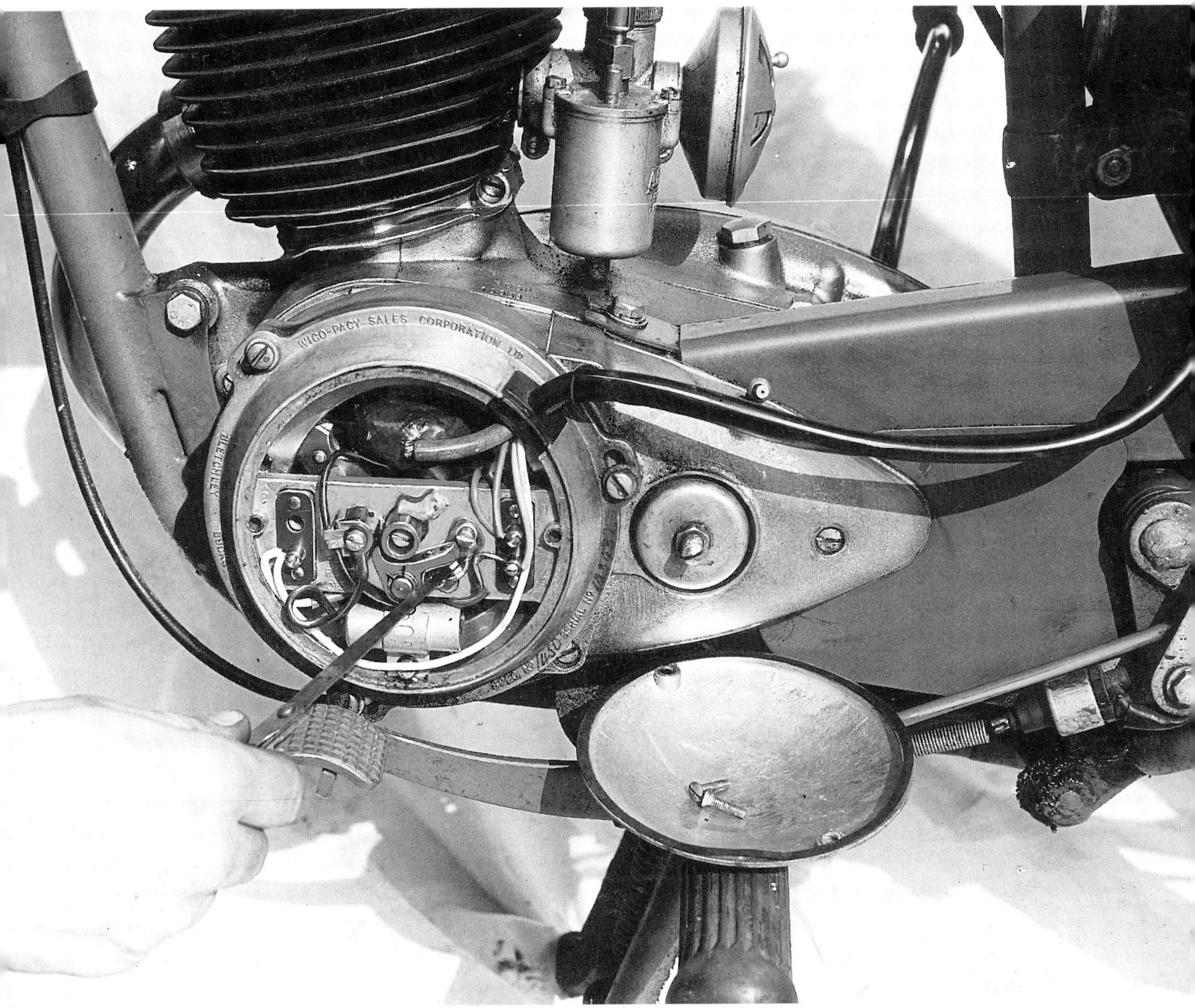

used, one on the C range and the other for all models with a mag-dyno.

These had the dynamo clamped to the magneto body and gear-driven from its armature. The C range had the dynamo held to the upper rear of the crankcase and driven by chain from the camshaft. The drive chain was 8 mm pitch, 5 mm roller diameter, 48 links long and endless. Its tension was adjusted by rotating the dynamo in the clamp band.

Dynamo testing

This can begin on the machine by disconnecting the leads to the dynamo. Then join the two terminals, D and F, and connect a voltmeter from the join to the dynamo body. Run the machine so the dynamo speed is up to 1000 rpm and look for the voltage reading to rise smoothly and quickly to 10 volts. Don't run the dynamo faster in an attempt to push the volts value up. If there is no reading at all, look to the brush gear; if it is about 0.5 volts the field winding is suspect, and if between 1.5 and 2 volts then the armature winding is the likely culprit. For any further work the dynamo will need to be dismantled.

Dynamo service

Mark parts before taking them apart and proceed with some delicacy as some items are rather brittle. Clean all the connections to reduce contact resistance, and check that all wires are in good order and not frayed in any way. Examine the brushes and replace if worn down to about $\frac{5}{16}$ in. Make sure the brushes, whether old or renewed, can move freely in their boxes and that the brush springs are strong enough to hold them in contact with the commutator.

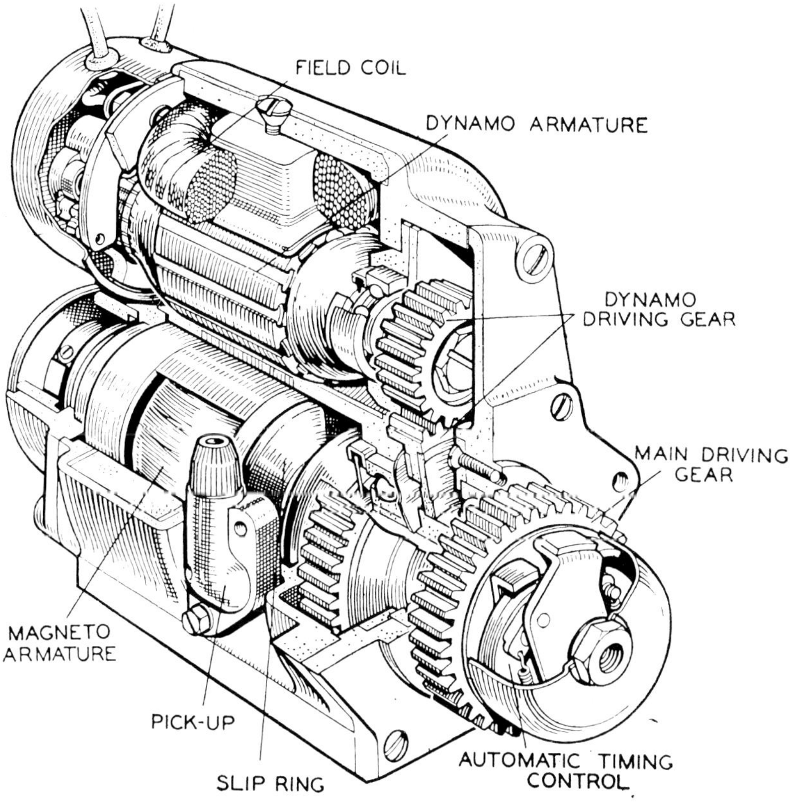

LEFT *Cutaway drawing of an early post-war mag-dyno showing details of its construction*

LEFT *The Wipac magneto as fitted to the Bantam from 1950 and well known to thousands of owners. The points pin can work loose and this one is on a 1956 D3*

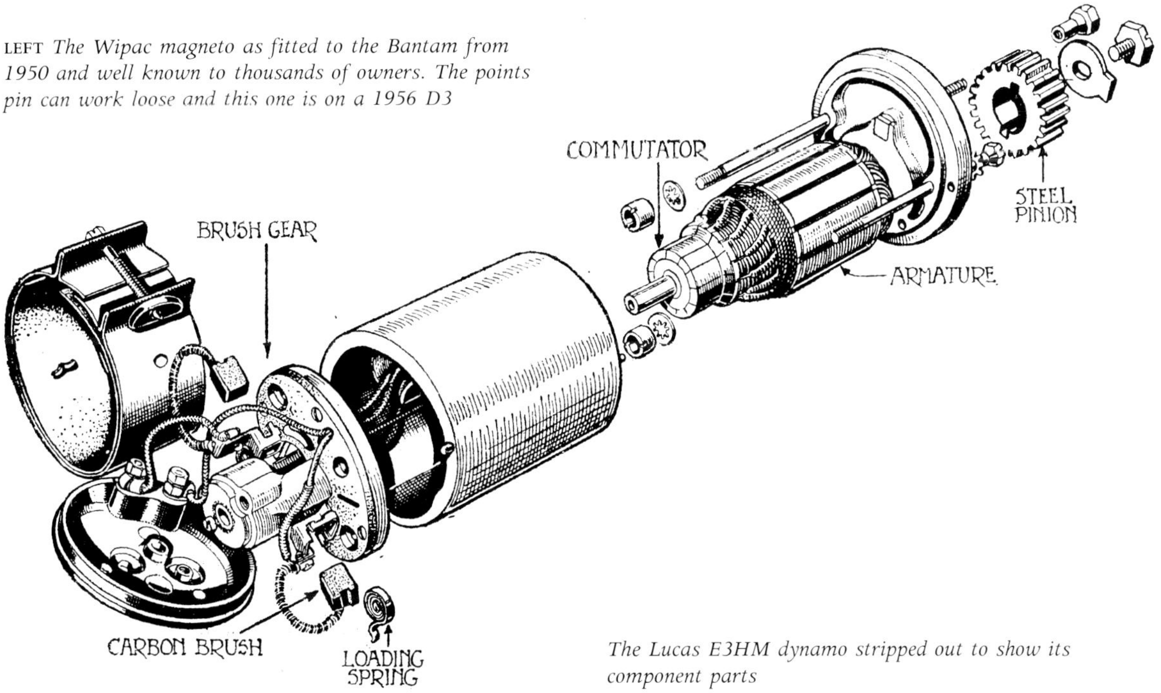

The Lucas E3HM dynamo stripped out to show its component parts

This last will need cleaning and if burnt may need machining to restore it to true round. Should this be needed, remove the minimum of material and be prepared to undercut the commutator segments. Also examine the wire connections to the segments for any signs of overheating which may indicate problems in the armature. Clean out all the carbon dust as this can short out the insulated wires.

Armature rewinds and field coil replacement are best left to specialists due to the equipment required. Grease the two ball races, but not too much or it will be all over the commutator. Reassemble with care to ensure everything goes back where it came from.

The finished result can be tested off the engine by connecting it to a battery so that it becomes an electric motor. This is done by joining the F and D terminals

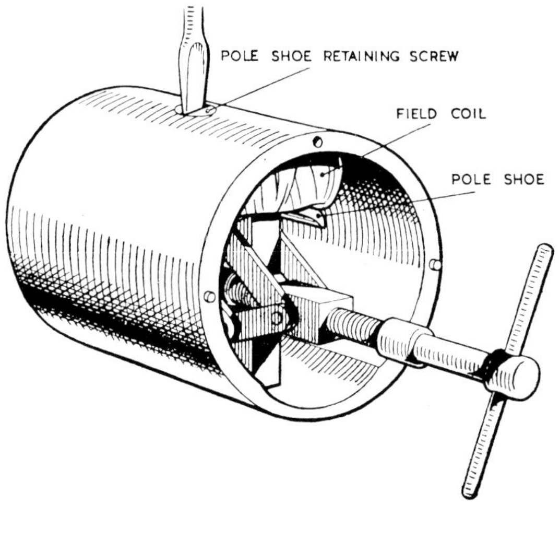

ABOVE *Fitting a field coil using an expander tool to locate it firmly into place*

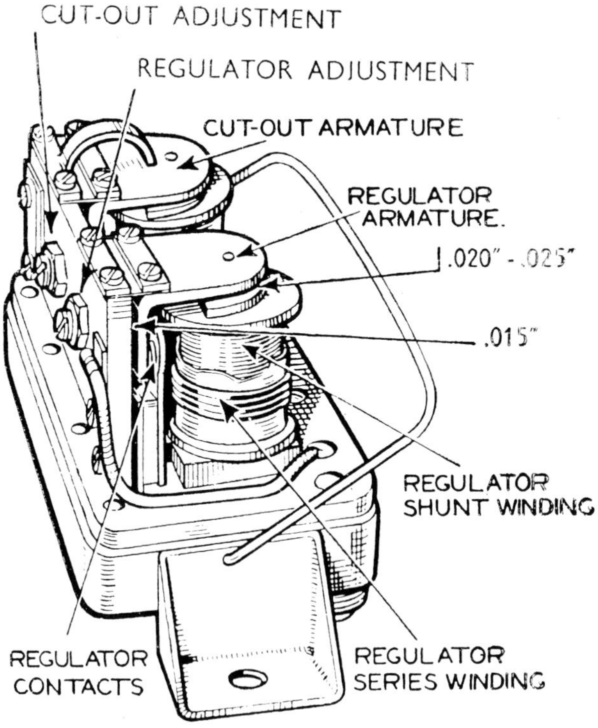

RIGHT *The MCR1 Lucas regulator showing its various features*

and connecting the join and the dynamo body to a 6-volt battery. The body connection is to the normally-earthed terminal and if all is well the armature will revolve.

Regulator unit

This is also known as the compensated voltage control unit, or cvc, and has one control coil plus the cut-out under the lid. It has four terminals in a row and the connecting plug cannot be reversed.

The early singles used the MCR1 regulator, but from 1949 the MCR2 was fitted. This differed in that the control resistor became a carbon disc fitted to the main frame behind the coils and can be recognized by a swelling in the back of the cover put there to clear it. On these two models the terminals were labelled FADE, but about 1958 the unit was changed to an RB107 which had its connections in the order FAED.

The cvc is a delicate electro-mechanical assembly and must be treated as such. It can be set up and adjusted by the owner, but this must be done precisely or the system will not work as it should. It is really no different from valve clearances or ignition timing.

Regulator function

Two jobs are done inside the cvc unit. The regulator side switches a resistor into series with the field coil to reduce the field current and thus the generated output. It is in a state of vibration while doing this. The cut-out is simply a switch which disconnects the dynamo from the battery when needed to prevent the latter trying to motor the former, which would discharge the battery.

Confusion with the unit usually arises because the theoretical circuit diagram, practical wiring diagram and the unit itself all look completely different. Further confusion arises in that the internal frame is used as part of the electric circuit but is not an earth. In truth, it connects via the cut-out points to the battery supply line, so it is insulated from the mounting frame.

Regulator service

If you decide to work on the cvc, trace out the electrical circuit first so you know where each part fits into the scheme of things. It will then be much easier to check each item for continuity or open circuit using your meter. In most cases, the only problem will be the mechanical aspects of the contacts, their cleanliness and their adjustment. With those taken care of, all the circuits are likely to function as they should.

Looking at the coils, the one on the left with a few turns of heavy-gauge wire about its middle is the regulator. The first adjustment is by moving the armature, which is the bent-steel part pulled by the coil magnetism and carrying one of the contacts; the next adjustment is made by bending the fixed contact on the MCR units; finally, an adjuster screw at the rear needs setting.

Air gaps are required between the vertical leg of

the armature that carries the contact and the frame, and between the horizontal leg and the bobbin core on the MCR units. The first should be 0.015 in. on the MCR1 and 0.020 in. on the MCR2. The second figure is 0.020 in. for both but with a tolerance of plus 0.005 in. on the MCR1 and minus 0.008 in. on the MCR2. On the MCR1, with the armature held against the bobbin core, the points gap should be between 0.002 and 0.008 in., and on the MCR2 between 0.006 and 0.017 in.

The RB107 has a different method of adjustment. The armature screws are undone, a feeler gauge of 0.015 in. put between the armature and the bobbin, and the screws done up. The contacts are then adjusted so they just touch with the feeler gauge still in place.

The remaining adjustments are made with the cvc wired to the machine. Put card between the cut-out points and disconnect the lead from terminal A. Insert a voltmeter between D and E and run the dynamo at about 3000 rpm. At 10 degrees Celsius the reading should be 8.0 to 8.4 volts, and can be adjusted with the screw at the rear. If the temperature rises, deduct 0.2 volts for every 10 degrees Celsius, and if it falls add it. Then run the dynamo at about 4500 rpm when the reading should not exceed 8.9 volts. Do all this quickly or errors will occur. If in doubt, do it in steps. The readings for the RB107 regulator should be 7.7 to 8.1 volts and the deduction 0.1 volts per 10 degrees Celsius from that ambient.

Cut-out setting

For the MCR1 and MCR2, the armature-to-frame air gap should be 0.014 in. and to the bobbin core 0.011 to 0.015 in. With these two gaps held correct by gauges, press the armature down on them and check that the gap between armature and stop-plate arm is 0.030 to 0.034 in. Bend the arm to adjust, then place a 0.025 in. gauge between armature shim and core face and check that the contact gap is between 0.002 and 0.006 in.

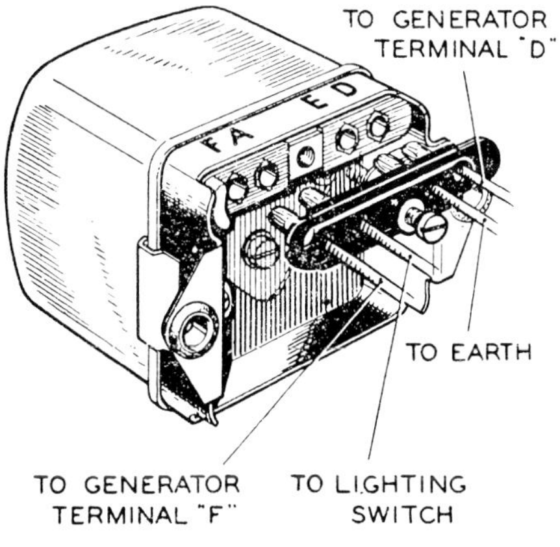

The later RB107 regulator with different terminal arrangement

Bend the fixed contact bracket to adjust.

The RB107 is set by pressing the armature down to the core face and checking the gap between its stop arm and its tongue, which should be 0.025 to 0.030 in. Bend the stop arm to adjust, then adjust the fixed contact blade to give a blade deflection of 0.01 to 0.02 in. when the armature is pressed firmly down on the core face.

Cut-out checking

This is done on the machine and a full test covers both cut-in and cut-out. For the first, connect an ammeter in the lead from dynamo D to cvc D, and a voltmeter between there and E. Gradually bring the engine speed up and watch for the voltmeter pointer to flick back as the points close. This should occur at 6.2 to 6.6 volts on the MCR1 and 6.3 to 6.7 volts on the MCR2 and RB107. It is adjusted by the screw, which increases the setting when turned clockwise. The ammeter should show a charge when the points close. When the engine stops, the ammeter discharge reading is taken and should be between 3 and 5 amps when the contacts open.

The cut-out check is done by detaching lead A from the cvc and connecting a voltmeter between terminals A and E. Run the dynamo up to 3000 rpm and then let its speed slowly die away. The voltage should be between 4.8 and 5.5 volts when the contacts open and the reading drops to zero.

Regulator oddments

The resistance used in the cvc, which is placed in the field circuit, can be measured if you have a good meter. The value for a carbon one is 36–45 ohms, while the wire-wound type of the MCR1 is 27–33 ohms.

If your machine has the short E3 dynamo fitted in error, it ought to have an MCR1 cvc. If this is not available, the MCR2 listed under part number 37144A should be used.

You can use the machine without the battery as long as the cvc is working correctly. This may not be fully legal in some cases, but it can be useful in an emergency. However, if the battery is in circuit, it must be topped up or the control is fooled into providing excess current which can ruin battery, dynamo and cvc.

The contact points do get dirty and may need cleaning. If they do, they will definitely need re-setting.

Should the dynamo polarity have reversed itself, which does happen, just hold the cut-out points together for a second or two and then pull them apart.

Do make sure that dynamo D is connected to cvc D and F to F. Although the dynamo leads are held by a kidney-shaped plate and the cvc one is non-reversible, they could have been switched at some time. Detach and check by meter as they often run out of sight on the machine.

Modern regulators

By using modern electronic components, the problems of the electro-mechanical cvc can be removed with solid-state devices. This is electronic engineering quite outside most people's knowledge, but specialist suppliers make it easy for the rest of us.

A unit is available to replace the cvc and comprises a waterproof box that does the same job and enables the machine to be converted to 12 volts. Battery and bulbs also need changing but not the horn, and since the change boosts output, better lights can be fitted. The new assembly is small enough to tuck out of sight, so the alteration is not at all obvious for owners who wish to keep up appearances.

While this change departs from total originality, it is to be recommended for any machine used on a regular basis in modern traffic where good lights are essential. The move to 12 volts not only greatly improves the electrical efficiency of the system but also allows halogen lights to be used as a further bonus.

Alternator

BSA adopted the alternator on the C range in 1954, the B range in 1958 and for all unit models from their start in 1959. Effectively, the Bantam had this form of generator from the start. With it came the advantages of no touching parts and other delights, but these included control problems and boiled batteries so all was not quite as good as it might have been. In time the zener diode came along and with it better control and 12-volt systems.

The C10L was fitted with a Wipac unit but all the others used Lucas equipment with an RM13 on the C11G and an RM13/15 with longer rotor on the C12. The B31 and B33 fitted an RM15 from 1958, and the unit models began with an RM13 on the C15 for 1959–61 which also went on the competition models for the same year. For 1962 they changed to an RM19 while keeping to energy-transfer ignition, and the C15 changed to an RM18 which was also fitted to the SS80 and the later C15 Sportsman. The SS80 had fitted the RM13 for 1961, its first year.

The B40 began with an RM13/15 for 1961 but changed to an RM19 for 1962 which also went on the SS90. For the police models of the C15 and B40, the RM20 was fitted. The RM19 went on the B44 models from 1965, with the GP and VE versions having energy-transfer ignition. For the C25, B25, B44VS, B44VR and B44SS up to 1968, the RM19 in its standard form was used, and from 1969 the RM21 with encapsulated windings went on the B25, B44SS and B44VS. This unit continued in use on the last of the B25 and the B50 models, but not the B50MX which fitted the RM22.

Alternator checking

There is not a great deal that can be done other than cleaning and inspection. Check that the rotor has been running clear of the coil poles and look at the wiring for any damage. Use a meter to check continuity and insulation, and establish which coils are connected together and how the wires attach to them. Compare this with your wiring diagram and keep notes on this aspect as these may help a good deal when sorting out the connections to the rectifier.

It is possible for the rotor centre to become loose within the assembly and this can give rise to a nasty knocking noise in the engine. A cure is to machine away the alloy side enough to allow the core to come out and then to refit it using a Loctite gap filler.

Rectifier

Early alternators had their output turned into direct current by massive selenium-plate rectifiers. The original boxes soon became a smaller set of four plates on a single central bolt and, in time, this assembly was replaced by a similar silicon-diode rectifier.

All the four-plate types give full wave rectification, and the centre stud is one of the direct-current connections and must be treated as such. It connects to the earthed side of the battery. The three-plate connections have the other direct-current line in the middle, flanked by the two alternating-current ones. These last two may connect either way round as reversal at that point will not affect the rectifier operation at all.

The rectifier can be cleaned and its electrical function checked for the correct working of each diode. These must pass current one way but not the other, and a meter or battery and bulb will act as a tester. Do not move the central clamping nut or the device will fail. The nut tension controls the efficiency of the unit and must be left alone. Care is therefore needed when fixing the device to the machine.

A special two-element selenium-plate rectifier was specified for the Lucas IA45 generator used on some early Bantams which also gave full alternator output for battery charging.

Alternator control

On the face of it, the stator coils connect to the rectifier, which connects to the battery to complete the circuit. Unfortunately, there are complications. First, the output needs to be controlled to suit the load, and second, it would be nice to be able to start even with a flat battery. Coping with these problems introduces complications in the switches and wiring, and confusion can be the result.

The control of 6-volt Lucas alternator systems is done by stator-coil switching. The basic control is that four coils are permanently connected, and with the lights off the remaining two are short-circuited to reduce the output of the four in use. With the pilot

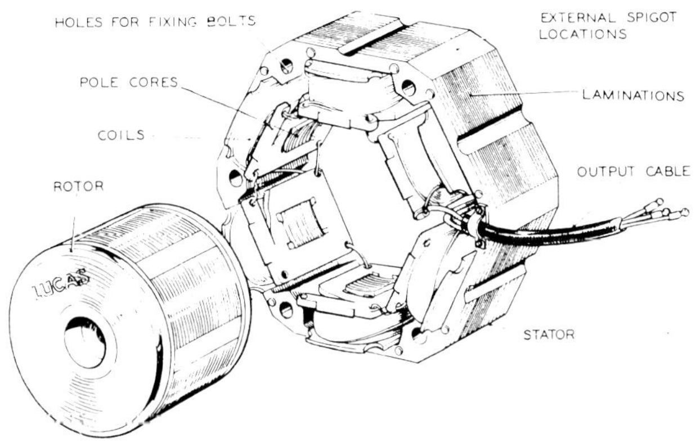

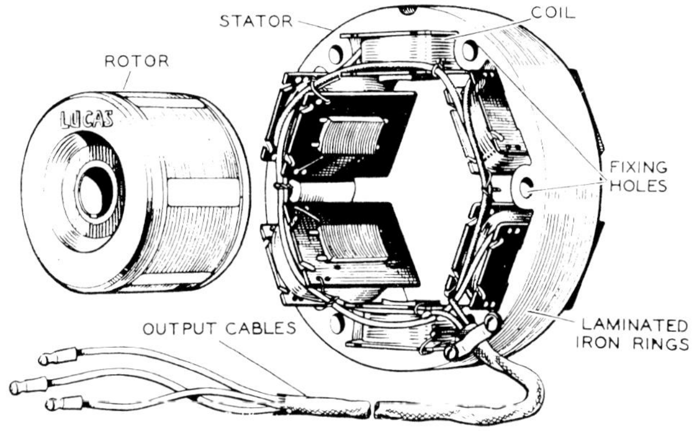

Top is the RM14 alternator, with the round RM15 below it. Both have six coils and various wiring options

light on, the two are open circuit so they don't affect the other four, and with the headlight on all six are connected. This means that the light switch has to be joined electrically to the charging circuit. For emergency ignition, four coils supply the ignition circuit direct, leaving two to assist the battery; a similar, but not identical, arrangement was used by the Wipac design fitted to the C10L.

A 12-volt system was used for the road models from 1967 onwards and for them a zener diode was employed for control. The 1967–70 models had a heat sink mounted under the bottom fork yoke to dissipate the excess energy of the alternator, but from 1971 the zener was mounted in the electric components box and used this case as the heat sink.

The Bantam with Lucas generator type IA45 differed from the Wipac models in having switch control of the output in conjunction with a half-charge resistor mounted in the headlamp. This had a value of 6.5 ohms.

Complications and problems can arise because of dirty contacts, poor earths, wire colour changes, owner alterations and all manner of odd circuit variations used by Lucas over the years. To sort it out you have to use the full circuit diagram and trace out each section in turn so that you really *do* know what is happening.

Alternator voltage conversion

A useful change as the 12-volt system is more efficient and simplifies the wiring. All the coils are permanently connected to the rectifier which has the zener diode fitted between its supply terminal and earth. The actual details vary according to the machine circuit, but can be sorted out using the wiring diagram and the information already established for the switches.

When first introduced, the zener diodes that were then available could not cope with controlling the full output when there was no headlight load, so the switched connection was still needed. This had two coils permanently on for machines fitted with a magneto, and four where coil ignition was used. Modern zeners can cope.

Battery, ignition coils, bulbs, rectifier and ignition condenser will need changing. The horn is not essential, but any ancillaries need to be remembered.

Coil ignition

This was used on all the C-range models right from the start, but did not go on the B31 or B33 until 1958. It appeared on some D7 Bantams in 1964 but was then standard for the road D10, D14 and D175 Bantams from 1967 onwards. All the unit road models and the B44VS for 1968–70 had coil ignition, while from 1971 this was backed up by a capacitor system. The latter allowed the machine to run without a battery at all.

Ignition points and advance mechanism

The points were either located in their own housing or installed in the timing cover. The first style was used by the C range up to 1953, the B range and the unit models up to 1964. After these dates the C range, unit models and Bantams had the points in the timing cover or on the chaincase.

The early C range had the points cam skew-gear-driven, as did the unit models, but the B range simply mounted the housing in place of the magneto and used the same gear drive, even if the detail part was new. Except for the Bantam, all had an advance mechanism built in between the drive and the points cam.

The points are replaced as a matter of course, and the advance mechanism needs to be checked in case the springs are tired or the small pivots worn. The housing and its cap should be checked for damage or cracks and any bearings must be in good order. Make

The finned zener-diode mounting used in 1967 on the singles

sure the cam spindle can turn freely, and double-check that the points' wire connection is to the correct side of the insulation washers, as this is a common mistake.

Energy-transfer ignition

This system has some of the alternator windings connected directly to a special ignition coil. This allows the machine to run without a battery, but the ignition timing and its relation to the alternator coils is critical.

The arrangement was first seen on the C15T and C15S models and was quite troublesome due to the backlash in the skew-gear drive, which made the timing critical. The timing-cover points system was better and modern owners often change to a capacitor system to bypass the problems. ET ignition went on the two competition C15 models, B40E, B44GP, B44VE, B44VS for 1967 only and B50MX. A Wipac version was used by the D10, D14 and D175 Bushman and Pastoral models.

Ignition timing

This is often a source of great concern to owners. In one sense it is important, but on the other hand the actual figure used may be less so. What is often forgotten is that the engine may be 20 or more years old, worn in various ways and running on a different blend of fuel to that available to it when new.

Therefore, while the original figure makes a good starting point, it is not sacrosanct. The old-fashioned technique of advancing the setting until the engine pinks on a rising road and then backing it off a little still works, even if it is awkward to carry out on some models.

Check the timing you decide to use on full advance. The retard figure is much less important so may be

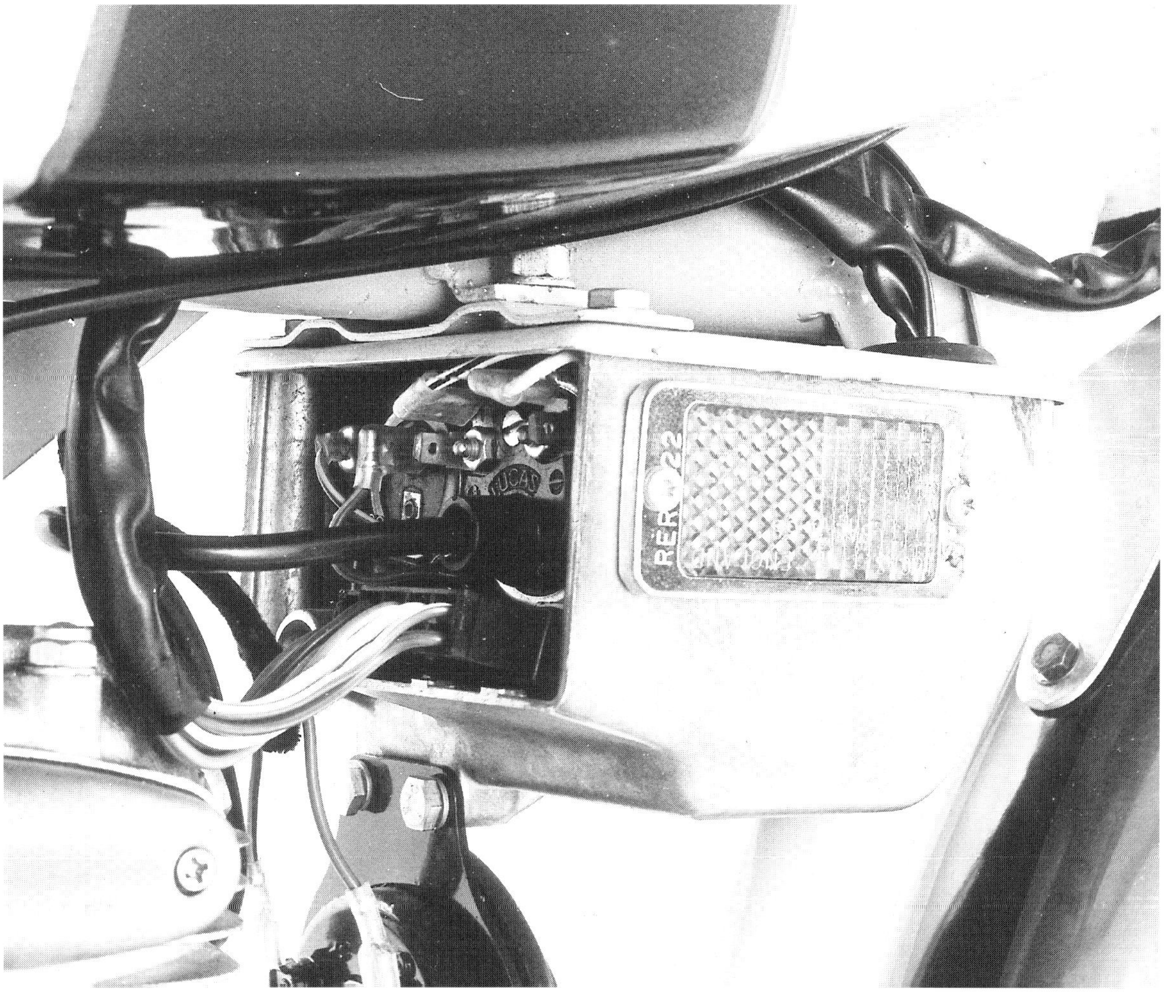

The electrical box used from 1971 on the singles to carry most of the components, seen here on a B25T

ignored, although the more particular among us will check it to be sure. Beware of slack in the drive when checking and for slack in distributor bearings which can give a false reading. Recheck if in any doubt.

Electronic ignition

This is a worthwhile modification for late-type machines and is available in various forms to replace magneto or coil ignition. It is also possible to adapt them to existing parts to retain the original drive system.

The installation instructions supplied with the kit should be carefully followed, especially regarding the timing. Electronic advance is normal, so the mechanical device must be discarded or locked, and the timing will have to be checked with a strobe. Therefore, a timing mark will be needed; this must be checked with a timing disc before the ignition is set up.

A further option is capacitor ignition using the alternator as a power source, a 12-volt zener-diode control, a storage capacitor, and the original points and advance mechanism. This is effectively a variation of the earlier energy-transfer system but is much better in use and is, in essence, the same as that installed from 1971 onwards as a stand-by.

Sparking plug, cap and lead

The plug should be replaced by a modern equivalent, although many owners do like to keep the original if it is to hand. Check that the plug top is tight as it can cause a misfire if slack. Grades are listed in an appendix.

The cap should be the type that contains a suppressor and the lead must be in good condition. Make sure the ends are clean and make a good connection or an odd misfire may occur.

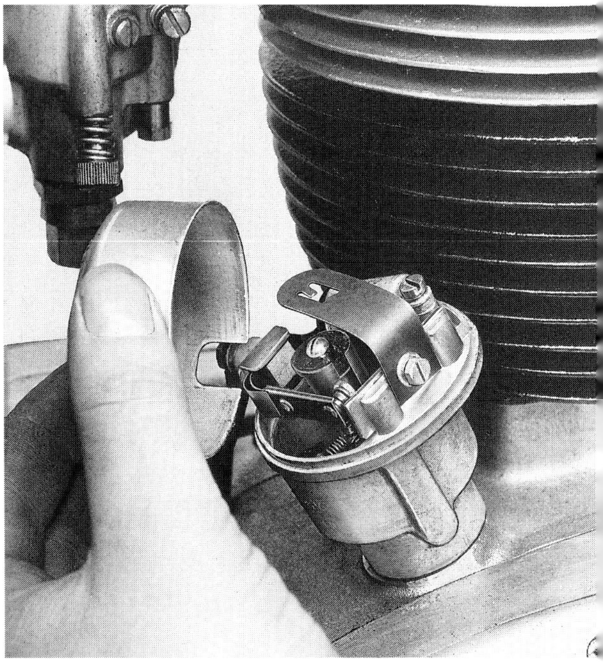

ABOVE *Points housing of the unit singles for 1958–64 and here on a 1961 B40*

ABOVE LEFT *The 1965 points in timing-chest style used by the singles from that date*

LEFT *The points housing of the 1966-onwards Bantams, shown here on a D10 Supreme of that year. The cam is not keyed to the shaft*

Using a strobe to check the ignition timing on a 1971 B25SS. The rotor marks should first be checked statically as correct

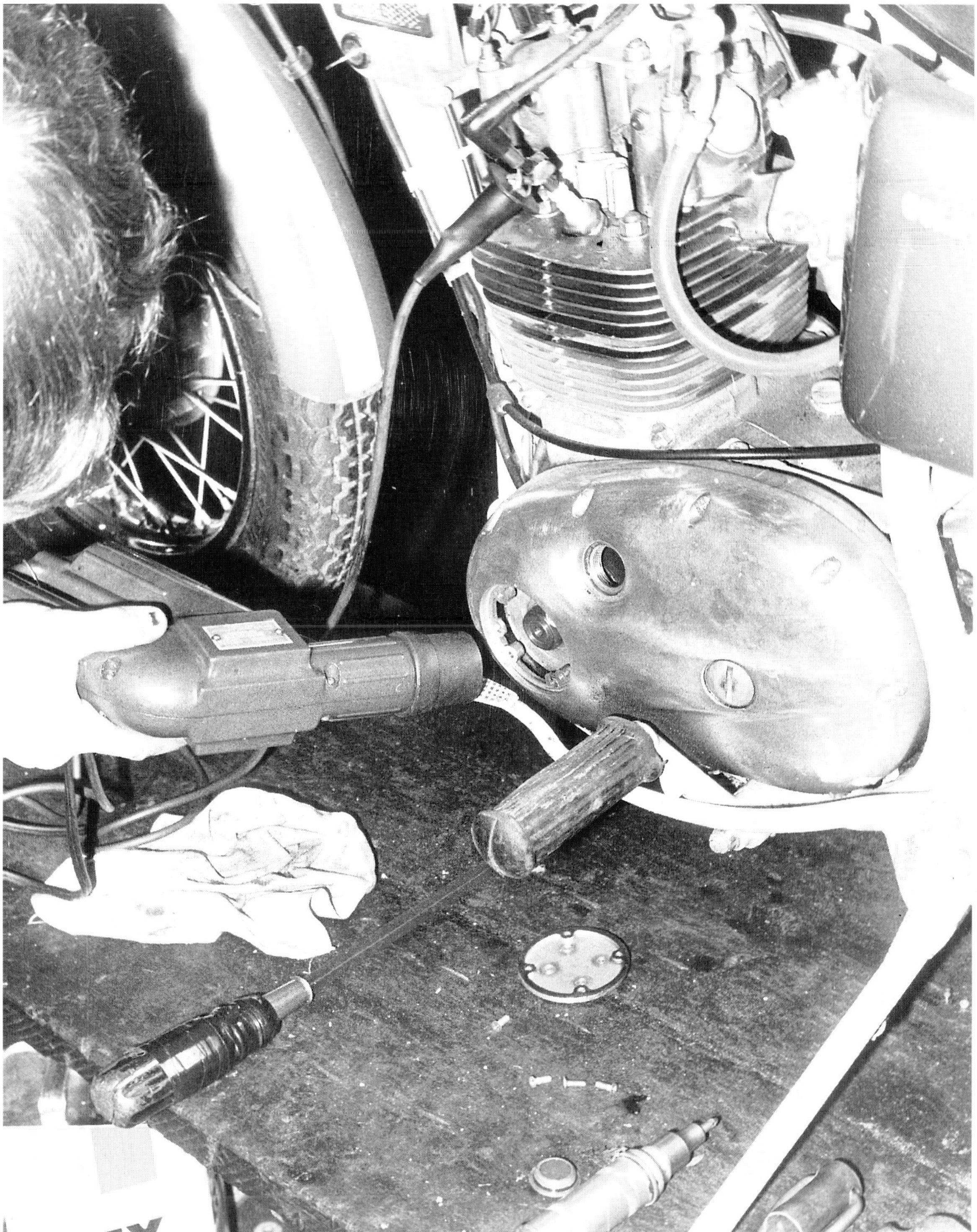

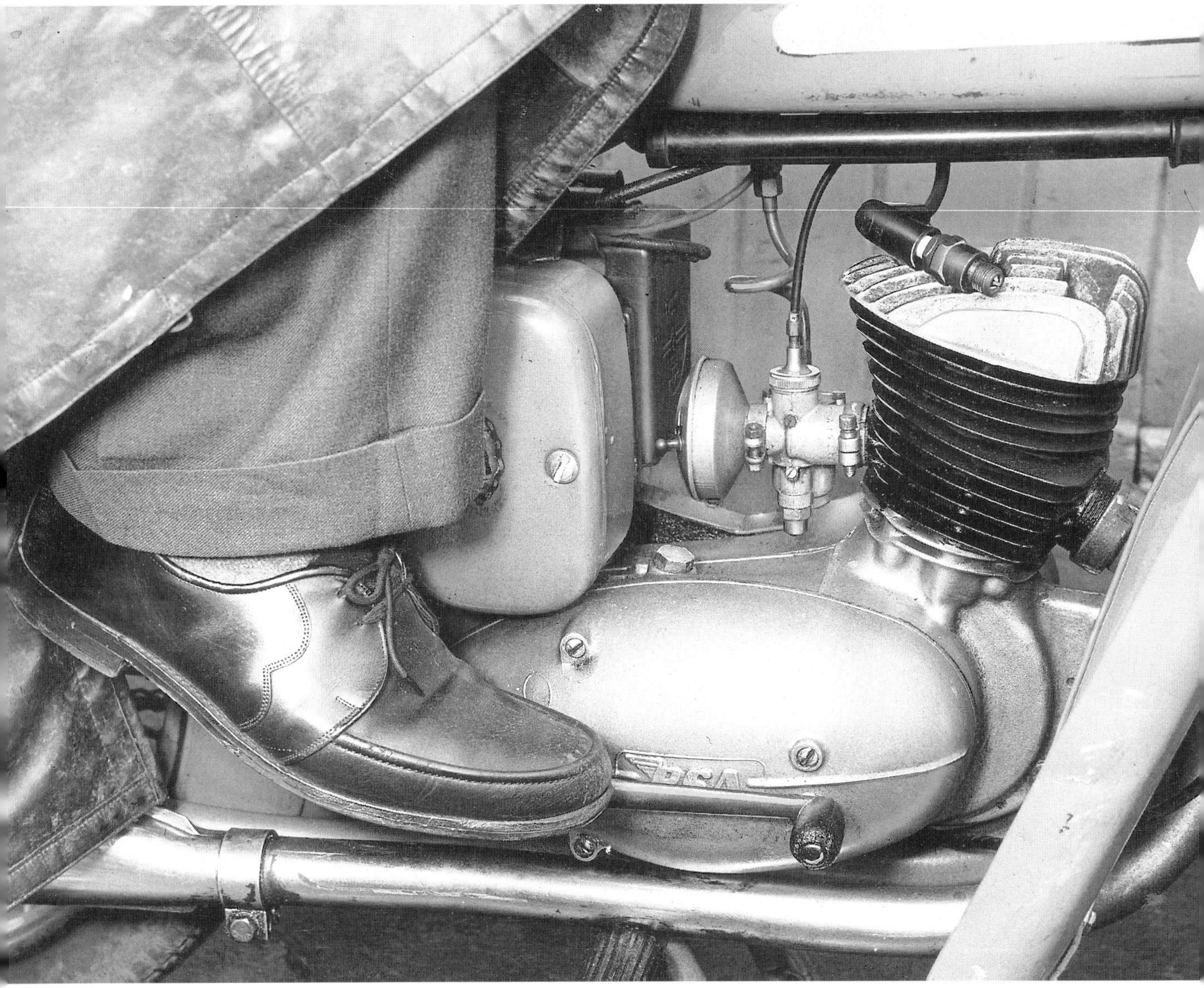

ABOVE *Searching for a Bantam spark on an early D1 with the plug laid on the head in traditional manner*

LEFT *Headlamp with toggle switch, ammeter and warning lamp on a 1968 single*

RIGHT *The 1953 C10 with side valves and the rather ornate tank panels used that year*

Headlamp and switch types

The early B and M models were built in the traditional manner with a separate headlamp shell with a small panel set in it. This carried an ammeter with the light switch to its rear. Initially the M models had an 8 in. lamp and the Bs a 6 in., but in time both moved to a common 7 in. one and this arrangement was used up to 1952. A cowl was fitted to the B and M models for 1953 and this carried the light switch on the left and the ammeter on the right, either side of the speedometer, while the headlamp shell had an underslung pilot lamp. This last feature was dropped for 1955, but otherwise the arrangement continued up to 1957.

For 1958 the B range had a nacelle with the ammeter now left and light switch right of the speedometer. An ignition switch was incorporated into the light switch. The M range lost its cowl and reverted to the arrangement it had used for 1946–52 with a small panel in the shell carrying the ammeter and light switch. This arrangement was used by all Gold Star models equipped for the road from first to last, with only the headlight itself being altered to keep up with changes in technology.

The C range up to 1953 had a very similar arrangement, except that an ignition switch was built into the centre of the lighting one, and for 1953 a warning light was added between the ammeter and switch. For 1954 the range gained a headlamp cowl with a single combined lighting-and-ignition switch, but no ammeter was fitted. For 1956 the C10L changed to two switches in the headlamp shell, while the C12 had its combined switch set in a side panel on the right of the machine and an ammeter in the headlamp shell.

The unit models began with the headlamp in a nacelle with ammeter to left and light switch to right, while the ignition switch went on the centre panel between the oil tank and battery compartment. This layout was used by the C15, B40, SS80 and SS90 in turn, with a detachable ignition key appearing for 1962.

The C15T had a small separate headlamp shell with on/off and dip-switches fitted in it, and this arrangement also served the B40E, B44VE and 1967 B44VS. For 1968 that model changed to a toggle switch for the lights, gained a red main-beam warning light in the shell, and also an ignition switch which went under the seat nose on the left. A further warning light in green appeared for 1969–70, but only one would seem to have been connected, this being the green for main beam.

The 1966 C15 Sportsman moved away from the nacelle of the road models to a long separate shell with ammeter to right and light switch to left, while the ignition switch stayed where it was on the centre panel. This arrangement was also used by some models destined for the USA but with the shell fittings as on the C15.

The C25 and B44VR adopted a similar layout, but with the ammeter and light switch in line along the shell, and the ignition switch under the seat nose on the left. The ammeter sat ahead and a red main-beam

warning light went on the left of the lighting switch.

For 1968 the lights were controlled by a toggle switch, and for 1970 the B25 only was fitted with a green warning light in addition to the red one. The green became the main-beam warning, while the red was for low oil pressure. On the B44SS, from 1969, the red was fitted alone and was the main-beam warning.

The layout changed for 1971 and the B25 had a headlamp shell with a simple turn switch in the centre for the lights. Around it went warning lights in red for low oil pressure, green for main beam and amber for indicators, while the ignition switch went in the left side of the electrical box under the front of the tank. The B50 was as for the B25 except that there was no red warning lamp.

The Bantam had a unique arrangement up to 1951 when fitted with Wipac equipment, as the switch was in the headlamp shell but controlled by a lever mounted on the left handlebar. This had four positions and was connected to the switch slider by cable.

The machines with Lucas parts were simpler in that they just had a light switch in the top of the headlamp shell. This arrangement was adopted for the Wipac models in 1952 and went in turn on the D1, D3 and D5 models up to 1958 whether they had direct or battery lighting. It was also used by the direct D7 models up to 1966 but the battery-lighting ones changed to a system with two switches for 1964.

From 1954 the Bantam models had a cowl added to the forks and round the headlamp shell, while all D7 models, except the Trail, had a nacelle from their start in 1959.

The D10 Bantam series continued with a nacelle for the Silver and Supreme models, which had two switches in the shell plus a main-beam warning lamp. The Sports and Bushman models had a separate, and rather long, headlamp shell with the same layout, while the Pastoral model had just a single central switch.

For 1968 the D14 series took over and continued as the D10 except that the D14 Bushman became as the D10B Pastoral. The next year brought the D175 which was equipped as the D10S with separate shell and two switches but no warning light, while the D175B was as the D14B with a single switch.

All bulbs should be as per the list.

Stop and tail lamp

The singles fitted the same small, round rear light as used by most English machines in 1946, with only the M range differing in detail. It fell into line with the B and C models in 1949, and all changed for 1953 to the rectangular Lucas 525 with stop and tail function.

This had a separate reflector fixed below the rear number plate, but for 1956 this went when the function was incorporated into the lamp lens, and this later tail light was used for many years. In the 1960s it

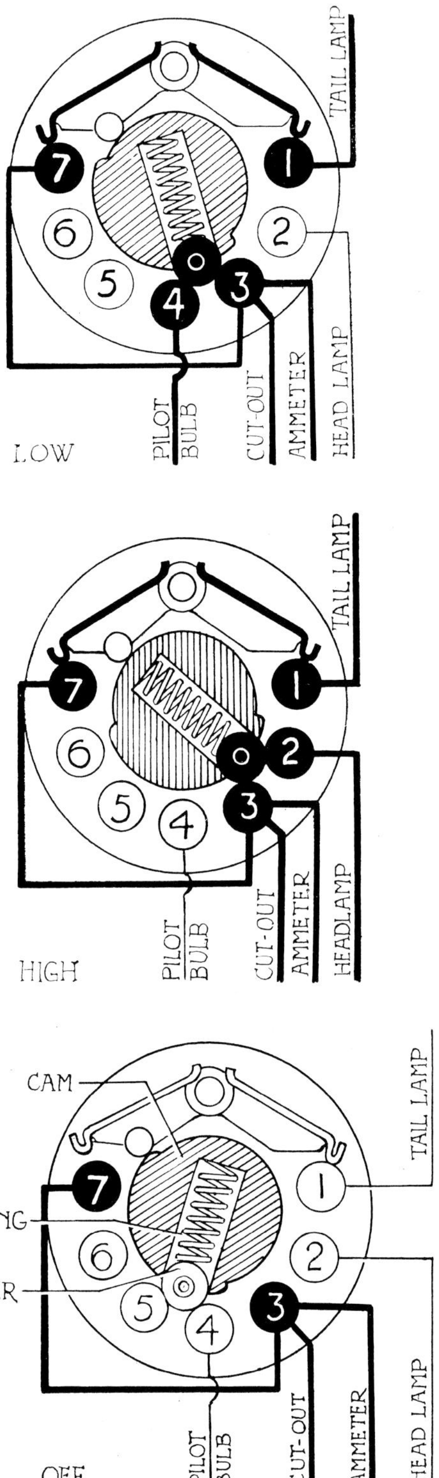

ABOVE *Connections and roller positions of the old-type Lucas headlamp switch. Post-war the tail lead was from terminal 5*

RIGHT *The 1965 B40 showing the ignition switch with key in the centre panel and points housing*

was joined by another form for the US market which then became the standard fitment.

Exceptions included the C10L which fitted Wipac parts, with one for 1954 and another from then onwards; also the Bantams which had both makes and various types. The D1 began with a small round lamp with the lens body held in place by a screw, but later changed to a bayonet fitting. Some Wipac lamps had a twin filament bulb, but a design with one tail and two stop bulbs in one assembly was more usual. This type then continued in use with styling changes.

Bulbs should be as listed in all cases. Where direct lighting is fitted, it may be worth protecting the bulbs from excess voltage with a clipper diode.

Turn signals

These were fitted to the B25 and B50 from 1971. They should be treated in the same way as similar lights, while the flasher unit may also need to be checked over.

Remember that the bulb wattage must be correct or the signals will either flash at the wrong rate or not at all.

Horn

Trouble with the horn may occur in the part itself or be a fault in the button or wiring. The problem should be bypassed by checking with direct wiring between horn and battery. If current is reaching the horn and nothing is happening, it may need adjustment. This may be by a screw in the back or a nut under a cover. However, some horns may have no adjustment facility at all.

Where provided, the adjuster should be moved not more than one or two notches at a time. On a scale of 24 notches equals one full turn of the screw. Six notches from just not sounding should be about right, but the current flow should also be monitored and anything over 5 amps indicates a need for specialist attention.

Don't move the centre screw as this controls the basic points setting and needs special equipment to set. Given this and care, the horn may be stripped and the case renovated in the same way as any other part.

Battery

The problem on some models is appearance, as while the battery lived outside enclosing panels, its looks were an important aspect of the left side of the machine. It is possible to obtain facsimiles of the early black-bodied 6-volt battery, which is one solution.

Another is to adapt an old battery by cutting out the interior and fitting a modern one inside it.

For the rest, keep it clean, check the specific gravity and smear protective jelly on the terminals to keep corrosion at bay. Keep the battery working, if off the machine, by running it down with a 3-watt bulb and then recharging it. This will prevent it from collapsing when asked to do some real work.

Up to 1966 all singles had a 6-volt system, but from 1967 all the four-strokes, other than the C15, changed to 12 volts. The last C15s and all Bantams stayed with 6 volts.

Ammeter

There is not much one can do to repair one of these, so either you have one working or it just acts as a dummy to keep the original appearance. In this case, one terminal can be used as a junction point, but if the insulation of the case is in any doubt it is best to keep the wiring away from it altogether.

Wiring and switches

The wiring is a prime source of electrical troubles with poor connections, poor earths and intermittent leaks to earth being the major problems. Switches can also cause many headaches if the contacts are not clean and making good connections. It must all be carefully checked over.

Switches must be checked using a meter for their correct operation. The older type can be taken apart for cleaning but watch for rollers with springs behind them that can fly out and roll all over the floor. Recheck the operation after assembly. Draw the connections on your wiring diagram so you can see how the components connect up in each switch position.

Any machine with direct lighting must have a dip-switch with make-before-break contacts. If it does not, there is a point when neither headlamp filament is in circuit, and for that brief time all the current goes to the tail light. This then blows unless protected by a clipper diode, but the correct dip-switch is a better answer.

BELOW LEFT *Rear end of the 1968 singles showing the lamp housing and side reflector along with the number-plate support*

BELOW *The wire clip and catch used to retain the battery lid on a 1966 D10 Supreme*

Stop-light switch for front brake cable on a 1969 B25. The cable adjuster is well out and the fairing support tubes can be seen

Earthing

All the older machines rely on the cycle parts to do this job, which is why they often have problems. Having carefully restored the protective paintwork of frame, forks, mudguards and panels, it is rather a shame to damage this finish to complete the earth return.

The answer is to run an earth wire from each item back to the battery or to a suitable junction point. The wires must be of a gauge able to carry the current from all items they are collecting for, and are best earthed both to the frame and the engine at one point.

Fuses

These were not fitted to early machines but are a good insurance for all. At the very least, a single 35-amp fuse in the main battery line can save the day in the event of a short circuit.

7 The finish

This is the process that produces the final appearance whether that is polished, plated or painted, and the result always depends on preparation. The final top coat is the easy stage—it is the work necessary to bring the surface to the required standard for that coat that takes time and effort.

The production finishes used by BSA were either to polish castings or leave them as cast, to plate certain major items and the details with either chromium or cadmium, and to paint the steel parts that made up the bulk of the cycle side along with certain cast-iron items using the stove-enamelling process.

Petrol tanks and wheel rims were both chrome-plated and painted on the earlier models, while the plastic and rubber items were as moulded. Transfers were added as a final touch at certain points.

Cleaning the parts

This can be done mechanically or chemically, depending on the surface smoothness desired and the shape and area in question. Some of the chemicals are not readily available in the small quantities needed by the amateur, and all must be treated with caution and only used when protective clothing is worn. Read the instructions carefully, including the warning notes and what to do if you splash yourself.

Detergents

A household washing powder straight from the kitchen is most useful for cleaning castings. They are best done in a heated saucepan, but before immersion all steel items must be removed. Don't leave the parts in for longer than is necessary as many of these products are acidic in nature and will attack the castings. When the cleaning is complete, wash all the detergent away with hot water and then dry the casting.

Mechanical

At its simplest, this involves scraping the finish, usually paint, away with a knife or some similar tool. This is slow, tiring and tedious but will get you down to the bare metal in time. It can also damage the surface if you are not careful to prevent the knife digging in.

More usually it means some form of blasting process, where small particles are blown at the item to be cleaned so they knock the finish off. The speed, severity, substrate damage and visual finish depend on the abrasive material used.

For removing rust, paint and corrosion, aluminous-oxide grit blasting is suitable for motorcycle parts. Iron grit or shot are not suitable and would badly damage castings and blow holes in sheet metal, so avoid them. A less common and more delicate process is vapour blasting, which carries the abrasive medium in water, but the most popular method for smaller items is bead blasting. This uses glass beads and so does not take material away. It is also used on castings that have been grit-blasted as that process tends to open the metal pores. The beads close them up again, flatten the surface out and give it a polish that can range from matt to gloss.

All parts should be thoroughly cleaned before blasting. Threads, cylinder bores, tight tolerance holes, headstock bearings, oilways and tapped holes will all need protecting to make sure nothing is trapped which could cause damage later.

Blanking off can be done using nuts, bolts, pieces of tube or several layers of masking tape. Items such as headstocks in frames can be sealed using a length of studding, two metal discs and rubber discs cut from an old inner tube. Don't forget a screw for the grease-nipple hole.

The alternative to blasting is to remove paint, rust and, inevitably, some metal using emery. The manual method involves cloth strips which can be useful on frame tubes, but for most items mechanization is essential. This takes the form of an electric drill and an emery flap wheel which is used to remove deep scratches from the metal and to blend the damaged area into the rest. For the best results, you should let the tool do the work without forcing it. Don't use a sanding disc as it will take off too much and most likely score the surface.

The extension of this type of work is to finer and finer grades of abrasive, so that you finish up with a polished surface. This was normally applied to the timing cover, gearbox end cover and outer primary chaincase, but may be extended by owners to many more castings.

Polishing can be done by hand, with mops or by a combination of the two. Industrial polishers use large mops driven at speed and can round off edges and draw out holes in a very short time. If you do have access to such equipment, though, practise first.

Small mops can be used in an electric drill and must be kept charged with mop soap. Again, proceed with care, especially where there are sharp edges you wish to keep. Before mopping the easy areas you should deal with the awkward crevices. It is very tempting to do the job the other way round but not advisable.

The manual way of polishing involves wet-and-dry emery cloth in paraffin. You need a medium-grade cloth and then two grades of fine, and it is a tedious, dirty job. The recesses can be done with an emery-stick, which may be driven by a drill. The major areas can be done using a Loyblox—this is a block of rubber impregnated with emery-grit which can be used wet or dry.

The final touch is a polish with Solvol Autosol or Belgom Alu, applied with a soft cloth.

Chemical

There are chemical cleaners available for light-alloy parts and, as with the detergent mentioned above, after use they must be washed away well. Most are acidic in nature, so care is necessary when using them and the instructions must be followed closely.

More usually, chemical cleaning means a paint stripper. This is another messy operation but one that is quick and effective. Wear protective clothing and avoid contact with the fluid by wearing gloves and eyeshields. It is a nasty substance.

Spread out plenty of newspaper, put out the parts for stripping, and paint the liquid on. After a while, the paint will start to bubble up and often comes away in sheets. A scraper may be needed to help it along, and all the old paint must come away.

The parts will need to be cleaned with water if the stripper is so based, or thinners and wire wool. You *must* make sure that all the old paint and stripper is removed or the new coat will lift within days of application.

At this point you may find that under the paint there were patches of filler from some long-distant repair. These will all have to come away so you can get down to bare metal and check on the exact damage.

The factory line in 1951, with visitors from the West African distributors seeing a D1 receiving its final touches. It was a popular model and many were sold in their homelands

ABOVE *The 1968 B44SS Shooting Star*

BELOW RIGHT *A rather special 499 cc Gold Star prepared for the 1949 ISDT and ridden by Fred Rist as a member of the Trophy-winning British team*

Rust

You now have the steel parts in an ideal state for them to rust. However they have been cleaned, they will begin to oxidize immediately, and any handling only makes matters worse due to the acids of the skin, so proceed to the next stage quickly.

Parts that are due to be painted should be given one coat of etch primer as soon as possible after the blasting or stripping process. This will keep the rust at bay while you draw breath. Parts for plating can just be greased.

Restoring the surface

If the part is to be plated, a metallic surface is essential and defects cannot be resin-filled as they can for painted items. Thus, it may be necessary to weld or braze, depending on the material, in order to obtain the required surface.

This technique will work for castings and the heavier steel parts, but sheet-steel components in general, and the petrol tank in particular, need sheet-metal skills. If you have these, you will have the hammers and dollies to do the work; if you don't, you had best farm out all but the simplest tasks.

During preparation it is well worth rounding off the sharp corners of items such as engine plates and frame lugs as this will reduce any tendency to chipping. This usually starts from a sharp edge, so their removal will improve the appearance in the long term.

Filling

Steel or iron parts which have been left for years are likely to have a pitted surface, and it is not practical to fill these with braze or clean the surface down to remove them. The former would take forever, and the latter would weaken the part far too much. One answer is a resin filler, which may come as a brushed-on liquid or a two-part resin-and-hardener kit.

An alternative is lead filling as used for cars. The area to be treated has to be tinned first, which is done using a flux with powdered lead in it. This is brushed on and warmed with a blowlamp.

Then continue with the lead, which comes as an alloy of lead and tin in sticks. The blowlamp will allow the lead to be kept movable without running about, and a hardwood spatula will let you push it about. Wear a mask, try not to put too much on (remember you can always add more if needed), and finally dress down with a file and flattening paper.

The surface then has to be rubbed down, which is done using 320-grade wet-and-dry emery, used wet. It is a tedious job as the aim is a smooth, even surface that blends in with the rest of the part without bumps or hollows. This is not easy to get completely right first time, but hollows can always be given another coat of filler, so you have another chance.

Pinholes in the surface are dealt with using stopper in a similar way.

Once you are quite certain that the entire surface of the part is perfect, you can move on—but don't delude yourself. Any mark or imperfection will shine through, no matter how many coats of paint you put on.

Painting

The traditional method of applying paint is by a number of brushed-on coats, the surface being rubbed down between each. This was far too slow for mass-produced machines, so the job was speeded up using spray or dip techniques and stove-enamelling paint. This gave a hard finish with a deep gloss that stood up to knocks well.

In contrast, a brush finish either took a great deal of time to apply or looked poor and was easily damaged. Fortunately this is not the case any longer, although time and care are needed if a really good finish is wanted. It is now easy to obtain good coverage, a deep gloss and a hard surface that won't chip easily, and even if it is damaged it can be touched in without too much trouble.

Most restorers, therefore, use a synthetic enamel, and the most common make is Tekaloid which is favoured by many professional men. Others simply shop at a high-street store and produce very good results using either the enamel as it comes or as a two-part product.

A short drying time is characteristic of cellulose, which is normally used for spraying. It has to be mixed with thinners, is volatile and flammable, and must be handled with care as it can be medically dangerous.

A short drying time is desirable as it helps to combat the home restorer's greatest enemies when painting, which are dust and midges. For this reason, some do use a cellulose, but in the end the finish depends far more on the preparation, clean atmosphere and operator care than the paint type.

To achieve this there are certain guidelines to follow. Paint after rain has washed dust from the atmosphere. Choose a warm, still day and damp down the working area. Wear clothes that do not harbour dust, so avoid wool. Work in an area free from draughts and don't open the door once you have begun. However, don't forget you do need air to breathe! Don't breathe on the work, and hang it from wire, not string, with the least important face pointing upwards. Use a tack rag on the surface immediately before you start, and leave the working area as soon as the painting is finished.

The paint is applied by a brush and the name Hamilton is the one that comes up most often. A 1 in. wide brush will cover most items, but a $\frac{1}{2}$ in. version may be needed for details and a 2 in. one for mudguards or large panels. Run the brushes in on something unimportant, and wash out dirt with clean paraffin in several stages until it is really clean. Tap the handle against a piece of wood to shake the surplus out, do not finger the bristles or wipe them with a rag. After use, clean the brush in paraffin, wash in warm soapy water, then clear water, and leave to dry.

Lightweights in the Isle of Man in 1950, as used by The Motor Cycle's *Arthur Bourne, Bill Banks and Roy Morton. All are 125 cc machines*

To do the actual painting, pour some paint into a clean cup and load the brush from that. Do not put the brush in the paint tin. Apply with long flowing strokes with the brush running down the part under its own weight to avoid brush marks. A light touch will give a lovely finish.

Two or three coats are usual, and between each the surface has to be rubbed down using 500-grade wet-and-dry, used wet. This gives a smooth surface and allows you to see where the next coat has to go—not

always easy on a dark, glossy surface.

There are two areas where the above will not work so well. One is where there is heat, so brake drums and cylinder barrels are better stove-enamelled, which means masking off and filling using materials that will cope with the baking temperature. The other is the petrol tank where the problem is resistance to petrol and staining. It is fine if you never spill anything when refuelling, and the cap seal does its job, but otherwise consider going to an expert.

Some restorers give the tank a coat of polyurethane lacquer, but this is not advisable as it will react with any spilt petrol and act as a paint stripper.

Paint colour

Black is black for most of us, but colours seem to come in so many shades and suffer from fading, which leads to matching problems.

Also remember that all paints are not the same, and while you can spray synthetic on to cellulose, it won't

MOK 751

ABOVE *Phillip Palmer, winner of the 1954 Junior Clubmans, with his CB Gold Star during a post-race press test*

ABOVE LEFT *The engine unit of a 1967 C25 Barracuda with the square-finned head and barrel*

LEFT *A B34GS prepared for the 1952 ISDT with extra cables and a good deal of fine detail work to speed repairs up*

work the other way round. Using a sealer or isolator may work, but don't expect too much. It is better to get back to the basic surface.

Keep to one type of paint for all stages and colours, including any lining you do.

Paint colours are given in an appendix which is more detailed than that of *BSA Gold Star & Other Singles* and so should take precedence over that volume with regard to the information given. Matching is another matter, and an area of original paint that has been shielded from the light will act as the best guide. The inside of the toolbox or the underside of a clip are possible places, but if your machine has been fully repainted at some time, this matching is lost.

It may be possible to judge what you are after from a brochure or a contemporary magazine advertisement, but otherwise you will have to find a machine to study. Museums, shows and meetings are all possible sources, or you may be able, if lucky, to find a part in its wrapper in the right colour, which will be worth buying whether you need it or not, just for the match.

Once you know what colour you need, you have to get the paint shop to mix it for you. Start from the British Standard Colour Chart as this should get you near, but expect to have to experiment a little. Persevere on odd parts until you are satisfied you have it correct or to the shade you want it to be.

Spraying

This takes more cash to get the equipment, and tends to be expensive in paint as much goes past the work on to the walls. The technique has been much described but, as with the brush, practice, preparation and no dust are the keys to success.

TOP *The 1970 D175B Bushman Bantam*

ABOVE LEFT *A well-modified Gold Star with sidecar, prepared to a really high standard*

ABOVE *Not a Gold Star, but a 1953 B34 with all-alloy engine in a rigid frame*

Investigate paint types as some give off a lethal vapour and are not for the amateur at all. Learn how to operate the spray gun, the effects of your techniques and changes to them. Practise first.

Observe all safety precautions, these being more stringent for spraying due to the fire risk and the fumes. Keep a fire extinguisher of the correct type to hand. Make sure ventilation is good, don't have naked flames, gas heaters or open radiant fires, and check on your electrics in case anything can spark. Wear a mask when working.

Coatings

Alternatives to painting are plastic coating or powder coating. These will not give the gloss required by the perfectionist, but the coats are tough.

Again, preparation is important and will reflect in the final appearance. Dip coating can be done at home on items such as stands, the main requirements being a means to heat the part up to around 300 degrees Celsius and a container for the powder into which the part is dipped.

Plating

Plating, like painting, depends on preparation for a good result. This means cleaning the surface and polishing it without damaging it. Once again the files, emery and elbow grease are needed, but with some of the smaller parts the biggest problem is holding them.

After preparation, the trick is to find a good plater who is interested in your motorcycle work, and for this recommendations should be sought. Whether or not you are aiming for a concours job, expect to pay for good workmanship as this is always less expensive in the long run than a cheap job.

The major plated parts are finished with chromium but other plating processes are needed as well. Nuts and bolts that are not chromed are normally either cadmium- or zinc-plated. Bright nickel may be found on the spoke nipples.

Lining and transfers

Signwriters do this freehand, and one solution used by many restorers is to farm out the job. Alternatives are plastic tapes which are simply laid on and either left at that or varnished. Masking with pvc tape will give the outline required or, for straighter lines, car lining tape may be used. This has a centre strip which is removed to leave two outers parallel to each other.

Don't forget that the lining paint must be the same type as that it is being applied to, or you will have trouble. Remove the tape before the paint is fully dry so it can flow smooth. Gold lining will then need a clear coat to protect it and yacht varnish is often favoured.

Transfers are the final touch to a machine and should be applied with care, according to their directions. Make sure they go in the correct place, and protect with a thin coat of clear varnish when dry.

Fibreglass

This material was used for some petrol tanks and side covers, and it poses its own set of problems for finishing. In addition, the use of the material for petrol

The D7 Bantam in its first year, 1959, and with a good number of changes from the previous D5

Fitting out a 1951 D1 for the Post Office. Years later the Bantam Racing Club was to buy such machines for members to base racers on

tanks was always suspect and was banned in the UK during 1973. From that date tanks were legally required to be made in metal, but some authorities think this always applied and was retrospective. Modern EEC regulations allow the use of non-metal tanks, but at the time of writing this does not apply to the UK.

This leaves certain BSA owners in a quandary if they want to use their machines on the road. There does not appear to be any easy answer if the original appearance is to be kept. Possible solutions are to remake the tank in metal, or to bond a metal tank into the original shell, but either is expensive. A change to another BSA tank in metal loses originality but is likely to be the easiest solution. However, check clearance underneath to make sure all will be well.

The repair and finishing of fibreglass are different to parts made in metal—so different, in fact, that they are really not the same jobs at all. Metal is hard and unaffected by paint stripper or paint solvents. Fibreglass is a mixture of glass and resin, and the latter can be attacked all too easily. Being soft, it is easy to mark and scores can be produced readily.

When the material was first introduced we were told that repairs would be easy, which is true if you simply want to join up a crack or fill a hole. If you also want a good smooth surface for your final paint, the job takes much longer as tissue layers have to be used to build up the surface before it is shaped, smoothed and rubbed down.

Painting also takes much longer as each coat must be left for a week, sometimes two, to make sure any interaction is complete. If this is not done, the result will be nice for a month but then all the repairs will show through.

Practise your technique on a scrap part and allow as much time as you can between steps to make sure all the chemicals have done their job and stopped reacting. This is golden rule one when dealing with any fibreglass part. Making sure you use the correct materials has to be rule two, and reading the instructions *first* is number three.

8 Frame and stands

With these items you have something solid to work on, so most minor repairs are easy to do. Bent brackets can be heated and returned to their correct position, and cracks around them welded. Holes may need welding and redrilling if elongated, or tapping out if their threads are damaged at all.

The real work on the frame is to check its alignment, which can be done with string and straight edges, but does take a good eye to spot areas where there is a problem. Crash damage is easy to see, but not the twist of five years of sidecar work.

Rigid and plunger frames

The first post-war frames were rigid and comprised two or three sections which bolted together using the engine and its mounting plates to make a structure. The B, M and C ranges all had front frames which comprised the top, down and seat tubes brazed into their lugs, but the rear parts differed more. The B type did not extend the lower tubes along the crankcase but the M did, so it had the right tube kinked to clear the oil-pump bulge in the engine. For the C range there was a chainstay and separate backstay assembly.

The B range had one front and rear frame section, but the M had two of each as one was for solo use and the other incorporated the sidecar lugs. From 1948, only the sidecar frame was listed which thus went on to the M33, although this first type was only there for the one year.

There were considerable changes for 1949, due in part to the appearance of the plunger rear suspension. The new B-range frame front differed from the earlier part in that the frame lug in front of the crankcase was shorter and only spanned the top two bolts. It was only amended for 1955 when a steering-lock lug was added to the headstock.

This new front took a choice of rear assemblies, and that for the rigid B models was little changed from the earlier part. New were the plunger rear end for the B models and a similar part for the Gold Star. This latter differed in having additional lugs on the chainstays for rearset footrests and brake pedal. These parts all continued as they were to the end of their runs: the rigid B in 1954, the plunger in 1955 and the Gold Star in 1952. The exceptions were the B32 and B34 for 1954–55 which had a new rigid frame with twin downtubes and one-piece construction.

The M models also changed for 1949 with a new frame front whose downtube stopped at the first crankcase bolt it came to. The front continued to be fitted to the 1946-type rear with sidecar lugs until that end was revised for 1951. At this point, both rigid and plunger assemblies were listed with the first much as before and the second with the plunger lugs. Neither was to change but a third was listed for the M21 supplied to the AA. At the front the frame changed for 1955 when the steering-lock lug was added, and an alternative was listed for the AA.

The C models had their first change to the frame front in 1946 when the forks were altered from girders to telescopics, but otherwise this part stayed as it was up to 1953. The chain- and backstays began with one for each model, but from 1947 the C11 parts also went on the C10. Where a four-speed gearbox was fitted, the frame front was different, as was the rear half when equipped for plungers; both these variations appeared for 1951.

There was a complete change for 1954 with a simple one-piece frame with plunger rear suspension for the C10L. This was revised for 1956 when the new four-speed gearbox was introduced and a steering lock became an option.

The C11G had more complication with a rigid frame front for 1954 with chain- and backstays. This was used with the three-speed gearbox and for 1955 was revised to have a steering-lock lug and to suit the plunger rear half. In addition, there were frame fronts to suit the four-speed gearbox for both years, with and without the lock lug but both to go with the rear suspension. Just one rear assembly served all versions and both years.

The Bantam began with a simple, rigid welded frame which served all direct-lighting models and was thus used up to 1955. In 1950 it was joined by three more and, of these, the rigid one differed only in having a lug on the underside of the top tube for the ignition coil. It went on models fitted with the Lucas generator and served up to 1953.

ABOVE *The 1955 Daytona Gold Star, still with the rigid frame to suit the unusual circuit that the event was run on*

BELOW *A mixture which is from the 1949–52 period and is either a B31/B33 with competition mudguards or a B32/B34 with a road exhaust system*

ABOVE *The 1953 BB Gold Star with the small-finned engine in the pivoted-fork frame*

BELOW *The first Bantam in a pivoted-fork frame was this 1956 D3*

The two plunger frames brought in for 1950 duplicated this arrangement, but after 1953 it was the one with the lug that remained in use up to late 1963. Thus, only early plunger frames with direct lighting lacked this feature. All frames had a new headstock gusset plate and the rear stay tubes changed from 16 swg to the thicker 14 swg for 1952.

Pivoted-fork frames

This type should be checked as for the rigid one, plus inspection of the rear fork and its pivot. These can be a real problem where the pivot pin is a press-fit in a frame lug which the fork ends straddle. If neglected, the bushes and spindle wear badly or, worse, seize so the spindle turns in the frame.

The pivot is a drive-fit and should drift out, but often a hydraulic press will be needed to do the job. If the frame hole is worn this will need attention, and none of this is easy.

The Gold Star led the way to the pivoted-fork frame in 1953 and this was revised for 1954 when the big-fin engines first appeared. A very similar frame went on the road B models for 1954 and gained the steering-lock lug in 1955. A frame on the same lines, but without the silencer and pillion-rest loops, went on the B32 and B34 for 1956–57.

The C12 had a built-up frame with a front section of three tubes and a rear of two loops joined by a cross-pressing. These sections bolted together and, with the engine and its mounting plates, made a rigid structure. The parts were common to all years.

The unit models began with built-up frames and the C15 had the subframe bolted on at the seat nose and rear fork pivot. The front section was modified a little for 1965 but not the rear. The competition models each had their own frame front halves with a common rear, which differed from the standard one in having an extra lug on each angled side tube and mudguard brackets pointing out from the rear loop rather than in. The front half of the scrambles frame was much as the standard one, but minus lugs on the top, to the rear of the headstock. The trials model differed more in having a separate front tank mounting, fewer seat-tube brackets and other detail changes.

For 1963 the competition models both changed to a common one-piece frame. While this continued with the single downtube, it had duplex seat tubes to accommodate the central oil tank.

The B40 had a frame very similar to the C15 but with the front tank supports in line with the top tube rather than below it. It had its own rear half and the front section was amended for 1965. The sports SS80 and SS90 used the C15 and B40 frames, so the C15 Sportsman simply continued this practice.

The Victor Grand Prix had its own special frame, but the B40E used the 1963 C15 competition one with the duplex seat tubes which also went on the B44VE for 1966–67 and the B44VS for 1967 only. For 1968 the B44VS had some extra lugs and brackets added to its frame, and for 1969–70 fairing mounting tubes were welded to the front of the headstock.

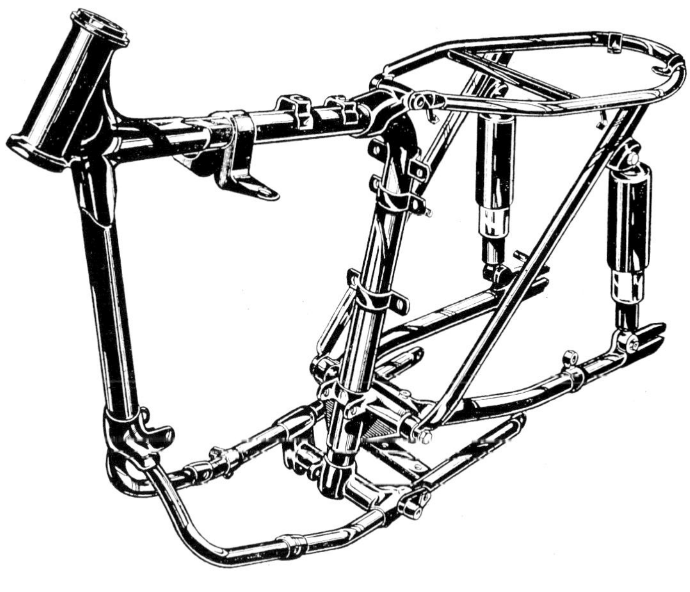

The C15 frame as introduced in 1958

The road models went over to a one-piece assembly for the frame in 1967. One frame served the C25, B25, B44VR and B44SS for the 1967–68 period, and was modified to add the fairing lugs for 1969–70. For the USA version of the B25 in 1970, the same frame was listed but without a centre stand.

The year 1971 brought the oil-in-frame design with one for the B25, one for the B50MX and a third for the other B50 models. The motocross model lost its tank support brackets in its 1973 form.

The Bantam first had a pivoted-fork frame for the D3 in 1956, which comprised a front loop and bolted-on subframe. Both changed for the D5 in 1958 with a cross-tube between the subframe members, in place of a pressing, and detail alterations for the front part.

The design of the fork pivot changed to a pressed-in pivot pin on the D7 for 1959, so there were new parts for front and rear. The subframe became a seat loop with two support tubes, and the front altered to suit the fork pivot and the footrests. The version supplied to the GPO had a different front frame.

The basic three-speed D10 of 1967 continued with the D7 frame, and the front part was also used by the D10S, but the D10B had its own front with altered lugs on the seat tube. At the rear the D10S had its own subframe, as did the D10B which had extra lugs on the rear of the support tubes.

The year 1968 brought the D14 series with the D7 frame still in use for the D14/4, but with a new front

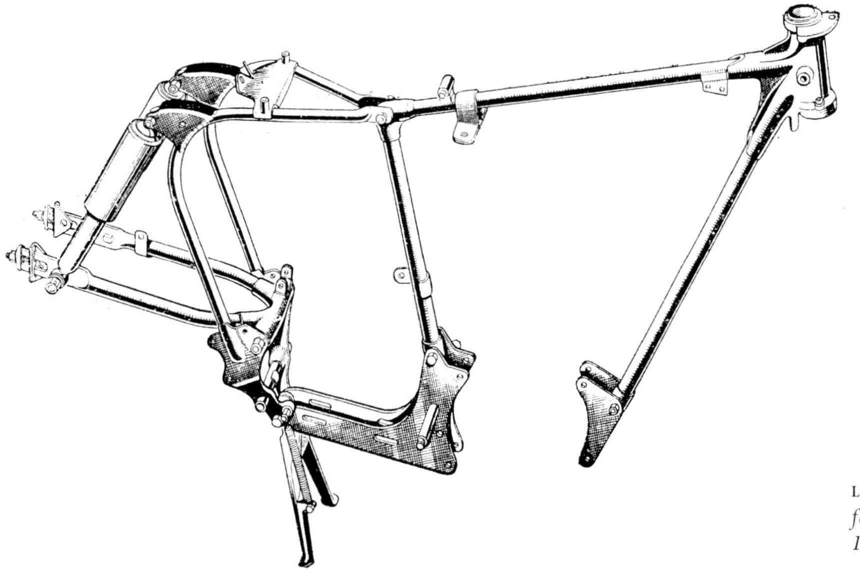

LEFT *The pivoted-fork frame used for the C12 when it appeared for 1956 to replace the plunger C11G*

BELOW *A 1964 D7 Super de luxe*

each for the D14/4S and D14/4B. Both these fitted the subframes from their D10 versions. For 1969 some of the frame threads were Unified and there were new fronts for both the D175 and D175B models. The subframe for the first remained that used by the earlier models since the advent of the D7 in 1959, and the Bushman kept the one first used by the D10B in 1967.

Rear fork

Expect to replace the bushes when checking this part. Both bronze and Silentbloc bushes were used, up to 1970, and the first will need reaming to fit. From 1971 there were needle races and if these are worn expect to replace the spindle as well.

The first rear fork went on the Gold Star in 1953 and then on to the B range for 1954. On the Gold Star it changed in detail for 1958 and this part was used by the competition B models for 1956–57. The road B models had a change for 1956 to suit the option of a full rear chaincase and new hubs, with another for 1958

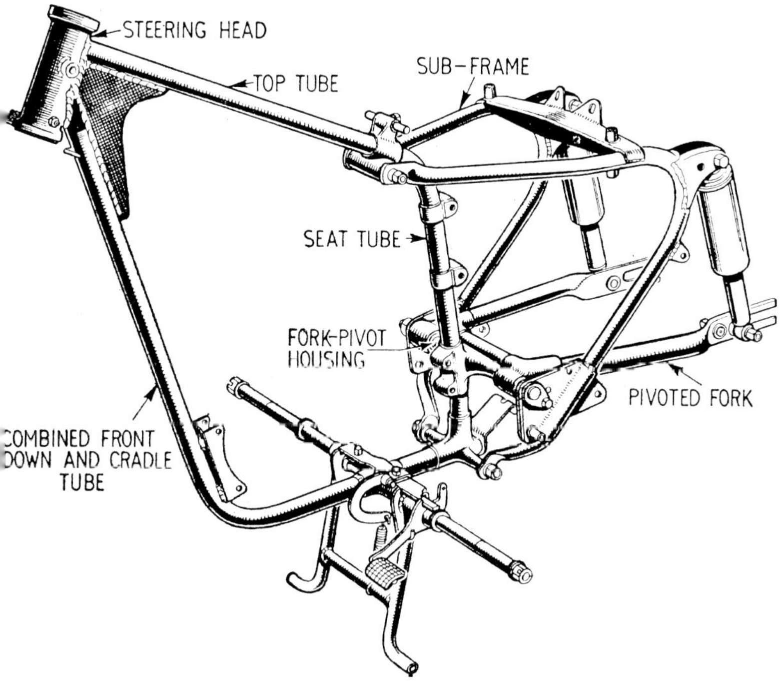

LEFT *The D3 pivoted-fork frame which differed from both the D5 and later D7 types, but retained the early D1 centre stand*

BELOW *The 1971 B25T Victor 250 with small front brake and sprung front mudguard*

when the hubs were again changed. All had Silentbloc bushes.

The C12 had just one part for all years and it moved on Silentbloc bushes.

The unit models differed and had bronze bushes at first on the various C15 models and the B40. The fork used on the C15S and C15T also went on the B40, but not the basic C15. The competition models alone changed to a similar fork with Silentbloc bushes for 1963, and this fork went on to the B40E, B44VE, B44VS, C25, B25, B44VR and B44SS for the 1965–68 period. It was modified for 1969–70 by the addition of a small bracket on the front end of the left leg and this part went on all models.

The B44GP had its own rear fork which pivoted on Silentbloc bushes. From 1971 all models had the same fork with needle bearings and cross-tubes at the ends of the legs for the wheel spindle, as chain adjustment was done at the pivot point.

The Bantams began with Silentbloc bushes in 1956 and changed to bronze bushes for the D7 in 1959. At the same time, the rear unit attachment studs moved to a position above the wheel centre and the rear brake anchor became a clip on the left leg. This design was amended in detail for the GPO D7, the D10 and D14 of 1967–68, and further altered with a Unified thread on the unit studs for 1969.

Head races

Expect to renew these.

The B range began with a set of cups and cones, with a total of 48 balls of $\frac{3}{16}$ in. diameter split between the top and bottom. Both cups were the same but the cones differed. This first type was used for 1946–48 but for 1949 it was changed to that used by the M range from 1946. This again had one cup type and two cones, but turned on 40 balls of $\frac{1}{4}$ in. diameter. The cone difference lay in the bore size, this being larger in the bottom cone to aid assembly. This type continued on all B, M and Gold Star models from then onwards.

The C range used the M-range cups and cones with the 40 $\frac{1}{4}$ in. balls on the machines fitted with girder forks. When these were changed for telescopics in 1946, the head races became those of the B range of that year and thus had 48 $\frac{3}{16}$ in. balls. This arrangement continued to 1958.

The unit models began with the same size and number of balls but with their own cups and cones. One type of the first and two of the second served the C15, B40, their sports versions and the competition ones up to 1962. These last changed for 1963 to the M-range cup and a new pair of cones with 40 $\frac{1}{4}$ in. balls. This set-up went in turn into the B40E, the C25, B25 and all B44 models up to 1970. For 1971 a pair of taper-roller bearings was used for all models.

The Bantam had the same cups for all models, and these were as used by the B range in 1946 and all the C range. Thus all Bantams have 48 $\frac{3}{16}$ in. balls in their head races. The cones differed a little but began as two of the B-range top cones, and this continued on all road D1 models to the end in 1963. The D3 and competition machines from 1954 had heavier forks and these had the bottom cone changed to the lower 1946 B-range type. This duly went on to the D5 in 1958, but for the D7 the next year there was a change to the lower cone of the C15, although the top one remained as it had been from 1949. It stayed in place right through to 1971, but the lower one altered once more for 1969.

Centre stand

This may need attention to its pivots and feet as both can wear badly.

The B range began with a stand with a single central pivot which was modified a little for 1950. The competition models had their own stand which changed for 1950, but from 1951 used the standard B road-model item. This stayed in use on the plunger and rigid frames except that the competition models went to another type from 1954 onwards.

This last went on the Gold Star that year after it had fitted another stand for the preceding one. It was also fitted to the road B range in the pivoted-fork frame for 1954–57 but was then altered to a type with roll-on feet.

The M models in the plunger frame had just one stand for all years, but the M21 for the AA had a different part. One stand spring served the M range and all the B range in rigid or plunger frames, and a second served those in pivoted-fork frames.

The C range fitted the road B stand for 1946–49 and had the same change as the B stand, and so continued to share it on the rigid frames for 1950–54. On the plunger models the C10 fitted the stand from the 1950 B32 and B34, while the C11 used the one from the plunger M models. This last went on to the C11G as well, but both the C10L and C12 had new items, although the first came from a Bantam. The C10L had its own stand spring but all the others used the one from the early B range.

The unit models had their own series of stands with one for the C15, one for the C15T and two for the B40, with the change occurring for 1965. The C15 Pastoral had yet another type and this went on to the C25 and B44 road models for 1967–68. It was amended for 1969 and revised for 1971 to suit the new frame design.

Several springs were used with these stands, with one for the C15 and C15T, and a second which first appeared on the C15 Pastoral and then went on the road models from 1967 onwards. Further springs came in 1971, one for the B25 and another for the B50.

The Bantam stand was clipped into place for its first year but from 1950 was held up by a spring. The first stand served all the road rigid- and plunger-frame models, but there was another for the competition ones and it was this that was fitted to the C10L. A new

Checking the operation of the prop stand on a 1970 B44SS. The footrest and brake pedal suggest that it went down the road during this road test

stand appeared for the D7 in 1959 and also went on the road D10 models and the D14/4 of 1968. Another version was used for the 1968 D14/4S and the 1969-onwards models. One stand spring served for 1950–58 and another from 1959 onwards.

Prop-stand

These were an option until well into the 1960s, but were a good investment as few BSA centre stands allowed the machine to roll on to them with ease.

The first prop-stand went on to all the M range and the B and C ranges up to 1955. Another served the B range and Gold Star models with the pivoted-fork frame, another the B32 and B34 rigid-frame models of 1954–55, and one more the C12, the C10L not having the option offered. One spring served all the stands.

The unit models all had similar legs and one served the C15 and B40 models plus their sports versions. There was another for the competition models, fitted as standard, and this one also went on the B40E and the 1966–67 models of 247 and 441 cc. These last had a new part for 1968–69, this also going on to the B44VR for 1967, and there was another part for 1970. The new frames of 1971 brought two more, with one each for the B25 and B50. These frames also had a new spring while all the others kept to just one item.

A prop-stand was not listed for the Bantams until 1954 and then that item continued for all the rigid and plunger models to their end. It went on the D3 and D5 as well, but no stand was listed for the D7 at first. When this did occur, for 1962, there were two available, one for each side, and both remained available right through to 1971. There was also a special stand for the D7 Trail model and another for the D10 Bushman and Pastoral machines of 1967.

The stand spring used for 1954–67 was that used by the B, C and M models, but another was used from 1968 onwards.

Rear stand

Only one rear stand was made, and it and its spring were used on the rigid-frame M range only, and thus for 1946–55.

9 Suspension

Front suspension was initially by girder forks for the C range in 1946 and the M range up to 1948, but from then onwards and for all other models it was by telescopic forks. These were fitted with a styling cowl in 1953 for the B and M ranges, but not until 1954 for the C and D. From 1958 the B range changed to a nacelle and this design went on the Bantam and C15 for 1959 but was phased out in the mid-1960s. This brought a return to the separate headlamp of the past.

At the rear, plunger suspension first appeared for 1949 on the B range and went on Bantams for 1950 and both C and M ranges for 1951. Prior to that time the machines had rigid frames, but these had all been dropped by the end of 1955. The plungers continued on the D1 and M21 into the 1960s, but from 1954 the other models all turned to pivoted-fork rear suspension, controlled by two hydraulically-damped spring units.

Girder forks

These are easy enough to dismantle and assemble but more tricky to repair and adjust. The main girder needs to be checked for alignment and damage just like the frame itself, and repairs are carried out in the same way. The side links also need checking for straightness and the condition of the holes and threads.

Expect to have to renew the spindles and their bushes, which may call for machining facilities. Adjustment begins by assembling the parts loosely, minus the steering and fork dampers. The four spindles and the head race then need to be brought into their correct positions in stages, where the parts are just free to move. All spindle nuts must be tight when checking and care will be rewarded by better steering.

The main fork fitted to the M range in 1946 was modified for 1948 with the removal of one or two redundant lugs, but otherwise there were no changes.

Telescopic-fork types

Most of these are similar and the manual will detail their work procedure. Roll the legs on a flat surface to check for bends and fill minor pits with epoxy resin which is rubbed down when hard. Expect to renew fork bushes and seals and check the springs in case they are tired and have settled down. If this has happened, try to find new springs of the correct rate as packing is not the best answer.

Assemble according to the book, making sure the head races are correctly adjusted and that the fork legs are parallel, so they can move freely without binding. Fill with the correct grade of oil and try to get the same amount in each leg.

BSA kept to one basic fork type for many years for the larger singles, but this had a good many detail changes to suit external fittings, such as the headlamp or the mudguard stays.

The B-range fork went on all models and first changed for 1948 with the shrouds revised to suit a larger headlamp shell, a new fork spring and chrome-plated fork seal holders, the latter being a useful identification feature. The shrouds were altered again for 1949 along with the lower legs and the main tubes.

The legs changed from a single stay fixing at the rear of the leg spindle lug to one front and rear, plus a lug with two holes for the mudguard bridge which had previously fitted to two studs on the leg. The main tubes were changed, but the new items were soon further revised for the Gold Star only, from frame YB31-3451, along with new bushes. The new B-range fork went on to the M range and a sidecar spring was listed for them.

For 1950 there was a new fork assembly for the Gold Star only, with a new right lower leg to take the 8 in. front brake fitted that year to the Clubmans, road-racing and touring models. In addition, there was a change to the M sidecar spring, and new shrouds without headlamp supports for the competition B models.

ABOVE RIGHT *Preparing a Gold Star for the 1951 Junior Clubmans at Small Heath*

RIGHT *A 1958 DBD Gold Star scrambler at Small Heath before going out to Uganda with owner Mike Younghusband, plus spares to allow it to run on grass and in hillclimbs and road races*

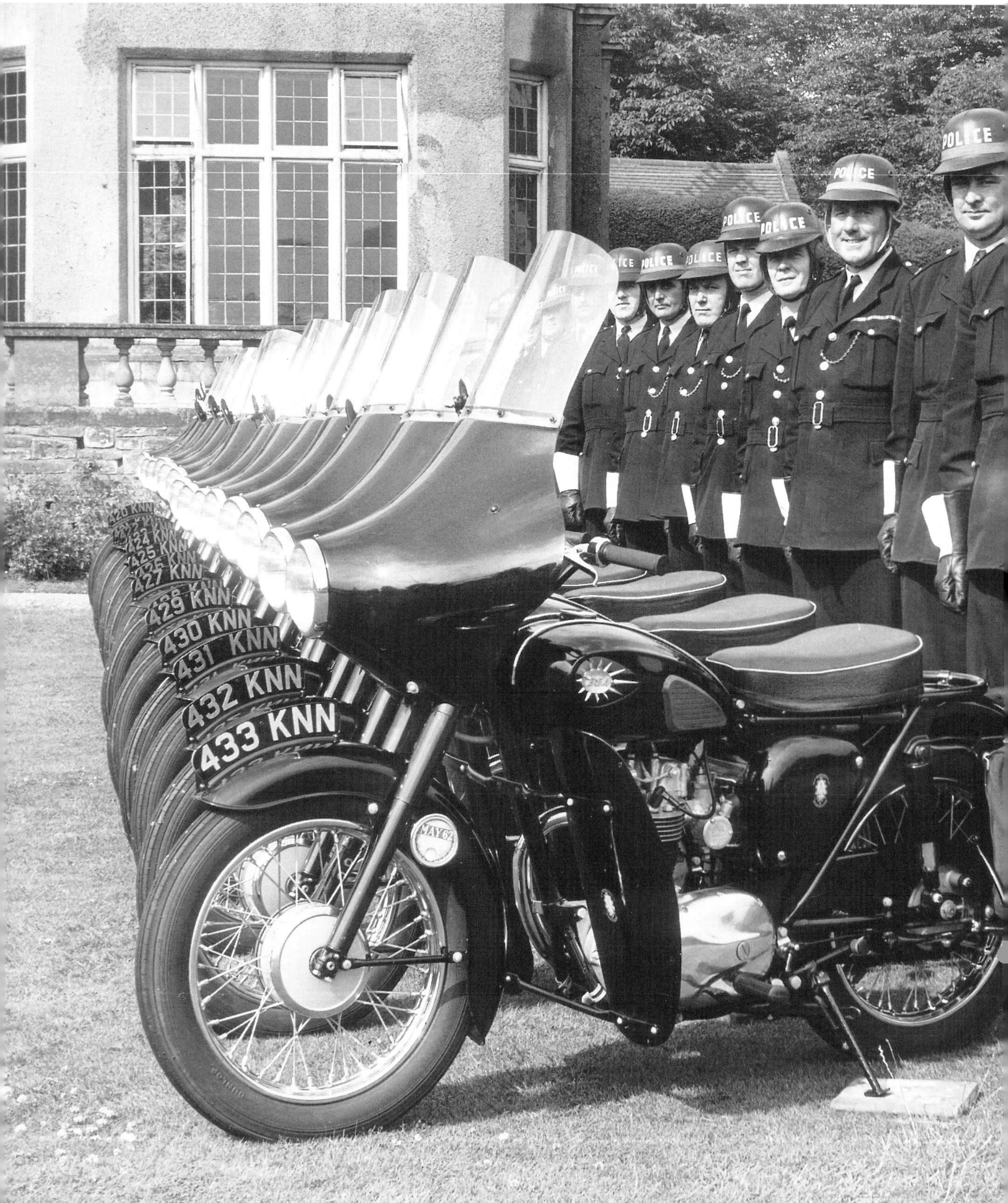
POLICE
POLICE
POLICE
POLICE
POLICE
427 KNN
429 KNN
430 KNN
431 KNN
432 KNN
433 KNN

The next change came in 1953 with the cowl for the headlamp. As this supported the shell, the competition shrouds went on to all the models except the Gold Star, which kept to the earlier design for all years. There was also a new right lower leg for the B33, as that year it went to the 8 in. front brake.

For 1954 the Gold Star became available with clip-ons and thus fork shrouds which fitted beneath the lower yoke. To go with them was a special main tube, which also went on the competition B models of 1956–57. The top nut that held the tube into the top crown was altered for the AA M21 about this time to add a filler plug, but the rest continued with the original part.

The M21 and M33 were fitted with the 8 in. brake and fork leg to suit for 1956. At the same time, the B-range legs were altered to suit the full-width hubs used for that year and the next. The legs of the B range changed again for 1958 when they were both fitted with detachable end caps. These replaced the left-hand thread in the right leg and split clamp in the left which had been a BSA feature from 1946; the new design accommodated a new hub. At the same time, a nacelle was introduced to carry the headlamp and switches. The M range kept to the old fork type and lost its headlamp cowl after 1957, and so reverted to the earlier layout but with the 8 in. brake.

The Gold Star kept to the original design with a new arrangement of headlamp support bracket. The Clubmans models continued with the clip-ons and short shrouds, and the scrambler with the 7 in. brake, right fork leg to suit, no lights, and shrouds without headlamp supports.

The C range began with girders but soon moved to telescopic forks of a similar but lighter nature, with one or two detail parts from the B type. The shrouds changed for 1948 when the oil-seal holder became chrome-plated (as it was one of the B details), and for 1949 there were new fork legs. These were amended only in having two mudguard-stay lugs in place of one.

The next change came for 1954 when the C10L adopted Bantam forks and the C11G stayed with the existing type. The latter did have new shrouds to suit the arrival of a headlamp cowl, and the C10L had its own yokes and upper legs. For 1955 the C11G changed its lower fork legs, but otherwise this fork remained as it was and went on to the C12. For 1956 the C10L changed to the same type of fork with many common parts.

The unit models began with three versions of the same design of fork with some parts from the earliest B model. The road models had a nacelle as on the B

Notts police line up in 1961 with a run of C15 machines fitted with special seats and other police equipment

OPC 70D
BSA

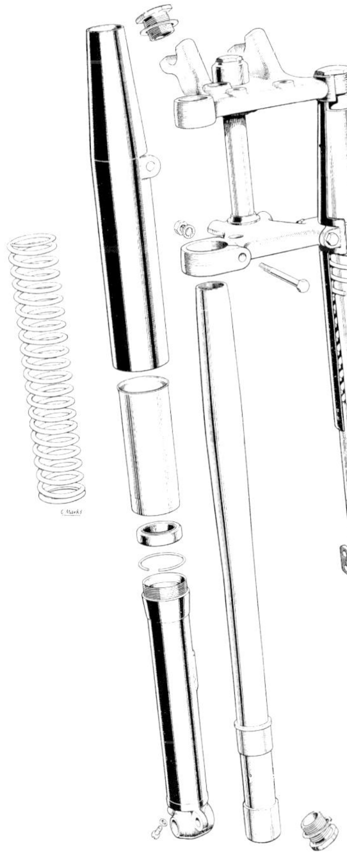

ABOVE *The 1965 SS80 sports single in its final year*

LEFT *A 1966 B44VE Victor Enduro with some alterations but showing its slim lines*

RIGHT *The BSA front fork as used on most of the range up to 1963*

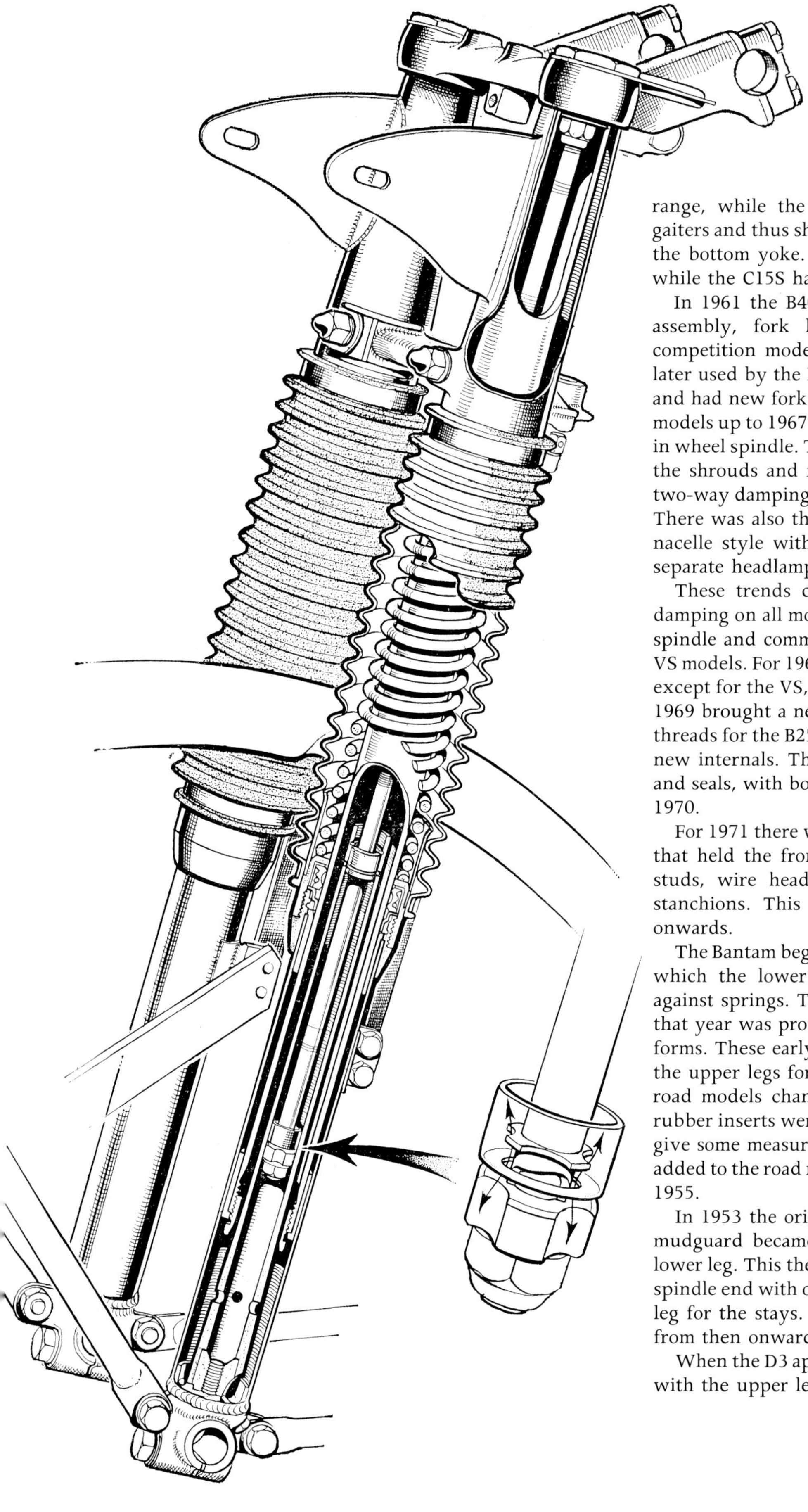

The 1966 BSA fork with two-way shuttle damping

range, while the competition ones both had fork gaiters and thus shrouds which terminated just below the bottom yoke. The C15T had headlight brackets, while the C15S had plain shrouds.

In 1961 the B40 arrived and had its own shroud assembly, fork legs and springs. For 1962 the competition models had new fork legs which were later used by the B40E. The B44GP appeared in 1965 and had new fork legs which went on the VE and VS models up to 1967 and reverted to the old-type screw-in wheel spindle. There were also revisions to many of the shrouds and most important on the B44GP was two-way damping, later adopted by the other models. There was also the start of the move away from the nacelle style with the C15 Sportsman which had a separate headlamp.

These trends continued for 1967 with two-way damping on all models, common legs for the screw-in spindle and common shrouds except for the VE and VS models. For 1968 it was back to fork legs with caps, except for the VS, and gaiters on all models. The year 1969 brought a new fork-leg shape with Unified cap threads for the B25 and B44SS, both of which also had new internals. There were also new shrouds, shafts and seals, with both shafts and legs being revised for 1970.

For 1971 there was a new fork design with the caps that held the front wheel spindle retained by four studs, wire headlamp brackets and exposed fork stanchions. This fork remained in use from then onwards.

The Bantam began with a very simple fork design in which the lower legs slid within the upper ones against springs. This gained gaiters for 1950 and for that year was produced in standard and competition forms. These early forks had a stud set low down in the upper legs for the mudguard cross-stay, but the road models changed from this for 1953. For 1952 rubber inserts were added in the competition forks to give some measure of damping, and this feature was added to the road models in 1954. It was not used after 1955.

In 1953 the original, sprung and deeply-valanced mudguard became unsprung and supported by the lower leg. This then had a bracket added at its wheel-spindle end with one hole in front and two behind the leg for the stays. These continued in use on the D1 from then onwards.

When the D3 appeared in 1954 it had heavier forks, with the upper legs enlarged where they fitted into the yokes. Both D1 and D3 models had a cowl for the headlight, and the heavier D3 forks minus the cowl were also fitted to the competition models. The D5 continued with the same forks.

The D7 had a redesign on the lines of the larger machines, with lower legs sliding on the stanchions and a nacelle to support the headlight and carry the switches. This design stayed with the road D7 and the D7 Pastoral, but the D7 Trail version fitted the D1 forks with special yokes.

The D10 kept the D7 fork but the D10S modified it with shrouds to support a separate headlamp, and the D10B had the same arrangement but with short shrouds and fork gaiters. The D14/4 was as the D10, but the D14/4S and D14/4B had gaiters and a welded-on mudguard-stay lug on each fork leg. Both were revised to a new form of lug for 1969 and kept the gaiters, although these too were new.

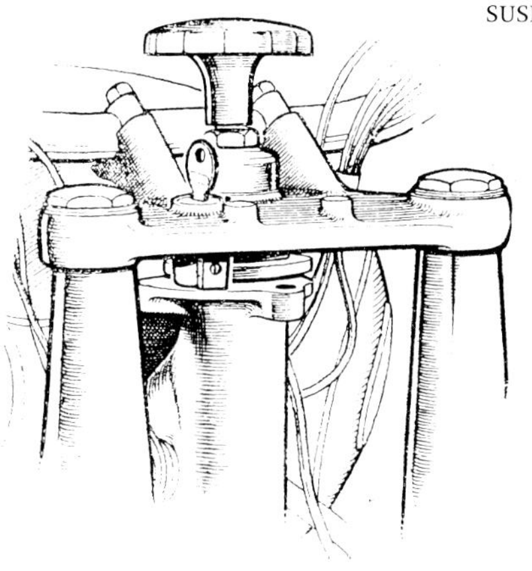

ABOVE *The new fork crown adopted for 1955 with steering lock*

BELOW *The plunger rear suspension of the D1 Bantam in 1952 with the typical rear hub and brake details*

Steering yokes

These are also known as crowns and should be checked for damage or distortion. Those of the early C and M models were to suit the girder forks, and the first pair of telescopic-fork yokes were for the B range of 1946–48 and were to suit the early head races.

For 1949 a new pair was introduced and the top yoke differed in having two tapped holes for the speedometer bracket. It went on the road B models and Gold Stars for 1949–52, and the competition B machines for one further year. The bottom yoke served the Gold Star for the same period, but went on the road B models for 1949–53 and all the M range from 1949 onwards.

The M-range top yoke for 1949–54 was also used on the B road models for 1953–54, but both ranges changed for 1955 when a steering lock was added in the yoke. This new part went on all the M models from then onwards, other than the AA M21 machines which had their own part, and the rigid and plunger B models of 1955.

The pivoted-fork-frame Gold Star of 1953 had a new top yoke which remained in use on it from then onwards and also went on the rigid competition B models of 1954–55. The B range with pivoted-fork frame had a new top yoke for 1954 which also went on the competition ones in this frame type, but was changed for 1955. The new part served the road models from then onwards but was only used for that one year on the competition models. They had another part for 1956–57.

The pivoted fork and rear units of a 1956 D3 Bantam, plus the dualseat fittings

The lower yoke had fewer changes, with a new part appearing in 1953 for the Gold Star trials and scrambles models. It stayed with them to the end and for 1954 went on all the B-range machines up to 1957. These had a new part for 1958–60 and there was one further bottom yoke for the Gold Star Clubmans and road-racing machines of the 1953–63 period.

On the C range there was just one bottom yoke for all models for 1946–58 except the C10L. This had a part to suit its Bantam-type forks for 1954–55 and another with a steering lock set in it for 1956–57. There was more variety with the top yokes, with the original 1946 one modified for 1949 and gaining two holes for the speedometer bracket in 1953. It was modified for the C11G of 1954 and had a lock added for 1955, this last part going on to the C12 as well. The C10L had two similar top yokes to match the two bottom ones.

The unit models began with one pair of yokes for the C15, which later went on to the SS80, and another for the competition models which went on to the B40E. A third set appeared for the B40, and later for the SS90 in 1961, much as those of the C15.

The top yoke of the competition models had two extra holes for a speedometer bracket and went on to the C25 of 1967 and the B44 models of 1965–67, including the Victor Grand Prix. The competition lower yoke went on the B44VE but the Grand Prix had its own part, and the two 1967 road models had one with an extra hole for the zener-diode head sink.

For 1968–70 there was one pair of yokes for all models and then the forks were redesigned for the new frame of 1971. One pair of yokes was used for the road models and there was a second top yoke without lock for the B50MX. This model had both yokes revised for 1973.

The D1 had one bottom yoke for all years but the top one changed for 1950 and 1954. The D3 had heavier forks with crowns to suit and these were also fitted to the competition models for 1954–55. A second bottom yoke was used for the pivoted-fork D3 and this, plus the top one, went on to the D5 for 1958.

There were new parts for the D7 in 1959 and these were revised for 1962, the latter items continuing in use on the D10 and D14/4. The other D14 models had new yokes and these were changed again for 1969. In addition there was a special pair of yokes for the D7 Trail model and a lower crown with an extra hole for the GPO D7.

Handlebar fixing

Just one part served many models but not the ones with girder forks for which there were two parts, one for the C range and the other for the M. Otherwise two of the one-part fixings served to clamp the bars to the top yoke of the B and M ranges, the C range except the C10L, the unit models for 1959–70, and the Bantams from the D7 onwards.

It was also used with a seat on the D1 for 1950–63 and the D7 Trail model. The D1 did have something else for its first year, when the clamp was formed from strip steel instead of bar material, and the seat also differed. The only other variation of this form of clamp was for the unit models of 1971–73 when a modified, but similar, part was listed.

The arrangement for the C10L and certain Bantams was different with a one-piece, light-alloy clamp complete with four downward-facing studs. This was held in place by nuts under the top yoke and went on all C10L machines, with the same part on the D3 and D5 Bantams with battery lighting over the 1954–58 period. A second similar part with a central hole was used on the direct-lighting D3 and D5 Bantams, plus the D1 and D3 competition versions of 1954–55. The added hole was for the bulb horn which screwed into the top of the steering column on Bantams of that period.

Steering damper

The various parts need to be renovated as required. Note that the damper knob is screwed on to its rod and locked with a cross-pin which must be removed first.

The damper was used by the B and M ranges, plus a sidecar version of the B40. Most of the detail parts were common to all years with just a change to the damper rod and friction plate for 1948. There was a new anchor plate to the frame for the Gold Star in 1953 and the same part went on the B range for 1954, but was modified for the B31 and B33 for 1956. These models reverted to the 1954 part in 1958. The damper rod and plate were new for the B40, but other details came from the older models.

The Gold Star models had a locking plate fitted from 1950. This was held by the handlebar clip bolts and its purpose was to stop the damper from unwinding from its setting during a race. The original plate was modified for 1953 and the new one used from then onwards, and also on the B32 and B34 models for 1954–57.

Plunger frames

These first appeared on the Gold Star and for the B range in 1949, then went on the Bantam in 1950 and the C and M ranges in 1951. The first lasted to 1952, the B to 1955, and the C to 1957, but the M and D1 continued to 1963.

The plunger units need to be checked and can be dismantled without tools if care is taken. Make sure the covers do not scrape, or the finish will go as soon as you ride the machine.

The only differences between the B and M parts were the springs and the plunger columns. The latter were altered on the M range for 1956. The C range used Bantam parts except for the springs, and these too became D-range items for the C10L of 1954, although the C11G continued with the older type.

The 1966 D10 Supreme Bantam with chrome-plated and painted tank, lined mudguards and twin mirrors

That same year the plunger columns were changed for both C and D ranges.

Rear-suspension units

BSA fitted sealed rear units to their singles and these offer limited scope to the restorer. In all cases, the outer covers and springs can be removed but the actual damper unit is sealed. The rubber mounting bushes can be renewed, but repair of the unit requires that it is dismantled, which for most people is not possible.

Replacements can usually be found and these should have a better performance plus other advantages. In all cases, check that the eyes at the ends of the unit and frame attachments are in good order and will carry the loads they are called upon to support.

The pre-unit models all had rear-suspension units with complete covers that hid the springs from view. This practice was continued on the unit models until 1966 when the B44VE had top covers only. This also continued on the 1967–68 models, while for 1969 there were no covers and the springs were fully exposed.

The Bantam kept complete covers on its rear units until 1967 when the Sports and Bushman models left them off to fully expose the springs. The next year the D14/4S and D14/4B did the same, as did the D175B for 1969. The D14/4 and D175 remained with their complete covers.

It is well worth fitting covers or gaiters to rear units to keep road dirt off the damper rods and away from the unit seals.

10 Painted parts and plated details

This chapter covers the mass of major parts and minor fittings that are mostly steel pressings and are nearly all painted. A few are forged or die-cast and some are plated with chromium or cadmium.

The problems in this area arise not so much with the repairs, as these are usually straightforward, but in collecting all the parts and ensuring that what you have gathered up is correct for your model. Machines built up from parts can be expected to have cycle details from many models included, and worst of all are the basket jobs. These last need very careful checking over from the first.

The following sections are not concerned with the repair of the parts, which follows stock procedures, but with their correct identification. Knowledge of part numbers and changes will all help to ensure that the cycle spares bought from a dealer or autojumble will be correct for your project.

Engine and gearbox plates

These parts acted as frame members as well as supporting the mechanics in the early pre-unit models, so the fit and condition of the holes is important.

At the front of the early B engines went a pair of flat plates held to the crankcase at three points and the frame at two, the lower frame hole being higher than the lowest engine one. These served all the rigid and plunger models, including the Gold Star, except the B32 and B34 of 1954–55. These had the same plates as were used by the pivoted-fork models and again these went on the Gold Star. They were similar to the early type but handed with a washer attached at one hole.

The M models of 1946–48 had front plates much as the B range, except that the lower frame hole was below the lowest engine one, which extended the plate. For 1949 there was a new design with three frame holes, of which the top two were close together.

At the rear went plates to support the crankcase and provide the slotted holes for the gearbox bolts. The first B models of 1946–48 had the plate with the crankcase holes as a separate part attached to the remainder. For 1949 this assembly changed to one flat plate with the stand stop attached and handed for the left and right. This pair of plates served the rigid and plunger models plus the early Gold Stars, but again not the B32 and B34 of 1954–55. These had their own pair on the lines of those fitted to the pivoted-fork B range. This range had two plates to each side, making four in all, arranged to surround the gearbox and thus give better support. The B-range set were also used by the Gold Star.

The rigid M range just used a pair of flat sheet plates, but the plunger ones were handed. This was done by the stand lugs and by a stand spring pin on the right side plate.

With the plates went covers to enhance the appearance, and at the front on the B range this was a small channel pressing on top of the plates. This served the rigid and plunger frames, with the exception as above, and went on the Gold Star.

The pivoted-fork frame had a cover bent to run up the front edge of the plates and across their top. A total of six tabs were bent in from it for fixing and this part served the B range, B32 and B34 of 1954–55, and the Gold Stars from 1958 onwards. An alternative went on the 1953–57 Gold Star.

The M range followed a similar pattern, with the 1946–48 models using a part much as the B range. From 1949 a cover went on the front of the plates held by four bent tabs to the studs.

As well as a front cover, there was also one at the rear on some pivoted-fork models. This was a curved pressing used to cover the gap between the plates. One served the B range and Gold Star for 1954–57, with nothing being fitted to the latter in its first year in that frame. It was modified to suit the coil-ignition B range of 1958, and another version went on the Clubmans models only from that date.

The C range had just one front-engine-plate type for all models except the C10L, which differed in having two close-spaced frame holes and two engine ones. The other had only one frame hole and two engine holes, thus three in all. At the rear the C10L plates formed part of the frame.

The other models began with a flat rear plate for the rigid frames and the plunger ones with three-speed gearbox. When a four-speed box was supplied, the

F 724

ABOVE *The 1947 M20 with all-iron engine, girder forks and serrated footrests without rubbers*

LEFT *Unit single fitted with Motoplas screen, legshields and mirrors*

rear plates were handed at the rearmost hole. There were new plates for the C11G with two of one part going on the rigid model. The three-speed plunger frame had one of these, but the right side had a bush welded on the outside of its rearmost hole. The four-speed version had handed plates but the C12 went back to flat ones, although of a revised shape.

The C range had a rear cover over the plates and bent down on the right side. Two were listed for the C10L with the 1954–55 one having a slot in its top rear edge. The one for the three-speed C11G had a plain rear edge and a pointed rear corner to the right side, but that for the four-speed had a cutaway at the rear and a radiused corner. The C12 was similar with a stud added to the right side.

The unit models did not have engine plates until 1971, except for the B44GP, and these were handed and went at the rear of the gearbox with one pair for the B25 and another for the home B50. The T, SS and MX models shared one of the B25 parts, but a new pair was used for the B50MX of 1973.

The Bantam had rear plates only on the pivoted-fork-frame models. Just one plate served all except the 1967 D10 Bushman, which had a variant.

Engine torque stays

These link the top of the engine to the frame and must fit well if they are to do their job.

The B range, in rigid or plunger frame, had a nearly straight tubular stay from the rear of the cylinder head to the frame. The same part served the Gold Stars with small-fin engines and for them there was also a curved part which was used when the twin-top-feed TT carburettor was fitted. This same part also went on the 1954–57 B34 under the same circumstances.

The pivoted-fork frames had a small, triangular plate with one for the road B models and the 1954–55 competition models, one for the latter for 1956–57, and a third for the big-finned Gold Stars. This last was only fitted to the CB, DB and scrambles model from 1956 as it did not appear on the DBD34 Clubmans model.

The M side-valve range had a simple stay with its end holes at right angles to one another. This was modified for 1956 when one end was bent a little. To go with these basic parts were formed ones for use when a right-hand sidecar was fitted. The M33 had its own curved stay which was not the standard B one, despite the ohv engine.

The C range did not have a stay until 1954 when the C10L fitted one with the ends at right angles. The stay ran from a special cylinder-head stud to the headstock gusset plate. The C11G and C12 had a flat strip stay which ran from the cylinder head to a clip on the frame downtube.

The unit models began with a clip round the tank tube, a simple stay and a bracket bolted to the top of the engine. This arrangement went on the C15, and for the competition models there was another stay and a

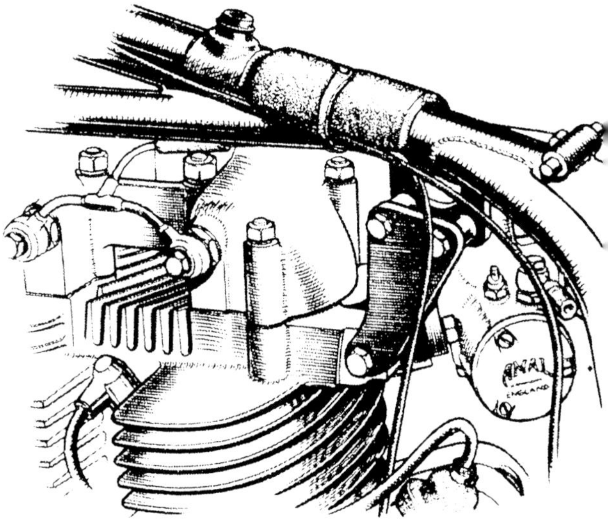

TOP *The 1954 CB32 Gold Star with big-finned engine, swept-back exhaust and rearsets*

ABOVE *Cylinder-head torque stay as used on the later Gold Star in scrambles form*

RIGHT *The 1966 C15 Sportsman with the Victor bottom half*

The B40 Military model, during a road test in 1967, showing its non-standard parts, often from the off-road models

bracket incorporating a lug for the exhaust-valve lifter cable. This feature was to go on all such models. The B40 had its own bracket at first but changed, while the C15 Pastoral model linked the bracket to the headstock with a tubular stay.

This arrangement with a horizontal stay replaced the first design and went on the competition C15 models and the B40E with a new stay. The same bracket with the early stay went on the B44GP, B44VE and 1967 B44VS. For the last model there was a new stay for 1968–70. There were new parts for the 1967–68 247 and 441 cc road models, and for 1969–70 the B25 retained the bracket but had a new stay with a further lug welded to it. The B44SS went to the original bracket from the competition C15 and used its own stay on the lines of the B25 one.

It was all change for 1971 on the B50 with a new bracket and stay, but the B25 kept to the 1967 bracket although its stay was new. There were no further changes and the Bantam did not have a torque stay.

Silencer bracket

These were only used on some unit and Bantam models as the others supported the exhaust system with welded-on brackets, which bolted directly to the frame.

Brackets did not appear on the unit models until 1965, and they had two fixings to the silencer and one to the frame. One went on the C15, B40 and SS90, while another went on the SS80 and a third on the C15 Pastoral. The 1967–70 road models had a simple rectangular plate with four holes, but the 1969–70 B44VS had a larger bracket with a joggle in it. Similar, but modified, brackets went on the USA version of the B25 for 1969 and 1970. The final unit-model bracket was for the 1973 B50MX and was designed to support the twin silencers of that model.

The Bantam brackets were all essentially triangular and first appeared in 1962. The same part went on the D7, D10 and D14/4, with another for the D175 and a third for the D14/4B and D175B. The other brackets were longer with flanged edges, with one for the D10S, one for the D10B and a third for the D14/4S.

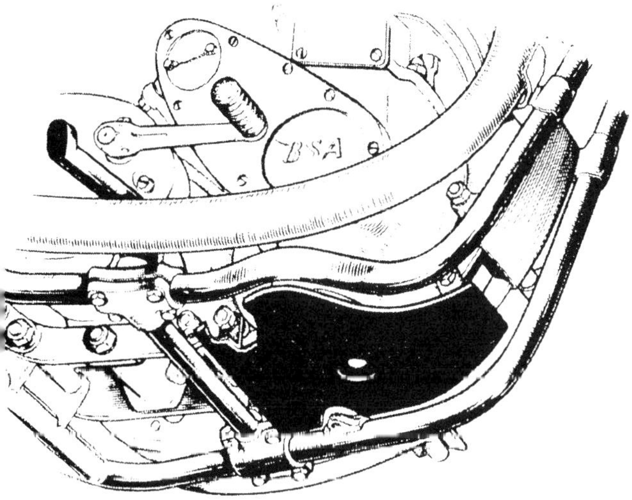

Undershield

This was listed from the start for the competition B models, and up to 1953 they used a pressing with flanged sides and four fixing lugs. The same part also went on the Gold Star, but from 1953 that model had another shield. This was a curved sheet, again with four lugs, and went on the B models from 1954.

The unit competition models each had an undershield which was modified for the new frame in 1963. This curved sheet, with two clips welded to it, went on the B40E, B44GP, B44VE and 1967 B44VS.

LEFT *The fitting of the footrests and crankcase shield to the DBD scrambles Gold Star*

BELOW *A 1956–58 C12 fitted with Patrol panniers and legshields*

There was another for the C15 Pastoral and a further version for the 1968–70 B44VS. This had to be amended for the 1971 frame and the new part went on all models, including the road ones, from then onwards.

The Bantam first had an undershield on the D7 Trail and Pastoral models, and this same part went on all the Bushman and Pastoral models from then onwards.

Drip shield

This was only fitted to the C11 and then only for one year, 1948. Its purpose was to stop petrol dripping on to the dynamo and it went between carburettor and cylinder head. The part itself was that also fitted to the A7 twin.

Distributor shield

This was part of the legshield option for the C range and bolted to the right shield which was cut away a little to clear the distributor. It was only available in this form for the C10 and C11 of 1946–53 and was there to keep road spray off the ignition.

Float-chamber supports

These were only listed for the Gold Star and were used when the float chamber was separate from the carburettor and flexibly hung on a stud. This allowed the float height to be set, and the same flexible mount was used from 1953 onwards.

For 1953 only, this was held so its centre-hole axis was vertical and directly held the chamber stud. Its two support brackets were formed to suit this, but for 1954 their ends were bent up and the mount turned so its centre hole was horizontal. A small eye stud was added to take the chamber stud. An alternative existed for the DBD34 scrambles model when this was fitted with a GP carburettor and competition magneto.

Headlamp cowl and nacelle

The cowl was first fitted to the B and M ranges for 1953 and was a single, complex pressing. It went on both ranges up to 1957 and was then changed to a nacelle for the B range but not the M. The new item comprised a tubular shell section which bolted to a pressing wrapped round the fork tubes between the yokes. A decorative ring went between the two and a dished cover went on the top to clean that area up. This went on all the B models of 1958–60. Neither cowl nor nacelle appeared on any Gold Star.

The C range adopted a cowl for 1954 with a simple curved pressing for the C11G and C12. The C10L had an assembly with this form of pressing attached to short shrouds which fitted over the fork tubes between the yokes. This was only fitted for 1954–55.

The unit models began with their own form of nacelle on the C15, while for the B40 revised top and light support shell parts were introduced. These also went on to the SS models, but not the Sportsman.

The Bantams first fitted cowls in 1954, and the D3, and later D5, used the C10L part. The D1 fitted a similar one which remained on that model up to 1963. The D7 changed to a nacelle on the lines of the C15 one

The 1955 DB34 Gold Star in Clubmans trim, with clip-ons and rearsets

The 1954 D1 Bantam with plunger frame, direct lighting and big-finned head and barrel

but with its own parts, except for the decorative ring. The main pressing and its top remained common on the D7, D10 and D14/4 models, the nacelle not being fitted to the Sports or Bushman machines of 1967–68 or any 1969 or later ones.

The lamp cowl was altered for 1964 to suit the models with twin switches and another was listed for the GPO Bantams. These also had their own decorative ring and this part was used by the D10 and D14. There was a second main pressing for the D7 Pastoral model.

Headlamp shell

These are all fairly similar as they all have to carry a light unit, but there are variations in light, size and shell piercing for switches.

The B, C and M models all began with shells which had a small panel for the ammeter and light switch. For 1953 the B and M gained a cowl and a shell with underslung pilot, but this later feature went for 1955. From 1958 the B models had a nacelle and thus no shell, but the M returned to the 1946 arrangement, though with a more modern light unit. All Gold Star road models had this arrangement, but the shell supports varied.

The C range continued in 1954 with a shell for each model with a single switch, but for 1956 the C10L had two switches and the C12 an ammeter only as the switch went to a side panel.

The unit models began with a nacelle with an ammeter on the left and a light switch to the right of the speedometer, and this applied to most of the models based on the C15. The C15T had a small shell with two switches while the C15 Sportsman of 1966 had a deeper one. This carried an ammeter and a light switch, and a similar arrangement went on the road models of 1967–70. There was variation in the switch type and number of warning lights, while the B40E, B44VE and 1967 B44VS kept to the C15T style. From

The first of the unit singles in the form of a 1959 C15

ABOVE *The 1969 B25 Starfire with twin-leading-shoe front brake and chrome-plated headlamp and mudguards*

LEFT *Nacelle and headlamp with single switch on a 1962 D7 Super Bantam*

BELOW *The stays supporting the headlamp of the 1956 and later Gold Star in Clubmans form*

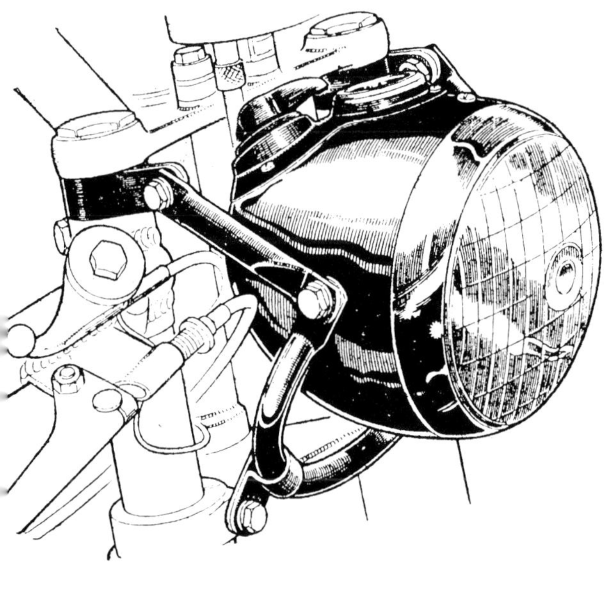

1968 the B44VS was as for the road models. The arrangement was further revised for 1971–72.

The Bantam began with a deep alloy shell for Wipac models with the separate handlebar switch and a more normal one for the Lucas models. From 1952 the Wipac type changed, involving a move of the switch to the shell where it stayed until the nacelle appeared in 1959.

For 1967 the Sports and Bushman models had a long shell and from 1969 this was the only type used. Either one or two switches were fitted, and a warning light was fitted for 1967–68.

Headlamp brackets

These were used on the C and M models fitted with girder forks and for the first were four strips, all the same. The M model did warrant tubular stays in two lengths and there was a second set used for the AA models. For 1948 only, these went on to the standard machines until they switched to telescopic forks.

The Gold Star adopted a set of brackets when it became available with clip-ons in 1954 and at first these were four different tubular stays. For 1956 a new arrangement was used with a curved stay running under the headlamp shell and held by two clips on to the bottom-yoke clamp bolts. The stay ran up and out to the shell bolts, where it was braced by two short stays clipped round the fork tubes just below the top yoke.

The unit models had supports for the headlamp for 1971–72 which were formed in wire. They were

ABOVE *The Gold Star prepared for the 1958 ISDT and ridden by Brian Martin*

BELOW *The 1967 D10 Sports model with flyscreen, waist exhaust and decorated tank, as well as full-width brakes front and rear*

RIGHT *The machine on which Jeff Smith won the 1964 500 cc Motocross World Championship, on view at the Earls Court Show that year. Caron Gardner, a* Goldfinger *Bond girl, is the model*

BSA
SPORT STAR

handed and fitted to the fork yokes via rubber bushes to insulate them from vibration.

The Bantams only had a headlamp bracket in their early days and it was a simple pressing which fitted to the bottom-yoke clamp studs. There were three in all: one for a machine with a Wipac system up to 1953, one for the Lucas model up to the same year, and one for the 1954–55 competition models,

Flyscreen

This was an attempt to jazz up the styling of the ageing Bantam and is to be found only on the D10S and D14/4S of 1967–68. It may well be cracked and few are likely to have survived.

Mudguards, their stays and front stand

All these parts are associated together and care is needed to ensure you have the correct parts from the many made. Above all else, do make sure the mudguards are properly secured and cannot revolve round the wheel. Also check that they sit with a good line to the tyres.

Front mudguard

The B range began with a guard for each model but only the B31 had the rear stay doubling as a front stand. This model had a blade guard with a minimal valance and was held by a front loop stay, a centre bridge and the stand with its two attachment lugs. The B32 had its own chrome-plated blade, stays and bridge, and the parts from each machine went on the B33 and B34 for 1947. Both sets changed the bridge piece for 1948 to suit the change of fork-leg fixing.

All changed for 1949 with new parts in all locations. Of the road models, the B31 kept to these in rigid form and only changed the bridge in 1955 for the last plunger models. The B33 went to a valanced mudguard for 1953 and for this had a new front stay and stand. For 1955 it shared the B31 bridge.

The pivoted-fork B road models appeared for 1954. The B31 kept to its minimal valance, although in revised form, until 1956 when it adopted the B33 valanced guard, this being the one it had fitted from 1953. Its stay and stand were common to all applications up to 1957, but the bridge varied. The B31 was special at first, while the B33 used the 1949 pattern, but for 1956 both went to the 1955 plunger-frame type. For 1958 onwards the mudguard and bridge remained the same but the stay and stand were modified.

The competition models had new parts for 1949 but the front stay was not to change again. The blade did for 1954 with one for the rigid models and one for those with a pivoted rear fork. Both had a new common bridge and a rear stay, which was now the same part as the front one.

The Gold Star began with the 1949 B32 items but had new blades for 1953. For the models with a 19 in. front wheel there was a new set of parts, including a front stand with single fixing lug. The second blade was for a 21 in. front wheel as used for trials and scrambles, and this had the front stay and bridge as on the 1954 B32 and the stand from the pivoted-fork B31 of that year. By 1955 the stands had gone and only front and rear stays were used, each model having its own which was used in both locations.

ABOVE *A 1959 M21 for the AA, equipped with massive legshields, radio and panniers*

ABOVE LEFT *A competition Bantam prepared to run in the 1949 ISDT. Note the decompressor in the cylinder head*

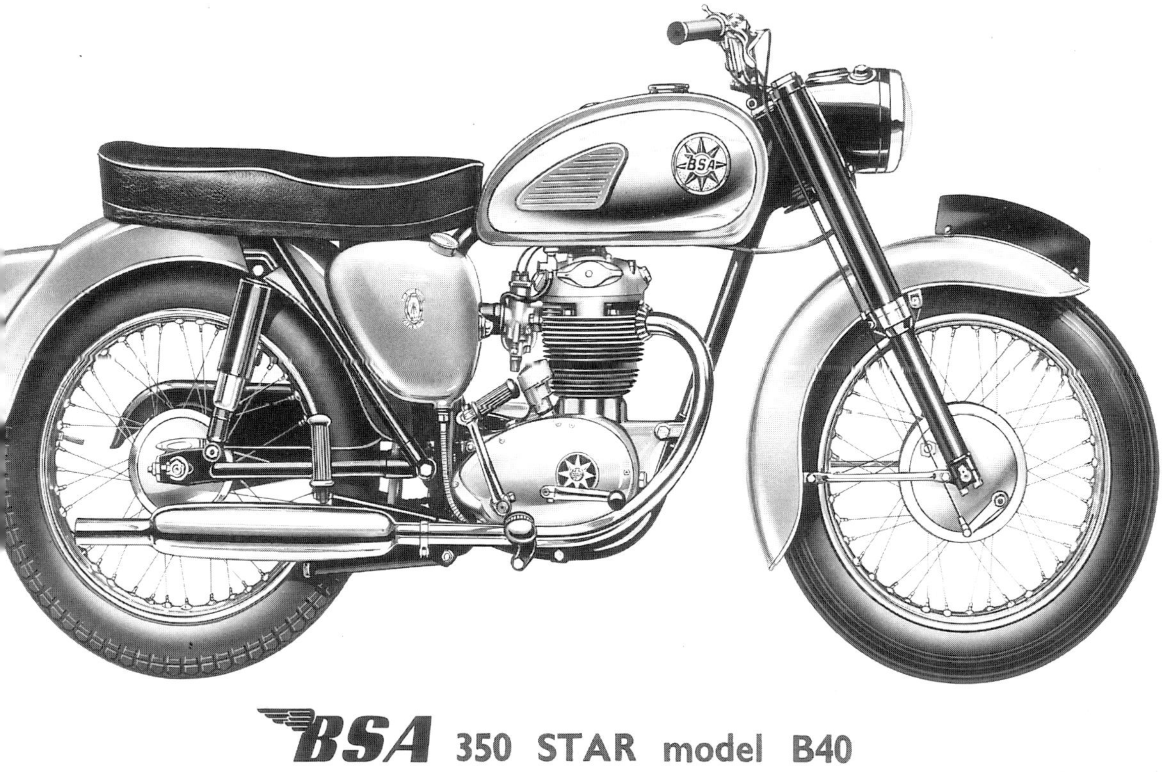

ABOVE *The 1961 B40, much the same as the smaller C15*

ABOVE LEFT *A 1958 B31 with alternator electrics, nacelle and new brakes*

LEFT *The 1959 scrambles C15S with road-style tank and open exhaust*

The M range began with its own blade, stay and stand to suit its girder forks. For 1949 it changed to the B-range parts, and in 1956 it went to the valanced guard and supports as used on the B road range of that year. These were also called for by the AA on their M21 machines.

The C range also began with a mudguard to suit girder forks but moved to telescopics and new parts that same year of 1946. The guard and stays were altered for 1949 and went on to the C11G in 1954, both stays being the same part. The same design, but with different parts, was used for the C12.

The C10L began with all Bantam parts and had the guard supported by a bridge loop attached to the bottom end of the fork legs and two pairs of stays, front and rear. Only the stays were altered for the revised forks in 1956.

The unit C15 had its mudguard supported by two brackets from the fork legs and two rear stays. The same arrangement served the SS80, but for 1965 this model changed to a chrome-plated guard and new stays. The B40 had its own guard and stays but used the common bracket, as did the SS90 which again had its own chrome-plated guard and stays.

The competition models had chrome-plated guards supported by a one-piece loop that acted as both front and rear stays, plus a bridge loop. Certain special versions had three loop stays with some from the late B32 model, and there were minor variations to suit the USA market. For 1963 the competition models changed to light-alloy guards held by a bridge loop and two rear stays.

The B44GP had this style of guard and fixing which then went, with a new blade, on to the B44VE and B44VS. For this last, there was a change of bridge loop for 1968.

The road models went to a choice of guards, drilled for a number plate or not, and three new loop stays for 1967. The front and bridge stays both bolted to the same lug high up the fork leg to revise the style. The same blades stayed in use up to 1970, although the choice was only available for the B25 from 1969. The front stays were altered for 1968 and the rear one for 1969.

The year 1971 brought a new style of guard, with built-in stays rubber-mounted to the fork leg on the road models. The trail model had the guard bolted to a bracket, which in turn attached to the bottom fork yoke. This bracket was changed for the 1973 B50MX

and there were three different guards of this type, with one each for the B25T, B50T and B50MX. The road style came in two forms: one for home use, drilled for the number plate, and a second for export.

The Bantam began with a sprung front mudguard with a massive valance, and this was held by a cross-stay on each side and two clips on to the fork legs. The competition model had a blade held by bent cross-stays and the same two clips, chrome-plated for their first year only. There was also a modified version of the standard blade for Australia for 1950 only.

The competition parts continued as they were up to 1955, but the road D1 changed to an unsprung blade for 1953. This had no valance and was held by a bridge loop and a pair of stays to front and rear. These parts continued on all D1 machines from then onwards, and also went on the D3 for 1954–57 and D5 of 1958.

There was a new blade for the D7 in 1959 with a bent cross-stay on each side and a pair of fork-leg clips. These changed to a type with two clamping bolts for 1962, but the other parts remained as they were and all went in turn on the D10 of 1967 and D14/4 of 1968. The D7 Trail model had its own blade held by a bridge loop and two pairs of stays.

The D10S was listed with the same pair of mudguards as the 1967 unit road models, but had its own set of stays. One blade was for the Sports model and the other for the USA Sportsman. The D10B had another pair of blades and used the front and bridge stays from the road unit models with its own rear loop.

For 1968 the D14/4S fitted the blade from the D10 Sports using the front and bridge stays from the D10B and its own rear loop. The D14/4B fitted the Sportsman's blade with the same stays from the unit models, including the rear loop from the same source. This remained for the D175B model as well. The D175 had a new blade with new pairs of front and rear stays, while its bridge support was part of the mudguard assembly.

Rear mudguard

The B31 and B33 began with a rear mudguard with tail, all supported by a combined loop stay and lifting handle, vertical stays and rear stay. For 1949 the main guard section changed, as it did again for 1953, but the supports remained the same on these rigid models.

The plunger version had a guard with hinged tail and the supports bolted to the tops of the suspension units with a single bent stay on each side. The guard was revised for 1953. There was a new guard for the pivoted-fork model of 1954 and this was supported by a pair of bent stays and attachment plates fixed to the top rear-suspension-unit mounting. The guard and stays were both changed for 1955 onwards.

The B32 and B34 had a chrome-plated guard with two support loops. The guard was altered for 1949 on the rigid models and another guard with new supports appeared for 1954. The plunger-frame models had their own guard with a pair of rear stays and a small loop support bolted to the top of the suspension braces. The pivoted-fork models used the road-model system and attachment plates with their own blades and bent stays, which were altered for 1956.

The Gold Star began with the B32 parts but changed to the pivoted fork design for 1953, using the same attachment plates for the trials and scrambles models from then onwards and for the others of that year alone. The blades and supports also differed between the off-road and racing models, with one pair for 1953 and a second for 1954 onwards. The later off-road stays were as used by the 1954 pivoted-fork B32.

The M models had a mudguard plus tail at first, and these were supported by a loop stay and two pairs of stays. For 1951 the guard only was altered and was joined by one for the plunger frame with its own pair of bent stays to hold it.

The C range began with a mudguard with tail, supported by a loop stay and two pairs of stays. The loop and a single backstay were altered with the change to telescopic forks, and the loop changed for 1950. It and the guard changed once more for 1953, and the guard was revised for the rigid C11G of 1954 but kept the same supports.

The plunger models were introduced for 1951 with bent stays on the lines of the larger models. The blade was altered for 1953 and for the C11G of 1954, with a further change to blade and stays for 1955. The C10L had its own parts with a choice of blades to suit saddle or dualseat fitment, and a new blade for 1956. The C12 had its own guard and a different design of support stays.

The C15 had two mudguards listed, one of which was used when a lifting handle was fitted. Another form was introduced for 1965. The SS80 also had two guards listed, one for home and one for the USA. In similar style the original B40 guard was replaced by two, one to be used with a handrail, while there were three for the SS90 to cover home, handrail and USA fitments.

There were a variety of guards listed for the competition and off-road variants, and for the UK use the C15T and C15S fitted alloy parts from 1963. The B40E and B44GP had their own parts. Two guards were listed for the B44VE, and the same parts were also listed for the B44VS and road models of 1967. The road machines had a support rail fitted and one part served all models for 1967–70.

New guards were fitted for 1968 and again for 1969, except for a few early B44VS machines. The B25 continued to have a choice of two guards listed, of which only one went on the B44SS and the other on the B44VS. There were new guards and support rail

ABOVE LEFT *The Military B40 with external oil filter and special carburettor as well as a useful rear chaincase*

BELOW *The 1966 C15 Sportsman with its humped seat and separate headlamp shell to distinguish it from the SS80*

for 1971, with the latter made to carry a pair of side reflectors. Individual guards were listed for the B25, B50T, B50SS and B50MX, the last changing for 1973.

The Bantam rear mudguard was supported by the rear carrier so there were only two rear stays when in this form. When a dualseat was fitted, extra stays were added to replace those of the carrier. For the first year the rear stays were handed, but quickly became two of the same part.

The original mudguard used by the rigid machines was changed for 1955. The plunger model had its own two guards, one for saddle and the other for dualseat, which were altered for 1954. Of these, the saddle fitment came from the C10L, but it was the dualseat type that became common for 1955 and remained in use on the D1 from then onwards.

The competition D1 had its own guard supported by two loop stays with a second set of parts for the plunger-frame version. The D3 version of all the road and competition models used the same parts as the D1, but the pivoted-fork D3 had its own mudguard supported by two new stays.

The D5 copied the D3 but had its own set of parts, while the D7 had a new mudguard. For 1962 it was revised and joined by a second type pierced to take a handrail. These two guards then went on the D10, D14/4 and D175 in turn. The D7 Trail and D7 Pastoral models each had their own guard, as did the GPO D7.

There were two guards listed for the D10S with one for the Sportsman and another for the Sports, this one also going on to the D14/4S. In the same way there were two for the D10B, with the USA one going on to the D14B. There was a new guard for the D175B.

Front number plate

This is no longer a legal requirement in the UK, but many owners like to keep it and either display the registration number or the model type and year.

LEFT *The Bantam D7 Silver from 1966, with economy finish to reduce its price*

RIGHT *Rear-end details of the 1971 B50SS showing fittings and conical rear hub*

Most B models had the same plate, but from 1954 the B32 and B34 had one set across the front forks and bolted to the base of the competition plate fitted that year. The M range had one plate for its girder forks and then used the B plate with the telescopics. The C range did the same except for the C10L, which had its own plate (this changing for 1955). When a valanced mudguard was fitted, there was no plate as the sides of the guard were used to carry the mark.

The unit road models had a change of plate for 1965 and there were alternatives for the off-road and competition models. From 1962 these went across the front of the forks on the C15T. The whole range had a new plate for 1967 which was changed for 1971.

The Bantam began with its numbers on the side of the valanced guard, but had the standard B-range plate for the competition model. It remained in use up to 1961 and also went on the D7 Trail model and the D10S. It was replaced on the D7 from 1962 and this new plate also went on the D10, D14/4 and D175. There were further plates for the GPO D7, D10B, D14/4S and D175B, this last fitting across the fork legs. In the early days there had been a front plate for use in Australia.

Rear number plate

This is still required in the UK but has always been governed internationally by local regulations so that, in the end, the company just provided the mounting below the rear light and left it to the dealer to find and fit the necessary plate. This was not so in earlier days when white numbers were painted directly on the plate, to be followed later by transfers, plastic self-adhesive numbers, pressed-aluminium, and finally the modern reflective version in yellow.

There were a considerable number of rear plates used on the B range, with the first having the small, round Lucas rear light of the time. Another went on the competition models, and for 1950 revised ones able to take a stop and tail light were available. For 1953 the road models had the plate boxed into the rear guard with revisions for 1956 and 1958. The competition models had their changes for 1954 and 1956.

The Gold Star began with a plate as used by the B32 and changed to one with a rear-reflector mounting hole for 1953. This went on the trials model for 1954 but the Clubmans model fitted the 1953 B-range part. Both changed for 1955 and the Clubmans again for 1958.

The M range had its own plate at first but used the boxed-in B type for 1953 and had a further change for 1956. The C range was similar but fitted the B-range plates for all years, with changes for 1951, 1953 and 1956.

The unit models had a plate for the tourers and one for the competition models, both of which changed for 1965. The SS models had their own plate, as did the off-road types. A new plate came in for the B44VE in 1966 and went on all the 1967 models. A deeper plate appeared for 1968 and there were two styles listed for 1969. There was a further plate for 1970 and another plus new brackets for 1971–72.

The Bantam had a single plate for its first year but two for 1950, one to suit Wipac and the other Lucas lamps. For 1954 it was back to one revised plate, but the 1955 competition models went back to a 1950 plate and the D1 had a further revised plate for 1956 which it kept from then onwards.

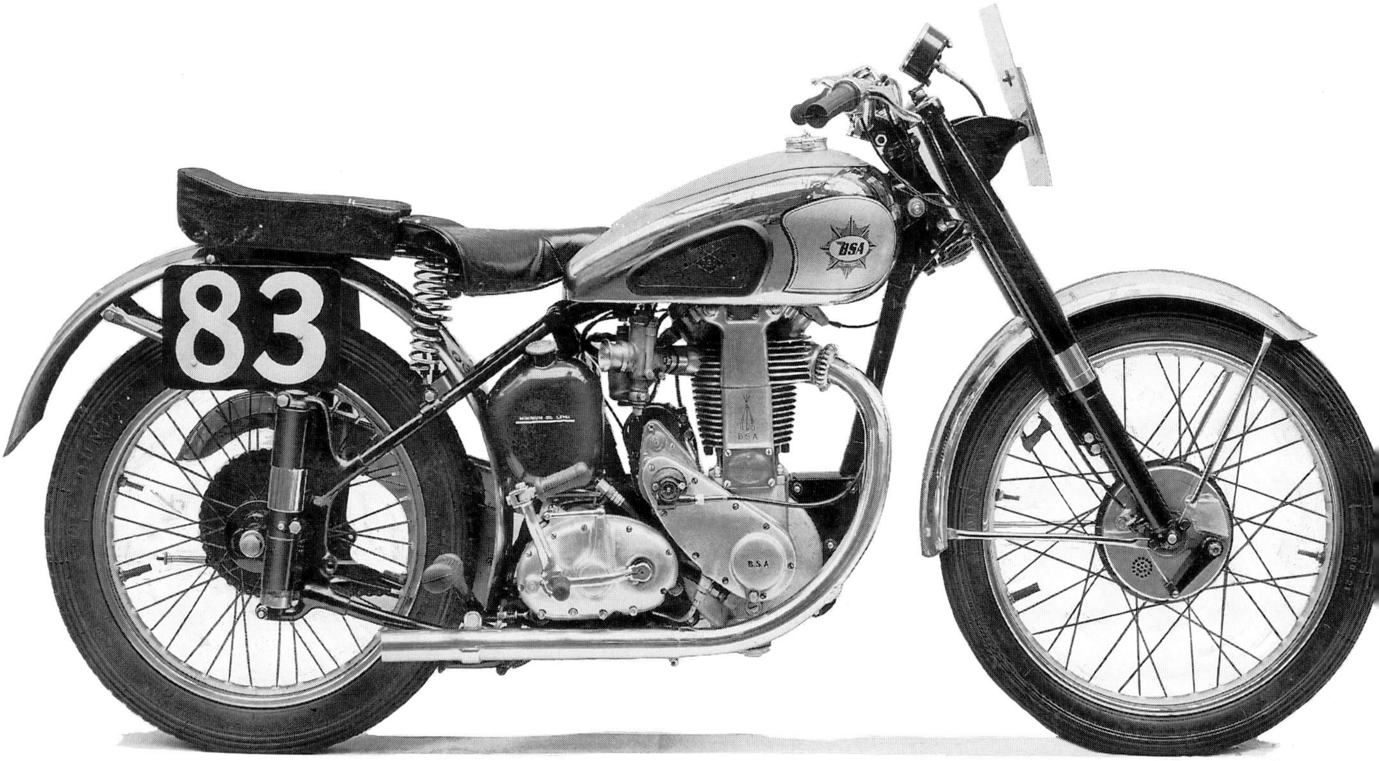

ABOVE *The 348 cc Gold Star ridden into 17th place in the 1949 Clubmans by Jack Difazio*

RIGHT *A B40 at an early-1960s show*

The pivoted-fork D3 had a different plate which also went on the D5, but there was another for the D7 and D7 Trail models. The road one was changed for 1962 and this plate went in turn on the D10, D14/4, D175 and D175B. The GPO D7 had its own plate, while the D10S and D14/4S fitted the rectangular type from the four-strokes. The D10B had the 1968 four-stroke plate.

Competition plate

This item first appeared in 1954 on the B32 and B34 to carry the rider's number in an event. It was a plate which was held to the front forks by the bottom-yoke clamp bolts and a small bracket attached to the top yoke. The plate was drilled at the base for the registration plate and the style was normal for most trials models. The part was also listed for the scrambles Gold Star from 1958 onwards.

Another competition plate was listed for the Victor Grand Prix and was of oval shape to suit the scrambles use. For the B50MX the side panels were modified to act as competition plates, and for 1971 there were two pairs listed. For 1973 a left one continued to be fitted and was joined by a new right.

Rear light support

For most models the rear light was attached to the top of the number plate, but this changed from 1966 on the B25 and B44 ranges. They had a pressing bolted to the mudguard, a plate for the light unit and a strip to carry the number plate. Of these parts the plate was common to all models for 1966–70.

The pressing first changed for 1968, when side reflectors were added, and again for 1969, when the first few B44VS machines had another part before altering to one common to the other models. This part continued for 1970. The number-plate strip was amended for 1968 but returned to the 1966 part for 1970.

There was a new, one-piece pressing for all road models in 1971 which was designed to take the turn-indicator stalks but not the side reflectors, which were mounted on the rear-mudguard support rail.

Lifting handle

This was a necessary aid for pulling the machine up on to its centre stand, as most BSA models were hard to raise. On small and rigid models the rider was expected to manage, but for the plunger frames a handle was provided, bolted to the left side of the frame between the saddle and the rear plunger lugs. One served the B range and early Gold Stars, another the M range and a third the C models, although it was

350cc
STAR
Model B40

changed for 1953. Both C-range handle types continued on the C11G.

The pivoted-fork B range had a new lifting handle for 1954 and the C12 had two listed, one for each side. The C15, B40 and SS models had a handle listed from 1962 onwards.

Side and centre panels

These are only found on Bantams and unit models as, with one exception, the job of enclosing the centre area of the machine of pre-units was done by the oil tank on the right and the toolbox on the left. For the Bantams the toolbox and battery carrier served the same duty. The exception was the C12 which had a panel on the right to carry its electrical switch.

The unit models began with a centre panel which joined the oil tank and toolbox cover into one clean shape. The centre panel of the C15 went on to the SS80, B40 and SS90, but for the larger-capacity models changed its top fixing lugs for 1965. The competition models had their own centre panel up to 1962, after which they fitted a central oil tank. One toolbox cover served all the road models and on the competition ones a similar pressing acted as the air-filter lid.

Side panels first appeared on the B44GP in 1965 with one on each side, but for the B44VE there was only one, on the left, which acted as the air-filter lid. The same part also went on the B44VS in 1967, but for 1968–70 this model had a panel held in place by two Oddie stud fasteners of different lengths.

The 247 cc road models of 1967 began with two well-shaped left side panels in fibreglass, one for the home market and the other for the USA, each of which went on the left of the machine to match the oil tank. Two more similar panels were listed for the 441 cc road model and in both these cases only one panel went on for 1968.

For 1969 the left panel was joined by a similar right one which fitted over the oil tank and had a hole for the filler cap. Both were retained by Oddie studs and there was one pair for the B25, one for the USA B25 and one for the B44SS. For 1970 the road models adopted the left-side-only cover of the B44VS, so for that year all had the same fitting.

The redesign of 1971 brought a new pair of side covers for both road models plus a pair for the B50MX. The latter acted as competition plates and the right was altered for 1973.

The Bantam only had panels on pivoted-fork models and the first went on the left side of the D3 in 1956 to enclose the rectifier and horn. A similar part went on the D5 in 1958, but the design was revised for the D7 to comprise centre and left panels with the matching right, being the toolbox lid. This last went on to the D10 and D10S but the left was changed for 1962, although it too continued on to the D10 models. The centre was joined by a second type for the de luxe models and it was this that went on to the D10.

ABOVE *The side panel and other details of a 1970 D175B*

LEFT *Ignition lock and other items of a 1970 B25 Starfire*

The D7 Trail model had its own pair of panels as did the D10B, and there was another pressing without an air-hose cut-out for the D7 Pastoral model. The D10 Pastoral had a different pair of panels which also went on the D14/4B and D175B. The left also went on the D14/4 and D14/4S, but the right was altered as it now covered the air filter which was housed on that side. The two models had different right covers but that of the D14/4 also went on the D175—however, that model had its own left cover.

Battery carrier

This is often the most corroded item on the machine as it may have been subject to battery fumes as well as the weather. If the acid has attacked it, the parts must be fully cleaned off or the trouble will occur again. The damage may be severe but can usually be repaired, while measures should be taken to stop it happening again.

One battery carrier served all the rigid and plunger B models plus the Gold Star, while another assembly of tray and straps went on the pivoted-fork models. There were three carriers for the M range, all much as the early B type, with one for 1946–47, another for 1948 onwards, and the third for the M21 used by the AA.

The C range had one carrier for the rigid frames and a second for the plungers up to 1953. For 1954–55 there were three assemblies to suit the C10L, the three-speed C11G and the four-speed C11G. From 1956 there was a new assembly for the C10L and another for the C12.

The C15 carrier went behind the seat tube and comprised a bracket with a wire over-centre strap to hold the battery. This arrangement was used on all this series until the C25 and B44VR of 1967. These had a tray for the battery and an elastic strap which clipped to it. The tray was modified by the addition of a bracing angle for 1968 and this part continued to be fitted up to 1970, also going on to the B44VS that year. There was a new tray with hanging support strap and insulated mountings for 1971–72.

On the Bantam the first carrier of 1950 was used on machines with Lucas electrics and was similar to those on the other ranges. It had changes to its mounting for 1954 and 1955, but for 1956 took the form it was to keep to the end of the D1. These parts also went on the

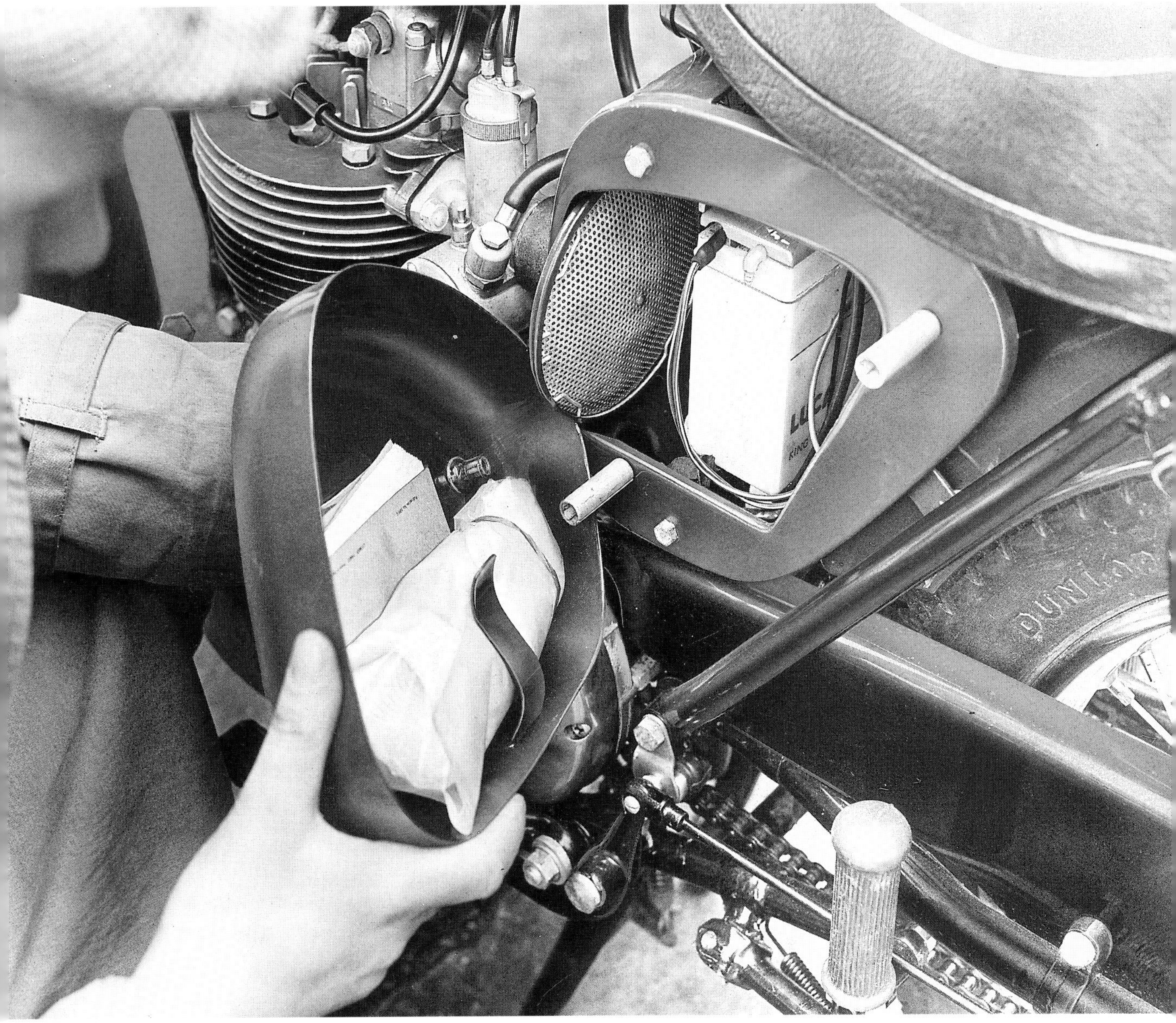

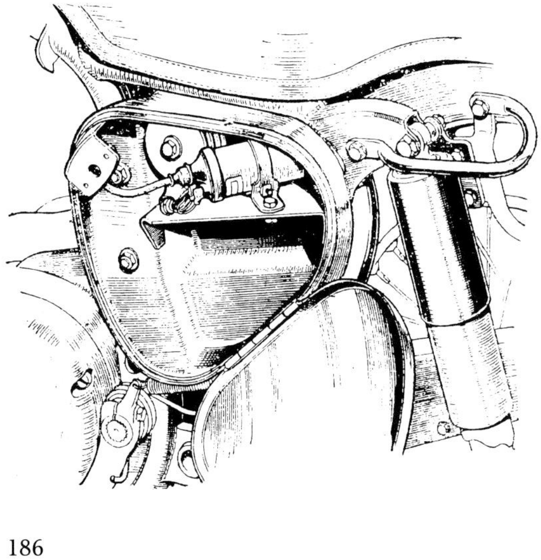

ABOVE *Toolkit, battery and air cleaner as installed on a 1961 B40*

LEFT *Toolbox stowage of coil and rectifier on the 1958 B range with alternator electrics*

plunger D3, but the pivoted-fork model had its own design bolted to the seat tube and this went on to the D5 and D7 as well. It was superseded by a revised type with over-centre wire strap in 1962, which went on to the late D7, D10, D14 and D175 models.

Toolbox

The early models had a triangular toolbox set between the rear chainstays on the right. One box served all the rigid B models but the one for the plunger machines was changed for 1953. The first type went on the 1949 Gold Star but this was changed to another for 1950.

The pivoted-fork models had the box in the angle of the subframe on the left and the Gold Star type was used by the road B models at first; both then had a change for 1958 when the box lid was domed to match the oil tank.

The B32 and B34 had their own box and this was changed for 1952 and 1954, while no box was fitted after 1955. The M range began with its own box but changed in 1948 to the one also used by the 1950 Gold Star. The plunger model had its own box.

On the C range one part served both rigid and plunger models and was altered for 1953. It was replaced by two in 1954, one for the C10L and the other for the C11G, and both of these were altered for 1956, the second to fit the C12 on the left.

Matters were less clear on the unit models as the toolbox lid was a side panel, covered above, which left an inner panel to complete the box. On the C15 this went on the left and was linked to the centre panel. It also had a large hole in it to provide access to the battery which went inboard of it, next to the oil tank. The competition machines had similar parts which were part of the air-filter system and are dealt with below.

The arrangement changed for the road models in 1967 when the new series adopted a box bolted to the left of the frame for the tools. This was beneath the side panel and the same part was used on the B44VS from 1968 and remained in place up to 1970. For the new range of 1971 a tooltray was bolted to the frame on the left, again concealed beneath the side panel.

The Bantam began with a small toolbox bolted to the frame seat tube on the right side of the machine. The lid was held by two special screws. A modified toolbox was fitted on the machines with Lucas electrics but remained on the right. For 1953 both changed to a single lid screw but, from 1954, models with battery lighting had the toolbox fitted on the left and the box was drilled on its forward side for a wiring harness clip. In this case, the lid retained its single screw and the box remained in use to the end. The direct-lighting models kept the box on the right and went back to two lid screws until 1958, when they fell into line with one.

The rigid and plunger D3 was as the D1, but the pivoted-fork model had its toolbox mounted on the right, as did the D5. For the D7 the design became as for the C15 but with the tools stored under the right cover. This fitted to an inner panel, which matched to the centre one, and this inner one was amended for 1962. The new part then went on the D7 Trail, GPO D7, D10 and D10S models.

The D10B had a different inner panel with a hole to accommodate the air filter, while the D10 Pastoral moved it over to the left side with its own cover. This left panel did the same job on the D14/4B and D175B, while a version with a battery access hole went on the D14/4, D14/4S and D175.

Air-cleaner housing

This is only found on a few models as most had the air cleaner attached directly to the carburettor. However, one did appear on the Gold Star scrambles models with the central oil tank.

The part occurs on the competition C15 where it replaced the toolbox inner panel of the standard model. This was because the air filter was housed in this area and the panel had a small hole in it for this reason. Another panel was listed for the C15T Pastoral with a very large hole to accommodate the drum-type air cleaner. The B40 fitted the C15 part at first but for 1965 the rear fixing hole had become a slot. The parts were common to the SS models.

For 1963 the competition C15 machines changed to a wedge-shaped filter mounted above the central oil tank. A suitable box and lid were used to house it. For the B44VE the air box went to the left of the machine alongside the oil tank and this part also went on the B44VS for 1967. From then onwards drum filters were fitted, but for 1971 a new housing was introduced for the road models and a second design for the B50MX.

Most Bantams had the filter directly fitted, but not the D14/4, D14/4S or D175. For these models a triangular element was fitted under the right side panel to an inner plate. This was positioned as the toolbox inner had been before it and was connected by hose to the carburettor intake.

Electrical box

This was fitted to the 1971–72 road models and contained most of the electrical components. It went under the front of the petrol tank and comprised a light-alloy box plus lid. The lid was common to both models but not the box, which carried different side reflectors and was thus drilled to suit on each side. The B25 had rectangular reflectors and two fixing holes, while the B50 had round ones and an extra hole for their fixing.

The B50MX had its electrics attached to a mounting plate which was modified for 1973.

Bulb horn

This needs to work for the machine to be street legal if it is all that is fitted. It was found on the B44VE and

B44VS in 1967 only, and early Bantams with direct lighting, but was unusual in the latter case as the bulb was screwed into the top of the steering column and the outlet into the bottom. The bottom part was dropped by 1954 but the arrangement continued on all direct-lighting models.

Chainguard and chaincase types

The B31 and B33 rigid models had a simple guard for all years as did the M range, both items being similar in appearance. The M range had the additional benefit of a lower guard as well. The plunger versions of both ranges fitted a common part which was extended down on the inside at the front to give more protection.

The pivoted-fork-frame B road models had a similar style of guard modified to suit the new design. This was altered for 1956 to extend the inner wall to provide it with four fixing holes, and these were matched by the mountings of the optional full chaincase. This was introduced that year and was built up from front, top and bottom sections plus a cover for the rear half of the wheel sprocket. The guard and chaincase option continued as they were to the end.

The competition models had their own chrome-plated guard which had an extended inner wall. This first part was used on the rigid models up to 1953, but for 1950 was joined by another in black. This had a small guard added to its top and a pair of tyre pump clips, and was fitted when the standard tank was replaced by a two-gallon one. This type in a revised form went on the rigid models for 1954–55.

The plunger-frame competition machines began with their own chrome-plated version of the road guard and this was joined for 1950 by one with a tyre guard and clips. These items also went on the Gold

ABOVE LEFT *The tank and engine top half of the 1971 B50SS, plus the electrics box with ignition key*

LEFT *The 1958 B33 with alternator and points in the old magneto position*

ABOVE RIGHT *Starting a 1972 B50T, which was not too easy unless the correct drill was followed*

Star for those years, and for 1951 both changed to an amended type still with the tyre guard and clips. When they went into a pivoted-fork frame, both fitted the guard to be used by the 1954 road B range but with a chrome-plated finish. It was revised for the Gold Star for 1958.

The C range had two similar guards for 1946 but the next year both fitted the C11 part which continued in use on the rigid C11G in 1954. The plunger frame used a guard without the lower rear lug and this went on to the sprung C11G. The C10L had a rather slim guard, while the C12 one had rather more line.

The unit models had a similar guard for the road machines and an abbreviated one for the competition models. The first went on the C15 and SS80 and was joined by another for the two 343 cc machines. The second was amended for 1963.

Another guard went on the B40E and also the B44VE, but for 1967 the latter changed to the original C15T guard. This was also fitted to the C25 that year and the B44VS for the following one as well. The B44VR had a very similar part for 1967 and this went on the B25 and B44SS for 1968.

For 1969 there was a smaller guard for the two road models but the B44VS stayed with the earlier type, although it was modified with a bracket added near its tail; this continued for 1970. For 1971 there was a new guard in two parts, one to bolt to the left fork leg and the other to the frame as an extension. These parts went on all road models.

The Bantam began with a simple guard with front and rear fixings. It carried a transfer with the gear positions marked as a scale for a small indicator linked to the gearbox mechanism. In 1950 it was joined by three more guards, one similar for the plunger frame and two, each with an extended inner wall, for the rigid and plunger competition models.

All changed for 1954 when the transfer went and the plunger-frame one remained in use up to 1963. The rigid one went after 1955 and the competition ones

continued to differ in form and rear fixing. The rigid one had an angle bracket at the rear and a rectangular extension, while the plunger had an inset tube and a curved rear edge to the inner wall.

The pivoted-fork D3 appeared for 1956 with a new style of guard and a small extension which bolted to its front end, low down. The D5 guard differed in having a bracket about halfway along its top but the extension remained the same. For the D7 the guard lost its inset-tube mounting and the extension plate changed its shape and was also joggled at one corner. It was to continue in this form up to 1971.

The guard was amended for 1962 but then continued as it was on all road models. The D7 Trail model had its own guard with two brackets attached to its top surface, and a final guard with a smaller single bracket went on the D10B, D14/4B and D175B.

Chainguide

This was only found on the competition unit and D7 Trail models. For the latter it comprised a pivoted chain tensioner of the type more usually found within a primary chaincase, and it was only listed for that one Bantam model.

For the unit models the guide was formed in strip steel and bolted to the left leg of the pivoted fork to help the chain stay on its sprockets. It was first seen on the C15S and the same part was also fitted to the C25 in

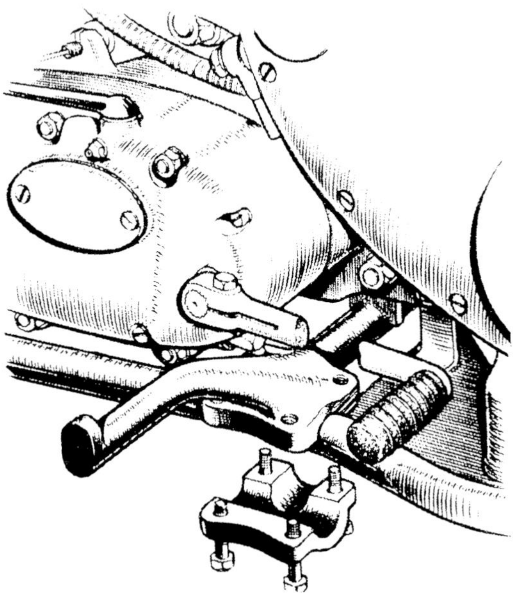

ABOVE *Late scrambles Gold Star footrest which clamped on to the frame tubes and was locked to prevent movement by a cross-tube*

TOP *Folding footrest as fitted to the 1971 B50MX*

1967, B40E, B44VE, B44VS up to 1968 and B44VR for 1967 only.

A new part with only one fixing bolt was fitted to the B44VS for 1969–70, while for 1971 the feature became part of the rear-brake anchor arm. One version was fitted to the B25T and another to the B50 trail, motocross and export street scramblers. It did not go on the home and general export SS models.

Footrests

These are nice sturdy items that can usually be repaired. If worn, they can be built up again and then reshaped with a file.

Footrests were often common on the B range and one pair served all the rigid and plunger road models. The pivoted-fork version used one type of right rest, but the 1954 left rest was altered for 1956 and 1958. The competition machines began with the standard rests but for the rigid 1954 models went to a new pair of revised shape. These were also fitted to the pivoted-fork model for 1956–57, but for 1954–55 this one fitted the road-model pair.

The Gold Star began with its own pair of rests but for 1950 changed the right one to the stock B-model type. In addition, rearsets were available for this model, and while the left rest remained the same part, it was mounted from a more rearward lug. The right one was moved to match and also made to fold up to allow the kickstarter to be used.

From 1953 both forward and rear rests were listed with the first of those listed for the 1954 road B range. The rearsets changed to a pair of the 1950 folding type but were modified from a tapered to a regular form for 1958, at the same time having washers welded to their outer ends.

In addition, there were special rests for the trials and scrambles models from 1954 onwards and each was a two-part forging. These clamped to the lower frame tube at a point where there was a cross-tube, which was also clamped on to prevent the rests from rotating or sliding. This was used from then onwards, with a folding version developed for the USA market from 1959.

Just one footrest rubber was used by the B range, with one more for the 1958-onwards Gold Star rearsets. The first went on all the B road models, the competition ones for 1946–53, and the pivoted-fork B32 and B34 for 1954–55. The others had bare rests which suited their purposes. The first rubber also went on all the Gold Stars with forward footrests and the rearsets up to 1952. The latter then went without until 1958 when another type was used to suit the modified rests.

The M range began with ex-wd serrated rests without rubbers, but from frame XM20-7390 in 1947 changed to using two of the right-side B-range rests and the B-range rubbers. The latter continued from then onwards, but the rests changed to the B-range pair for 1949. The AA models had their own special rests and rubbers to suit the legshield normally fitted.

The C range had two footrest rods so the footrests hung down on the right but ran back on the left, except on the C10L and C12. The rests were handed on most models and the left one was common to all machines and years. The right on the original rigid frame also went on the three-speed plunger and the equivalent C11G model.

The four-speed model had a different right rest and this was also used on the similar C11G and C12. The C10L differed in fitting the same left rest on the right as well. All models had footrest rubbers with the B range one being fitted up to 1953 and another from 1954 onwards.

The unit models all had rigid rests for the home market but a folding version was listed from early on. The early rigid pair went on the C15, B40 and SS models with a modification for 1965. Another was used on both sides of the competition models but became a pair for 1963, while there was a further pair for the C15 Pastoral.

The B44GP had its own special rests but the B40E used the original folding rest. This continued on to the B44VE, B44VS, USA B25 for 1969–70 and B44SS for 1969–70. The 247 cc for 1967–69 and road 441 cc for 1967–68 had one rest type fitted to both sides on all models. For 1970 a rigid pair went on to the home B25.

For the new range of 1971 there was one pair of rigid rests for road use and a second folding type for the trail and scrambles models. The 1973 B50MX had a completely new pair of folding, spring-loaded, serrated footrests.

The road footrest rubbers were at first the stock B-range type, but there were two others for the USA-style off-road models, one of which went on to the B44VE and B44VS. The 1967 road models had a new rubber which was changed for 1969 but returned for 1971. There was an alternative for the folding rests from 1969 onwards and this also changed for 1971 when the B44VE type was used again.

The Bantam had a footrest bar which ran through a lug on the bottom frame tube and carried various distance tubes, on to which went the centre stand, rear brake pedal and a pair of footrest rubbers. Although there were detail changes to one or two parts over the years, the design remained the same, as did the rubbers for all road D1 models in rigid or plunger frames, the D3 in these and pivoted-fork form, and the D5.

The rigid D1 and D3 competition models differed only in the rod and the rubbers which were as on the C range and thus changed for 1954. The plunger competition model differed from the rest in having separate raised footrests which were both the same as the part fitted to the left on all the C range. The rubbers were as for the rigid version, again with the 1954 change.

A new system was introduced for the D7 with each rest being bolted to a frame lug beneath the engine. The one part served both sides and went on all but one model from then onwards. The exception was the D7 Trail model which had a pair of raised rests. The rubbers for all models were the early B type at first, with a change in 1967 to the road four-stroke type, so the range matched.

Footrest rubbers are always best replaced on any restoration, as new ones will make a nice finishing touch.

Pillion rests

The rests were optional on rigid- and plunger-frame models but became a standard fitment on the pivoted-fork frame. The pivot should be just tight enough to hold the rest in position.

Most of the early models fitted the same part, which was the folding footrest as used on the 1950 Gold Star right side as a rearset. It went on the B, C, M plunger and Gold Star models up to 1954, and did not have a rubber fitted to it. From 1955 all these models fitted the 1958 Gold Star footrest and its rubber. The rigid M models had their own pair of more solid pillion rests with their own rubbers and these were used for all years.

The unit models began with the 1955-onwards B-range rest and rubber, and this went on all the road models and the C15 Pastoral until a change of rest for 1965. This also went on the B44VE for 1967, but the other models of that year had a revised rest. This had its outer ends turned out to act as a retainer for the rubber, and this part remained in use for all to the end. The rubber was altered for 1969 but went back to the earlier type for 1971.

The Bantam had the same rests and changes as the other models, with the early type changed in 1955 to the one with rubber. The latter continued in use from then onwards and the rest was altered for 1962 and 1967 to use the same parts as the rest of the range. The D10B and D14B both used the folding footrests from the 1967–70 unit models as their pillion rests plus the rubbers to go with them.

Pillion-rest supports

In most cases, the rests were fitted to a suitably positioned frame lug, but in some cases a mounting plate was used. In the case of the C10L, this was simply a channel section which ran vertically between two chainstay lugs to carry the rest. On the C12 there was a plate on each side to do this job and also, in one case, to support the silencer.

On the unit models a plate appeared on the C15 Pastoral to do this job and it bolted to the right frame by the rear fork pivot. This same part then went on the right side of the road models for 1967 to hold the silencer and the pillion footrest. On the left a similar plate became part of the rear fork pivot and held the left rest. It was also bolted to the frame to prevent it rotating.

ABOVE *Sports Bantam with D10S air cleaner but D14/4S exhaust-pipe shield. In fact, a 1968 D14 Sports*

LEFT *The 1970 Shooting Star B44SS with simpler side panels and shaped kneegrips*

The assembly of pivot and plate went on all models for 1967–70, but the right plate was changed for 1969 when the silencer bracket was altered. The B44VS had its own right plate for all years and this part was also fitted to the B25 for the USA during 1969–70.

The Bantam had channel supports for the rigid and plunger models similar to the C10L, but for the D7 used plates which also braced the rear fork pivot to the frame. The right plate was common to all road models but the left was altered for 1962. The D10B had its own pair of plates which also went on the D14/4B, but for the D175B the right was modified, although the left remained common to the earlier Bushman models.

Brake pedal

This is another part that is often damaged but is not too hard to repair. The pivot may need to be machined and bushed if worn, as may the rod end hole. Heat to straighten and build up worn surfaces, so they can be filed to shape.

The B range had their first change of pedal for 1949 when the plunger frame was introduced, and with it came two new pedals. From 1950 the rigid one went on the plunger frame as well, while there was a new pedal for the pivoted-fork models in 1954. This remained in use on the B32 and B34, but for 1956 the road machines changed hubs and brake pedals. In their new form the pedal was splined to a cross-shaft within the rear fork pivot, which had a lever at its right end to operate the brake cable. The pedal was revised in detail for 1958. The rigid B32 and B34 had their own pedal for 1954–55.

The Gold Star began with the plunger B-range pedal for 1949 and like them changed for 1950–52. In addition to the normal pedal, a rearset one was also listed which splined to a short cross-shaft with lever that pivoted in a frame lug. It was amended for 1952.

The pivoted-fork Gold Star fitted the same pedal as the 1954 B range for the trials and scrambles models of 1953 and the trials and road ones of 1954 onwards. The scrambles model was changed and had its own pedal for 1954, which was fitted from then onwards. For the Clubmans and road-racing machines there was a special rearset pedal which was common to all for 1953–63.

The rigid M models had their own pedal but the plunger ones fitted the 1950 B-range part. The AA version had a special pedal from as early as 1948. The C range had their pedal splined to a short shaft, as on the early rearset Gold Star, and this was used on all models up to 1955 except the C10L. This had its own pedal as did the C12 which joined it for 1956.

The unit models had a conventional pedal for the road models of 1959–66 plus a variation for the competition ones, which was revised for the new frame of 1963. The C15 Pastoral kept to the standard C15 part, but the B40E used the 1963 competition one. The B44GP had its own pedal while that of the B44VE also went on the 1967 B44VS. For that year the C25 had a pedal with two stop-pin holes in its vertical lever, and for 1968 it, and the other models, changed to a common and similar pedal. This was used until the new frame in 1971 brought a new pedal style.

The Bantam only had two main styles of brake pedal; the original 1949 one went on all the rigid and plunger road D1 and D3 models, the plunger competition D1 for 1950–53, the pivoted-fork D3 and the D5. A modified version was used on the rigid competition D1 and D3 models plus the 1954 plunger version. A new pedal, without the stop cut-out, appeared on the D7 in 1959 and remained in use up to 1971 on the road models. For the Bushman machines from 1967 onwards there was a modified version of this.

Rear brake rod

This needs to be straight with the thread and fork hole in good order.

The B range had one brake rod for the rigid models with another for the plunger ones. The rigid B32 and B34 of 1954–55 had their own rod, but the pivoted-fork version used the same part as the similar road models. The latter changed to a brake cable for 1956 and this was modified for 1958.

The Gold Star fitted the plunger B rod at first with an option listed for the rearset brake pedal. From 1953 all Gold Stars used the pivoted-fork B-range part, but

it was chrome-plated to suit the application.

The M range had its own rod for the rigid machines but the plunger ones used the plunger B-range part. The C range used the 1946 B-range rod on all models except the C10L. This had its own rod while the other was listed with a chrome-plated finish for the C11 de luxe.

The unit models also began with the 1946 B-range rod which also went on the B44VE for 1966. It had a new part for 1967 and this also went on the B44VS that year. The B44GP had its own rod and a new one was introduced for the road models in 1967, this also going on to the B44VS in 1968. Standards dropped in 1971 when a rod with a bent end replaced the older type with a proper yoke, and this part stayed in use from then onwards.

The Bantam had a second type of rod introduced for the plunger models in 1950, but by 1951 these were fitting the stock rigid-frame part which stayed in use on them up to 1963. The pivoted-fork D3 had a different arrangement with two brake rods. The first short one connected the pedal to a small lever and the second longer one ran back from there to the brake. The lever was positioned so that the front end of the rear rod coincided with the rear fork pivot in order that rear wheel movement did not react on the pedal.

ABOVE *Adjusting the rear brake of a 1961 B40, which had many parts in common with the C15*

RIGHT *The AA on patrol with a 1958 M21 with all the usual fitments needed to assist road users*

The D3 design went on the D5, but for the D7 the pedal was moved so that only one brake rod was needed. This then went on all models from 1959 to 1971, except the D10B which had its own rod.

Rear carrier

For some models this part was also a mudguard stay, but for most it simply bolted to the rear mudguard or its supports.

The road B range had one for each frame style, although the part was seldom seen on a pivoted-fork model, since to fit it the standard dualseat had to be changed for a saddle. However, the option remained to the end. Each carrier had a frame with a single cross-bar and four short supports. On the plunger model the

UYO
97

front pair were vertical but all others leaned in a little.

The M range used the plunger B part for its own plunger models but had its own carrier for the rigid ones. On this the front legs were again vertical. The C range had one carrier with lean-in legs for all models up to 1954, but fitted the rigid B one on the 1955 C11G plunger and the C12. The C10L had its own part with two cross-bars.

The unit models had a carrier which mounted behind the dualseat and this was listed for the C15, B40 and SS models. It had three bars running fore and aft within the main frame with vertical supports from two of these. A further small carrier was listed to go with panniers on the B40 and SS90.

The Bantam had a greater variety of rear carriers than the others and on the first model the part was the vertical stay for the rear mudguard to which it was bolted. This carrier had no cross-bar and went on all rigid models, while a second type with one cross-bar was used on the de luxe and Colonial rigid machines. A third version with two cross-bars went on the plunger models and was also used by the C10L.

A carrier with four short legs was introduced for the pivoted-fork D3 and a similar one went on the D5. Nothing was listed for the D7 at first and then two appeared, one to go with panniers. The other had three fore-and-aft bars and both continued to be listed for the D10, D14/4 and D175.

There were also two pressed-steel carriers, each with a single cross-bar. The first had this running along the machine and went on the GPO D7 and the D10B, while the second had it across and was used by the D14B and D175B.

Legshields, crash bars, mirror and panniers

All these items were options and none are essential to a restoration, but the fitment of one from the correct period can set off a machine very well.

The legshields in various forms were listed for B and M models from 1949 onwards, the unit road models for 1959–66, and all C and D models. Crash bars were available by themselves or to go with the legshields for

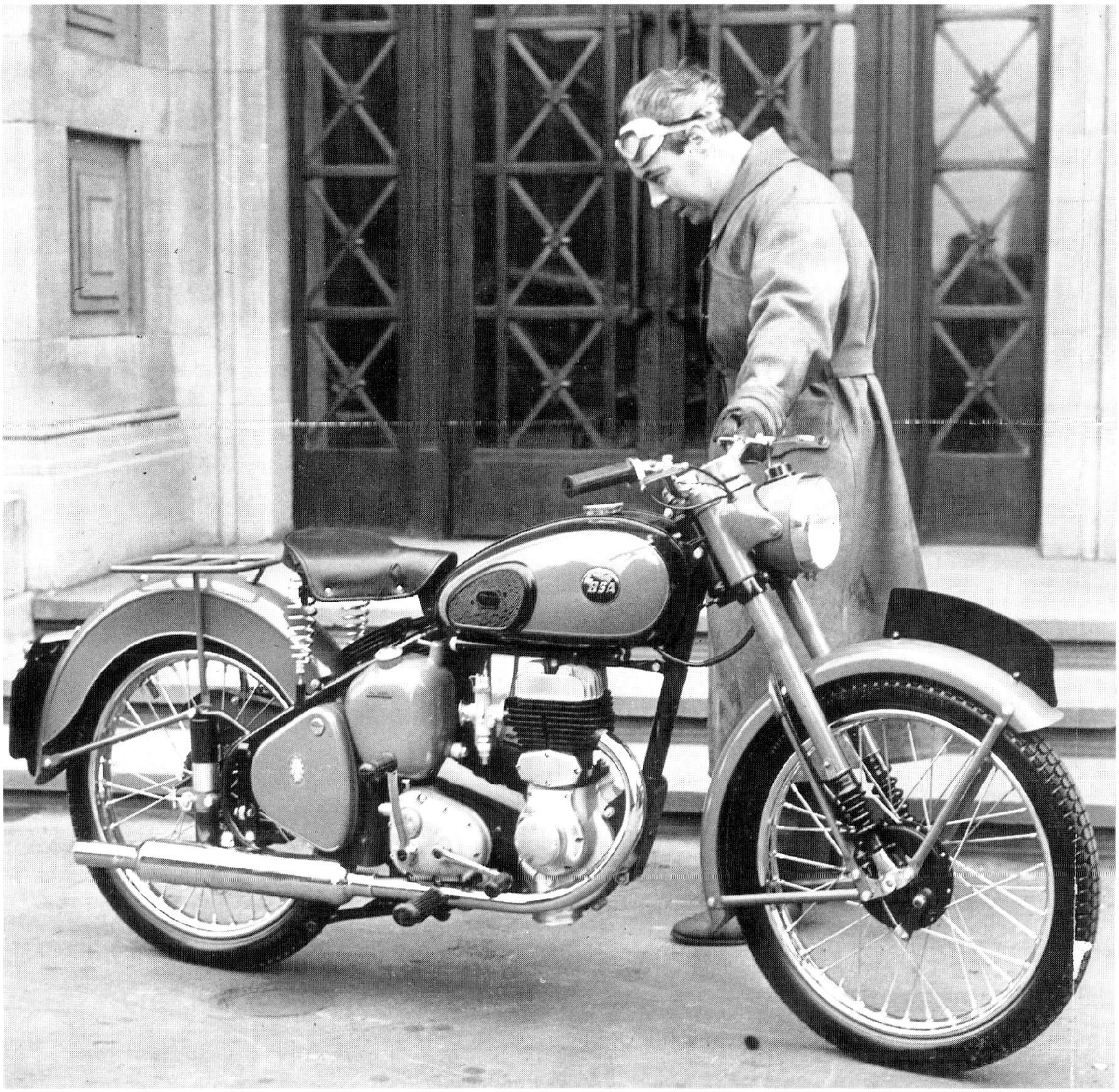

ABOVE *Bill Nicholson outside the BSA front door with a 1954 C10L*

LEFT *Mirrors fitted to a 1966 D10 Supreme which has twin switches in the headlamp shell and ball-end levers*

the same years on the M, unit and D models, but not the B or C until 1954.

Panniers were listed for the B range from 1956, the D from 1962 and the unit models for 1965–67 only. The mirror was fitted to the D10 and D14/4 Supreme models only.

11 Wheels and brakes

This is an area where a good few operations have to follow one another in a definite sequence. Due to this an early start is advised to avoid a hold-up later on when it may not be convenient. Once the machine is without wheels it becomes very hard to move about unless reduced to parts.

Spoking pattern and rim offset

Before doing anything else, get your notepad out and measure the rim offset and draw the spoke pattern. This first is a vital piece of data and the second will give you real problems if you have to work it out from scratch.

The rim offset is taken by placing a straight edge across the mouth of the brake drum and measuring from it to the edge of the rim. Just to make sure, also measure from a firm point at the other end of the hub and take the rim width. Take more than one measurement in case there is a variation, and if really stuck find another machine and measure that.

For the spoking pattern, first check to see if the rim is handed to suit an offset hub. Next note where the valve hole is, how the spoke to one side of it runs, whether its head points out from the wheel or into its centre, and any feature of the hub which will enable you to locate that spoke into the same hole.

Relating the rim, spoke lay and hub for that first spoke will give the key to the wheel build. From it the others will fall into a pattern. Working round the rim the spokes will alternate from one side of the hub to the other. Every third spoke will be laid the opposite way to the first and its head will face the reverse way unless straight spokes are fitted. Every fifth will echo the first in angle and lay. Note the spoke cross-pattern.

Wheel dismantling

If you want to repaint the hub you will have to dismantle the wheel. Note that there can be up to four types of spoke in each wheel, with a difference in length and head angle as well as diameter. Keep the spokes in batches and note which goes where on your spoke diagram. Note that for some wheels certain spokes cannot come away until others have been removed, and the rebuild will have to be done in the reverse order.

Hub, drum and rear sprocket

The bearings, spindle, drum and sprocket teeth are the things most likely to need attention. Replacement is the easiest way to repair most damage, but with the drum it may be necessary to skim it to remove scores or any belling or oval out-of-truth. Check the rivets of the crinkle hub as these are known to work loose.

Front-hub types

The whole range began with similar offset hubs in 1946, and that of the B31 had a 7 in. diameter brake that was used in all versions up to 1955. The same hub was also used by the B32 and B34 for all years and the B33 up to 1952. This last then changed to a cast-iron hub with an 8 in. brake which was modified for 1955 but for the Gold Star only.

The B31 and B33 changed to a full-width, light-alloy hub with 7 in. brake for 1956–57 and again for 1958. This last hub was of composite construction with a cast-iron drum supported by two conical pressings riveted to it and welded to the central bearing housing. An embellishing disc went on one side to match the brake plate.

The Gold Star had the B31 hub for 1949 and this remained in use for the trials models up to 1955 and scrambles ones up to 1953. For the latter it was modified for 1954 and continued to be fitted in this form to the end. The other models all had an 8 in. brake for 1950 and this was the type fitted to the B33 in 1953. It was amended for 1955 when it gained three cooling fins round the drum and 12 holes in the drum wall, six of $\frac{3}{4}$ in. diameter and six more of $1\frac{1}{2}$ in. These latter were then blanked off with light steel discs pressed into place, which could be removed for Clubmans or road-racing use. In 1956 it was joined by the full-width hub with 190 mm brake, both of these continuing to be listed to the end.

The M range began with its own version of the hub with 7 in. brake to suit the girder forks but for 1949 changed to the B31 hub. This was used up to 1955, and thus the end of the M20, after which the hub with 8 in.

ABOVE *A fine study of D. F. Thompson practising for the 350 cc Clubmans in 1956 at Union Mills*

RIGHT *The full-width front brake design adopted in 1958 by the B range and later used in a smaller size for the C15*

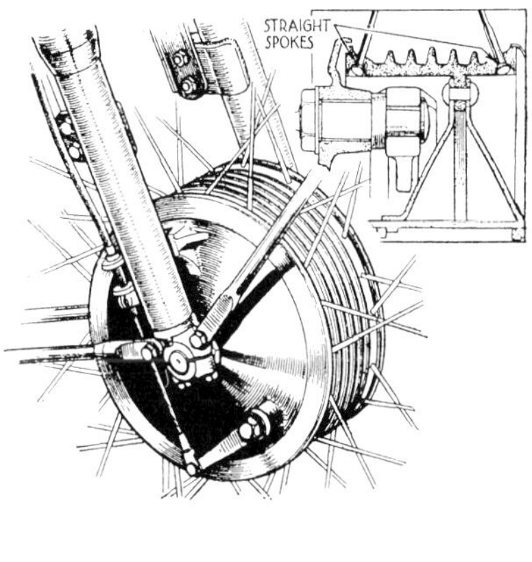

brake, as used by the 1955 B33, was fitted. This hub was listed for the AA M21, and the 1950 8 in. type was in the parts list for all models up to 1955, although there was no mention of it as an option in the brochures.

The C range had a $5\frac{1}{2}$ in. diameter brake in its offset hub and, as with the M range, there was one for the girder forks and another for the telescopics. This was used for all up to 1953, the C11G for 1954, and the C10L for 1956–57. A similar size hub went on this last model for 1954–55, but the 1955 C11G had a hub with 7 in. brake similar to that of the B31. The C12 had the same size brake but in a full-width hub.

The unit models began with a full-width hub with straight spokes and a 6 in. brake which went on the C15, SS80, C15 Sportsman and the competition models. These last changed to an offset hub with 7 in. brake for 1962 and used that from the 1955 C11G. This same hub also went in the B40E, B44VE and the 1967 C25, B44VR and B44VS.

The B40 fitted a full-width hub with 7 in. brake which also went on the SS90, while the B44GP had its own part. For 1968 the road models went back to full-width hubs with 7 in. brakes for the B25 and 8 in. for the B44SS which also had wider brake shoes. For 1969–70 both shared a twin-leading-shoe 7 in. brake in a new full-width hub. The B44VS continued with its offset hub for 1968 but with an 8 in. brake.

The full-width hubs all had embellishing discs with one for the C15 hub and another for the B40, this being the one used by the last of the B range. New discs came in for the B25 and B44SS in 1968, but for 1969–70 they shared a new common part.

For 1971 two new conical hubs were introduced with either a 6 in. or a twin-leading-shoe 8 in. brake. The smaller went on the B25T, B25SS export, B50T and B50MX, while the 8 in. one was fitted to the B50SS and home-market B25SS.

The Bantam had an offset hub with 5 in. brake and this one part was used by all road D1 and D3 models. The competition D1 began with the same hub but from frame YD14758 changed to one with taper-roller bearings, although the drum size stayed as it was. For 1954 it changed again to a $5\frac{1}{2}$ in. brake which went on both D1 and D3 competition machines.

The D5 had a new hub with a 5 in. brake of greater width, but the D7 went to the $5\frac{1}{2}$ in. diameter, though in a new hub as the number of spokes went up to 40. This hub served all the D7 models, the D7 Pastoral,

RIGHT *The Starfire B25 of 1968, which was still with the single-leading-shoe front brake*

BELOW *Conical front hub adopted in two sizes for the 1971 range, this being the larger 8 in. version with twin-leading-shoes*

D10, D10B and D14/4. The D7 Trail used the D1 hub to match its forks.

The D10S had a full-width hub but the same size brake, and a revised version was used for the D14/4S and D14/4B. The D175 and D175B went back to an offset hub with one new part common to both models.

Rear-hub types

All B and M models had hubs with 7 in. brakes and most were offset, the exception being the B road models of 1956–60. The B range began with a one-piece hub which incorporated the sprocket teeth, and this type went on all rigid-frame road models with an amendment for 1949. The competiton models used the same hubs up to 1953.

The plunger frame appeared in 1949 and was fitted with the quickly detachable (qd) rear wheel with the famous crinkle hub and one-piece brake drum and sprocket. This went on all plunger-frame machines, including the Gold Star. For this model in 1953, and the B range in 1954, a revised version appeared with new spindle and other details to suit the pivoted-fork application. This was used by Gold Stars up to 1954, the road B models up to 1955, and the competition ones to their end. It was also used by the rigid B32 and B34 of 1954–55.

There was a new light-alloy, full-width hub for the road B models in 1956 to match the front which had a separate sprocket held to it by four special nuts. In this way the qd facility was retained. It was changed for 1958 to another full-width hub which matched the new front one.

The Gold Star had its rear hub altered for 1955 to match the front. It was also finned but, unlike the front, had the fins machined in a light-alloy ring bonded on to the drum. A revised hub was fitted for 1958 which had no cooling holes, catered for the wider rear chain, and had the fins machined in the drum itself.

The M range began with a qd hub which had the one-piece drum and sprocket held to the hub by three bolts and the drive transmitted by three studs. This was changed in 1949 for a one-piece design similar to the B range but in both these cases the brake-shoe width was greater for the M range. The plunger models all used the B plunger rear hub with the same size of brake shoe.

All the plunger models had the same brake drum which went with the crinkle hub, and all the pivoted-fork models used this form of construction. The 1946–48 M type was alone in using bolts to hold the drum to the hub. There were two drums listed for the 1953 Gold Star, one with 42 teeth and the other with 46 for scrambles use. The first was used by the B road range for 1954–55 and the competition one for 1954–57. The Gold Star kept the 46-tooth one for

scrambles up to 1957, while the other was altered for 1955 with the cooling fins and holes. From 1958 a common drum with 46 wider teeth was fitted.

The C range with girder forks fitted a hub with riveted-on sprocket, but with the change to telescopics came a hub with a bolted-on sprocket. This was used for all rigid frames and a similar one served all the plunger ones other than the C10L. This had a smaller (5 in.) brake and used a Bantam hub which was modified for 1956. All the other C models had a $5\frac{1}{2}$ in. brake, including the C12 which had a full-width hub and its sprocket riveted in place.

The unit models began with a full-width hub similar to the front with straight spokes and a 6 in. brake, and for the road models a combined drum and sprocket was bolted to it. Two were listed for the C15 with 45 or 46 teeth, and there was a third for the B40. The competition models used a similar hub, but in their case the sprocket was bolted to the drum and so could be replaced by itself or changed in size. This type was modified for 1963 and was also used on the B40E and 1966 B44VE. The SS80 used the C15 hub and the SS90 the B40 one. The B44GP had its own hub and also its own end plate with all the other full-width hubs using the same C15 part.

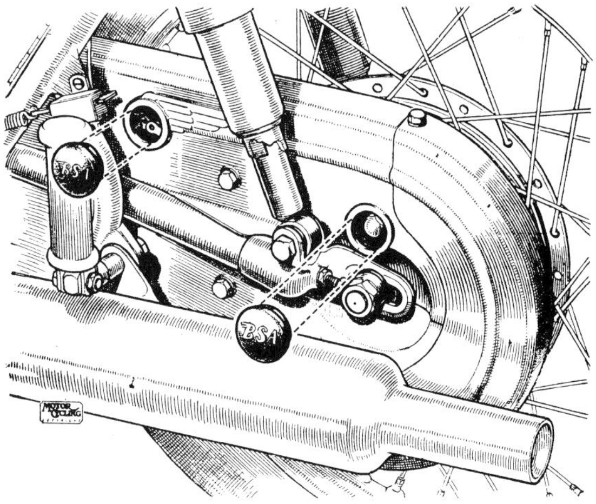

ABOVE *The fully-enclosed rear chaincase introduced for 1956 as an option for the range and here shown as on a twin*

TOP *The full-width rear hub of the 1961 B40 which matched the front and drove the speedometer*

For 1967 all models changed to the old-style qd wheel with crinkle hub and separate drum and sprocket. The hub was common to all, as was the brake drum, but the sprockets differed with 47, 49 or 52 teeth. For 1971 there was a change to a conical-hub design with bolt-on sprocket for all models, with a small variation for the B50MX. Sprockets with 47 or 52 teeth were used.

The Bantam began with a hub built up from steel pressings with a 5 in. brake and a 47-tooth sprocket riveted to it. For competition use it had one with 58 teeth and both these were modified to have a larger-diameter spindle for plunger use. All racing Bantams used the latter as the first was known to break under duress.

The plunger hub was used by the pivoted-fork D3 and continued on the D1 to the end. The D5 had the same hub but only 46 teeth on its sprocket. The D7 had a new cast-iron hub taken from the Triumph Tiger Cub, with bolted-on sprocket. It had a $5\frac{1}{2}$ in. brake and was used by the D7, D10, D10B, D14/4 and D14/4B models with 46-, 47- or 58-tooth sprockets. The D7 Pastoral had the 58 teeth but the D7 Trail was shown as using a special 80-tooth sprocket.

The D10S and D14/4S both had full-width hubs but kept to the brake size and bolted-on 47-tooth sprocket. For 1969 there were two new hubs similar to the D7 type, with 47 or 58 teeth to suit the road and Bushman models.

Wheel bearings

Most models used ball races but there were some with taper rollers and others with cup and cone. The crinkle hubs had two races in the hub itself and a third in the chainwheel and drum assembly.

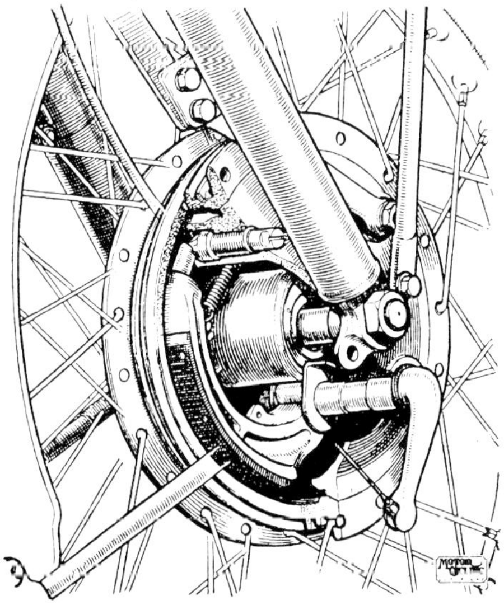

RIGHT *The full-width alloy hub fitted to the B range for 1956 with wedge brake adjuster*

BELOW *The 1956 C12 with switch panel on the right of the machine*

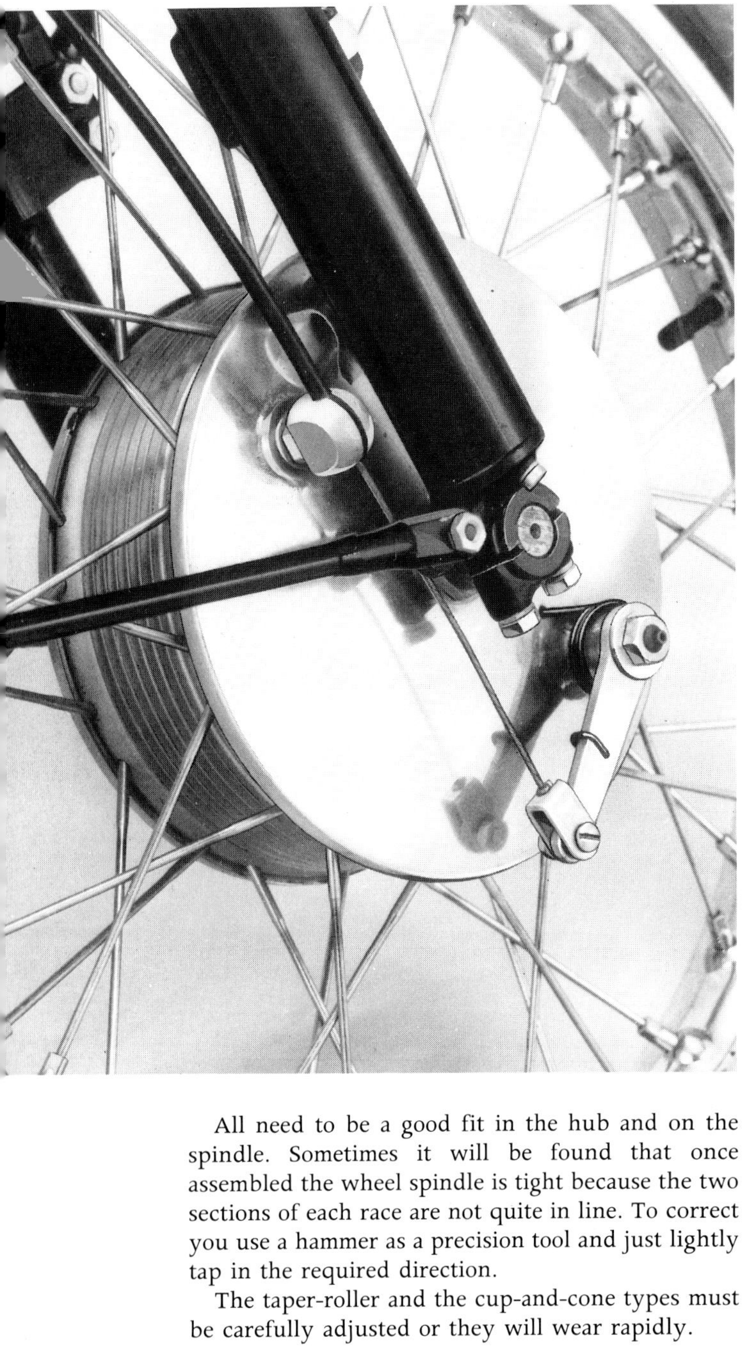

All need to be a good fit in the hub and on the spindle. Sometimes it will be found that once assembled the wheel spindle is tight because the two sections of each race are not quite in line. To correct you use a hammer as a precision tool and just lightly tap in the required direction.

The taper-roller and the cup-and-cone types must be carefully adjusted or they will wear rapidly.

Brakes

Most are single-leading-shoe, but regardless of type they require the same check over. If you fit new brake shoes or reline, first check that the brake drum is the standard diameter and has not been skimmed at some time.

Should you go to an expert, he will want the wheel and backplate so he can check the drum and correct this first of all. Only then will he reline the brakes with oversize liners and turn them to match the drum.

Front-brake types

The B range began with a simple single-leading-shoe brake of 7 in. diameter which went into the B31 up to 1955, B33 up to 1952, and B32 and B34 up to 1957. For the last two models the backplate was chrome-plated and the same brake went into the 1949 Gold Star and continued to be used for all trials and scrambles versions of that model.

An 8 in. brake with polished light-alloy backplate was introduced for the Gold Star in 1950. It was retained by an anchor strap and was used by the road, Clubmans and racing versions as well as the B33 for 1953–55. From 1956 the Gold Star had the option of the 190 mm full-width brake and this had its own alloy backplate and anchor.

For 1956–57 the B31 and B33 shared a common 7 in. brake and alloy backplate and anchor strap. This had a wedge adjuster at the shoe pivot end and the shoes themselves were special to suit the design. The cam lever had an internal pull-off spring linked to it. There was a further change for 1958–60, and for these final years the backplate was a casting restrained by a lug and painted black with a polished rim to match the hub.

The M range had a 7 in. brake with one backplate for the girder forks and the B31 type for the telescopics. From 1956 the 8 in. brake with backplate anchor was fitted. The C range began with a $5\frac{1}{2}$ in. brake and again had one backplate for the girder forks and another for the telescopics which was used up to 1954 with a modification from 1949. The C10L kept to the same brake size but used a Bantam-style brake for its first two years, reverting to the 1949 type for 1956–57. The C11G changed to a 7 in. brake for 1955, in the style of the B31, and this continued on the C12.

The unit models continued the single-leading-shoe type with a 6 in. brake and a cast backplate with

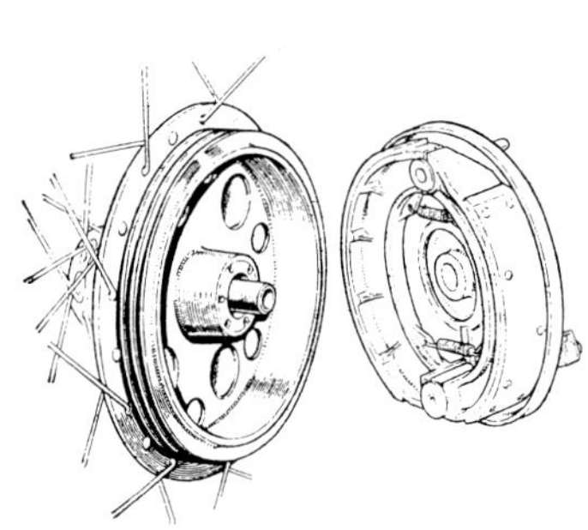

ABOVE *The 1955 Gold Star front hub with bonded-on fins and cooling holes, some of which carried blanking discs for road use*

ABOVE LEFT *The full-width hub with single-leading-shoe brake of the 1968 B25 Starfire*

RIGHT *The fork leg with four studs and 8 in. twin-leading-shoe brake of the 1971 B50SS. The cam levers work better if lengthened*

LEFT *The fully-floating front brake shoes introduced for the unit singles for 1962*

BELOW LEFT *The 6 in. conical hub and single-leading-shoe brake fitted to the 1971 B50MX*

BELOW RIGHT *Rear wheel of the C15 as built for 1959–61 to a typical BSA design*

polished rim and black centre. This was used by the C15, SS80 and competition models, and these last changed to a 7 in. brake for 1962 with a chrome-plated backplate. The B40 and SS90 were in the same style as the C15 but with a 7 in. brake, and for 1962 this was altered to a floating brake-shoe design so it became self-centring.

There was a new backplate in 1966 for the B44VE and this also went on the other models for 1967. This did not last for long and for 1968 there were new brakes and backplates for all, with different parts for each model. The road models kept to their 7 in. brakes, but the B44VS went up to 8 in. with the 1950 Gold Star backplate and anchor strap.

It stayed with this, but the road models went over to the BSA and Triumph group's twin-leading-shoe 7 in. brake with bell-crank cable lever for 1969–70. For 1971 there were new backplates to go with the new conical hubs and the 6 in. one was a normal single-leading-shoe type with an anchor strap for the backplate. The 8 in. brake had an air scoop built into the backplate along with exit vents, and was fitted with Lockheed shoes. These were twin-leading and the two levers were moved by a single control cable, with the outer pushing on one and the inner pulling the other. They were too short to be fully effective and it is worth adding an inch to their length.

Early Bantams had the pressed-steel backplate restrained by a riveted attachment that straddled the fork leg and provided a cable-stop anchor point. This system was used by all D1, D3 and D5 models with either 5 in. or $5\frac{1}{2}$ in. brakes. For the D7, D10 and D14 models, except the D14/4S and D14/4B, the design was changed to a stud held to a lug on the fork leg by a nut. The exceptions had a short anchor riveted to the backplate which located over a lug cast on the fork leg, while the D7 Trail model used the D1 fork and backplate. The D14/4B part went on to both D175 models.

Rear-brake types

All were single-leading-shoe and of straightforward design and construction. All B and M models had 7 in. rear brakes and the first B rigid machines had a backplate with a stud for an anchor strap. The competition plates were chrome-plated to match the front ones.

The plunger frames had a backplate with a slot which engaged with a lug on the left suspension slider, and the same brake went into the Gold Star. The backplate was modified for the pivoted-fork frame and returned to an anchor strap with the same part going on to all Gold Stars from 1953, the road B range for 1954–55 and the competition models in that frame type.

The road B models had an alloy backplate with wedge adjuster for 1956–57 to match the front, and a further change for 1958 onwards for the same reason. These continued to use some form of anchor strap to restrain them. The rigid competition models of 1954–55 had their own backplate to suit their new frame.

The M range in the rigid frame had a backplate with a further plate riveted to it with a single hole for the long anchor strap which ran beneath the chainstay. It was amended for 1949 and was joined by one with a slot for the plunger frame in 1951, this being similar to the B-range type.

The C range had different backplates for its girder-fork model, and its 1946-onwards and 1949-onwards models in rigid-frame form, but all had a $5\frac{1}{2}$ in. brake and were located by a lug in a slot. The plunger models had a different type with a slotted pressing attached to the plate to locate on a frame lug. Similar designs were used by the C12 and the C10L, but the latter had a smaller brake of 5 in. diameter.

The unit models began with a 6 in. brake and a backplate with anchor strap. This was used by all models up to 1966 other than the B44GP which had its

own part. All, including this competition model, changed to a 7 in. brake for 1967 and continued with this up to 1970. For 1971 there was a new backplate with leading and trailing shoes to suit the conical hub, but the size stayed the same, as did the fitment of an anchor strap.

The Bantam began with a 5 in. brake and a backplate with an open-ended location slot in it. This and a variation served the rigid and plunger models, and for the pivoted-fork D3 the location part was extended. For the D5 this part had a joggle formed in it and fitted wider brake shoes. The D7 had a $5\frac{1}{2}$ in. brake and a backplate with a long anchor arm with a slot in its forward end for a bolt. This part was used up to 1968 and revised in detail only for the D175.

Spokes and nipples

These need to be straight and with good threads. It is false economy to just replace some if more than one or two are past redemption; better to respoke completely. Check carefully the length, gauge and head angle you require before shopping, and inspect what you buy to make sure you do get what you want.

Wheel rims

All BSA singles had steel rims of the WM section form. Diameters used were 17, 18, 19, 20 and 21 in., and width numbers 1, 2 and 3. Most had 40 spoke holes, but the D1, D3, D5, D7 Trail front, C10L rear and C10L front for 1954–55 had 36.

Light-alloy rims were listed as an option for the Gold Star for all years. All are listed in an appendix along with the tyres fitted to each model and some modern equivalents.

Wheel rebuilding

This is an area that many people fight shy of, but with care and patience good results can be obtained. Work in the correct order of assembly and make sure the rim is the right way round.

Fit the first spoke and start its nipple so it cannot shift and scratch the rim. Then continue this process until you have all in place. It will be obvious if you have made a mistake.

You can now try to true the wheel. Set it vertical so you can spin the rim and place a marker just clear of this. Try it for truth and adjust the spokes to get the radial position correct first. Then go on to deal with the sideways error. At the end you can still let an expert carry out the final tweak if you wish.

Tyres, tubes and rim tapes

You have a choice here between something in the old style which was current when your machine was new or a modern low-profile type. The choice will depend to some extent on the use to which you put the machine and your riding style and habits.

Do fit a new rim tape after you have checked the spoke ends and filed down any protruding from the nipples, while a new inner tube really is mandatory. The tyre must suit the rim section, and the front and rear must be compatible. The faster the machine, the more important this is.

If you fit modern tyres, check the clearance for the fatter section. Fit with care and use your slim, smooth, polished tyre levers. Don't forget the security bolts but do forget the tyre pressure table in the old manual, as the figures have no relevance to modern tyres.

12 Cables, controls and instruments

There are few things that look worse on a restored motorcycle than cables drooping in loops and obviously far too long or with their adjusters unscrewed fully and hanging on the last thread. There is nothing more dangerous than cables that are tight and which could be pulled by the forks as they move.

The control cables should be the proper length, run on the right route, be neatly clipped out of harm's way, and in correct adjustment. They should also be of the correct gauge for the job or the throttle will feel heavy and the front brake full of sponge.

Soldering

This is the technique used to attach the nipple to the wire, and the secret of success is having clean parts. Solder will not adhere to surfaces that are dirty, tarnished or greasy, but is no problem on a clean surface.

The tools you need are a soldering iron, solder and flux. The first can be electric, heated over a gas flame or heated by butane. The solder you use comes in a stick. Do not use flux-cored electrician's solder as it is not up to the job. The flux can be a paste in a tin or a liquid. My own preference is for the former as it is convenient to be able to open it and dip the iron and cable in.

To cut an inner to length you use sharp, heavy-duty cutters, but before cutting you must tin the cable. Once this is done, you can cut the wire and solder a nipple on the end. To do this successfully you have to splay the wire ends out to sit in the countersink in the nipple and then apply the solder. Once it has cooled give it a good tug, as it is better for it to fly off in the workshop than on the road. File to shape and make sure it fits its lever and can turn if necessary.

Cable making

There are two ends to a cable, so there are two soldering jobs to do on each. On the machine there will be at least three, and as many as six, cables, so it takes some time to make a full set from scratch.

Once complete, the cables need to be lubricated. Funnels round the end are a common method, but I prefer a pressure device which is messy but works well.

Controls

The handlebars to which these are fitted varied to some extent, and the B, M and C ranges all changed to a common bend for 1948. Prior to then, the C had one bar for the girder forks and one slotted at its right end for a straight-pull twistgrip.

The common bar went on the road B and all M models to their end, the competition ones up to 1955, the 1949–50 Gold Star, and the trials and scrambles Gold Stars from 1951 onwards. The B competition models had a change of bend for 1956, and the Gold Star Clubmans models listed their own for 1951–52 and 1953–57. In addition, this model had clip-on bars listed from 1954 onwards and Western bars from 1954, with a change for 1958.

There was a special bend for the AA M21, and on the C range the common 1948 bend was only fitted for two years. For 1950 one with welded-on clutch and brake-lever blocks was used, and for 1951 this was modified to fit the horn button in the top of the brake block. This bar went on nearly all the range from then onwards, except for the 1956–57 C10L which had another bend.

The unit models began with bars with welded-on blocks but also had the option of Western bars to which the controls were clamped. The B40 had its own bend at first but went over to the C15 one in time, while the SS models had different bends with clamped-on controls.

The B40E used the C15T bend, while the C15S changed to a braced bend for 1962 which was also fitted to the B44GP and 1966 B44VE. This last changed to the 1959 C15 competition bar for 1967, and this bend was fitted to the B44VR, B44SS and B44VS for 1967–70. In addition, it was listed as the Western bar for the B25, but this model also had a standard bend for these years. New, braced bars were listed for 1971, with one for road and another for off-road models.

The Bantam models began with bars with welded-on clutch and brake blocks in two types. The original was used up to 1957 and went on models with direct

ABOVE *The 1945 B31 showing the tank-mounted speedometer and collection of levers and buttons on the handlebars*

LEFT *The handlebars of this girder-fork 1946 C11 were much cleaner with no advance or air levers and a hidden throttle cable*

RIGHT *By 1953 the C10 had the horn button far out of reach, but the other controls fell to hand as they said*

lighting. The other had an additional hole in the brake block and went on models with Lucas electrics or battery lighting. It was the bend fitted to the C range for 1951–58.

The D5 used the bend from the C10L of 1956–57, while the D7 had a new bend plus a Western-bar option which was altered for 1962. At the same time, a third bend was listed which later went on the C25 in 1967 and the GPO D7 of that year. This last continued in use on the Bantam and went on the D10, D14/4 and D175 in turn.

There were two bends listed for the Sportsman and Sports versions of the D10S, with the latter going on to the D14/4S as well. The D10B fitted the 1959 competition C15 bend, as also used by the 1967–70 441 cc models, and this went on the D14/4B and D175B models.

The controls also varied over the years and a careful study of the parts list needs to be made to ensure the correct item. Some machines had two controls mounted together while the 1971-onwards models used combined lever housings and electric switches. Each control needs to be checked over and care will be rewarded by smooth operation and a pleasant feel.

Instruments

The ammeter has been mentioned already, which leaves the speedometer and rev-counter. Two types of mechanism were used in the speedometers and rev-counters fitted by BSA, with the chronometric type being superseded by the magnetic in 1964.

The first was generally held to be the more reliable in the long term but is complex. If you are an instrument fitter you can tackle one, but a mechanic should best stop at the mileage recorder. The later magnetic type is easier to work on but only once you get the bezel off. For repair, the rev-counter is simply a speedometer mechanism minus the distance recorder.

Depending on the model and year, the speedometer was driven from the front wheel, rear wheel or gearbox, and the rev-counter had two drive schemes, one from the magneto gear nut and the other, used on the unit models from 1969, from the crankshaft oil-pump skew gear.

Speedometer types

The first point on any speedometer is the direction of rotation of the needle which must match the cable. Next is the maximum scale reading, then whether in miles or kilometres and, most important, the revolutions-per-mile figure.

This is normally written on the scale just under the part number, and for many models a figure around 1600–1700 can be expected if it is calibrated in miles,

ABOVE *Classic Gold Star control layout with clip-ons, ball-ended levers and twin instruments*

RIGHT *The 1961 B40 with valve lifter and air lever to clutter the bars, but rather neat combined horn and dip-switch*

reducing to about 1000 for the metric measurement. This is also the cable speed in rpm at 60 mph since at that speed travelling one mile takes one minute.

The final points to consider in speedometer selection are the presence of total and possibly trip distance recorders, the method of returning the trip recorder to zero, and the mounting of the instrument.

The B range all began with the speedometer mounted in the tank where it was held from below by a clamp plate. It was driven from the gearbox and this was true for all years, but for 1948 the instrument was moved on to a bracket attached to the top fork yoke, this bracket becoming a marque standard part.

For 1953 the road B model adopted a headlamp cowl and the speedometer was set in this and held by a clip. This arrangement continued for the nacelle adopted from 1958, but the competition models kept to the 1948 bracket in all cases.

The Gold Star used the speedometer bracket from the B range where only that instrument was fitted. From 1954 there was a second bracket which was used when a rev-counter was fitted by itself, and this angled the instrument to make it easier to read when in a road-racing crouch.

From 1954, and where both instruments were fitted, two of the 1948 brackets were used and these were mounted, in turn, on a single plate. This stretched across the top of the forks and was held by the two top fork-leg nuts. It was simplified for 1956.

The M range began with the speedometer mounted on the top of the girder forks, offset to one side, and driven from the front wheel. During 1947 a second bracket was listed to position the instrument centrally and only this was used for 1948.

The range went to telescopic forks for 1949 and changed to the B-type bracket with gearbox drive for the instrument. For 1953 it copied the B range in turning to a cowl-mounted speedometer, but in 1958 went back to its 1949 arrangement.

The C range also began with the speedometer driven from the front wheel, but had it mounted centrally on the girder forks on the 1948 M bracket. With the change to telescopics the speedometer was moved into the petrol tank where it was held by the same clamp plate as the B range and driven from the rear wheel.

When a four-speed gearbox was fitted, as available from 1951, the drive was taken from this, and for 1953 the speedometer was moved on to the top of the forks on the 1948-marque general bracket. The C11G and C12 continued this arrangement with rear wheel or gearbox drive, depending on the number of gears, and

they both used the same mounting bracket.

The C10L had a D-shaped speedometer which bolted directly to the top fork yoke and it was rear-wheel-driven at first, but gearbox-driven from 1956.

The unit road models continued the B-range nacelle style with the speedometer set in it but driven from the rear wheel. The competition ones used the 1948-marque bracket or, on the C15T, a variation to suit a D-shaped speedometer, but all changed for 1964 to a round magnetic type. The B40E had its instrument mounted in a moulded cup on the fork top.

For 1967 all models had the speedometer in a moulded cup and driven from the rear wheel. The road models had a drive box with 2:1 ratio and the cup fitted to a round mounting plate attached to the fork

ABOVE *D10 Sports of 1967 with flyscreen to mask speedo and chequered decor on tank top*

ABOVE RIGHT *The controls of the 1965 SS90, which were much as those of the other unit singles of the period*

RIGHT *American-style bars and controls as for the unit singles in 1968*

BSA

The controls, headlamp and speedometer of the 1971 B50SS fitted with turn indicators

top yoke. The B44VS had a 1.25:1 ratio box and its own style of mounting plate. For 1968 all three models changed to a new common plate.

A rev-counter became available as an option for 1969 and a new moulded cup was used for either instrument. Two mounting plates were listed, one the 1968 type for use with the speedometer alone, and the other a wider one to take both instruments. The B44VS was the same, except for the ratio of the rear-wheel-drive box, and stayed as it was for 1970 when the road models had a change of speedometer head.

This new head, which was of 80 mm diameter, was listed for the B25T and B50SS models for 1971, the B50T having the same part with a reversible trip, and the B25SS having a 60 mm diameter head in place of the 80 mm one. To match, the rev-counter was listed in both diameters for the B25. Both instruments went in new rubber cups mounted in individual plates held by the fork top nuts, and again there were two sizes for the B25 models. The rear-wheel-drive box had a 21:10 ratio for the T models and 2:1 for the others.

The Bantam in D1, D3 and D5 forms had a D-shaped speedometer mounted on the top fork yoke and driven from the rear wheel. For the D7 the head was round and went in the nacelle with a change to the magnetic type in 1964. The D10 and D14/4 used the same arrangement, but the D10S, D14/4S, D175 and D175B mounted the speedometer into the top of the headlamp shell. The D10B and D14/4B had the same lamp mounting but a different rear-wheel-drive box.

When hunting for a replacement speedometer, most of the requirements are easy to determine and to check, except for the important revs-per-mile needed to match the machine. For front- or rear-wheel drive, the factors are the tyre revs-per-mile and the ratio between wheel and cable. If from the gearbox, the tyre, final-drive gearing, sleeve-gear ratio and layshaft skew-gear pair all play their part. Use the data to calculate the optimum cable speed and this is the figure to seek on any replacement speedometer.

Rev-counter types

Both chronometric and magnetic types were fitted, with the first being driven by a right-angle gearbox bolted to the outside of the timing cover and driven by the timed breather bush. This arrangement was officially available for the Gold Star from 1954 onwards, but was to appear on the earliest models when built to Clubmans specification, and in this case the drive was from the magneto gear nut which was extended and slotted to suit.

The second type was driven from a shaft meshed with the crankshaft oil-pump skew gear and was listed as an option from 1969 onwards. For 1969–70 it matched the speedometer and for 1971 was available in two diameters for the B25 models.

13 Petrol tank

The tank is truly the crowning glory of any motorcycle, so its finish is important if you want the machine to look nice, but not to the extent that it does not match the rest of the machine. If the general paintwork is reasonable but a touch shabby, a super tank job will stand out and show up against it. It may be better to leave the tank to blend in with the rest, or you may find yourself renovating all the paintwork you meant to leave alone for a season or two.

All tanks need to be fully checked over, repaired and finished as required. This work must include the filler cap and the removal of any rust on the inside. A handful of sharp stones or nuts and bolts dropped in and shaken around can help a good deal. They should be followed by a wash and treatment with a rust inhibitor. Finish off with Petseal which is a two-pack sealer.

For any panel-beating work you may need a specialist, and for cracks welding will be necessary. Removing the petrol and its fumes is a problem and there are many horror stories about this. Methods vary and range from washing out, steam cleaning, feeding the car exhaust into it or lengthy techniques with special gear.

One of the above should suit, and many follow this by standing well back and pointing the welding torch into the tank. If there is a bang, you know the tank will need to be cleaned out better next time.

Tank types

The B range began with a tank which had a large hole right through it for the speedometer and its drive, but changed for 1948 to one without that feature. For 1953 the shape was revised a little, but up to that point the one tank, with various finishes, was used by all models. In addition, there was an optional two-gallon tank listed for the competition models for 1948 and 1950.

This option became one of the tanks listed for the Gold Star in 1949, along with a three-gallon one, and both differed from the standard part in having a breather tube fixed to the tank top just ahead of the filler cap. At first this was a simple tube on to which a pipe was pushed, but it quickly became a tapped hole for a banjo connection and short curved pipe.

There was a further tank for the rigid and plunger road B models of 1954–55, with a recess in the side for a round plastic badge. At the same time a tank was introduced for the pivoted-fork models, and this had a centre bolt fixing which the company was to use for many years.

The standard tank held four gallons, but there was also an option available that took two and which was used by the pivoted-fork competition models for 1954–55. In their rigid form these had a two-gallon light-alloy tank with centre bolt fixing, and this was fitted as standard to the 1956–57 models which went into a pivoted-fork frame. The road models continued with the two-gallon option to the end, but the standard four-gallon was modified for 1958 with slight alterations to its shape and a change of petrol tap.

The Gold Star had the two tanks listed for 1949, but for 1950–51 the smaller was fitted for off-road use and the larger for the rest. The year 1952 saw the appearance of a tank brace under the front end and a four-gallon tank for road or racing use as an alternative to the three-gallon one. It was finished with a transfer as usual, although some export models would seem to have been fitted with a round plastic badge late in the year. Off-road, there was the choice of two or three gallons.

The pivoted-fork-frame model of 1953 had two tanks listed with two- and four-gallon capacities, each in two forms, one for petrol and the other to be fitted when alcohol fuel was used. The tanks had the round plastic badges and the centre bolt fixing. Both were amended for 1954 and the larger again for 1958, while the light-alloy two-gallon tank used by the competition B models was listed as an option from 1956. From 1956 a five-gallon light-alloy tank was also available as an option for racing or Clubmans use.

In contrast, the M range had few tank changes. It began with a hinged filler cap, but for 1948 was altered to a tank with the quarter-turn cap used by other ranges. This tank was common to all three models and had one further change, for 1954, when round plastic badges were fitted. For the AA there were alternative tanks, but these differed only in finish and a lack of badge holes at first. The change to the quarter-turn cap came for 1949 but was not in favour for long, as it was soon replaced by the hinged type, though with this to one side of the aperture.

The C range had a conventional tank on the models with girder forks, but with telescopics came one with the speedometer set in it. It was not until 1953 that this feature moved to the forks and the tank was changed. There were also special tanks for the C10 machines sold to the GPO, with one for those with girder forks and a second for those with telescopics up to 1948.

There were new tanks for 1954 with one for the C10L with a small, round plastic badge and another for the C11G with a larger badge. The latter tank went on to the C12 and both were held by a front cross-bolt and separate rear bolts. Beading was fitted to the tank upper-surface weld joints from 1955 and each length was held by the tank bolts.

The unit models began with one tank for the road C15 and a second two-gallon one for the competition models, both with pear-shaped badges and a centre bolt fixing. The road model had beading strips on its two weld seams and the tank was revised twice over the years. Its second change came for 1964 when its capacity was increased to three gallons and the kneegrips went on supports held in place by screws.

The SS80 and B40 both began with similar tanks with round badges, but the SS80 for 1963 and the B40 for 1964 both changed to the 1964 C15 tank with pear-shaped badges. The SS90 fitted this tank to all years.

The competition C15 models changed to a light-alloy tank with a transfer for 1962, but prior to then one was listed as an option. The Pastoral model had its own tank which was similar to that of the early competition ones, while the B40E had an alloy tank with centre bolt fixing and transfers. The B44GP had its own special tank with just enough capacity for the events it ran in.

The use of an alloy tank continued on the B44VE and B44VS for 1966–70, with one tank serving both models and all years. In 1967 the road model went to small fibreglass tanks of a sculptured shape which continued to have pear-shaped badges and a centre

ABOVE *A pair of 1950 D1 Bantams at a test in Australia where one managed no less than 213 miles to the gallon*

LEFT *Eddie Dow in the 1953 Senior Clubmans in which he crashed while lying second. He won in 1955 and became famous for his range of goodies for Gold Stars*

BSA
500 O.H.V.
GOLD STAR

bolt fixing. Four were listed for 1967 for the C25, B25, B44VR and B44R.

The tank numbers changed for 1968 with just two listed for the B25 and B44SS, both really as before but fitted with light-alloy badges in place of the plastic ones. They were enlarged for 1969 to $3\frac{1}{4}$ gallons and their material changed to steel, although the shape remained much as it was. One was listed for both models and continued in use for 1970. A smaller alternative was available for the B25 in the USA and was modified for 1970. Beading was used from 1969 onwards.

New tanks and beading appeared for 1971 to suit the new frame, but the centre bolt fixing was retained in principle. The tanks of the trail and MX models were in light alloy but the others were in steel with two- or three-gallon capacities available for road use. The trail models had two-gallon tanks and the scrambles model a one-gallon tank.

The D1 and D3 Bantams all had similar tanks, with two weld seams either side of a central strip and the filler cap on the left. The original was quickly joined by a de luxe type which had a chrome-plated sheet clipped over the centre strip. From 1950 a revised tank with such a sheet was fitted to all models up to 1953. For 1954 they returned to the original tank but with chrome-plated beads over the tops of the two weld seams, and this tank remained in use for the D1 and D3 from then onwards.

The D5 had a new, and slightly larger, tank with a single seam and the filler on the right. A similar tank went on the D7 for 1959–60 and this had a plated bead on the central seam. The same tank was fitted to the D7 Pastoral and a modified version to the D7 Trail for 1963 only.

For 1961 the D7 tank was altered to take pear-shaped badges and had no centre bead. It was used up to 1965 but during that year there was a change to a new tank shape with knee recesses and round badges. This tank form had two weld seams with plated beads to conceal them and a central filler cap. It was used for the remaining D7 models.

This last D7 tank was amended for 1967 by changing the rear fixing holes to slots, and in this form went on the D10, D14 and D175 models, apart from the Bushman versions. These last used a similar tank without the badge recesses, and the same part also went on the 1967 GPO D7.

Filler cap

All B and C road models had the same quarter-turn bayonet cap, which was also used by all M models from 1948 onwards. Prior to then, the M range had a hinged cap with wing-nut fastener and another of the same type was specified by the AA. This last was used by all Gold Star machines except where they had an alloy tank, which usually had a snap-action cap. This was also used by the competition B range from 1954 onwards—prior to then they used the standard B-range cap.

This cap went on all the unit models at first, but for 1962 the competition ones changed to alloy tanks with snap-action caps. This type also went on the B40E and B44E, while the 1967 range had a revised form which was used up to 1970, except on the USA version of the B25 for that year. That model had a quarter-turn cap and this type was used by all the 1971 models except

ABOVE LEFT *The 499 cc Gold Star late in 1952 with round tank badges*

LEFT *The central tank fixing adopted for the pivoted-fork-frame models from 1953 and used for most from then onwards. Here seen on a 1954 B31*

RIGHT *The tank used for the 1958 D5 Bantam with central seam and more capacity than that of the D3*

the B50MX, which kept to a snap-action one.

The Bantam filler cap incorporated an oil measure and this was altered to suit changes in the petroil ratio. As the part could always be cut short, the owner is advised to measure the actual capacity to avoid errors. All caps were of the quarter-turn type and the first change was made for 1954, this cap remaining in use on the D1 to its end.

There was a new cap for the D5 in 1958 which was also used by most years of the D7. When the tank with the knee recesses appeared in 1965, it had a new cap with a short oil measure. This was to allow it to clear the tank tunnel in its new, central position in the tank top. This new cap was used on the D10 and D14 models as well, but there was a new one without any oil measure for the D175 in 1969.

Tank badges

These are delicate and should be handled with care. Check them for damage and fit to the tank, and that their fixing screws fit their holes and won't bottom in them when assembled.

The road B and M range had the same badges for each year and began with a small, rectangular, winged BSA one held by two small screws. Early in 1952 these were replaced by larger badges with a circular section at the front and a flowing tail that ran back to the kneegrip. For 1953 this badge became a two-part item,

ABOVE *The C15S scrambler of late 1962 with alloy tank, but still fitted with a protruding exhaust pipe*

ABOVE RIGHT *Sculptured tank of the 1967 C25 Barracuda*

RIGHT *The 1966 C15 Sportsman which replaced the SS80 and retained the standard tank*

BSA

BSA

LEFT *The tank with die-cast badges adopted for 1968 and seen on a B44SS which carried several transfers and had a snap-action cap*

RIGHT *The Victor Special B44VS of 1970 with its alloy tank and off-road features*

but was replaced for 1954 by a round plastic badge with the piled-arms motif. This was used by both ranges from then onwards.

The competition B models began with the small rectangular badge, but from 1954 used a star-form transfer with '350' or '500' to suit the machine size. These models were also fitted with tanks with a 'BSA' transfer and, for export, with the round plastic badge as on the road models.

The Gold Star began with transfers, as used by the late B competition models, but changed to a round plastic badge on some models late in 1952, and for all for 1953. This was the same size as that used on the road B range, but with a star motif, and was used by all from then onwards except, where applicable, when transfers were employed. For 1953 alone there was a small, round plastic badge for the trials and scrambles version and this just had the letters 'BSA' on it.

The C range used the same rectangular badge as the B and M at first and continued to share with these models the changes for 1952 and 1953. The C10L fitted a small, round plastic badge which was amended for 1955, while the C11G and C12 both used the larger round badge from the B and M ranges.

The C15 had pear-shaped plastic badges for all years which went on the competition models for 1959–61, the SS80 from 1963, the B40 from 1964, and the SS90 as well. The earlier SS80 and B40 machines had a round plastic badge and from 1962 the competition C15 models had a transfer which also went on the B40E.

The B44GP had transfers on both the top and sides of the tank, and the latter were similar to the 1946 badges with a rectangular form of the flying BSA, but enlarged. The side transfers were used on the 1967 B44VE along with another top transfer, but for 1966 this model had side transfers only and these were in a star form.

Three pairs of plastic badges were listed for 1967 in the pear shape, with one each for the C25, B25 and B44VR. The last two had a tank top transfer as well, each in a form to suit the model. The B44VS used the top and side transfers from the B44VE and kept to these for 1968.

The road models changed to die-cast light-alloy badges for 1968 but kept to the pear shape. They were revised for 1969–70 and joined by another pair for 1969 only for the USA version of the B25. The B44VS had new top and side transfers for 1969 but the next year went back to the older side type alone, without the top one.

With the changes for 1971 came new transfers for the B25 and B50, with another for the B50MX. The home-market B50 was listed with a badge and the B50MX had a change of part for 1973.

The Bantam had transfers for many models but used the C15 pear-shaped plastic badges on the D7 for 1961–65. During 1965 a round badge began to be fitted which was the type that the B40 and SS80 had used. It remained for the road models from then onwards, but the Bushman machines had a transfer which was introduced for 1967.

Kneegrips

These were a feature of machines from the 1920s and gradually became more common as speeds rose and the need for something to clamp on to became more

pressing. As tanks fattened in the 1930s, they served also to protect the finish.

The B, M and C ranges all shared one pair of grips up to 1953 and a second from 1954 to the end of their production runs. The Gold Star fitted grips up to 1953 on the Clubmans and road models but not the alloy tanks, and the same applied to the competition B models.

The road unit models fitted kneegrips from 1959–65 in general and up to 1967 in the case of the C15 and C15 Sportsman. Grips next appeared on the 1969–70 road models and were shaped to match the knee recesses these machines had in their tank sides. No kneegrips were used on the 1971–73 unit models.

No Bantam models of any year had kneegrips fitted.

Taps

These may have a cork seal or taper-cock fitting and must be checked for leaks and petrol flow. Some came complete with their petrol pipe and this must not be damaged in any way.

The B range began with a tap which had a push/pull bar and a lever to turn the reserve on. For 1954 the road models changed to a type with cork plunger which pulled out for 'on' and turned for 'reserve', while the competition ones fitted a taper-cock tap. This last was fitted to all Gold Star models for all years.

The M range began with a simple push/pull tap which continued for machines for the AA. The rest changed to the early B-range tap for 1948, and for 1954 continued to mirror the road B range, so using the cork-plunger tap. The C range began with the same tap as the M models and changed for 1953 to a type similar to the 1954 B type. For 1954 this was amended to a push-on pipe and from 1955 was listed complete with the pipe in two forms, one for the C10L and the other for the ohv models.

The C15 began with a tap much like that of the C12, and this was used by all the unit range up to late 1961. The road models of 1962 changed to a tap with cork plunger, horizontal body and exit thread which was thus in line with the plunger. The competition models had a similar tap with extended body but changed to the road-model type by 1965.

This 1962 C15 tap was also fitted to the B40E, B44VE and B44VS for all years. The B44GP had the taper-cock tap as used by the Gold Star and this went on the road models as well for 1967–68. For 1969–70 they had a new style of this form of lever tap and a further new pair was used for the road models of 1971–72. One of these alone served the B50MX.

The Bantam began with the push/pull tap as used by the C and M models and copied the C range for 1953 and 1954, with a simple pull tap with threaded connection for the first year and push-on pipe from then onwards. This then applied to the D1 models, and the above to the D3 series.

The D5 fitted the same tap and pipe as the C12 and this went on most D7 models. For late 1965 to 1966 it was replaced by a new form which no longer included the pipe. The road D10 models had a simple pull tap complete with pipe which had an end fitting to suit the float-chamber connection. A similar assembly was listed for the GPO D7 and another for the D10B. This last was used by all D14 and D175 models.

14 Seating

The seating on BSA singles consisted of a saddle and optional pillion pad at first, with this arrangement being standard on most rigid and plunger models. A dualseat first appeared as an option in 1952 and as standard the next year. In time, all models were fitted with a dualseat, but the saddle remained as an option for some into the 1960s. A handrail was offered for some models.

Saddle

A saddle is an assembly and can thus be renovated just as any other. In some cases, the underfelt may have gone altogether and must be replaced.

The most usual wear point is the hole in the frame for the saddle nose bolt. Seldom greased, it may need repair and this one job will ensure a good, stable seat.

Saddle types

The B range had one saddle for all rigid-frame road models and the competition ones up to 1953. These last then had another for 1954–55 and a third for 1956–57 when they used a pivoted-fork frame. There was a different saddle for the plunger-frame models and one more listed as an option for the road machines in a pivoted-fork frame.

The Gold Star fitted the plunger B saddle and for 1950–51 also had a special Clubmans saddle listed for racing use. From 1953 onwards the pivoted-fork B saddle was an option for the Gold Star and would have been fitted as standard on the trials model.

The M range used the plunger B saddle from the start until it was amended for 1955. The same part went on rigid- and plunger-frame models. For the C range there was a single saddle for the C10 and C11, and then one each for the C10L and C11G. One further was listed as an option for the C12.

There were no saddles on the unit models, although some had short or single seats. The Bantam had a saddle on all D1 and rigid and plunger D3 models. There was one for 1949 which was used by the earliest competition models but there was another for the next year. This went on rigid, plunger, standard, competition, D1 or D3 models. For the competition versions it was raised by a pair of stays common to all years. A further saddle was available as an option for the pivoted-fork D3.

Pillion seat

This may be built up much as a saddle or can be a simple moulded pad, which is what BSA went for. Often a proprietary seat was fitted instead of the BSA one and can be treated as the saddle if of built-up construction. The moulded type will need replacement if water has penetrated the inside or if the cover is torn.

One pillion pad was listed for the B, C and M ranges for 1946–49, with a second for 1950 to the end of the model runs, this being 1955 for the B and M, but 1957 for the C. One further pad was listed in 1949 only for the plunger B models and the Gold Star. Once the dualseat became the standard fitment, the pillion was no longer listed to go with the then-optional saddle.

A further racing pad was listed for the early Gold Stars for use when they were in Clubmans trim, and there was one for 1949 and another for 1950–51. No pillion was listed for the Bantam models fitted with a saddle.

Dualseat types

The part comprises a steel pan which can rust, a moulded interior which can rot, and a cover which may tear or split. The inside is the main problem as the other parts can usually be repaired.

One dualseat was listed as an option for the B, M and Gold Star in 1952, and remained as such for the rigid and plunger B range to 1954, all the M range, but only up to 1953 for the Gold Star, by which time it was a standard fit.

For 1953 only, the Gold Star had a second dualseat listed for the Clubmans and road-racing models, while

ABOVE RIGHT *Vic Willoughby and Harry Louis sampling the Gold Star on which D. T. Powell had won the 1953 Junior Clubmans*

RIGHT *The 1948 B31/B33 road model with its saddle, which was the normal wear at that time*

39
NEL 284

BSA

ABOVE *John Draper riding in the 1949 Bemrose trial on a B32 with rigid frame*

ABOVE RIGHT *A 1963 D7 on the move*

RIGHT *The 1964 C15T Trials Cat built for the USA market and based on the trials model with added lights*

325 KBM

BSA
BANTAM
4
SPORTS
SEP 67

BSA
STARFIRE
250

the B range had another type as the 1955 option.

The pivoted-fork machines had different seats with one for all Gold Stars of 1954–63, one for the road B range for 1954–60, and one as an option for the competition B range for 1954–57. There was also a Feridax racing seat listed as an option for the Gold Star from 1956 or even earlier.

The C range listed the 1952 dualseat as an option for 1953–54 but changed to its own types for 1955 onwards. One each was listed for the C10L, rigid C11G, plunger C11G and C12, this being the only model to fit the dualseat as standard. All the others only had it as an option.

The unit road models all had a dualseat but they did change on occasion. Also the colour of the top or the side was varied to give different styling effects. There was a seat change for 1962 which applied to the C15, SS80 and B40, with this new seat also going on to the SS90. The competition models had a short or single seat which was changed for 1962, and an option of a dualseat for some years. The single seat could likewise be fitted to the road models.

The C15 Sportsman had a seat with a rear hump which was fitted to all the 1967 models. Prior to then the B40E had used the 1962 competition-model single seat, and this also went on the B44VE for 1966. The B44GP had its own seat. The humped seat continued in use for 1968 and was modified for 1969–70.

The new frame of 1971 meant new seats and these discarded the rear hump. Three were listed in all, with one for the B50MX, one for the home market, and the third for the SS and T models.

The Bantam listed the 1952 dualseat as its option for 1953–54 on the D1 and D3, but had a revised one for the rigid and plunger models from then onwards, though always as an option to the standard saddle. The dualseat was first fitted as standard to the pivoted-fork D3 in 1956, with a change for the D5 in 1958 and the D7 in 1959.

The D7 seat was revised for 1962 and again during 1965 to match the change in tank shape and badge. In addition, there was an optional short seat listed which was fitted as standard to the machines for the GPO.

LEFT *The 1967 D10 Sports Bantam with humped seat and separate headlamp shell*

BELOW LEFT *Starfire B25 from 1970, the last year before the major restyling*

BELOW *One year older, this is the 1969 B25 which was not exactly the same set of parts*

Bray Hill in 1952 with H. Hunter on a 348 cc Gold Star

This same seat also went on the D10 Pastoral, but the D10 Bushman used the same seat as the D10 Silver. The D10 Supreme had another type which went on the D14/4 the next year, while the D10S had a seat with a rear hump which was also fitted to the D14/4S for 1968. The D14/4B used the D14/4 seat. A new seat with Unified thread studs was used from 1969 onwards.

Handrail

This is an optional, tubular part with chrome-plated finish, bolted to the machine to lay round the rear of the seat. It was only listed for pivoted-fork models and was first available in 1954.

One was for the road B range and another for the Gold Star and 1954–55 competition B range. Both were similar, as a loop to match the seat rear with the ends ran forward to terminate as fixing lugs. Two more lugs were welded on the underside further back to provide four-bolt fixing.

Both types changed for 1958 to continue for the road B range and the Clubmans Gold Star, with the first continuing on the C15 for 1959–61. The C12 which preceded it had its own part and these were all in the original style.

The C15 had a new part for 1962 which differed in that the loop ends were now straight and no longer turned down at the front. The same part went on the B40, but the two SS models had another with the rear lugs welded to the top of the main loop. A new shape in the style of the C15 type was introduced for the new models of 1967 and was used by all of them from then to 1970.

A handrail similar to that of the B range was listed as a Bantam option for the pivoted-fork D3 of 1956 and also went on the D5. A revised shape went on the D7 from 1962, the D10, D14/4 and D175, but not the Sports or Bushman models.

15 Assembly

This is often the most satisfying part of a restoration or rebuild, culminating in that heady moment when you swing on the kickstarter and the engine bursts into life.

It is also a time for making haste slowly, as rushing matters can easily damage something you have spent time, money and effort on. Slow and sure is best, with plenty of reference to your notes so that you work in the right sequence. In the build-up to the final assembly, you should have checked the fit of bolts to holes as you went along, and all this work will now pay off in a straightforward fitment of the parts without snags.

The greatest problem is protecting the finish you have lavished so much care on, so cover, pad and mask where necessary and work slowly to avoid damage. Have a think about the order in which you intend to assemble the parts and arrange the items of each stage so they are together. It is good practice to do this as it is a further check that you have everything, and that each item has been reworked as required. It will also ensure that you are not caught off balance with something partly together and you short of a vital bolt but with no free hand to locate it. If this does happen, go back and dismantle rather than chance damage occurring while your back is turned.

Start the assembly with the frame and fit the rear fork, the head race cups and main stand. You can now put the skeleton on your machine bench and prop the front end up. Remember that most of the pre-unit frames used the engine as part of their structure and can collapse without it. The front and rear frame halves may need to be left a little slack at their main fixings to allow for the final alignment on fitting the engine, so until this is done further props may be needed. Check with care to avoid damage. If you have any doubt at all about the stability of the assembly, clamp the stand down.

Now fit the fork crowns and the forks themselves. Add the front wheel. If you fit the mudguard at this stage, it will definitely need protection, so it is best omitted for the time being. The rear guard may well have to be fitted early on, and it may be necessary to add the wiring harness at this stage or at least fit the rear section if this is threaded through frame and mudguard tubes and guides. If the machine is balanced on its centre stand, either fit the rear wheel or anchor the rear fork end to your bench.

Once you have a stable frame that is not going to rock about, fit the engine and gearbox while you have the most room in which to move. Don't forget to check that you have not left out anything that must be fitted first. Sort out all engine fixings, plates and spacers in advance and place to hand. Spare rods to locate on may well be needed.

You are more likely to damage something while fitting the engine than at any other time, so first protect everything you can. Don't try to lift the weight into place unless you have at least two helpers to take the load while you slide the fixings in. With only two people, something is sure to be scratched.

Blocks underneath are one way to take the strain, but better still is a means of lifting the engine from above. In view of the cost of a rebuild, it is well worth the price of a car engine hoist, which will be able to carry the load easily. Arrange the lifting sling so it is secure and holds the engine in the correct plane for its fixings to line up. If you have to tilt the engine to achieve this, you are more likely to have an accident and crushed fingers. It is better to adjust the sling so the engine just drops into place.

Then fit all fixings and tighten. As with any assembly work, it is best to complete a sequence fully and not leave the final tightening for later in case you forget. This is not always possible, however, in which case leave the nut undone and give it a marker to remind you. On pre-unit models add the gearbox before clamping the rear engine plates tight, and then go round all the frame bolts to make sure you have remembered to tighten them all.

Continue the assembly as you wish and as the design dictates, but leave the tank and seat as late as possible. Check wheel alignment once both are in place for good, and adjust the chain tension correctly.

Don't try to start the engine until all is ready and keep the battery on the shelf until near the end. Before connecting it, use your meter to check that the wiring is not shorting to earth somewhere, and make sure you

BSA
BSA
TRIUMPH

HOTEL
NORTH BAR
Aladdin
PINK
MICHELIN
POWER
FOE 588D

ABOVE *Swedish racing driver Yuge Rosqvist on a 1962 C15T fitted with lights*

LEFT *Two 1966 C15 Sportsman models stopped by some old-fashioned petrol pumps during the National Rally of that year*

PREVIOUS PAGE *Line of 1971 BSA models with one Triumph among them and at least two twins, all with common forks and other items*

connect it the right way round. It should be fine, but it is better to be sure than chance a spark at this stage. Disconnect the battery while you fill the oil tank and check the gearbox and primary-chain levels.

If the machine is still up on the bench, you will need help to get it down safely. Take care that you don't drop it at this stage, and give yourself plenty of room to work in. Once down, you can prepare to start up by opening the workshop doors to let the exhaust fumes out.

The petrol tank will have been best left off while you get the machine down to ground level, so now fit it, connect it up and pour a small amount of fuel in. Half a gallon, or two litres, is fine to start with. Turn on and check for leaks. Connect the battery and start the engine. Keep the engine speed low and check that oil is returning to the oil tank. Where the rocker supply comes from the return line, hold your finger on the pipe in the tank to force some into the rocker box as soon as possible. Check that the generator is charging.

Next put the machine on its stand and run it up through the gears to make sure all is well in that area. Have a good look round the pipe connections to make sure there are no leaks and do your ignition-timing strobe check if this is called for.

ABOVE *A 1953 D1 used by the police to check reaction time, seen here at the Schoolboys Exhibition*

LEFT *A BSA twin and a 1954 D1 passing the royal castle Amalienborg in Copenhagen in Denmark*

Try the machine gently in your drive to check the operation of the clutch and brakes. If you have done your paperwork, are insured and still taxed after all this time, you can now get your helmet and go for a ride. If not, you will have to put it away again for the time being.

For most owners in the UK that first ride of the restored machine is the prosaic one to the local dealer for its official test. Rather irksome after all your work, but look on it as a top mechanic may regard scrutineering at a race meeting—a check that nothing has been overlooked. It may help to go to a dealer who knows something about older machines and who will believe that, for instance, taper-roller-bearing wheels should have some side-play and that a 7 in. sls drum brake may lack the bite of a double disc with hydraulic operation.

A chat when booking the appointment is well worth the effort and can smooth the way to your pass.

When the machine is legal, enjoy a ride. After a few miles check the oil level and give the machine a look over to see if anything has worked loose. Get some more petrol before you run short and roll off some more miles.

Then take the machine back to the workshop. Check items such as chains, brakes and cables which may have settled down a touch. Go and do your carburation check.

Enjoy your BSA single.

16 Paperwork

In this modern age, ownership and use of any road vehicle involves pieces of paper, and some of these are documents issued by the authorities. This chapter concerns these in general and those specific to the United Kingdom in particular. Details for other countries will vary and must be checked as necessary.

The first piece of paper was mentioned in the opening chapter and is the receipt for the machine, or the bundle of receipts for parts if that was the way you obtained your model. It is very desirable that they contain the engine and frame numbers so you have proof of ownership of what you actually do have. Make sure they agree with what is stamped on the machine and beware of anything that looks altered.

The other documents you will need in the UK are a registration form, a test certificate and an insurance certificate. The first is currently known as a V5, the second as a VT20 and the last is obtained privately. With them you can then tax the machine for road use.

You should consider insurance long before you get to the road as the parts and the machine as a whole need to be covered against fire or theft as soon as you get them. Try to obtain an agreed value for the machine and make sure you adjust this in line with the market. The insurance will need to be extended to cover road risks before you ride in public, and it is worth shopping round for a company which specializes in older machines and caters for them. Otherwise, your relatively sedate B33 will be lumped in with modern 500 cc models of far higher performance and spares prices.

The V5 and VT20 are linked to an extent and also involve the number plate of your machine. Where a machine has been in use on a fairly continuous basis, its original buff or green log book will have been replaced by a V5 which will record the correct engine and frame numbers along with the original registration number as displayed on the number plate.

As nothing is perfect, there are even discrepancies when the documentation is all in order. For example, a BSA is bought from a dealer; it suffers an engine problem and the complete unit is changed. This is not recorded at the time, the machine is eventually withdrawn from use and finally sold off. The new owner rebuilds it and on coming to register it compares paper numbers with actual markings to find they don't tally—as they have not done for many years.

More difficult is a machine that has not been used for a period and has no V5. For the authorities to issue a form with a registration number appropriate to the machine's year, they need further proof, and the onus is on the owner to provide it. Only in cases of rare or historic machines, well-known past owners or some similar reason is there much hope of retaining the original number, but it is always worth trying with an application.

As part of this exercise to keep the original number, it helps to be able to link it to the machine, and for this old MoT certificates or old licence discs are acceptable. Where not available, or to back them up, a letter from a recognized authority confirming the date of the quoted engine and frame numbers, and stating whether or not they were likely to have begun life together, should be obtained. Acceptable sources are the owners club, Vintage MCC, service-page writers of the specialist magazines (I am one of these) or the holders of the original records of the firm.

It is not normally possible to trace the original registration number from scratch as much of the official record no longer exists. The procedure needed would be to look at the company's records to match engine and frame numbers. If this is in order, the records will then give the name of the dealer to whom the machine was sent. He in turn would then need to be sought out and his records could give the registration number. In practice, few dealers from those days are still in business, and fewer still will have kept such records for the 20 or 30 years likely to be involved.

So you have to call on your Local Vehicle Licensing Office and take all your documents with you. There you fill up a form, as you would expect to do at any government office. This will trigger off a series of events which will culminate with the issue of a V5 if all goes well.

The first thing likely to happen is a visit from the authorities or their agents to inspect your machine.

Earls Court in November 1952, with a Bill Nicholson replica drawing the crowds

YPD 937
LKJ882
L

ABOVE *A 1956 training-scheme school with a strong line-up of BSA models plus a Velocette and an Ariel sidecar. Three Bantams and a C12 show how the firm looked after the learner market*

LEFT *Fred Wallis on his Gold Star at Alton Towers in 1956*

This is done to check that the numbers all agree with those quoted on the form and that the machine is what you say it is and does exist.

This visit is not always carried out, but if it does take place the machine is best assembled to some degree. It is often desirable to register the machine long before the restoration is complete or there is any need to tax it for the road. At the very least, it allows you to get the number plate finished.

After the visit, and if all is in order, the vehicle documents can be issued. If the evidence is good, the original registration number, or mark as they call it, may, in rare cases, be retained and entered on the main computer at Swansea. Normally this is not so, but where there is evidence as to the age of the machine, the authorities will try to issue it an appropriate number for its period. Should there be no way of linking the machine to any period, which may happen with a hybrid, a number with a letter Q prefix will be issued.

Following this, the machine will have to go for its official test as mentioned in the previous chapter. Book the test, make sure you have insured the machine for road use, pass the test (after all this, I would be most disappointed if you did otherwise), and you can then tax the machine for the road.

Keep all the paperwork in case there are any queries at any time and to go with the machine should you ever come to sell it.

Now you have to decide what to restore next year.

A 1955 M21 which, by then, was fading from the scene as riders turned to more powerful and stylish models

APPENDICES

1 Engine and frame numbers

Up to the end of 1968 BSA used one style of numbering for both engines and frames. This comprised a year letter or two, followed by the model type and then the number itself. Engines and frames seldom matched and at times even the prefixes differed. Thus to determine the year of either, the whole of the number, including all prefixes and suffixes, is needed. The letter S was often used in the frame prefix to indicate rear suspension, while a C would be for competition, B for battery lighting and A for alloy engine. The 1969 and later data is given at the end of the sections dealing with each model range in turn.

Range	Year	Model	Engine	Rigid frame	Spring frame
D1	1949	D1 engine	UYD-101		
		D1	YD-101	YD1-101	
	1950	D1 engine	UYD-20001 (Wico)		
		D1 engine	UYDL-101 (Lucas)		
		D1	YD-20001	YD1-20001	YD1S-20001
		D1 (Lucas)	YDL-101	YD1-20001	YD1S-20001
	1951	D1	YD1-40001	YD1-40001	YD1S-40001
		D1 (Lucas)	YDL1-3001	YD1-40001	YD1S-40001
	1952	D1	YD1-63001	YD1-64001	YD1S-64001
		D1 (Lucas)	YDL1-8001	YD1-64001	YD1S-64001
	1953	D1	BD2-101	BD2-101	BD2S-101
		D1 (Lucas)	BD2L-101	BD2-101	BD2S-101
	1954	D1 direct	BD-101	BD2-14600	BD2S-14600
		D1 battery	BDB-101	BD2-14600	BD2S-14600
		D1 comp	BD-101	BD2-14600	BD2S-14600
	1955	D1 direct	DD-101	BD2-34701	BD2S-34701
		D1 battery	DDB-101	BD2-34701	BD2S-34701
		D1 comp	DD-101	BD2-34701	
D3	1954	D3 direct	BD3-101	BD2-14600	BD2S-14600
		D3 battery	BD3B-101	BD2-14600	BD2S-14600
		D3 comp	BD3-101	BD2-14600	BD2S-14600
	1955	D3 direct	BD3-5138	BD2-34701	BD2S-34701
		D3 battery	BD3B-5138	BD2-34701	BD2S-34701
		D3 comp	BD3-5138	BD2-34701	

Range	Year	Model	Engine Direct lights	Battery	Frame
D1	1956	D1	DD-4801	DDB-3301	BD2S-55001
	1957	D1	DD-	DDB-	BD2S-
	1958	D1	DD-8577	DDB-7849	BD2S-65001
	1959	D1	DD-10812	DDB-10628	BD2S-67581
	1960	D1	DD-12501	DDB-12501	BD2S-70501
	1961	D1	DD-14501	DDB-14501	BD2S-73701
	1962	D1	DD-15481	DDB-16413	BD2S-76680
	1963	D1	DD-16129	DDB-17606	BD2S-78746
D3	1956	D3	BD3-10401	BD3B-12801	CD3-101
	1957	D3	BD3-	BD3B-	CD3-
D5	1958	D5	ED5-101	ED5B-101	FD5-101

Range	Year	Model	Engine Direct lights	Engine Battery	Frame
D7	1959	D7	ED7-101	ED7B-101	D7-101
	1960	D7	ED7-1501	ED7B-7001	D7-8101
	1961	D7	ED7-3001	ED7B-15501	D7-18401
	1962	D7	ED7-4501	ED7B-23001	D7-27450
	1963	D7	ED7-5505	ED7B-26904	D7-33268
		D7 Police		ED7BP-26904	D7-33268
		D7A (USA)	ED7A-5505	ED7BA-26904	D7-33268
		D7 Trail	ED7-5505		D7-33268T
	1964	D7	ED7-6887	FD7-101	D7-38400
		D7 (USA)	ED7A-6887	FD7A-101	D7-38400
		D7 Trail	ED7-6887		D7-38400
	1965	D7	ED7-9001	FD7-3001	D7-42878
		D7 Pastoral	ED7-9001		D7-42878
		Trail Bronc	ED7-9001		D7-42878
	1966	D7 de luxe	FD7-101	FD7-9076	D7-49855 to 51960 & GD7-101 to 8616
	1966	D7 Silver	FD7-101	FD7-10127	D7-51320 to 51960 & GD7-101 to 8616

Range	Year	Model	Engine	Frame
D10	1967	D10	D10-101	D10-101
		D10S	D10A-101	D10A-101
		D10B	D10A-101	BD10A-101
D14	1968	D13 Supreme	D13B-101 to 780	D13B-101
		D13 Sports	D13B-101 to 780	D13B-101S
		D13 Bushman	D13C-101 to 780	D13C-101B
		D14/4	D14B-781	D14B-781
		D14/4S	D14B-781	D14B-781S
		D14/4B	D14C-781	D14C-781B

Range	Year	Model	C10 engine	C11 engine	Rigid frame
C	1946–47	C10, C11	XC10-101	XC11-101	XC10G-101 girders XC10T-101 teles
	1948	C10, C11	YC10-101	YC11-101	YC10-101
	1949	C10, C11	ZC10-101	ZC11-101	ZC10-101
		C10 Australia	ZC10-101		ZC10A-101
	1950	C10, C11	ZC10-4001	ZC11-8001	ZC10-10001
		C10 Australia	ZC10A-4001		ZC10A-10001
		C10 A. C. Cars	ZAC10-101		

Range	Year	Model	Engine	Rigid frame	Spring frame
C	1951	C10	ZC10-7001	ZC10-21001	ZC10S-101
		C10 4-speed	ZC10-7001		ZC10S4-101
		C10 Australia	ZC10A-7001	ZC10A-21001	
		C11	ZC11-16001	ZC10-21001	ZC10S-101
		C11 4-speed	ZC11-16001		ZC10S4-101
	1952	C10	ZC10-10001	ZC10-29001	ZC10S-2601
		C10 4-speed	ZC10-10001	ZC10-29001	ZC10S4-2001
		C11	ZC11-25001	ZC10-29001	ZC10S-2601
		C11 4-speed	ZC11-25001	ZC10-29001	ZC10S4-2001
	1953	C10	BC10-101	BC10-101	BC10S-101
		C10 4-speed	BC10-101	BC10-101	BC10S4-101
		C11	BC11-101	BC10-101	BC10S-101
		C11 4-speed	BC11-101	BC10-101	BC10S4-101
	1954	C10L	BC10L-101		BC10LS-101
		C11G	BC11G-101	BC11-101	BC11S-101

Range	Year	Model	Engine	Rigid frame	Spring frame
C	1954	C11G 4-speed	BC11G-101	BC11R4-101	BC11S4-101
	1955	C10L	BC10L-4001		BC10LS-4501
		C11G	BC11G-11501	BC11-801	BC11S-4001
		C11G 4-speed	BC11G-11501	BC11R4-501	BC11S4-8001
	1956	C10L	BC10L-7001		DC10S-101
		C12	BC11G-23001		EC12-101 or BC11S4-18001
	1957	C10L	BC10L-		DC10S-
		C12	BC11G-		EC12-
	1958	C12	BC11G-40001		EC12-16001

Range	Year	B31 engine	B33 engine	Rigid frame	Spring frame
B31	1946	XB31-101		XB31-101	
B31, B33	1947	XB31-101	XB33-101	XB31-101	
	1948	YB31-101	YB33-101	YB31-101	
	1949	ZB31-101	ZB33-101	ZB31-101	ZB31S-101
	1950	ZB31-9001	ZB33-4001	ZB31-9001	ZB31S-5001
	1951	ZB31-15001	ZB33-7001	ZB31-14001	ZB31S-10001
	1952	ZB31-21001	ZB33-11001	ZB31-19001	ZB31S-17001
	1953	BB31-101	BB33-101	BB31-101	BB31S-101
	1954	BB31-6001	BB33-2001	BB31-1386	BB31S-5895
		BB31-6001	BB33-2001		CB31-101
	1955	BB31-15001	BB33-5001		BB31S-12001
		BB31-15001	BB33-5001		CB31-6001
	1956	BB31-22001	BB33-7301		EB31-101
	1957	BB31-	BB33-		EB31-5819 to 8553
	1958	GB31-101	GB33-101		FB31-101
	1959	GB31-1909	GB33-662		FB31-2572
B33	1960		GB33-1001		GB33-101

Range	Year	B32 engine	B34 engine	Rigid frame	Spring frame
B32	1946	XB32-101		XB31-101	
B32, B34	1947	XB32-101	XB34-101	XB31-101	
	1948	YB32-101	YB34-101	YB31-101	
	1949	ZB32-101	ZB34-101	ZB31-101	
	1950	ZB32-3001	ZB34-2001	ZB31-9001	ZB31S-5001
	alloy	ZB32A-3001	ZB34A-2001	ZB31-9001	ZB31S-5001
	1951	ZB32-4001	ZB34-3001	ZB31-14001	ZB31S-10001
	alloy	ZB32A-4001	ZB34A-3001	ZB31-14001	ZB31S-10001
	1952	ZB32-5001	ZB34-4001	ZB31-19001	ZB31S-17001
	alloy	ZB32A-5001		ZB31-19001	ZB31S-17001
	sand-cast		ZB34A-4001	ZB31-19001	ZB31S-17001
	die-cast		ZB34A-5001	ZB31-19001	ZB31S-17001
	1953	BB32A-101	BB34A-101	BB31-101	BB31S-101
	1954	BB32A-201	BB34A-201	BB32R-12	CB31-101
	1955	BB32A-251	BB34A-301	BB32A-201	
	1956	BB32A-301	BB34A-351		CB34-101
	1957	BB32A-	BB34A-		CB34-

Range	Year	B32 engine	B34 engine	Rigid frame	Spring frame
Gold Star	1949	ZB32GS-101	ZB34GS-101	ZB31-101	ZB32S-101
	1950	ZB32GS-2001	ZB34GS-2001	ZB31-9001	ZB32S-2001
	1951	ZB32GS-3001	ZB34GS-3001	ZB31-14001	ZB32S-3001
	1952	ZB32GS-4001		ZB31-19001	ZB32S-4001
	Clubmans	ZB32GS-6001		ZB31-19001	ZB32S-4001
	sand-cast		ZB34GS-4001	ZB31-19001	ZB32S-4001
	die-cast		ZB34GS-5001	ZB31-19001	ZB32S-4001

Range	Year	B32 engine	B34 engine	Rigid frame	Spring frame
Gold Star	1953	BB32GS-101	BB34GS-101	BB31-101	BB32S-101
		BB32GS-101	BB34GS-101		BB32A-101 (s/a)
	1954	BB32GS-1001	BB34GS-1001		CB32-101
		CB32GS-101	CB34GS-101		CB32-101
		BB34GSD-101		CB32D-101	Daytona
	1955	BB32GS-2001	BB34GS-2001		CB32-1501
		CB32GS-501	CB34GS-501		CB32-1501
		DB32GS-101	DB34GS-101		CB32-4001
	1956		DB34GS-501	BB32R-301	

Range	Year	B32 engine	B34 engine	B34 DBD engine	Spring frame
Gold Star	1956	DB32GS-501	DB34GS-501	DBD34GS-2001	CB32-4001
	1957	DB32GS-	DB34GS-	DBD34GS-2963	CB32-
	1958			DBD34GS-3001	CB32-7001

Range	Year	B32 engine	B34 engine	Spring frame	Catalina frame
Gold Star	1959	DB32GS-1501	DBD34GS-3753	CB32-7873	CB32C-101
	1960	DB32GS-1601	DBD34GS-4601	CB32-8701	CB32C-351
	1961	DB32GS-1741	DBD34GS-5684	CB32-10101	CB32C-601
	1962	DB32GS-1794	DBD34GS-6504	CB32-11001	CB32C-741
	1963		DBD34GS-6881	CB32-11451	CB32C-857

Catalina models used the 499 cc engine only.

Range	Year	M20 engine	M21 engine	M33 engine	Rigid frame	Spring frame
M	1946–47	XM20-101	XM21-101		XM20-101	
	1948	YM20-101	YM21-101	YM33-101	YM20-101	
	1949	ZM20-101	ZM21-101	ZM33-101	ZM20-101	
	M21 Batavia		ZM21-101		ZM20-2201 to 2700	
	1950	ZM20-4001	ZM21-5001	ZM33-3001	ZM20-7001	
	M21 Dutch AA		ZM21-5001		ZM20D-8426 to 8445	
	1951	ZM20-6001	ZM21-8001	ZM33-4001	ZM20-10001	ZM20S-101
	1952	ZM20-10001	ZM21-10001	ZM33-5001	ZM20-14001	ZM20S-301
	1953	BM20-101	BM21-101	BM33-101	BM20-101	BM20S-101
	1954	BM20-1001	BM21-1601	BM33-501	BM20-1502	BM20S-1192
	1955	BM20-2501	BM21-4501	BM33-1301	BM20-4001	BM20S-4001
	1956		BM21-7501	BM33-2101	BM20-7001	BM20S-8001
	1957		BM21-	BM33-	BM20-	BM20S-
	1958		BM21-11001		BM20-10001	BM20S-11001
	1959		BM21-12033		BM20-10313	BM20S-12031
	1960		BM21-12901		BM20-10451	BM20S-12031

Range	Year	M21 engine	M21 alternator engine	Spring frame
M21	1961	BM21-14301	BM21A-14301	BM20S-14201
	1962	BM21-15453	BM21A-15453	BM20S-15061
	1963	BM21-15588	BM21A-15588	BM20S-15159

Range	Year	C15 engine	SS80 engine	Frame
C15	1959	C15-101		C15-101
	1960	C15-11001		C15-11101
	1961	C15-21251		C15-22001
			C15SS-101	C15-27644
	1962	C15-29839	C15SS-1101	C15-31801
	1963	C15-41807	C15SS-2705	C15-38035

Range	Year	C15 engine	SS80 engine	Frame
C15	1964	C15D-101	C15SS-3633	C15-42211
	1965	C15F-101	C15FSS-101	C15-45501

Range	Year	C15 engine	Sportsman	Frame
C15	1966	C15F-2089	C15FSS-2001	C15-49001
	1967	C15G-101		C15G-101
			C15SG-101	C15SG-101

Range	Year	C15S engine	C15T engine	Frame
C15C	1959	C15S-101	C15T-101	C15S-101
	1960	C15S-301	C15T-301	C15S 501
	1961	C15S-2112	C15T-1056	C15S-2701
	1962	C15S-3101		C15S-3601
			C15T-1451	C15S-10001
	1963	C15S-4001	C15T-2001	C15C-101
	1964	C15S-4373	C15T-2116	C15C-853
	1965	C15FS-101	C15FT-101	C15C-1601

Model	Year	Engine	Frame
C15 Star (USA 1 in. bore)	1963	C15B-409	C15-38035
	1964	C15DB-101	C15-42211
	1965	C15FB-101	C15-45501
C15 Police	1963	C15P-41807	C15-38035
	1964	C15DP-101	C15-42211
	1965	C15FP-101	C15-45501
	1967	C15PG-101	C15PG 101
C15 Trials Pastoral	1963	C15T-1602	C15A-137
	1964	C15T-2116	C15E-101
	1965	C15FT-101	C15E-136
C15 Trials Cat	1965	C15FT-101	C15C-1601
C15 Starfire Roadster	1963	C15-41807	C15C-101
	1964	C15SR-225	C15C-853
	1965	C15FSR-101	C15C-1601
C15 Starfire Racer	1963	C15R-101	C15S-4123

Range	Year	B40 engine	SS90 engine	Frame
B40	1961	B40-101		B40-101
	1962	B40-3601	B40BSS-101	B40-3511
	1963	B40-4506	B40SS-180	B40-5017
	1964	B40-5275	B40SS-426	B40-6668
	1965	B40F-101	B40FSS-101	B40-7775
	1966	B40F-1149		B40-9973
		B40G-101 (modified unit)		B40-9973
	1967	B40G-201		B40G-201

Model	Year	Engine	Frame
B40 Star (USA)	1963	B40B-563	B40-5017
B40 Police	1964	B40P-5275	B40-6668
	1965	B40FP-101	B40-7775
B40 Super Star (USA)	1964	B40B-1088	B40-6668
B40 Sportsman (USA)	1965	B40FB-101	B40-7775
B40 Enduro Star (USA)	1964	B40T-143	C15C-853
	1965	B40FE-101	C15C-1601
B40 Rough Rider	1969	HCB40-462M	HCB40-462M

Model	Year	Engine	Frame
C25	1967	C25-101	C25-101
B25	1967	C25-101	B25-101
	1968	B25B-101	B25B-101
B44GP	1966	B44-101	B44-101
	1967	B44-131	B44-267
B44VE	1966	B44E-101	C15C-3137
	1967	B44EA-101	B44EA-101
B44VR	1967	B44R-101	B44R-101
B44VS	1968	B44B-101	B44B-101VS
B44SS	1968	B44B-101	B44B-101SS

1969 and later

For this period a new coding system was introduced using a two-letter prefix for the month and model season year, plus model-type code and a number which began at 00101 for each model year, and ran on irrespective of the model it was stamped on. The model season was taken to start in August.

The first letter was the month and the code was:

A	January	D	April	H	July	N	October
B	February	E	May	J	August	P	November
C	March	G	June	K	September	X	December

The second letter was the model year and the code was:

C September 1968 (B25) and November 1968 (B44) to July 1969 (B25 & B44SS) and June 1969 (B44VS)
D August 1969 (B25 & B44SS) and July 1969 (B44VS) to July 1970
E August 1970 to July 1971
G August 1971 to July 1972
H August 1972 to July 1973

The model codes were:
D175, D175B, B25S, B44SS, B44VS for 1969–70
D175, B25SS, B25T for 1971
B50SS, B50T for 1971–72
B50MX for 1971–73

2 Model charts

Abbreviations: rig—rigid; pl—plunger; s/a—pivoted-fork; comp—competition; batt—battery; d/l—de luxe; 4S—4-speed gearbox; scr.spec.—scrambles special

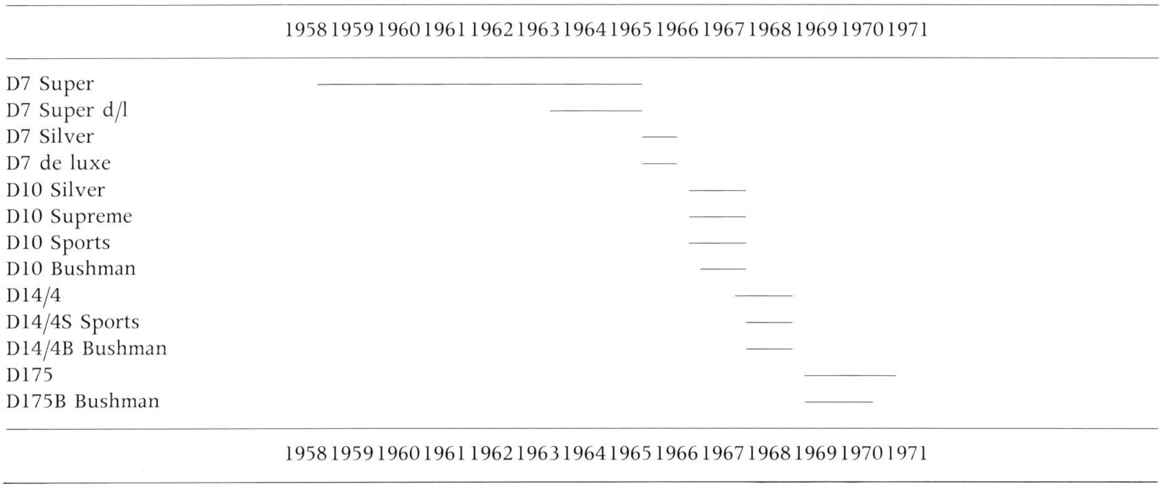

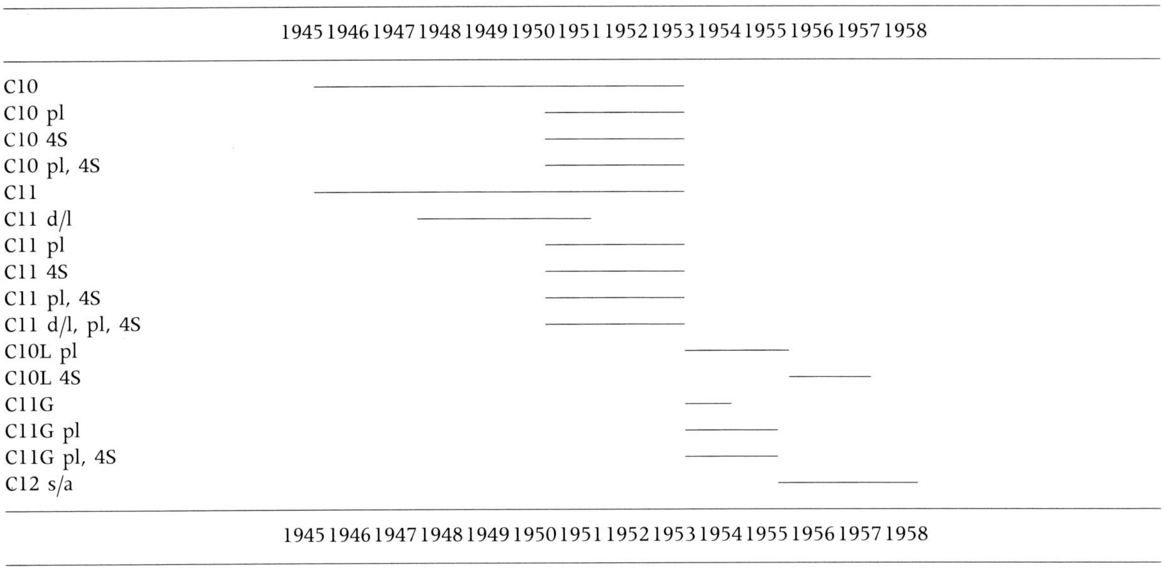
1945 1946 1947 1948 1949 1950 1951 1952 1953 1954 1955 1956 1957 1958
C10
C10 pl
C10 4S
C10 pl, 4S
C11
C11 d/l
C11 pl
C11 4S
C11 pl, 4S
C11 d/l, pl, 4S
C10L pl
C10L 4S
C11G
C11G pl
C11G pl, 4S
C12 s/a
1945 1946 1947 1948 1949 1950 1951 1952 1953 1954 1955 1956 1957 1958

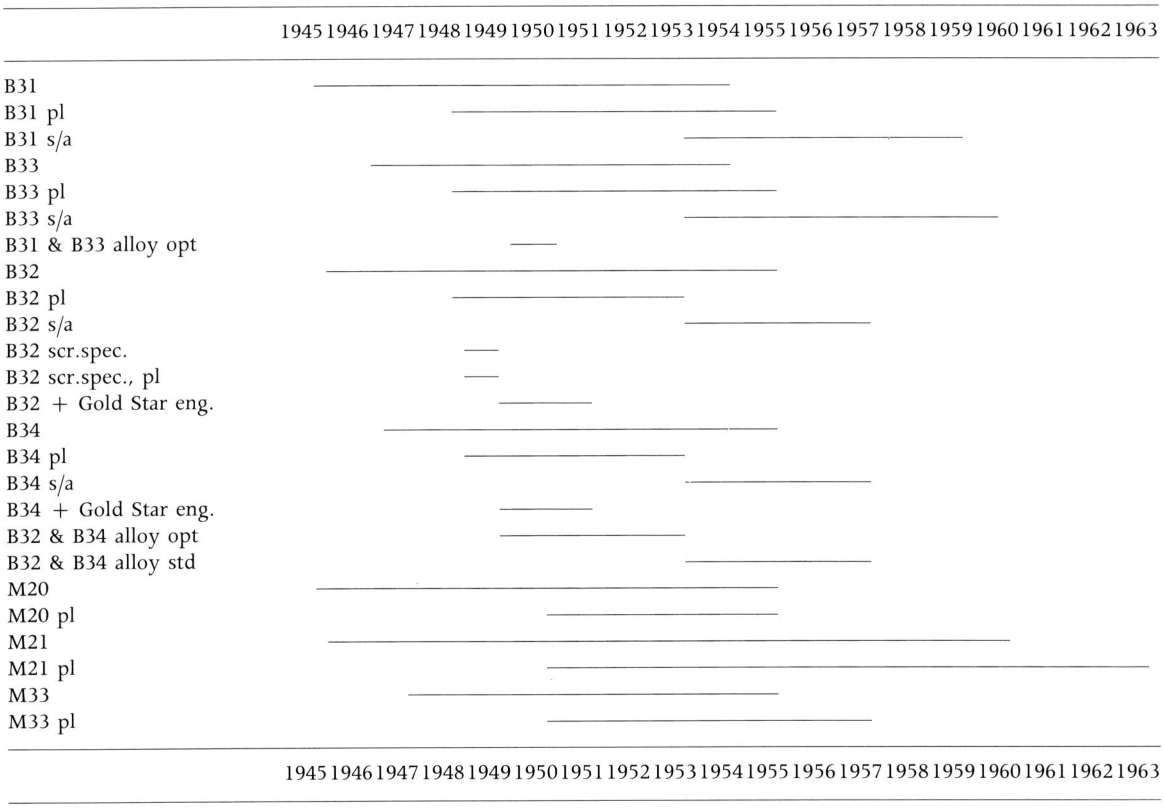
1945 1946 1947 1948 1949 1950 1951 1952 1953 1954 1955 1956 1957 1958 1959 1960 1961 1962 1963
B31
B31 pl
B31 s/a
B33
B33 pl
B33 s/a
B31 & B33 alloy opt
B32
B32 pl
B32 s/a
B32 scr.spec.
B32 scr.spec., pl
B32 + Gold Star eng.
B34
B34 pl
B34 s/a
B34 + Gold Star eng.
B32 & B34 alloy opt
B32 & B34 alloy std
M20
M20 pl
M21
M21 pl
M33
M33 pl
1945 1946 1947 1948 1949 1950 1951 1952 1953 1954 1955 1956 1957 1958 1959 1960 1961 1962 1963

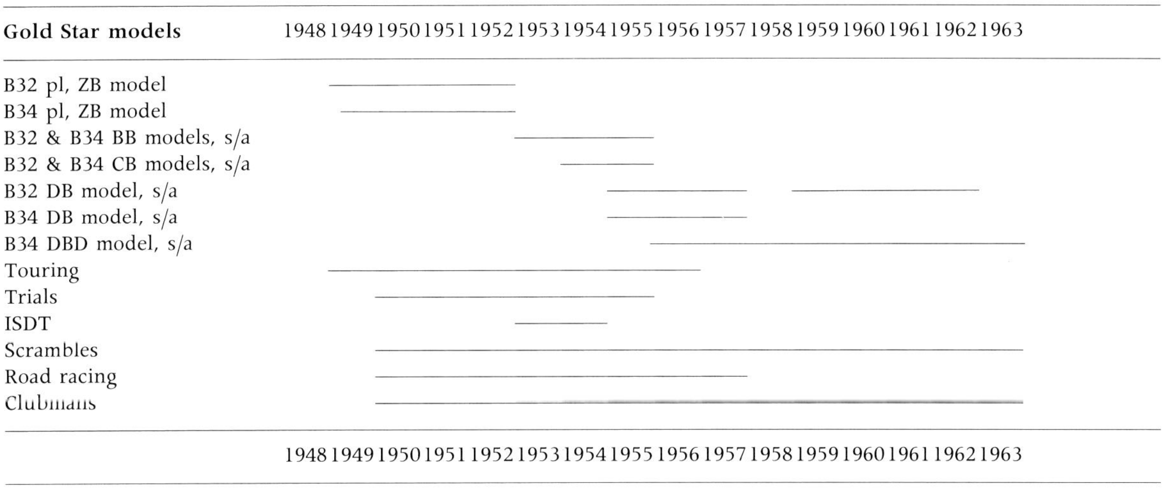
Gold Star models
1948 1949 1950 1951 1952 1953 1954 1955 1956 1957 1958 1959 1960 1961 1962 1963
B32 pl, ZB model
B34 pl, ZB model
B32 & B34 BB models, s/a
B32 & B34 CB models, s/a
B32 DB model, s/a
B34 DB model, s/a
B34 DBD model, s/a
Touring
Trials
ISDT
Scrambles
Road racing
Clubmans
1948 1949 1950 1951 1952 1953 1954 1955 1956 1957 1958 1959 1960 1961 1962 1963

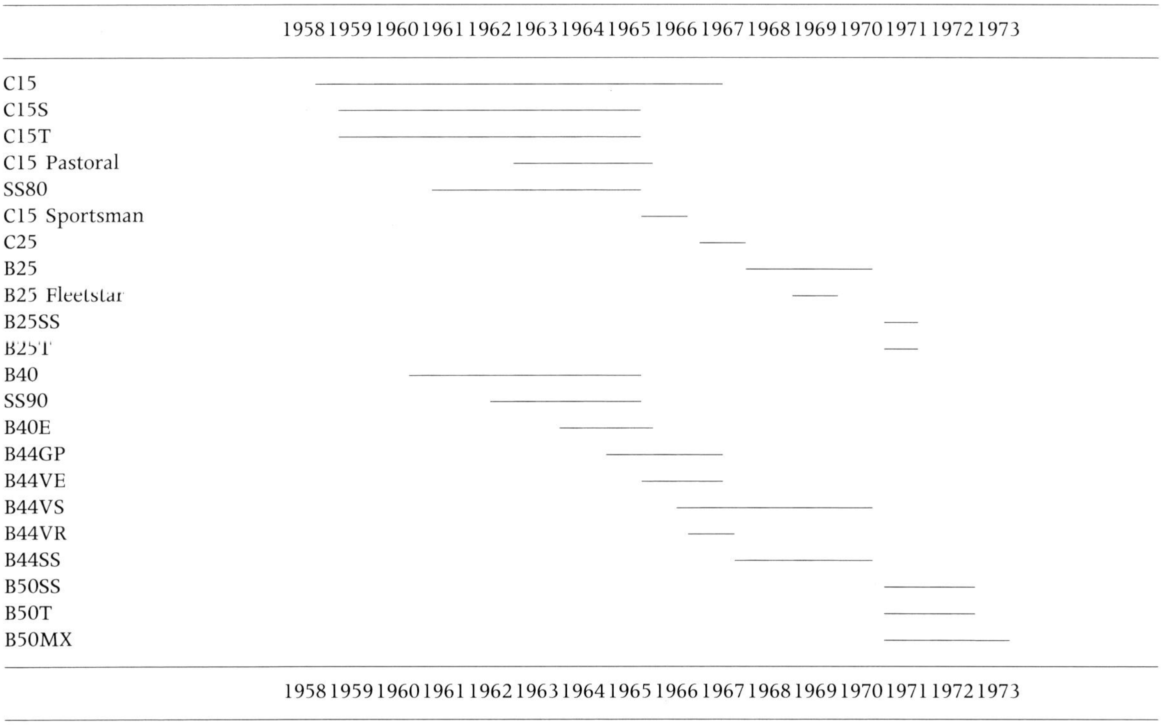
1958 1959 1960 1961 1962 1963 1964 1965 1966 1967 1968 1969 1970 1971 1972 1973
C15
C15S
C15T
C15 Pastoral
SS80
C15 Sportsman
C25
B25
B25 Fleetstar
B25SS
B25T
B40
SS90
B40E
B44GP
B44VE
B44VS
B44VR
B44SS
B50SS
B50T
B50MX
1958 1959 1960 1961 1962 1963 1964 1965 1966 1967 1968 1969 1970 1971 1972 1973

54

The experts final at the 1955 Columbus meeting, with Al Gunter taking his Gold Star round a BSA twin and another rider to win

3 Model recognition

These notes have been compiled from the main text and provide a quick guide to checking a machine for its year. The starting point should always be the engine and frame numbers, and the following is mainly concerned with external details that can be inspected when purchasing. The internal changes are not included as they are indicated in the main text and are seldom useful when checking a machine prior to purchase.

The words 'start' and 'end' are used to indicate when a model was first seen and when it was withdrawn. These both refer to the model year and not the calendar one, so allowance must be made for this.

The notes run on and are generally applicable to later models of the same series. If in doubt, refer to the main text.

Bantam

March 1948	Engine unit alone—start, Wipac with vertical HT lead outlet.
June 1948	D1—start, flat silencer, exhaust pipe under footrest, very well-valanced front mudguard, no fork gaiters, centre stand held up by clip, saddle, cable-operated light switch.
1950	Revised Wipac generator, exhaust pipe above footrest, fork gaiters, centre stand with spring to return and no clip.
	D1 competition—start, raised saddle, blade mudguards, decompressor, tilted exhaust and silencer, tyres to suit.
	Options of plunger rear suspension and/or Lucas battery electrics available for all models including competition ones. Thus a total of eight variations in build possible.
1952	Wipac light switch in headlamp, new headstock gusset.
1953	Unsprung front mudguard with little valance, dualseat option. Lucas option—end.
1954	D1 battery, D1 battery with plunger frame, D3 plunger, D3 batt pl, D3 comp, D3 comp pl—start.
	D1 models to replace the previous ones with Lucas electrics.
	All D1 road models with headlamp cowl, more fins on head and barrel, tubular silencer.
	D1 comp with more engine fins, heavier front fork, larger front brake, retains flat silencer.
	D3—as D1 with heavier front fork and larger front brake, tubular silencer for road models and flat for competition.
1955	End—D1 rigid, D1 comp, D1 batt, D3 pl, D3 batt pl, D3 comp, D3 comp pl.
1956	D3 s/a—start, pivoted-fork frame, long tapered silencer, dualseat standard, direct or battery lighting.
1957	D3 s/a—end.
1958	D5—start, as D3 with pivoted-fork frame, new tank, wider brakes, direct or battery lighting.
	D5—end.
1959	D7 Super—start, new frame, forks with nacelle, cast-iron hubs, cover over generator on left, direct or battery lighting.
1963	D1—end.
1964	D7 Super de luxe—start.
1965	D7 Super and Super de luxe—end.
1966	D7 Silver and D7 de luxe—start, centre panels altered, new tank shape with knee recesses and round badges.
	D7—end.
1967	D10—start, Concentric carbs, points on right set in primary chaincase, six-pole alternator, three- or four-speed gearbox.
	D10 Silver and D10 Supreme with three speeds, nacelle forks.
	D10 Sports with four speeds, separate headlamp shell, dualseat hump, waist-level exhaust, full-width hubs, flyscreen.
	D10 Bushman with four speeds, separate headlamp shell, waist-level exhaust pipe, trail tyres, revised gearing.
	D10—end.
1968	D14—start, larger-diameter exhaust pipe, four-speed gearbox.
	D14/4 Supreme as D10 other than gearbox.
	D14/4S Sports, full-width front and rear hubs, front backplate with torque arm, heavier forks with gaiters.
	D14/4B Bushman, front hub and forks as Sports, waist-level exhaust.
	D14—end.

1969	D175—start, central spark plug, offset hubs, exposed rear-suspension springs, low-level exhaust pipe.
	D175B Bushman—start, as D175 except waist-level exhaust pipe, undershield.
1970	D175B—end.
1971	D175—end.

C range

1945	C10, C11—start, girder forks, saddle, speedo on forks, 19 in. wheels for C10 but 20 in. for C11.
April 1946	Telescopic front forks, speedo mounted in petrol tank.
1948	C11 de luxe—start, special finish.
	C11 models, drip shield under carb added.
1949	Larger dynamo, no drip shield, light-alloy cylinder head for C10 during year.
1951	Horn button mounted on front brake block, options of four-speed gearbox and/or plunger rear suspension.
	C11 de luxe—end.
1952	C11, 19 in. wheels.
1953	Boxed-in rear number plate, speedo mounted on forks, underslung pilot lamp, dualseat option.
	C10, C11—end.
1954	C10L—start, plunger frame, three speeds, D3-type forks with cowl, alternator electrics.
	C11G—start, rigid or plunger frame, three-speed gearbox or four-speed with plunger, cowled forks, alternator electrics.
	C11G rigid—end.
1955	Monobloc carb, no underslung pilot lamp.
	C11G, steering lock, 7 in. front brake.
	C11G—end.
1956	C10L, four-speed gearbox, modified cylinder head with more fins and some angled, twin switches for lights and ignition.
	C12—start, C11G engine in pivoted-fork frame, four-speed gearbox, full-width hubs, 7 in. front brake, switch panel on right side of machine.
1957	C10L—end.
1958	C12—end.

B range—road

1945	B31—start, teles, rigid frame, speedo in petrol tank, saddle.
1947	B33—start, as B31 but with 499 cc engine.
1948	Speedo mounted on front forks.
1949	Larger dynamo, plunger-rear-suspension option, revised gearbox.
1950	B31 and B33—alloy-engine option start and end.
1952	Dualseat option.
1953	B31 and B33, boxed-in rear number plate, headlamp cowl, underslung pilot lamp.
	B33, 8 in. front brake, valanced front mudguard.
1954	B31 and B33, pivoted-fork frame with alloy chaincase and dualseat as standard, rigid and plunger models continued.
	B31 and B33 rigid—end.
1955	B31 and B33 plunger, steering lock, no underslung pilot lamp.
	B31 and B33 s/a, as plunger models plus Monobloc carb.
	B31 and B33 plunger—end.
1956	B31 and B33, full-width light-alloy hubs with 7 in. brakes, option of full rear chaincase.
1958	B31 and B33, alternator electrics, coil ignition, nacelle forks, domed oil tank and toolbox lid, new 7 in. iron hubs, roll-on feet for centre stand, $\frac{3}{8}$ in. wide rear chain.
1959	B31—end.
1960	Rear-brake cam lever positioned to point down.
	B33—end.

B range—competition

1946	B32—start, as B31, raised exhaust pipe, undershield, 21 in. front wheel.
1947	B34—start, as B32 but with 499 cc engine.
1948	Speedo mounted on front forks, folding kickstart.
1949	Larger dynamo, plunger-rear-suspension option, revised gearbox.
	B32 scrambles special—start and end.
1950	B32 and B34—Gold Star or alloy engine option start.
1951	B32 and B34—Gold Star engine option end.
1952	Dualseat option.
1953	B32 and B34—alloy-engine option end.
1954	B32 and B34, new rigid frame with duplex tubes, light-alloy engines as standard, pivoted-fork frame also available.
1955	B32 and B34 rigid—end.
1956	B32 and B34, central oil tank.
1957	Monobloc carb.
	B32 and B34—end.

Gold Star

1949	B32GS—start, alloy ZB-type engine, plunger frame, saddle, many options to suit many uses.
	B34GS—start, as B32GS but with 499 cc engine.
1950	8 in. front brake for all versions except trials and scrambles.
1951	Late in year B34GS engine changed to die-cast head and barrel with separate rocker box.
1952	Dualseat option, B32GS head and barrel as for 500.
	ZB engine type—end.
1953	BB models—start, pivoted-fork frame, dualseat standard, alloy chaincase, fat Girling rear units.

1954	BB models continued, slim Girling units. CB models—start, big-finned head and barrel, clip-ons, swept-back exhaust pipe, slim Girling units, flexibly-mounted float chamber.
1955	BB and CB continued. DB models—start, fins on vented brake drums, float-chamber mounting altered. BB, CB and trials versions—end.
1956	DBD version of B34GS—start, silencer with tapered front part, options of 190 mm front brake and five-gallon alloy petrol tank. Touring versions—end.
1957	DB32GS, DB34GS, road-racing versions—end.
1958	DBD34GS only available in Clubmans or scrambles form, domed oil tank and toolbox lid, $\frac{3}{8}$ in. wide rear chain.
1959	DB32GS available as 500 model fitted with 350 engine, central oil tank for scrambles models.
1962	DB32GS—end.
1963	DBD34GS—end.

M range

1945	M20—start, girders, rigid frame, saddle, no footrest rubbers.
1946	M21—start, as M20 but with larger engine.
1947	Footrest rubbers from frame XM20-7390.
1948	M33—start, as M20 but with B33, 499 cc ohv, engine fitted. Speedos mounted centrally on forks.
June 1948	Telescopic forks for all models, frame downtube pulled back for wheel clearance on full depression.
1949	Larger dynamo, revised gearbox.
1951	Plunger-frame option for all models, light-alloy cylinder head for M20 and M21.
1952	Dualseat option for all models.
1953	Boxed-in rear number plate, headlamp cowl and underslung pilot lamp for all models.
1955	Steering lock, Monobloc carburettor, no underslung pilot for all models. End—M20, M33 rigid frame.
1956	8 in. front brake and valanced front mudguard for M21 and M33.
1957	End—M33.
1958	No headlamp cowl so return to 1952 style with separate shell and small panel for light switch and ammeter.
1959	M21 in plunger frame only but some with rigid frame sold from stocks, all machines to special order only.
1960	End—M21 rigid frame.
1961	Alternator added on machines for AA.
1963	End—M21.

Unit models

1959	C15—start, unit construction of engine and gearbox, points behind cylinder, pivoted rear fork, dualseat, nacelle headlamp, full-width hubs, 17 in. rims. C15T—start, trials version, undershield, upswept exhaust system, optional lighting system. C15S—start, scrambles version, undershield, upswept open exhaust, short seat, fork gaiters, ball end levers.
1961	B40—start, no pushrod tube, valve lifter, 18 in. rims, 7 in. front brake.
April 1961	SS80—start, sports C15, clamped handlebar controls.
1962	Horizontal outlet fuel tap.
May 1962	SS90—start, sports B40. C15T—two-gallon alloy tank, alloy mudguards, 7 in. offset front brake. C15S—as C15T plus strutted handlebars, expansion chamber formed in end of exhaust pipe.
1963	C15 Pastoral—start. C15T, C15S—new frame with duplex seat tubes, central oil tank, inboard exhaust pipe, new air cleaner.
1964	B40E—start.
1965	B44GP—start, 531 Reynolds frame, chrome-plated cylinder bore. All models with points in timing cover and external clutch lever for rack-and-pinion mechanism. End—C15T, C15S, C15 Pastoral, SS80, B40, SS90, B40E.
1966	C15 Sportsman—start, as SS80 but separate headlamp shell and dualseat with hump. B44VE—start, trail model much as C15T but with 441 cc engine; small headlamp, upswept exhaust.
July 1966	C15, C15 Sportsman—Victor bottom half. End—C15 Sportsman.
1967	C25, B44VR, B44VS—start, square-fin barrel, 7 in. offset front hub, fibreglass tank, Concentric carbs. B44VE—Concentric carb, 7 in. rear brake. B44GP—7 in. rear brake. End—C15, C25, B44GP, B44VE, B44VR.
1968	B25—start, as C25 with 7 in. full-width front brake. B44SS—start, as B44VR with 8 in. full-width front brake. B44VS—8 in. offset front brake.
1969	B25 Fleetstar—start, fleet version of B25 with lower compression ratio and simpler finish to reduce price. B25, B44SS—7 in. twin-leading-shoe front brake, steel tank, rev-counter option. B44VS—rev-counter option. End—B25 Fleetstar.
1970	B25—oil warning lamp. End—B25, B44SS, B44VS.
1971	B25SS, B25T, B50SS, B50T, B50MX—start, new frame carrying oil within its tubes, conical front and rear hubs, 6 in. or 8 in. tls front brake, slim-line forks, cam rear fork pivot lock for chain adjustment. End—B25SS, B25T.
1972	End—B50SS, B50T.
1973	End—B50MX.

4 Finish codes

These are a series of suffix numbers that were added to a component part number to indicate the finish required. They were mainly used for petrol tanks, wheels, rims, mudguards and fork seal holders which could vary in appearance depending on the year of manufacture and whether an option finish had been taken up or not.

The suffix was separated from the part number by a stroke and thus the C11 petrol tank in 1948 was 29-7920/13 when in the standard chrome-plate with matt silver panels lined black, but 29-7920/14 when finished with blue panels lined in gold. Codes used by models other than singles have been included for interest and assistance.

1 Cadmium
2 Dull chrome
3 Bright chrome
4 Dull green Dutch
5 Sand (Egyptian)
6 Rustproof black
7 Black enamel
8 Service green (matt)
9 Green enamel
10 Khaki green
11 Khaki green (No. 3 gas proof)
12 Chrome-plate and Devon red, lined gold
13 Chrome-plate and matt silver, lined black
14 Chrome-plate and blue, lined gold
15 Chrome-plate and green, lined gold
16 Matt silver, lined black
17 Chrome-plate and black, lined gold
18 Mist green
19 Chrome-plate and matt silver, lined red
21 Polished aluminium
23 Polychromatic grey
24 Polychromatic silver beige
25 Swedish army grey
26 Chrome-plate, silver beige, lined red
27 Royal red or red (Post Office)
31 Silver
34 Devon red
36 Maroon and chrome-plate, lined gold
37 Maroon
38 Metallic green and chrome-plate, lined dark green
39 Metallic green
40 Dark green
41 Chrome rim and maroon hub
42 Chrome rim and dark green hub
43 Chrome rim and beige hub
44 Chrome rim and black hub
45 Chrome rim and mist green hub
48 Maroon with cream panels
51 Maroon and silver, lined gold
58 Dark green and light green, lined gold
59 Major grey
61 Chrome rim and major grey hub
64 Black and cream petrol tank
69 White
72 Maroon and cream petrol tank, lined gold and maroon (C12)
74 Dark green petrol tank with chrome panels, lined gold
78 Brilliant red and chrome
88 Nutley or sapphire blue
99 Bayard crimson petrol tank with ivory panels, lined gold
100 Almond green
101 Gunmetal grey
102 Princess grey
105 Bayard crimson
109 Royal red and chrome (tank)
110 Nutley or sapphire blue and chrome
112 Blue with double lining
120 Black and chrome (tank)
123 Royal red and chrome
125 Chrome rim and Bayard crimson hub
126 Black petrol tank with ivory panels, lined gold
127 Metallic grey and chrome (tank)
135 Red and silver
136 Black and silver
137 Royal red petrol tank with ivory panels, lined gold
142 Devon red and chrome (tank)
145 Nutley or sapphire blue and ivory panels, lined gold
146 Blue and chrome (tank)
162 Black and chrome
165 Silver
167 Flamboyant blue
168 Flamboyant blue and chrome
169 Nutley blue with ivory panels, double-lined
170 Flamboyant red
171 Flamboyant red and chrome
172 Blue and chrome
173 Red and chrome
174 Flamboyant blue and chrome, single white line

175 Flamboyant blue, single white line
176 Flamboyant red and chrome, single white line
177 Flamboyant red, single white line
201 Mandarine red
202 Mandarine red and chrome
208 Red and black
218 Yellow on polished alloy, white lines
221 Sapphire blue with silver panels, lined gold
223 Peony red, ivory panels, single gold line
226 Peony red
227 Flamboyant aircraft blue
228 Flamboyant aircraft blue, chrome panels, single white line
229 Flamboyant aircraft blue, single white line
233 Black, chrome panels, single white line
234 Black, single white line
235 Flamboyant electric blue
236 Flamboyant electric blue, chrome panels, white lines, white between weld seams on tank top
237 Flamboyant electric blue, white line
244 Bushfire orange
245 Bushfire orange and white, lined gold
248 Nutley or sapphire blue, lined gold
250 Peony red, lined gold
261 Firebird red
262 Matt black engine parts
263 Bushfire orange, moss gold centre strip, single black line
264 Bushfire orange, black line
265 Bushfire orange and white, lined black
266 Polychromatic aircraft blue
267 Polychromatic aircraft blue, chrome panels, lined white
268 Blue tank centre, white lining, chrome side panels (1970 A65L)
269 Blue tank centre, white lining, chrome side panels (1970 A65F)
270 Grey tank centre, white lining, chrome side panels
271 Blue (1970 A65L)
272 Blue (1970 A65F)
273 Polished alloy and yellow, polished cap
274 Grey
276 Flamboyant red, white lining
277 Flamboyant red tank centre, white lining, chrome side panels
280 Flamboyant aircraft blue, white stripes, red lining
285 Flamboyant red, black centre and side stripes, red lining
286 Flamboyant blue, white centre stripe
287 Flamboyant red, white centre stripe
288 Dove grey
291 Polished alloy sides, black centre and side stripes, red lining
293 Flamboyant red, black centre stripe
295 Polychromatic golden metallic bronze upper and white lower
296 Polychromatic golden metallic bronze
297 Sterling Moss polychromatic green upper and white lower
298 Sterling Moss polychromatic green
305 White
306 Instrument matt black
307 Silver sheen
314 Polished aluminium, white centre stripe, Flambordeaux side stripes
315 Hi-violet
322 Etruscan bronze
330 Chromed, Firebird red with white lining

A 1961 C15 poses for publicity

5 Colours

The numbers in brackets refer to BSA finish codes. The code for chrome plating is 3 and is not included below to save repetition. Note that during 1951 the nickel supply position began to restrict chrome plating and this finish was replaced by a painted one in many instances. For 1952 no changes in finish were announced, but during the year nickel continued to be in short supply so that tanks and wheels for most models were painted, with chrome plating restricted to the exhaust pipes, silencers and some minor fittings. This situation ceased by the end of the year, so for 1953 the range was back to its normal chrome-plated self. Each range is dealt with in turn.

Bantam

1949	D1—mist green (18) frame, forks, mudguards, wheel rims, hubs, toolbox, chainguard, headlamp, details. Petrol tank mist green with yellow side panels carrying Bantam transfer. Gear indicator transfer on chainguard. Chrome-plated exhaust, handlebars.
1950	D1—as 1949 with chrome-plated lower plunger spring boxes and strip on tank centre. Some export models in black (7) in place of mist green. Models with Lucas electrics with chrome-plated headlamp rim and points cover.
1951–52	D1—as 1950.
1953	D1—chrome-plated wheel rims on mist green hub (45) and chrome-plated beads on tank welds. Option in black (7) with chrome-plated wheel rims on black hub (44).
1954	D1—as 1953 except no gear indicator transfer or petrol-tank centre strip. Instead the tank welds had chrome-plated beadings fixed to them. D3—as D1 in Major grey (59) with chrome-plated rims on Major grey hub (61). Petrol tank with cream panels and Bantam Major transfer. Silencer fishtail painted for both models in green (18) or grey (59) to match.
1955	D1 and D3—as 1954. Export options in black (7) with tank in black with cream panels lined gold (64) and wheels with chrome-plated rims and black hubs (44), or in maroon (37) with tank maroon with cream panels lined gold (72) and wheels with chrome-plated rims and maroon hubs (41).
1956–57	D1 and D3—as 1955 with black or maroon options available to all.
1958	D1—as 1956. D5—in Bayard crimson with tank same with ivory panels lined gold (99) and wheels to match with chrome-plated rims and Bayard crimson hubs (125). Option in black (7) with black tank with ivory panels lined gold (126) and wheels with black hubs (44).
1959	D1—as 1956. D7—with black (7) frame, forks, chainguards, details. Royal red (27) mudguards, stays, centre panels. Tank in royal red with ivory panels gold-lined (137). Wheels with chrome-plated rims and black hubs (44). D7—option all in black (7) with wheels as above (44) and tank in black with ivory panels lined gold (126).
1960	D1—black (7) frame, forks, headlamp, toolbox, chainguard. Wheels with chrome-plated rims and black hubs (44). Petrol tank, mudguard and stays in mist green (18), black (7) or fuchsia red. D7—as 1959 in black (7) with signal red (27), sapphire blue (88) or black (7) mudguards and centre panels. Petrol tank with ivory panels and in red (137), blue (145) or black (126) with gold lining. Wheels as 1959.
1961–62	D1—as 1960. D7—as 1960 with tank option of chrome-plated side panels and in red (123), blue (110) or black (162).
1963	D1—as 1960. D7—as 1961 with silver sheen hubs and brake backplates.
1964–65	D7—as 1963.
1965–66	D7 Silver—black (7) frame, forks, chainguard; silver sheen (31) hubs, headlamp nacelle, mudguards; sapphire blue (88) centre panels. Petrol tank sapphire blue with silver sheen panels lined gold (221) plus round tank badges. D7 de luxe—black (7) frame, forks. Petrol tank flamboyant red with chrome-plated panels and white separating line (176). Mudguards flamboyant red with white line (177); centre panels flamboyant red (170).

1967 D10 Silver—black (7) frame, forks, nacelle; silver sheen (31) hubs; sapphire blue (88) mudguards, centre panels. Petrol tank sapphire blue with silver panels lined gold (221).
D10 Supreme—black (7) frame, forks; silver sheen (31) hubs; centre panels flamboyant blue (235); mudguards flamboyant blue with white line (237). Petrol tank flamboyant blue with chrome-plated panels and white separating line plus white between weld seams on top of tank (236).
D10S Sports—black (7) frame, forks; chrome-plate fork sliders, headlamp shell, mudguards; silver sheen (31) hubs; centre panels flamboyant red (170). Petrol tank flamboyant red with chrome-plated panels and white separating line plus chequered area between weld seams on top of tank (176).
D10B Bushman—black (7) frame, forks; white (69) mudguards; bushfire orange (244) centre panels. Petrol tank bushfire orange and white with gold separating line (245).

1968 D14/4—as 1967 D10 Supreme. Black option with centre panels black (7); mudguards black with white line (234); petrol tank black with chrome plating and white line (233).
D14/4S—as 1967 D10S Sports.
D14/4B—as 1967 D10B.

1969–71 D175—as D14/4 in black or as D10S except mudguards flamboyant red with white line (177). Also in polychromatic aircraft blue (266) with tank with chrome-plated panels and white line (267) in style of D10 Supreme.

1969–70 D175B—as 1967 D10B except tank separating line in black (265).

C range

1945 C10 and C11—black (7) frame, forks, oil tank, toolbox, mudguards, chaincase, details. Petrol tank chrome-plated with matt silver top and side panels lined black (13). Wheel rims chrome-plated with matt silver centres lined black (13). Chrome-plated brake backplates, handlebars, exhaust, headlamp rim, battery-carrier strap. In production wheel rims and brake backplates black (7).

1946–47 C10 and C11—as 1945.

1948 Standard C10 and C11—as 1945.
De luxe C11—as standard except tank and wheel rims chrome-plated with blue panels and centres respectively, both lined in gold (14). Chrome-plated fork seal holder and rear brake rod.

1949–51 C10 and C11—as 1948.

1951 C10 and C11—during year blue and beige in place of blue and chrome with wheel rims in matt silver with blue centres for C11 de luxe. C10 in black (7) with tank and rims in matt silver with black lining (16).

1952 C10 and C11—as 1951; in March new tank badge.

1953 C10 and C11—with all painted parts in maroon (37) and wheels with chrome-plated rims and maroon hubs (41); petrol tank in maroon with chrome-plated side panels lined in gold (36). Option in black (7) with wheels with black hubs (44) but tank remaining in maroon, chrome and gold lining (36).

1954 C10L—dark green (40) frame, lower fork yoke, stand, brake backplates, engine plates, plunger spring upper covers, chainguard. Light green forks, mudguards, headlamp shell, oil tank, toolbox. Petrol tank dark green with light green side panels lined in gold (58) and small round BSA badges. Wheels with chrome-plated rims and dark green hubs (42). Chrome-plated headlamp rim, exhaust system.
C11G—maroon (37) with petrol tank maroon with chrome-plated panels lined gold (36) and round tank badge. Wheels with chrome-plated rims and maroon hubs (41).

1955 C10L and C11G—as 1954 plus chrome-plated beading on tank weld seams.

1956–57 C10L—as 1955.
C12—maroon (37) with petrol tank maroon with cream panels lined gold (72) and wheels with chrome-plated rims, maroon hubs (41) and alloy hub centres. Chrome-plated beading on tank seam.
Option for C12 in black (7) with black tank with cream panels lined gold (64) and wheels with chrome-plated rims and black hubs (44).
Option of chrome-plated tank panels for C10L to give dark green, chrome and gold lines (74) and for C12 to give maroon, chrome and gold lines (36).

1958 C12—as 1956.

B range

1945 B31—black (7) frame, forks, oil tank, toolbox, mudguards, hubs, chainguard, details. Petrol tank chrome-plated with matt silver top and side panels lined black (13). Wheel rims chrome-plated with matt silver centres lined black (13). Chrome-plated brake backplates, handlebars, exhaust system, headlamp rim, battery carrier. Chaincase matt silver with black edge (16) to screw head channel.
In production wheel rims matt silver with black lining (16), backplates and chaincase black (7).

1946 B31—as 1945.
B32—black (7) frame, forks, oil tank, toolbox, details. Petrol tank chrome-plated with matt silver top and side panels lined black (13). Wheel rims matt silver with black lining (16). Chrome-plated mudguards, stays, rear chainguard, brake backplates, handlebars, exhaust system, headlamp rim.

1947 B31—as 1945.
B32—as 1946 except wheel rims chrome-plated with matt silver centres lined black (13).
B33—as B31 except wheel rims chrome-plated with matt silver centres lined black (13). From July mudguard centres lined with $\frac{1}{2}$ in. wide matt silver stripe.

B34—as B32 including 1947 wheel rims.

1948 B31 and B33—as 1947 except chrome-plated fork seal holders.

B31—option with tank panels and rim centres in Brunswick green lined gold (15), B31 rims also chrome-plated as B33.

B33—option with tank panels and rim centres in Devon red-lined gold (12).

B32—in B31 optional green (15) for tank panels and rim centres as standard, chrome-plated fork seal holders. Optional chrome-plated chaincase.

B34—as B32 but in B33 optional Devon red (12).

1949 B range—as 1948 except chrome-plated rear brake rod.

1950–51 B32 and B34—chrome-plated chaincase as standard.

1952 B range—as 1951 until restrictions on chrome plating had effect. New tank badges from March and at same time B31 adopted green tank and B33 a red tank, each gold-lined. Wheel rims were in silver with green or red centres to match.

B32 and B34—with matt silver tanks and wheel rims lined black (16).

1953 B31 and B33—maroon (37) for all painted parts with tank the same with chrome-plated side panels lined gold (36) and wheels with chrome-plated rims and maroon hubs (41). B31 with chrome-plated front brake backplate. Option of black (7) with wheels with black hubs (44) but tank remaining in maroon, chrome and gold (36).

B32 and 34—black (7) frame, forks, oil tank, toolbox. Petrol tank chrome-plated with matt silver panels lined black (13). Chrome-plated mudguards, stays, chaincase, chainguard. Wheels with chrome-plated rims and black hubs (44).

1954–55 B31 and B33—in maroon (37) with tank with chrome-plated panels gold-lined (36) and maroon hubs (41) as 1953 without the black option.

B32 and B34—as 1953 but alloy tank on rigid models and chrome-plated with silver panels lined maroon (19) for pivoted-fork ones.

1956 B range—as 1954 with all-black option for B31 and B33 as 1953 so tank to match with code (17) in black, chrome and gold lining. Alloy hubs for these models only.

1957 B31 and B33—as 1956.

B32 and B34—black (7) frame, forks; wheel with chrome-plated rims and black hubs (44); alloy petrol tank; chrome-plated mudguards, brake backplates.

1958–59 B31 and B33—black (7) frame, forks. Hubs black with polished rims to hub end and brake backplate. Oil tank, toolbox, mudguards, stays in almond green (100) for B31 and gunmetal grey (101) for B33. Petrol tanks to match with chrome-plated side panels and gold lining for B31 and red for B33. All-black option still available.

1960 B33—as 1958 except Princess grey (102) in place of gunmetal grey for petrol tank, oil tank, mudguards, stays, toolbox.

Gold Star

1949–51 Black (7) frame, forks, oil tank, headlamp shell, toolbox, details. Petrol tank chrome-plated with matt silver panels lined maroon (19) with Gold Star transfers. Wheel rims chrome-plated with matt silver centres lined maroon (19). Chrome-plated mudguards, stays, chaincase, chainguard, battery-carrier strap, brake backplates, rear brake rod, exhaust system, handlebars, fork seal holders, headlamp rim, plunger lower spring covers.

1952 Generally as before but petrol tank in matt silver with maroon lining and matt silver for mudguards, stays, chaincase, chainguard, brake backplates, handlebars.

1953–63 Black (7) frame, forks, rear fork, headlamp shell, upper damper covers, oil tank, toolbox, fork yokes, hubs except 190 mm, details. Silver grey damper bodies. Chrome-plated mudguards, stays, chainguard, wheel rims unless light alloy, lower damper covers, fork oil seal holders, headlamp rim, exhaust system, handlebars, kickstart and gear levers. Petrol tank matt silver with chrome-plated side panels lined maroon (19) and fitted with round Gold Star badges. Alloy tanks polished or finished as steel ones. Some models for the USA had royal or Nutley blue tanks with gold lining and rear dampers to match. This applied from 1958 onwards and varied with the year and whether for East or West Coast machines.

M range

1945 M20—black (7) frame, forks, oil tank, toolbox, mudguards, wheel rims, details. Petrol tank matt silver with panels outlined in black (16). Chrome-plated handlebars, exhaust system, headlamp rim.

1946 M20—as 1945.

M21—as M20.

1947 M20 and M21—as 1946.

1948–51 M33—black (7) frame, forks, oil tank, toolbox, mudguards, details. Petrol tank chrome-plated with matt silver panels lined black (13). Wheel rims chrome-plated with matt silver centres lined black (13). Chrome-plated handlebars, exhaust system, headlamp rim, fork oil seal holder.

M20 and M21—chrome-plated fork oil seal holder. Option of petrol tank and wheel rims in chrome-plate with matt silver panels and centres lined black (13) and thus as M33.

1952 M range—new badges in March, petrol tank silver with panels outlined in black (16), black wheel rims.

1953 M range—black (7) frame, forks, oil tank, toolbox, mudguards. Petrol tank maroon with chrome side panels gold-lined (36). Wheels

with chrome-plated rims and black hubs (44).
1954–55 M range—as 1953 except round tank badges.
1956–63 M range—black (7) frame, forks, oil tank, toolbox, mudguards. Petrol tank maroon with cream side panels lined to match both colours (48). Wheels as 1953. Option of tank as 1954 in maroon with chrome-plated side panels gold-lined (36).

C15

1959 C15—black (7) frame, forks, rear units, chainguard, stand, front-mudguard bridge stay. Petrol tank, oil tank, toolbox, centre panel, mudguards, front-guard rear stay fuchsia red (34) or turquoise green. Wheels with chrome-plated rims and black hubs with polished rim to both hub and backplate.
1960 C15—as 1959 except green now almond green (100).
1961 C15—silver sheen hubs and brake backplates, whitewall tyre option.
1962 C15—as 1961 in red (34), Nutley blue (88) or black (7) with petrol tanks to match, the blue one having ivory panels with twin lines (169). Black items as 1959, wheels as 1961.
1963 C15—as 1962 in red (34) or sapphire blue (88). Option of tanks with chrome-plated side panels in red (173) or blue (172).
1964 C15—royal red (27) in place of previous red and option tank with chrome-plated panel to match in royal red (109). Blue (88) and blue and chrome tank (172) continued.
1965 C15—as 1964 plus all-black (7) option. Tank in black with chrome-plated side-panel option (120) as further option.
1966 C15—as 1964 except tank panels chrome-plated as standard.
1967 C15—as 1966 plus all-black option with chrome-plated tank panels. Plating in new style and not under kneegrips.

C15 competition

1959–61 C15T and C15S—black (7) frame, forks, oil tank, toolbox, centre panel. Petrol tank sapphire blue with chrome panels (110), mudguards sapphire blue (88) with option of chrome-plate available. Wheels as C15.
1962 C15T and C15S—as 1959 until May when altered to black (7) frame, forks, oil tank, hubs. Rear hub as 1959 with polished rim. Chrome-plated wheel rims and front brake backplate. Light-alloy petrol tank and polished light-alloy (21) mudguards.
1963–65 C15T and C15S—as late 1962.

C15 USA models

1960–61 C15 (USA)—black (7) frame, forks; blue and ivory (145) petrol tank; sapphire blue (88) oil tank, toolbox, centre panel; blue with twin lines (112) mudguards.
1960 C15 Starfire Scrambler and C15 Road Scrambler (USA)—black (7) frame, forks, oil tank, toolbox; blue and chrome-plated (110) petrol tank; chrome-plated mudguards.
1962 C15 Pastoral—black (7) frame, forks, oil tank, toolbox; Nutley blue (88) petrol tank, mudguards.
C15 Starfire Roadster (USA)—black (7) frame, forks, oil tank, toolbox; blue and chrome-plated (172) petrol tank; chrome-plated mudguards.
C15 Star (USA)—black (7) frame, forks; blue and chrome-plated (110) petrol tank; blue (88) oil tank, toolbox; Nutley blue with twin lining (112) mudguards.
C15 Sport Star (USA)—black (7) frame, forks; red and chrome-plated (173) petrol tank; red (170) oil tank, toolbox; chrome-plated mudguards.
C15 Trials (USA)—as 1960 C15 Starfire Scrambler in black, blue and chrome.

SS80

1961 SS80—black (7) frame, forks, oil tank, toolbox, centre panel, mudguards. Petrol tank black with chrome-plated side panels (120). Wheels with chrome-plated rims and silver sheen hubs and backplates. Top fork yoke pressing chrome-plated. Option of chrome-plated mudguards.
1962–63 SS80—as 1961 or with flamboyant blue (167) oil tank, toolbox, centre panel. Petrol tank flamboyant blue with chrome-plated side panels (168); mudguards remained black or optional chrome-plated.
1964 SS80—as 1962 in flamboyant blue (167) only. Petrol tank in blue with chrome-plated side panels (168). Mudguards blue or option of chrome-plated.
1965 SS80—as 1964 except mudguards chrome-plated as standard.

C15 Sportsman

1966 C15 Sportsman—black (7) frame, forks; silver sheen (31) hubs and backplates; flamboyant blue (167) oil tank, toolbox; chrome-plated mudguards, headlamp shell. Petrol tank flamboyant blue with chrome-plated panels and white line (174).

B40

1961 B40—black (7) frame, forks. Petrol tank royal red with chrome-plated side panels (109). Royal red (27) mudguards, oil tank, toolbox, centre panel. Wheels with chrome-plated rims and silver sheen hubs and backplates.
1962–63 B40—as 1961 or all in black (7) with petrol tank black with chrome-plated side panels (162).
1964 B40—as 1961 in red or sapphire blue (88) with petrol tank blue with chrome-plated side panels (172).

1965 B40—as 1962 or 1964 and thus in red, blue or black.

SS90

1962 SS90—black (7) frame, forks; flamboyant red (170) oil tank, toolbox. Petrol tank flamboyant red with chrome-plated side panels (171); chrome-plated mudguards; silver sheen hubs.
1963 SS90—as 1962 plus option in black (7) with tank in black with chrome-plated side panels (120).
1964–65 SS90—as 1962.

B40E

1965 B40E—as C15T.

B44VE

1966–67 B44VE—as C15T in black, chrome-plate and alloy petrol tank.

C25/B25

1967 C25—black (7) frame, forks; white (69) or chrome-plated mudguards; bushfire orange (244) side cover, oil tank; chrome-plated headlamp shell. Petrol tank bushfire orange and white with black separating line (265).
1968 B25—black (7) frame, forks; chrome-plated mudguards, headlamp shell; Nutley blue with gold-lined (248) side cover, oil tank. Petrol tank Nutley blue with ivory panel lined gold (145).
1969 B25—black (7) frame, forks, oil tank, chrome-plated mudguards, headlamp shell. Flamboyant blue (227) petrol tank, side covers.
B25 (USA)—black (7) frame, forks, oil tank; matt black engine parts (262). Side covers bushfire orange with black line (264). Petrol tank bushfire orange, moss gold centre stripe and single black line (263).
1970 B25—as 1969 except black (7) side covers.
B25 (USA)—as 1969 except no matt engine parts, side covers white (69) and petrol tank flamboyant blue with white stripes and red lining (280).
1971 B25SS—grey (288) frame; exhaust system matt black; flamboyant red (170) side covers; flamboyant red with black centre stripe (293) mudguards. Petrol tank flamboyant red with black centre and side stripes red-lined (285).
B25T—as B25SS except petrol tank in polished aluminium with black centre and side stripes lined red (291).

B44VR and B44SS

1967 B44VR—as 1967 C25.
1968 B44SS—as 1968 B25 except side cover and oil tank in peony red with gold lining (250), and petrol tank in peony red with ivory panels and gold lining (223).
1969 B44SS—as 1970 B25 except peony red (226) petrol tank. Thus black side covers.
1970 B44SS—as 1969 except petrol tank flamboyant red (170).

B44VS

1967 B44VS—black (7) frame, forks, oil tank, hubs; chrome-plated mudguards. Petrol tank polished alloy with yellow panels and white lining (218).
1968–69 B44VS—as 1967 plus black (7) side covers.
1970 B44VS—as 1968 except petrol tank with polished cap (273).

B50

1971 B50SS—as B25SS.
B50T—as B25T.
B50MX—petrol tank as B25T (291), mudguards in stainless steel; side covers in race colour of yellow for England and white (305) for USA; matt black exhaust system.
1972 B50SS—black (7) frame; matt black exhaust system; black instrument finish (306) front brake backplate. Petrol tank, mudguards, side covers hi-violet (315).
B50T—black (7) frame; otherwise as 1971.
B50MX—black (7) frame; petrol tank polished aluminium with white centre stripe and Flambordeaux side stripes (314); otherwise as 1971.
1973 B50MX—as 1972.

10

Ken James on the 348 cc Gold Star with which he and I. Lloyd won the 1956 Thruxton 9 Hours

6 Pistons

Bantam

Model	Year	Bore (mm)	Piston number	Compression ratio
D1	1949–63	52	90-337	6.5
D3	1954	57	90-789	6.4
	1955–57	57	90-873	6.4
D5	1958	61.5	90-1305	7.4
D7	1959–61	61.5	90-1305	7.4
	1962–66	61.5	90-1459	7.4 3 rings
D10	1967	61.5	90-1516	8.65
D14	1968	61.5	70-7805	10.0
D175	1969–71	61.5	70-9784	9.5

C range

Model	Year	Bore (mm)	Piston number	Compression ratio
C10	1945–53	63	29-2561	5.0
C11	1945–53	63	29-2568	6.5
C10L	1954–57	63	29-2561	5.0
C11G	1954–55	63	29-2568	6.5
C12	1956–58	63	29-2568	6.5

B range

Model	Year	Bore (mm)	Piston number	Comp. ratio	Rod length (in.)
B31	1945–52	71	65-758	6.5	$7\frac{3}{8}$
	1953–59	71	65-809	6.5	$7\frac{3}{8}$
B32	1946–52	71	65-758	6.5	$7\frac{3}{8}$
	1953–57	71	65-1679	6.5	$6\frac{7}{8}$
B33	1947–52	85	65-1244	6.8	$7\frac{3}{8}$
	1953–57	85	65-1692	6.5	$6\frac{7}{8}$
	1958–60	85	65-1660	7.5	$6\frac{7}{8}$
B34	1947–57	85	65-1244	6.8	$7\frac{3}{8}$

B-range options

Model	Year	Bore (mm)	Piston number	Comp. ratio	Rod length (in.)
B31	1947	71	65-754	7.25	$7\frac{3}{8}$
	1948–50	71	65-754	7.5	$7\frac{3}{8}$
	1955–57	71	65-754	7.5	$7\frac{3}{8}$
	1947–50	71	65-790	7.75	$7\frac{3}{8}$
	1949–50	71	65-793	9.0	$7\frac{3}{8}$
	1947–50	71	65–775	12.5	$7\frac{3}{8}$
B32	1947	71	65-754	7.25	$7\frac{3}{8}$
	1948–50	71	65-754	7.5	$7\frac{3}{8}$
	1947–50	71	65-790	7.75	$7\frac{3}{8}$
	1949–50	71	65-793	9.0	$7\frac{3}{8}$
	1947–50	71	65-775	12.5	$7\frac{3}{8}$
B33	1947	85	65-1264	7.4	$7\frac{3}{8}$
	1948–50	85	65-1264	7.5	$7\frac{3}{8}$
	1953–57	85	65-1660	7.5	$6\frac{7}{8}$
	1950	85	65-1284	8.0	$7\frac{3}{8}$
	1947–50	85	65-1256	8.5	$7\frac{3}{8}$
	1950	85	65-1531	9.0	$7\frac{3}{8}$
	1954–55	85	65-2581	11.0	$6\frac{7}{8}$
B34	1947	85	65-1264	7.4	$7\frac{3}{8}$
	1948–50	85	65-1264	7.5	$7\frac{3}{8}$
	1954–57	85	65-1264	7.5	$7\frac{3}{8}$
	1950	85	65-1284	8.0	$7\frac{3}{8}$
	1954–57	85	65-2323	8.0	$7\frac{3}{8}$
	1947–50	85	65-1256	8.5	$7\frac{3}{8}$
	1950	85	65-1531	9.0	$7\frac{3}{8}$

Gold Star

Note that 348 cc engines had three rod lengths: early ZB at $7\frac{3}{8}$ in., late ZB from engine 6001 and BB at $6\frac{7}{8}$ in., and CB or DB at $6\frac{15}{32}$ in. Model BB thus includes late ZB engines in the table. The 499 cc engines only had two rod lengths: ZB and BB at $7\frac{3}{8}$ in., and CB, DB and DBD at $6\frac{15}{32}$ in. Pistons for the ZB34 and BB34 will interchange but will not fit the later engines.

Model	Year	Bore (mm)	Piston number	Compression ratio	Rod length (in.)	Model
B32GS	1949–52	71	65-1473	6.5	$7\frac{3}{8}$	ZB
	1953–54	71	65-1680	6.5	$6\frac{7}{8}$	BB
	1954	71	65-2275	6.5	$6\frac{15}{32}$	CB
	1955	71	65-1921	7.25	$6\frac{15}{32}$	CB
	1949–50	71	65-1476	7.5	$7\frac{3}{8}$	ZB
	1951–52	71	65-1615	7.5	$6\frac{7}{8}$	BB
	1949–50	71	65-1479	7.75	$7\frac{3}{8}$	ZB
	1953–54	71	65-1615	8.0	$6\frac{7}{8}$	BB
	1954	71	65-2254	8.0	$6\frac{15}{32}$	CB, DB
	1953–54	71	65-1666	8.5	$6\frac{7}{8}$	BB
	1954	71	65-2281	8.5	$6\frac{15}{32}$	CB
	1949–52	71	65-799	9.0	$7\frac{3}{8}$	ZB
	1953–54	71	65-1673	9.0	$6\frac{7}{8}$	BB
	1954–55	71	65-2287	9.0	$6\frac{15}{32}$	CB
	1955	71	65-2479	9.0	$6\frac{15}{32}$	DB
	1949–50	71	65-1482	12.5	$7\frac{3}{8}$	ZB
	1953–54	71	65-1686	12.25	$6\frac{7}{8}$	BB
	1954	71	65-2293	12.25	$6\frac{15}{32}$	CB
B34GS	1949–54	85	65-1464	6.8	$7\frac{3}{8}$	ZB, BB
	1953	85	65-1244	6.8	$7\frac{3}{8}$	ZB, BB
	1955	85	65-1930	7.25	$6\frac{15}{32}$	CB
	1949–54	85	65-1467	7.5	$7\frac{3}{8}$	ZB, BB
	1950	85	65-1290	8.0	$7\frac{3}{8}$	ZB, BB
	1954	85	65-1290	8.0	$7\frac{3}{8}$	ZB, BB
	1950	85	65-1460	8.0	$7\frac{3}{8}$	ZB, BB
	1954	85	65-2307	8.0	$6\frac{15}{32}$	CB
	1955–63	85	65-2544	8.0	$6\frac{15}{32}$	DB
	1949–50	85	65-1470	8.5	$7\frac{3}{8}$	ZB, BB
	1949–50	85	65-1450	8.5	$7\frac{3}{8}$	ZB, BB
	1954	85	65-2260	8.5	$6\frac{15}{32}$	CB
	1955–63	85	65-2553	8.5	$6\frac{15}{32}$	DB
	1958–63	85	65-907	8.75	$6\frac{15}{32}$	DB
	1950–54	85	65-1537	9.0	$7\frac{3}{8}$	ZB, BB
	1950	85	65-1540	9.0	$7\frac{3}{8}$	ZB, BB
	1954–55	85	65-2300	9.0	$6\frac{15}{32}$	CB
	1961–63	85	65-2247	10.0	$6\frac{15}{32}$	DBD
	1949–50	85	65-1278	11.0	$7\frac{3}{8}$	ZB, BB
	1954	85	65-1278	11.0	$7\frac{3}{8}$	ZB, BB

M range

Model	Year	Bore (mm)	Piston number	Comp. ratio
M20	1945–53	82	66-1190	4.9
	1954–55	82	66-1193	4.9
M21	1946–53	82	66-1198	5.0
	1954	82	66-1215	5.0
M21 AA	1954–57	82	66-1198	5.0
M33	1948–52	85	65-1244	6.8
	1953–57	85	65-1692	6.5

Model	Year	Bore (mm)	Piston number	Comp. ratio
M33 opt	1948–52	85	65-1264	7.5
	1953–57	85	65-1660	7.5
	1950	85	65-1284	8.0
	1948–50	85	65-1256	8.5
	1954–55	85	65-1256	8.5
	1950	85	65-1531	9.0
	1954–55	85	65-1278	11.0
	1954–55	85	65-2581	11.0

Unit models

Model	Year	Bore (mm)	Piston number	Comp. ratio
C15	1959–63	67	40-	7.25
	1964–67	67	40-630	8.0
C15T	1959	67	40-258	7.5
	1960–65	67	40-341	6.4
C15S	1959–60	67	40-347	9.0
	1961	67	40-444	10.0
	1962–65	67	40-644	10.0
SS80	1961	67	40-644	10.0
	1962–65	67	40-637	8.75
C15 Sp	1966	67	40-637	8.75
C15 (USA)	1960–61	67	40-359	8.0
	1962	67	40-630	8.0
C15 Road Scrambler		67	40-347	9.0
C15 Starfire Scrambler		67	40-444	10.0
C15 Starfire Roadster		67	40-644	10.0
C15 Trials (USA)		67	40-630	8.0
C25/B25	1967–70	67	40-970	10.0
B25	1971	67	71-1801	9.5

Model	Year	Bore (mm)	Piston number	Comp. ratio
B40	1961–65	79	41-075	7.0
SS90	1962–65	79	41-242	8.75
B40E	1964–65	79	41-250	8.0
	1964–65	79	41-242	8.75
B40 Military		79	47-041	7.0
B40 Rough Rider		79	47-041	7.0
B44GP	1965–67	79	41-570	
B44VE	1966–67	79	41-570	9.0
B44VR	1967	79	41-793	9.0
B44SS	1968	79	41-793	11.44
	1969–70	79	41-793	9.4
B44VS	1967	79	41-691	9.0
	1968	79	41-793	11.44
	1969–70	79	41-793	9.4
B50	1971–72	84	71-2745	10.0
B50MX	1973	84	71-2745	8.5
C15 opt	1960–61	67	40-258	7.5
	1960–61	67	40-264	8.5
B25 opt	1971	67	71-1953	8.5
B40 opt		79	41-250	8.0

A Gold Star in preparation for the 1950 Daytona race with rider Tommy McDermott on the right

7 Camshafts

C range

Model	Year	Camshaft	Timing	Set at	Inlet	Exhaust	Remarks
C10	1945–53	29-2164	25,70,70,25	0.010	0.004	0.006	
	1945–53	29-2078	29,84,80,28	0.015	0.012	0.015	ramp cam
C11	1945–53	29-2286	25,70,70,25	0.010	0.003	0.003	
	1945–53	29-2079	29,84,80,28	0.015	0.010	0.012	ramp cam
C10L	1954	29-1993	25,70,70,25	0.010	0.004	0.006	
	1955–57	29-2075	34,78,74,38	run	0.012	0.015	ramp cam
			29,84,80,28	0.015	0.012	0.015	ramp cam
C11G	1954	29-2025	25,70,70,25	0.010	0.003	0.003	
	1955	29-2076	34,78,74,38	run	0.010	0.012	ramp cam
			29,84,80,28	0.015	0.010	0.012	ramp cam
C12	1956–58	29-2076	as C11G				

Note that 29-2078 and 29-2079 were replacement camshafts for the C10 and C11 with ramp cams and may be used in any engine with the appropriate adjustment to the valve gaps.

Cam 29-2075 went into the C10L at engine BC10L-3562 and cam 29-2076 went into the C11G at engine BC11G-10438 late in 1954; both were of ramp form. The timings given are both to be found in BSA literature. The cams may be used in 1954 models if desired.

B and M ranges

Model	Year	Camshaft	Timing	Inlet	Exhaust
B31	1945–59	65-2420	25,65,65,25	0.003	0.003
B32	1946–57	65-2420	25,65,65,25	0.003	0.003
B33	1947–60	65-2420	25,65,65,25	0.003	0.003
B34	1947–57	65-2420	25,65,65,25	0.003	0.003
M20	1945–55	65-2420	25,65,65,25	0.010	0.012
M21	1946–63	65-2420	25,65,65,25	0.010	0.012
M33	1948–57	65-2420	25,65,65,25	0.003	0.003

Options for B range

Year	Inlet	Exhaust	Remarks
1948–50	65-2438	65-2434	spec. order
1948–50	65-2438	65-2436	racing

Gold Star

In 1952 quietening ramps were added to Gold Star cam profiles and the replacements are listed below. These would need to be checked with the gaps set at .018 in.

Engine size	Year	Model	Inlet	Exhaust	Timing	Gaps	Note
350	1949	Touring	65-2438	65-2434		.001	
500	1949	Touring	65-2438	65-2436		.001	
350/500	1949–55	Trials	65-2420	65-2420	25,65,65,25	.003	
350/500	1949	Clubmans	65-2438	65-2436		.001	
350/500	1949	Scrambles	65-2438	65-2434		.001	
350	1950–51	Clubmans	65-1346	65-1348		.001 *	
500	1950	Clubmans	65-1346	65-1348		.001	
350	1950–51	Racing	65-2438	65-2436		.001 *	
500	1950–51	Racing	65-2438	65-2436		.001	
500	1951	Clubmans	65-2440	65-1348		.001	
350	1952	Tourer	65-2448	65-2452	43,73,64,34	.008/.01	
350	1953–55	Tourer	65-2448	65-2450	43,73,64,34	.008/.01	BB
500	1952–55	Tourer	65-2448	65-2450	43,73,70,45	.008/.01	BB
350/500	1952	Scrambles	65-2448	65-2450	43,73,70,45	.008/.01	
350/500	1953–55	Scrambles	65-2454	65-2450	50,80,70,45	.008/.01	BB *
350/500	1952–55	Clubmans	65-2444	65-2446	60,85,80,55	.008/.01	BB *
350/500	1952–55	Race-dope	65-2448	65-2450	43,73,70,45	.008/.01	BB *
350	1954	ISDT	65-2448	65-2450	43,73,64,34	.008/.01	BB
500	1954	ISDT	65-2448	65-2450	43,73,70,45	.008/.01	BB
350	1954–55	Clubmans	65-2444	65-1891	60,85,85,60	.006	CB *
350	1955	Clubmans	65-2444	65-1891	60,85,85,60	.006	DB
350	1956–57	Clubmans	65-2442	65-2491	65,85,95,50	.006	DB
500	1954–55	Clubmans	65-2442	65-2446	65,85,80,55	.006	CB *
500	1955–63	Clubmans	65-2442	65-2446	65,85,80,55	.006	DB, DBD
350	1956–57	Race	65-2442	65-1891	65,85,85,60	.006	DB *
500	1955	Race	65-2442	65-1891	65,85,85,60	.006	DB
500	1956–57	Race	65-2442	65-2446	65,85,80,55	.006	DB, DBD
350	1954	Tourer	65-2444	65-1891	60,85,85,60	.006	CB
350	1955	Tourer	65-2448	65-2450	43,73,64,34	.006	CB
350	1955–56	Tourer	65-2448	65-2450	43,73,70,45	.006	DB
500	1954	Tourer	65-2442	65-2446	65,85,80,55	.006	CB
500	1955–56	Tourer	65-2448	65-2450	43,73,70,45	.006	CB, DB
350	1954–55	Scrambles	65-2444	65-1891	60,85,85,60	.006	CB
350	1955–57	Scrambles	65-2454	65-2450	50,80,70,45	.006	DB *
500	1954	Scrambles	65-2442	65-2446	65,85,80,55	.006	CB
500	1955–57	Scrambles	65-2446	65-2446	63,72,80,55	.006	CB, DB
500	1956–63	Scrambles	65-2446	65-2446	63,72,80,55	.006	DBD

Note Column gives model series type and * indicates the use of the special crankshaft pinion part 65-696 which gave timing 10 degrees earlier or advanced and was only used on the 348 cc models. Valve timing of all cams with .008/.01 or .006 gaps should be checked with these set at .018.

Replacement cam list as at 1952:

Old cam	New cam	Old cam	New cam
65-1346 by	65-2444	65-2436 by	65-2450
65-1348 by	65-2446	65-2438 by	65-2448
65-1354 by	65-2454	65-2440 by	65-2442
65-2434 by	65-2452		

Cam-lift data

Cam	Number	Opens	Closes	Cam lift**
Inlet	65-2420	25	65	.300
	65-2442	65	85	.442
	65-2444	60	85	.428
	65-2446	63	72	.400
	65-2448	43	73	.386
	65-2454	50	80	.415
Exhaust	65-1891	85	60	.428
	65-2420	65	25	.300
	65-2446	80	55	.400
	65-2450	70	45	.385
	65-2491	95	50	.428

** This lift figure includes the .018 in. checking gap.

Unit models

Note that all models changed their camshaft for 1965 due to the points moving into the timing cover.

Model	Year	Camshaft	Timing	Inlet	Exhaust	Set at
C15	1959–64	40-103	26,70,61.5,34.5	0.008	0.010	0.02
	1965–67	40-677	26,70,61.5,34.5	0.008	0.010	0.02
C15T	1959–61	40-335	41.5,62.5,62.5,41.5	0.004	0.004	
	1962	40-477	51,68,78,37	0.008	0.010	0.015
	1963–64	40-103	26,70,61.5,34.5	0.008	0.010	0.02
	1965	40-677	26,70,61.5,34.5	0.008	0.010	0.02
C15S	1959–60	40-335	41.5,62.5,62.5,41.5	0.004	0.004	
	1961–64	40-477	51,68,78,37	0.008	0.010	0.015
	1965	40-706	51,68,78,37	0.008	0.010	0.015
SS80	1961–64	40-477	51,68,78,37	0.008	0.010	0.015
	1965	40-706	51,68,78,37	0.008	0.010	0.015
C15 Sp	1966	40-706	51,68,78,37	0.008	0.010	0.015
C25	1967	40-958	51,68,78,37	0.008	0.010	0.015
B25	1967–69	40-958	51,68,78,37	0.008	0.010	0.015
	1970	71-1276	51,68,78,37	0.008	0.010	0.015
	1971	71-2297	51,68,78,37	0.008	0.010	0.015
B40	1961–64	40-103	26,70,61.5,34.5	0.008	0.010	0.02
	1965	40-677	26,70,61.5,34.5	0.008	0.010	0.02
SS90	1962–64	40-477	51,68,78,37	0.008	0.010	0.015
	1965	40-706	51,68,78,37	0.008	0.010	0.015
B40E	1964	40-103	26,70,61.5,34.5	0.008	0.010	0.02
	1965	40-677	26,70,61.5,34.5	0.008	0.010	0.02
B40 Military		40-677	26,70,61.5,34.5	0.008	0.010	0.02
B40 Rough Rider		40-677	26,70,61.5,34.5	0.008	0.010	0.02
B44GP	1965–67	41-584	63,72,80,55	0.015	0.015	0.015
B44VE	1966–67	41-595	51,68,78,37	0.008	0.010	0.015
B44VS	1967–68	41-595	51,68,78,37	0.008	0.010	0.015
	1969	41-958	51,68,78,37	0.008	0.010	0.015
	1970	71-1124	51,68,78,37	0.008	0.010	0.015
B44VR	1967	41-595	51,68,78,37	0.008	0.010	0.015
B44SS	1968	41-595	51,68,78,37	0.008	0.010	0.015
	1969	41-958	51,68,78,37	0.008	0.010	0.015
	1970	71-1276	51,68,78,37	0.008	0.010	0.015
B50	1971–72	71-1680	51,68,78,37	0.008	0.010	0.015
B50MX	1971–72	71-2567	63,72,80,55	0.008	0.010	0.015
	1973	71-1680	51,68,78,37	0.008	0.010	0.015

8 Ignition timing

The letter R indicates that the setting is taken on full retard. Note that some models changed the piston movement figure on occasion without changing the degree figure. Where this was close to tdc, the piston movement was very small and the variation would be minimal. In all cases, the advice in the electrics chapter should be heeded, and the machine set up to run happily in its current condition and present-day settings and fuel.

Model	Year	Timing (in.)	Timing (degrees)
D1	1949–63	$\frac{5}{32}$	26.5
D3	1954–57	$\frac{5}{32}$	26.5
D5	1958	$\frac{5}{32}$	26.5
D7	1959–66	$\frac{1}{16}$	17
D10	1967		19
D14	1968	$\frac{1}{16}$	16.5
D175	1969–71	$\frac{1}{16}$	16.5
C10	1945–53	$\frac{1}{32}$ (R)	12
C11	1945–53	$\frac{1}{32}$	12
C10L	1954–57	$\frac{1}{32}$ or tdc	12
C11G	1954–55	$\frac{1}{32}$ or tdc	12
C12	1956–58	$\frac{3}{64}$ or tdc	12
B31	1945–59	$\frac{7}{16}$	38
B32	1946–57	$\frac{7}{16}$	38
B33	1947–55	$\frac{7}{16}$	38
	1956–60	$\frac{3}{8}$	
B34	1947–55	$\frac{7}{16}$	38
	1956–57	$\frac{3}{8}$	
M20	1945–55	$\frac{7}{16}$	38.5
M21	1946–63	$\frac{7}{16}$	37.5
M33	1948–55	$\frac{7}{16}$	38
	1956–57	$\frac{3}{8}$	
C15	1959	$\frac{11}{32}$	33.5
C15T	1959–61	$\frac{9}{32}$	34
C15S	1959–61	$\frac{9}{32}$	34
SS80	1961	$\frac{9}{32}$	34
B40	1961	0.02 (R)	8.5 (R)
C15, C15T, C15S, SS80, B40, SS90	1962	$\frac{1}{16}$ (R)	15.5 (R)
	1963–64	0.007 (R)	5 (R)
	1965	0.280	33.5
C15	1966–67	0.280	33.5
C15 Sp	1966	0.280	33.5
C25	1967		35
B25	1968–71	0.342	37
B44GP	1965–67	0.265	28
B44VE	1966–67	0.265	28
B44VR	1967	0.265	28
B44SS	1968–70	.284/.323	29/31
B44VS	1967–70	.284/.323	29/31
B50	1971	0.303	30
	1972–73	0.385	34

Gold Star

Year	Model	Timing (in.)	Timing (degrees)
ZB and BB models			
1949	350	$\frac{7}{16}$	38
1950–51	350	$\frac{7}{16}$	38
	350 high cr	$\frac{3}{8}$	
	500	$\frac{1}{2}$	38
	500 high cr	$\frac{7}{16}$	
1952–55	350 tourer, MX, ISDT, trials	$\frac{7}{16}$	36 or 37.5
	350 racing, Clubmans	$\frac{15}{32}$	39
	350 racing with alcohol	$\frac{3}{8}$	34
	500 tourer, trials, ISDT, racing	$\frac{1}{2}$	40.5
	500 racing with alcohol	$\frac{7}{16}$	37 or 38.5
	500 Clubmans	$\frac{15}{32}$	39
1952–53	500 scrambles	$\frac{1}{2}$	40.5
1954–55	500 scrambles	$\frac{7}{16}$	38.5
1954–55	500 CB Clubmans, racing, MX	$\frac{13}{32}$	36
1956–57	350 DB models	$\frac{15}{32}$	38.5
	500 DB models except tourer	$\frac{13}{32}$	36
	500 DB tourer	$\frac{1}{2}$	40.5
1956–63	500 DBD models	$\frac{15}{32}$	39

9 Sparking plugs

Model	Year	Champion plug
D1	1949–54	L10
	1955–58	L10S
	1959–63	L7
D3	1954	L10
	1955–57	L10S
D5	1958	L10S
D7	1959–66	L7
D10	1967	N4
D14	1968	N9Y
D175	1969–71	N4
C10	1945–49	L10
	1949–53	N8
C11	1945–53	L10S
C10L	1954	N8
	1955–57	N8B
C11G	1954–55	L10S
C12	1956–58	L10S
B31	1945–59	L10S
B32	1946–53	L10S
	1954–57	NA8
B32 alloy engine	1950–53	NA8
B33	1947–59	L10S
	1960	L7
B34	1947–53	L10S
	1954–57	NA8
B34 alloy engine	1950–53	NA8
M20	1945–50	L10
	1951–54	N8
	1955	N8B
M21	1946–50	L10
	1951–54	N8
	1955–59	N8B
	1960–63	N8
M33	1948–57	L10S
C15	1959–67	N5
C15T	1959–65	N5
C15S	1959–65	N3
SS80	1961–65	N4
C15 Sportsman	1966	N4
C25/B25	1967–71	N3
B40	1961–65	N5
SS90	1962–65	N4
B40 Rough Rider & Military		N5
B44GP	1965–66	N64Y
	1967	N6Y
B44VE	1966	N64Y
	1967	N6Y
B44VR	1967	N6Y
B44SS	1968–70	N4
B44VS	1967–68	N6Y
	1969–70	N4
B50	1971–72	N4
B50MX	1971–73	N3

Gold Star

Capacity	Model	Year	Champion plug
350	All	1949	L10S, LA11, LA14, LA15
350	Warm up	1949	L11S when on alcohol fuel
350, 500	All	1950–51	NA8, NA10, NA12, NA14, NA19, L11S
350, 500	Tour, trials	1952–56	NA8
350, 500	ISDT	1952–54	NA10
350, 500	Scrambles	1952–55	NA12 (or NA14 for 350)
350, 500	Race, Club	1952–63	NA14 with petrol or alcohol fuel
350, 500	Scrambles	1956–63	NA14

Capacity	Model	Champion	KLG	Lodge
500 DBD	Touring	N5	FE70	HLN
	Trials	N5	FE70	HLN
	Scrambles	N3		
	Scrambles	N55R		
	Racing	N55R or N58R	731LR	RL51
	Warm up	L5	F80	HHN *

*When warming up using alcohol fuel, it is essential *not* to use a plug with a protruding nose.

Plug equivalents

Original make	Type	Modern NGK	Modern Champion
KLG	F80	B7HS	L82
	FE70	B5ES	N8
Lodge	HLN	B6ES	N4
	HHN	B6HS	L85
	RL51	B10EN	N54R
Champion	L10	B6HS	L85
	L10S	B6HS	L85
	L11S	B7HS	L5
	L5	B8HS	L5
	L7	B7HS	L85
	LA11	B9HN	L57R
	LA14	B10HN	L54R
	LA15	B11HN	
	N3	B8ES	N3
Champion	N4	B7ES	N4
	N5	B6ES	N5
	N8	B5ES	N8
	N8B	B6ES	N8
	N9Y	BP7ES	N9Y
	N6Y	BP8ES	N6Y
	N64Y	B77EC	
	NA8	B6ES	N5
	NA10	B8ES	N3
	NA12	B9EN	N57R
	NA14	B10EN	N54R
	NA19	B12EN	N52R
	N55R	B10EN	N54R
	N58R	B9EN	N57R

10 Alternators

Model	Year	Alternator
D1	1949	Wipac Geni-Mag
	1950–55	Wipac S55/Mk8
	1950–53	Lucas 47077
	1956–63	Wipac IG1452 or IG1454
D3	1954–55	Wipac S55/Mk8
	1956–57	Wipac IG1450 or IG1452
D5	1958	Wipac IG1450 or IG1452
D7	1959–61	Wipac IG1450 or IG1552
	1962–63	Wipac IG1452 or IG1552
	1964–65	Wipac IG1452 or IG1704
	1966	Wipac IG1704
D10	1967	Wipac IG1768
D10B	1967	Wipac IG1778 ET ignition
D14	1968	Wipac IG1768
D14B	1968	Wipac IG1791 ET ignition
D175	1969–71	Wipac IG1768
D175B	1969–70	Wipac IG1791 ET ignition
C10L	1954–55	Wipac 48 watt
	1956–57	Wipac 50 watt
C11G	1954–55	RM 13
C12	1956–58	RM 13/15
B31	1958–59	RM 15
B33	1958–60	RM 15
C15	1959–61	RM 13
	1962–67	RM 18
C15T	1959–61	RM 13 ET ignition
	1962–65	RM 19 ET ignition
C15S	1959–61	RM 13 ET ignition
	1962–65	RM 19 ET ignition
SS80	1961–65	RM 18
C15 Sp	1966	RM 18
C15 P	1962	RM 20
C25/B25	1967–68	RM 19
B25	1969–71	RM 21
B40	1961	RM.13/15
	1962–65	RM 19
B40 P	1962	RM 20
SS90	1962–65	RM 19
B44GP	1965–67	RM 19 ET ignition
B44VE	1966–67	RM 19 ET ignition
B44VR	1967	RM 19
B44SS	1968	RM 19
	1969–70	RM 21
B44VS	1967–68	RM 19 ET ignition 1967
	1969–70	RM 21
B50	1971–72	RM 21
B50MX	1971–73	RM 22 ET ignition

11 Carburettor settings

Model	Year	Type	Size	Main	Pilot	Slide	Clip	Jet
D1	1949	261	$\frac{5}{8}$	70		5	2	.106
D1	1949–50	261	$\frac{5}{8}$	75		5	2	.106
D1	1951–54	361/1	$\frac{5}{8}$	75		5	2	.106
D1	1955–61	361/8	$\frac{5}{8}$	75		5	2	.106
D1	1962–63	361/18	$\frac{5}{8}$	75		5	2	.106
D1 USA	1957–60	361/23	$\frac{5}{8}$	75		5	2	.106
D1 comp	1950	261	$\frac{5}{8}$	75		5	2	.106
D1 comp	1951–54	361/2	$\frac{5}{8}$	75		5	2	.106
D1 comp	1955	361/9	$\frac{5}{8}$	75		5	2	.106
D1 GPO	1962–63	363/13	.475	55	15	3	3	.103
D3	1954–57	523/1	$\frac{11}{16}$	90		5	2	.1075
D3 comp	1954–55	523/2	$\frac{11}{16}$	90		5	2	.1075
D5	1958	375/31	$\frac{7}{8}$	140	25	$3\frac{1}{2}$	4	.1055
D7	1959–61	375/31	$\frac{7}{8}$	140	25	$3\frac{1}{2}$	4	.1055
D7	1962–65	375/31	$\frac{7}{8}$	140	25	$3\frac{1}{2}$	2	.1055
D7	1966	375/60	$\frac{7}{8}$	140	25	$3\frac{1}{2}$	2	.1055
D7 de luxe	1962–66	375/59	$\frac{7}{8}$	140	25	$3\frac{1}{2}$	2	.1055
D7 Pastoral	1959	375/39	$\frac{7}{8}$	150	25	3	3	.106
D7 Pastoral	1960–63	375/40	$\frac{7}{8}$	150	25	3	3	.106
D7 Pastoral	1962–66	375/50	$\frac{7}{8}$	140		$3\frac{1}{2}$	2	.105
D7 West Coast	1962–66	375/56	$\frac{7}{8}$	110		$3\frac{1}{2}$	2	.1055
D7 East Coast	1962–66	375/31	$\frac{7}{8}$	140		$3\frac{1}{2}$	2	.1055
D7 GPO	1967	32/23	$\frac{11}{16}$	85	15	2	3	.104
D10 Silver	1967	376/323	1	180	25	$3\frac{1}{2}$	2	.1055
D10 Silver	1967	R626/2	26	150	25	3	2	.105
D10 Supreme	1967	376/323	1	180	25	$3\frac{1}{2}$	2	.1055
D10 Supreme	1967	R626/2	26	150	25	3	2	.105
D10 Sports	1967	R626/3	26	150	25	3	2	.105
D10 Sportsman	1967	R626/2	26	150	25	3	2	.105
D10 Bushman	1967	R626/2	26	150	25	3	2	.105
D10 Pastoral	1967	R626/2	26	150	25	3	2	.105
D14/4	1968	R626/12	26	160	25	3	3	.105
D14/4S	1968	R626/13	26	160	25	3	3	.105
D14/4B	1968	R626/12	26	160	25	3	3	.105
D175	1969–71	R626/17	26	180		$3\frac{1}{2}$	2	.105
D175	1971	R626/31	26	180		$3\frac{1}{2}$	2	.105
C10	1946–53	274/K	$\frac{25}{32}$	90		4/4	2	.1055
C10L	1954	274/BT	$\frac{25}{32}$	90		4/4	2	.1055
C10L	1955–56	375/2	$\frac{25}{32}$	120	25	$3\frac{1}{2}$	2	.1055
C10L	1957	375/30	$\frac{25}{32}$	120	25	$3\frac{1}{2}$	2	.1055
C10L air filter	1955–57	375/2	$\frac{25}{32}$	85	25	$3\frac{1}{2}$	2	.1055
C11	1946–48	274/L	$\frac{25}{32}$	80		4/4	3	.1055
C11	1949–53	274/AU	$\frac{25}{32}$	80		4/4	3	.1065
C11G	1954	274/BU	$\frac{25}{32}$	80		4/4	3	.1065
C11G	1955	375/4	$\frac{25}{32}$	140	25	$3\frac{1}{2}$	3	.1055
C11G air filter	1955	375/4	$\frac{25}{32}$	100	25	$3\frac{1}{2}$	3	.1055
C12	1956–57	375/4	$\frac{25}{32}$	140	25	$3\frac{1}{2}$	3	.1055

Model	Year	Type	Size	Main	Pilot	Slide	Clip	Jet
C12	1958	375/25	$\frac{25}{32}$	140	25	$3\frac{1}{2}$	3	.1055
C12 air filter	1956–57	375/4	$\frac{25}{32}$	100	25	$3\frac{1}{2}$	3	.1055
C12 air filter	1958	375/25	$\frac{25}{32}$	100	25	$3\frac{1}{2}$	3	.1055
B31	1946–50	276/AW	1	150		6/4	3	.1065
B31	1951–54	276/DR	1	150		6/4	3	.1065
B31	1955	276/GC	1	150		6/4	3	.1065
B31	1955–57	376/2	1	260	30	$3\frac{1}{2}$	2	.1065
B31 air filter	1956–57	376/3	1	200	30	$3\frac{1}{2}$	2	.1065
B31 home	1958–59	376/81	1	260	30	$3\frac{1}{2}$	2	.1065
B31 export	1958–59	376/82	1	200	30	$3\frac{1}{2}$	2	.1065
B32	1946–50	276/AW	1	150		6/4	3	.1065
B32	1951–54	276/DR	1	150		6/4	3	.1065
B32	1955–56	276/GC	1	150		6/4	3	.1065
B32	1957	376/2	1	260	30	$3\frac{1}{2}$	2	.1065
B32 scrambler	1955–57	376/43	$1\frac{1}{16}$	260	25	4	3	.106
B33	1947–54	289/G	$1\frac{1}{8}$	200		29/4	3	.1065
B33 air filter	1949–54	289/G	$1\frac{1}{8}$	170		29/4	3	.1065
B33	1955	289W	$1\frac{1}{8}$	200		29/4	3	.1065
B33 air filter	1955	289W	$1\frac{1}{8}$	170		29/4	3	.1065
B33	1955	389/3	$1\frac{1}{16}$	260		$3\frac{1}{2}$	3	.1065
B33	1955–57	376/10	$1\frac{1}{16}$	260	25	$3\frac{1}{2}$	3	.1065
B33 air filter	1955–57	376/9	$1\frac{1}{16}$	210	25	$3\frac{1}{2}$	3	.1065
B33 home	1958–59	376/85	$1\frac{1}{16}$	260	25	$3\frac{1}{2}$	3	.1065
B33 export	1958–59	376/84	$1\frac{1}{16}$	210	25	$3\frac{1}{2}$	3	.1065
B33 home	1960	376/241	$1\frac{1}{16}$	260	25	$3\frac{1}{2}$	3	.1065
B33 export	1960	376/240	$1\frac{1}{16}$	210	25	$3\frac{1}{2}$	3	.1065
B34	1947–54	289/G	$1\frac{1}{8}$	200		29/4	3	.1065
B34 air filter	1949–54	289/G	$1\frac{1}{8}$	170		29/4	3	.1065
B34	1955–56	289W	$1\frac{1}{8}$	200		29/4	3	.1065
B34 air filter	1955–56	289W	$1\frac{1}{8}$	170		29/4	3	.1065
B34	1957	376/10	$1\frac{1}{16}$	260	25	$3\frac{1}{2}$	3	.1065
B34 scrambler	1957	389/8	$1\frac{1}{8}$	240	25	3	2	.106
M20	1946–54	276/C	1	170		6/4	2	.1065
M20	1955	376/21	1	240	30	5	3	.1065
M21	1946–54	276/BR	$1\frac{1}{16}$	160		6/4	2	.1065
M21	1955–57	376/23	$1\frac{1}{16}$	250	30	5	2	.1065
M21	1958–63	376/88	$1\frac{1}{16}$	250	30	5	2	.1065
M21 AA	1949–60	276/DZ	$1\frac{1}{16}$	160		6/4	2	.1065
M21 AA	1960	376/251	$1\frac{1}{16}$	250	30	5	2	.106
M33	1948–54	289/G	$1\frac{1}{8}$	200		29/4	3	.1065
M33 air filter	1949–50	289/G	$1\frac{1}{8}$	170		29/4	3	.1065
M33	1955–57	376/10	$1\frac{1}{16}$	260	25	$3\frac{1}{2}$	3	.1065
B32GS	1949	276/DR	1	150		6/4	3	.1065
B32GS	1949–54	TT	$1\frac{1}{16}$	320		7	4	.109
B32GS alcohol	1949–51	TT	$1\frac{1}{16}$			7	4	.120
B32GS	1949–51	RN	$1\frac{1}{16}$	420		6	4	.109
B32GS std	1952–54	276/	1	150		6/4	3	.1065
B32GS std	1952–56	TT	$1\frac{3}{32}$	360		7	3	.109
B32GS trials	1952–54	276/	1	150		6/4	3	.1065
B32GS MX	1952–55	TT	$1\frac{3}{32}$	360		7	3	.109
B32GS race	1952–54	TT	$1\frac{3}{32}$	360		7	3	.109
B32GS alcohol	1952	TT	$1\frac{3}{32}$			7	4	.120
B32GS alcohol	1954–55	TT	$1\frac{3}{32}$	1200		7	3	.120
B32GS race	1952–55	RN	$1\frac{3}{32}$	450		6	4	.109
B32GS Clubmans	1952–54	TT	$1\frac{3}{32}$	360		7	3	.109
B32GS Clubmans	1954–55	GP	$1\frac{3}{32}$	210		6	3	.109
B32GS Cl, race	1956–61	GP	$1\frac{3}{16}$	280		5	4	.109
B32GS std	1955	RN	$1\frac{3}{32}$	450		6	4	.109
B32GS MX	1955–56	376/43	$1\frac{1}{16}$	260		4	3	.1065
B32GS Clubmans	1955	GP	$1\frac{3}{16}$	280		5	4	.109

Model	Year	Type	Size	Main	Pilot	Slide	Clip	Jet
B34GS	1949	289/G	$1\frac{1}{8}$	200		29/4	3	.1065
B34GS	1949–54	TT	$1\frac{5}{32}$	360		6	4	.109
B34GS alcohol	1949–51	TT	$1\frac{3}{16}$			6	6	.120
B34GS	1949–51	RN	$1\frac{3}{16}$	520		7	4	.109
B34GS std	1952–54	289/	$1\frac{1}{8}$	200		29/4	3	.1065
B34GS std	1952	TT	$1\frac{5}{32}$	360		6	4	.109
B34GS std	1954–55	TT	$1\frac{5}{32}$	360		7	3	.109
B34GS std	1956	TT	$1\frac{3}{16}$	360		7	3	.109
B34GS trials	1952–54	289/	$1\frac{1}{8}$	200		29/4	3	.1065
B34GS MX	1952–55	TT	$1\frac{5}{32}$	360		7	3	.109
B34GS race	1952	TT	$1\frac{5}{32}$	360		6	4	.109
B34GS race	1954	TT	$1\frac{5}{32}$	360		7	3	.109
B34GS alcohol	1952	TT	$1\frac{3}{16}$			6	6	.120
B34GS alcohol	1954–55	TT	$1\frac{3}{16}$	1700		6	4	.120
B34GS race	1952–55	RN	$1\frac{3}{16}$	520		7	4	.109
B34GS Clubmans	1952	TT	$1\frac{5}{32}$	360		6	4	.109
B34GS Clubmans	1954	TT	$1\frac{5}{32}$	360		7	3	.109
B34GS Clubmans	1954–55	GP	$1\frac{7}{32}$	260		7	2	.109
B34GS Cl, race	1956	GP	$1\frac{3}{8}$	330		7	4	.109
B34GS DB race		GP	$1\frac{3}{8}$	330		7	2	.109
B34GS std	1955	TT	$1\frac{3}{16}$	360		7	3	.109
B34GS std	1955	RN	$1\frac{3}{16}$	520		7	4	.109
B34GS MX	1955	389/8	$1\frac{1}{8}$	240		3	2	.1065
B34GS MX	1956–63	389/13	$1\frac{5}{32}$	320	25	3	2	.1065
B34GS MX	1958–61	GP	$1\frac{5}{32}$	240		5	3	.109
B34GS MX USA	1959–60	389/35	$1\frac{5}{32}$	320	25	3	2	.1065
B34GS MX USA	1961–63	389/61	$1\frac{3}{16}$	320	30	4	4	.106
B34GS Clubmans	1955	GP	$1\frac{3}{8}$	330		7	4	.109
B34GS Clubmans	1956–60	GP	$1\frac{1}{2}$	350		4	3	.109
B34GS Clubmans	1961–63	GP	$1\frac{1}{2}$	350	25	4	3	.109
B34GS race	1956	GP	$1\frac{1}{2}$	390		4	3	.109

There were two needles available for the GP carburettor: the standard GP and the GP6 which gave a weaker mixture. Each was listed in three forms to suit the carburettor type, and listed accordingly. Thus the 5GP and 5GP6 were the rich and weak needles for the 5GP2 carburettor, and the 3GP and 3GP6 for the 3GP2.

The DB32 was normally fitted with a GP6 needle whether with a silencer or megaphone exhaust, but on the DBD34 a GP needle went with the silencer and a GP6 with a megaphone. Around 1959–60 the DBD was delivered with a 3GP6 in all cases, but this was incorrect for road use and the 3GP should be fitted when a silencer is used.

In some cases, a standard needle was fitted for bench testing and supplied with the machine. This could give problems if the machine was raced unless it was changed for the weak, but always check on any setting to ensure it is correct for the engine it is supplying.

This need to check applies to all engines and carburettors as both will be of some age when being restored and neither is likely to be just as they were when new. In addition, the fuel being used now will not be quite the same as then.

Model	Year	Type	Size	Main	Pilot	Slide	Clip	Jet
C15	1959–67	375/34	$\frac{7}{8}$	140	25	4	3	.1055
C15T	1959–63	375/34	$\frac{7}{8}$	140	25	4	3	.1055
C15T	1964–65	375/51	$\frac{7}{8}$	140	25	4	3	.1055
C15T Cat	1965	375/51	$\frac{7}{8}$	140	25	4	3	.1055
C15 Star USA	1961–65	376/270	1	180	25	$3\frac{1}{2}$	3	.1065
C15S	1959–60	376/222	$\frac{15}{16}$	180	25	3	2	.106
C15S	1960–61	376/258	$1\frac{1}{16}$	240	25	$3\frac{1}{2}$	2	.1065
C15S	1962–63	376/295	$1\frac{1}{16}$	240	25	$3\frac{1}{2}$	2	.106
C15S	1963–65	376/304	$1\frac{1}{16}$	190	25	$3\frac{1}{2}$	2	.106
SS80	1961	376/270	1	180	25	$3\frac{1}{2}$	3	.106
SS80	1962–65	376/281	1	200	25	4	2	.106
C15 Sportsman	1966	376/281	1	200	25	4	2	.106
C15SS USA	1962–65	376/290	$1\frac{1}{16}$	210	25	$3\frac{1}{2}$	2	.106
C15T Pastoral	1962–65	375/51	$\frac{7}{8}$	140	25	4	3	.1055
C15 Police	1962–67	375/51	$\frac{7}{8}$	140	25	4	3	.1055
C15S (Special)		376/295	$1\frac{1}{16}$	240	25	$3\frac{1}{2}$	2	.106

Model	Year	Type	Size	Main	Pilot	Slide	Clip	Jet
C25	1967	R928/1	28	220	25	3	2	.107
B25	1968	R928/1	28	220	25	3	2	.107
B25 USA	1968	R928/1	28	190	25	3	2	.107
B25	1969–70	R928/8	28	260	25	3	2	.106
B25	1971	R928/20	28	200		$3\frac{1}{2}$	1	.106
B40	1961–63	376/253	$1\frac{1}{16}$	190	20	3	3	.105
B40	1964–65	376/280	$1\frac{1}{16}$	190	20	3	3	.105
B40 USA	1962–63	389/78	$1\frac{1}{8}$	160	30	$3\frac{1}{2}$	3	.106
SS90	1962–65	389/83	$1\frac{1}{8}$	200	30	$3\frac{1}{2}$	3	.106
B40E	1965	376/280		190	20	3	3	.105
B40 Rough Rider		L626/4	26	130	20	3	2	.106
B40 Military		L626/4	26	130	20	3	2	.106
B44GP	1965–66	389/221	$1\frac{5}{32}$	310	25	$3\frac{1}{2}$	3	.106
B44GP	1967	389/221	$1\frac{5}{32}$	260	25	$3\frac{1}{2}$	3	.106
B44VE	1966	389/235	$1\frac{5}{32}$	330	25	$3\frac{1}{2}$	3	.106
B44VE	1967	930/1	30	220	25	3	2	.107
B44VS	1967–68	R930/1	30	220	25	3	2	.107
B44VS	1969–70	R930/38	30	240		$3\frac{1}{2}$	1	.106
B44VR	1967	R930/11	30	230	25	3	2	.107
B44SS	1968	R930/11	30	230	25	3	2	.107
B44SS	1969–70	R930/38	30	240		$3\frac{1}{2}$	1	.106
B50SS	1971–72	R930/62	30	200		$3\frac{1}{2}$	1	.106
B50T	1971–72	R930/62	30	200		$3\frac{1}{2}$	1	.106
B50MX	1971–72	R932/18	32	250		3	2	.106
B50MX	1973	R932/28	32	180 or 250		$3\frac{1}{2}$	1	.106

12 Gold Star exhaust-system recommendations

	ZB		**BB**		**CB**		**DB & DBD**	
	350	**500**	**350**	**500**	**350**	**500**	**350**	**500**
Plain pipe—racing								
Length	49	49	45	41	41	37	41	37
Diameter	—	—	$1\frac{5}{8}$	$1\frac{5}{8}$	$1\frac{3}{4}$	$1\frac{7}{8}$	$1\frac{3}{4}$	$1\frac{7}{8}$
Plain pipe—scrambles								
Length	49	49	53	53	53	53	51	51
Diameter	—	—	$1\frac{5}{8}$	$1\frac{5}{8}$	$1\frac{5}{8}$	$1\frac{3}{4}$	$1\frac{5}{8}$	$1\frac{3}{4}$
Pipe for megaphone								
Length	38	38	$37\frac{1}{2}$	$37\frac{1}{2}$	36	$34\frac{1}{2}$	36	$34\frac{1}{2}$
Diameter	—	—	$1\frac{5}{8}$	$1\frac{5}{8}$	$1\frac{3}{4}$	$1\frac{7}{8}$	$1\frac{3}{4}$	$1\frac{7}{8}$
Megaphone								
Length	13	$13\frac{1}{2}$	$13\frac{1}{2}$	$13\frac{1}{2}$	$11\frac{1}{2}$	$12\frac{1}{2}$	$12\frac{1}{2}$	$12\frac{1}{2}$
Major diameter	$3\frac{7}{8}$	$4\frac{1}{2}$	4	$4\frac{1}{2}$	4	$3\frac{5}{8}$	$3\frac{5}{8}$	$3\frac{5}{8}$
Inverse cone								
Outlet diameter	—	—	—	—	—	$3\frac{1}{16}$	$3\frac{1}{16}$	$3\frac{1}{16}$

Notes:

Pipe diameters are external.

Lengths are measured round the outside of the bend.

All pipes are 16 swg (0.064 in.).

Where not given the pipe diameters are standard.

All dimensions are in inches.

DBD manual gives megaphone as 11 in. long and inverse cone as $\frac{3}{4}$ in. long to make $11\frac{3}{4}$ in. overall.

There is variation in the data from one source to another and the pipe lengths may need to be adjusted for the best results for any individual engine and to suit its piston, cams and timing.

13 Capacities

Petrol tanks
Size in UK gallons

Model	Year	Size
D1, D3	1949–63	1.75
D5	1958	2.0
D7	1959–65	2.0
	1966	1.87
D10, D14, D175	1967–71	1.87
C10, C11	1946–53	2.5
C10L, C11G, C12	1954–58	2.75
B31, B33 rig, pl	1946–55	3.0
B31, B33 s/a	1954–60	4.0, 2.0 option
B32, B34	1946–53	3.0
	1948, 1950	2.0 option
B32, B34 MX	1952–53	2.0
B32, B34	1954–55	2.0 alloy
B32, B34 s/a	1954–55	2.0
	1956–57	2.0 alloy
Gold Star	1949	3.0, 2.0 option
	1950–51	3.0
Trial, MX	1950–51	2.0
Road, race,	1952	3.0 or 4.0
Trial, MX	1952	2.0 or 3.0
Trial, MX	1953–63	2.0
Trial, MX	1956–63	2.0 alloy option
Road, race, ISDT	1953–63	4.0
Race	1956–63	5.0 alloy option
M20, M21	1946–47	3.5
M20, M21, M33	1948–63	3.0
C15	1959–63	2.5
	1964–67	3.0
C15T, C15S	1959–61	2.0
	1960–61	2.0 alloy option
	1962–65	2.0 alloy
B40, SS80, SS90	1961–65	3.0
C25/B25	1967–68	1.75
	1969–70	3.25 or 2.5 in USA
B44GP	1965–67	1.37
B44VE	1966–67	1.75
B44VS	1967–70	1.75
B44VR	1967	1.75
B44SS	1968	1.75
	1969–70	3.25
B25SS, B50SS	1971–72	2.0 or 3.0
B25T, B50T	1971–72	2.0
B50MX	1971–73	1.0

Oil tanks
Size in UK pints

Model	Year	Size
C10, C11, C10L, C11G, C12	1945–58	4
B31, B33 rigid and plunger	1945–55	4
B31, B33 s/a	1954–60	5.5
B32, B34	1946–53	4
	1954–57	3.2
Gold Star	1949	4
	1950–52	5
	1953–63	5.5
M20, M21, M33	1945–63	5
C15, SS80, B40, SS90	1959–67	4
C15T, C15SS	1959–62	4
	1963–65	5
B44GP	1965–67	4.2
B44VE	1966	5
	1967	4
C25, B25, B44VR, B44SS	1967–70	4
B44VS	1967–70	5
B25, B50	1971–73	4

Gearbox

Model	Year	Size in cc
Bantams—3-speed	1949–67	425
Bantams—4-speed	1967–71	570
C range 3-speed	1945–55	284
C range 4-speed	1951–55	568
	1956–58	285
B and M ranges	1945–55	568
B range	1956–60	400
M range	1956–63	370
Gold Star	1956–63	384
C15 and B40 ranges	1959–67	285
C25, B25, B44	1965–70	285
B25 and B50	1971–73	280

Primary chaincase

Model	Year	Size in cc
C, B and M ranges	1945–49	284
C range	1950–51	71
B and M ranges	1950–51	107
C, B and M ranges	1952–54	80
C range	1955–58	195
B and M ranges	1955	55
B31 and B33 s/a	1954–60	225
B32 and B34	1954–57	225
M range	1955–63	55
Gold Star	1949	284
	1950–52	107
	1953–63	225
All unit engines	1959–73	140

Front forks

Model	Year	Capacity cc
D1, D3 and D5	1949–63	Grease
D7, D10, D14/4	1959–68	70
D14/4S, D14/4B, D175	1968–71	175
C range	1945–58	142
C10L	1954–55	Grease
B range	1945–51	142
B31 and B33	1952–55	142
	1956–60	212
B32 and B34	1952–57	212
Gold Star	1949–51	142
	1952–63	212
M range	1948–63	142
C15, SS80	1959–67	100
C15T, C15S, B40, SS90	1959–65	190
C25, B25, B44	1965–70	190
B25, B50	1971–73	190

A 1967 B44VR Victor Roadster on show

14 Transmission

Gearbox internal ratios

Note that boxes with the same numbers of teeth on the gears may well not have the same detail part numbers, and these should not be mixed. It may also not be possible to change a complete box as it may not fit correctly.

Gearbox	Used	Mainshaft				Layshaft				Gear ratios		
		4	3	2	1	4	3	2	1	3rd	2nd	1st
D1 standard	1949–63		28	22	15		19	25	32		1.675	3.144
D1 race			24	22	19		23	25	28		1.186	1.538
D1 wide			28	21	15		19	26	32		1.824	3.144
D1 special			24	21	15		23	26	32		1.292	2.226
D1 special			28	22	19		19	25	28		1.675	2.172
D1 special			24	22	15		23	25	32		1.186	2.226
D3 standard	1954–57		28	22	15		19	25	32		1.675	3.144
D5	1958		28	22	15		19	25	32		1.675	3.144
D7-1	1959–61		28	22	15		19	25	32		1.675	3.144
D7-2	1962–66		26	22	15		21	25	32		1.407	2.641
D7 race	1959–66		24	22	19		23	25	28		1.186	1.538
D10	1967		26	22	15		21	25	32		1.407	2.641
D10/4	1967	29	26	22	17	18	21	25	30	1.301	1.831	2.843
D14	1968	29	26	22	17	18	21	25	30	1.301	1.831	2.843
D175	1969–71	29	26	22	17	18	21	25	30	1.301	1.831	2.843
C	1946–55		32	27	22		20	25	30		1.481	2.182
C4-1	1951–55	26	24	20	16	17	19	23	27	1.211	1.759	2.581
C4-2	1956–58	27	25	21	17	16	18	22	26	1.215	1.768	2.581
B1	1946–48	29	26	21	17	18	21	26	30	1.301	1.995	2.843
B2 ri & pl	1949–55	28	25	20	16	17	20	25	29	1.318	2.059	2.985
B-s/a	1954–60	26	24	20	16	17	19	23	27	1.211	1.759	2.581
B-close	1948	29	27	24	19	18	20	23	28	1.193	1.544	2.374
B32, B34	1954–57	26	22	17	14	17	21	26	29	1.460	2.339	3.168
GS	1949–52	28	25	20	16	17	20	25	29	1.318	2.059	2.985
GS-MX	1949–52	28	25	22	18	17	20	23	27	1.318	1.722	2.471
GS-Cl, race	1949–52	26	25	23	19	19	20	22	26	1.095	1.309	1.873
GS-STD	1953–56	26	24	20	16	17	19	23	27	1.211	1.759	2.581
GS-SC	1953–63	25	22	19	16	18	21	24	27	1.326	1.754	2.344
GS-DAY		26	25	22	18	17	18	21	25	1.101	1.460	2.124
GS-TRI	1953–55	26	22	17	14	17	21	26	29	1.460	2.339	3.168
GS-RRT	1953–55	25	24	22	18	18	19	21	25	1.099	1.326	1.929
GS-RRT2	1956–63	25	24	22	19	18	19	21	24	1.099	1.326	1.754
M1	1946–48	28	25	20	16	17	20	25	29	1.318	2.059	2.985
M2	1949–63	28	25	20	16	17	20	25	29	1.318	2.059	2.985
U1 C15	1959	30	27	23	18	20	23	27	32	1.278	1.761	2.667
U2 C15, B40	1960–64	26	27	23	18	17	23	27	32	1.303	1.795	2.719
U3 C15S, SS	1959–64	26	28	24	21	17	22	26	29	1.202	1.657	2.112
U4 C15T	1959–64	31	25	20	17	19	25	30	33	1.632	2.447	3.167
U5 C15S, SS	1965–66	26	28	24	21	17	22	26	29	1.202	1.657	2.112
U6 C15, B40	1965–66	26	27	23	18	17	23	27	32	1.303	1.795	2.719

Gearbox	Used	Mainshaft				Layshaft				Gear ratios		
		4	3	2	1	4	3	2	1	3rd	2nd	1st
U7 C15T	1965	31	25	20	17	19	25	30	33	1.632	2.447	3.167
U8 B25, B44, B50	1967–71	22	24	21	16	14	19	22	27	1.244	1.646	2.652
U9 C15, B44GP	1965–67	22	24	21	18	14	19	22	25	1.244	1.646	2.182
U9 B50MX	1971–73	22	24	21	18	14	19	22	25	1.244	1.646	2.182
U10 B40RR & M	1968	22	25	20	17	14	25	30	33	1.571	2.357	3.050

Sprockets, boxes and overall gear ratios

Model	Year	Sprockets				Overall ratio	Box type
		E	C	G	R		
D1	1949–63	17	38	15	47	7.004	D1 std
D1 comp	1950–55	17	38	15	58	8.643	D1 std
D3	1954–57	17	38	15	47	7.004	D1 std
D3 comp	1954–55	17	38	15	58	8.643	D1 std
D5	1958	17	38	16	46	6.426	D5
D7	1959–61	17	38	16	46	6.426	D7-1
	1962–66	17	38	16	47	6.566	D7-2
D7 Pastoral		17	38	14	58	9.260	D7-2
D7 Trail		17	38	14	80	12.773	D7-2
D10	1967	17	38	16	47	6.566	D10
D10S	1967	17	38	16	47	6.566	D10/4
D10B Pastoral	1967	17	38	16	58	8.103	D10/4
D10B Bushman	1967	17	38	16	47	6.566	D10/4
D14	1968	17	38	16	47	6.566	D14
D14B	1968	17	38	16	58	8.103	D14
D175	1969–71	17	38	16	47	6.566	D175
D175B	1969–71	17	38	16	58	8.103	D175

14-tooth gearbox option for D1 and D3 in 1950–55.

C10 & C11	1946–53	16	43	17	42	6.640	C
	1951–53	16	43	17	42	6.640	C4-1
C10L	1954–55	16	43	19	47	6.648	C
	1956–57	16	43	19	47	6.648	C4-2
C11G	1954–55	17	43	17	42	6.249	C
	1954–55	17	43	17	42	6.249	C4-1
C12	1956	17	43	17	42	6.249	C4-2
	1957–58	17	43	19	47	6.257	C4-2

17-tooth engine option for C10 and C11 in 1946–48.

B31	1946–48	17	43	18	42	5.902	B1
	1949–55	17	43	19	42	5.591	B2
	1954–59	17	43	19	42	5.591	B-s/a
B31 sidecar	1958–59	17	43	17	42	6.249	B-s/a
B32	1946–48	16	43	15	42	7.525	B1
	1949–53	16	43	16	42	7.055	B2
	1954–57	16	43	16	42	7.055	B32, B34
B32GS std	1949–52	17	43	19	42	5.591	GS
B32GS MX	1949–52	16	43	16	42	7.055	GS-MX
B32GS trials	1949–52	16	43	16	42	7.055	GS
B32GS race	1949–52	18	43	19	42	5.281	GS-C1, race
B32GS Club	1952	19	43	19	42	5.003	GS-C1, race
B32GS std	1953–56	17	43	19	42	5.591	GS-STD
B32GS MX	1953–57	16	43	16	46	7.727	GS-SC
B32GS MX	1959–62	16	43	16	46	7.727	GS-SC
B32GS trials	1953–55	16	43	16	42	7.055	GS-TRI
B32GS ISDT	1953–54	16	43	19	42	5.941	GS-STD
B32GS race	1953–55	18	43	19	42	5.281	GS-RRT

Model	Year	Sprockets E	C	G	R	Overall ratio	Box type
B32GS race	1956–57	18	43	19	42	5.281	GS-RRT2
B32GS Club	1953–55	18	43	19	42	5.281	GS-RRT
B32GS Club	1956–57	18	43	19	42	5.281	GS-RRT2
B32GS Club	1959–62	20	43	19	46	5.205	GS-RRT2
B33	1947–48	19	43	18	42	5.281	B1
	1949–55	19	43	19	42	5.003	B2
	1954–60	19	43	19	42	5.003	B-s/a
B33 sidecar	1958–60	17	43	19	42	5.591	B-s/a
B34	1947–48	17	43	18	42	5.902	B1
	1949	17	43	16	42	6.640	B2
	1950–53	20	43	16	42	5.644	B2
	1954–57	20	43	16	42	5.644	B32, B34
B34GS std	1949–52	19	43	19	42	5.003	GS
B34GS MX	1949–52	17	43	16	42	6.640	GS-MX
B34GS trials	1949–52	20	43	16	42	5.644	GS
B34GS race	1949–52	20	43	19	42	4.753	GS-C1, race
B34GS Club	1950–52	21	43	19	42	4.526	GS-C1, race
B34GS std	1953–56	19	43	19	42	5.003	GS-STD
B34GS MX	1953–63	17	43	16	46	7.272	GS-SC
B34GS trials	1953–55	20	43	16	42	5.644	GS-TRI
B34GS ISDT	1953–54	18	43	19	42	5.281	GS-STD
B34GS race	1953–55	21	43	19	42	4.526	GS-RRT
B34GS race	1956–57	21	43	19	42	4.526	GS-RRT2
B34GS Club	1953–55	21	43	19	42	4.526	GS-RRT
B34GS Club	1956–57	21	43	19	42	4.526	GS-RRT2
B34GS Club	1958–63	23	43	19	46	4.526	GS-RRT2

16-tooth engine option for B31 in 1946 and 16 to 19 teeth for B31, B33 and B34 in 1947–48; 15- and 17-tooth option for B32 in 1946–48.

Gold Star options were 16- to 23-tooth engine sprockets, 16- or 19-tooth gearbox and 43 standard or 44 option clutch. The 15-tooth engine option of the B32 was a Gold Star option for 1949.

Model	Year	Sprockets E	C	G	R	Overall ratio	Box type
M20	1946–48	19	43	18	42	5.281	M1
	1949–55	18	43	19	42	5.281	M2
M20 sidecar	1946–48	17	43	18	42	5.902	M1
	1949–55	16	43	19	42	5.941	M2
M21	1946–48	21	43	18	42	4.778	M1
	1949–63	20	43	19	42	4.753	M2
M21 sidecar	1946–48	17	43	18	42	5.902	M1
	1949–63	16	43	19	42	5.941	M2
M33	1948	21	43	18	42	4.778	M1
	1949–57	20	43	19	42	4.753	M2
M33 sidecar	1948	18	43	18	42	5.574	M1
	1949–57	17	43	19	42	5.591	M2

Options of 16- to 18-tooth engine sprockets for M20 in 1946–47 and 16 to 21 for 1948. For M21 options of 19 or 20 teeth for 1946–47 and 16 to 21 for 1948.

Unit engines

Model	Year	Sprockets E	C	G	R	Overall ratio	Box type
C15	1959	23	52	17	45	5.985	U1
	1960–64	23	52	17	45	5.985	U2
	1965–66	23	52	17	45	5.985	U6
	1966–67	23	52	17	45	5.985	U9
C15 sidecar	1962–64	23	52	16	46	6.500	U2
	1965–66	23	52	16	46	6.500	U6
	1966–67	23	52	16	46	6.500	U9
C15S	1959–61	23	52	16	56	7.913	U3
	1962–63	18	52	18	56	8.988	U3
	1964	23	52	15	60	9.043	U3
	1965	23	52	15	60	9.043	U5
C15T	1959–61	23	52	16	60	8.478	U4
	1962–63	18	52	18	56	8.988	U4
	1964	23	52	15	60	9.043	U4
	1965	23	52	15	60	9.043	U7
SS80	1961–63	23	52	17	45	5.985	U3
	1964	23	52	16	45	6.359	U3
	1965	23	52	16	45	6.359	U5
C15 Sportsman	1966	23	52	16	45	6.359	U5
	1966	23	52	16	45	6.359	U9
C25/B25	1967–70	23	52	16	49	6.924	U8
B25 Fleetstar	1969	23	52	16	52	7.348	U8
B25SS	1971	23	52	17	52	6.916	U8
B25T	1971	23	52	16	52	7.348	U8
B40	1961–64	23	52	19	46	5.474	U2
	1965	23	52	19	46	5.474	U6
B40 sidecar	1962–64	23	52	17	46	6.118	U2
	1965	23	52	17	46	6.118	U6
B40 Military	1968	23	52	17	49	6.517	U10
B40 Rough Rider		23	52	15	49	7.386	U10
SS90	1962–64	23	52	18	46	5.778	U3
	1965	23	52	18	46	5.778	U5
B44GP	1965–67	28	52	16	60	6.964	U9
B44VE	1966	28	52	18	52	5.365	U8
	1967	28	52	17	49	5.353	U8
B44VS	1967–70	28	52	17	49	5.353	U8
B44VR	1967	28	52	18	47	4.849	U8
B44SS	1968–70	28	52	17	47	5.134	U8
B50SS	1971	28	52	16	52	6.036	U8
	1972	28	52	17	47	5.134	U8
B50T	1971–72	28	52	15	52	6.438	U8
B50MX	1971–73	28	52	14	52	6.898	U9

Chains

C-range dynamo 1946–53: 8 × 5 mm diameter roller × 48 links

Primary drive

D range	1949–71	0.375 × 0.25 × 0.225 in. with 50 links
C range	1945–58	0.5 × 0.335 × 0.305 in. with 69–70 links
B range	1945–60	0.5 × 0.335 × 0.305 in. with 67–70 links
Gold Star	1949–63	0.5 × 0.335 × 0.305 in. with 66–71 links
M range	1945–63	0.5 × 0.335 × 0.305 in. with 68–70 links
Unit models	1959–73	0.375 × 0.25 × 0.225 in. duplex with 68–75 links

Model	Year	Links
D1, D3, D5, D7	1949–66	50
D10, D14, D175	1967–71	50
C range	1945–55	69
C10L	1954–57	69
C12	1956–58	70
B31	1945–55	69
B31 s/a	1954–59	67
B32	1946–53	68
	1954–57	67
B33	1947–55	70
B33 s/a	1954–60	68
B33 sidecar	1958–60	67
B34	1947–48	69
	1949–53	70
	1954–57	69

Gold Star

Model	Year	Links	Engine sprocket
B32GS	1949	68	
B34GS	1949	70	
B32GS, B34GS	1950–51	68	16
	1950–51	69	17, 18
	1950–51	70	19, 20
	1950–51	71	21
350 tourer	1952	69	
	1953–56	67	
350 trials	1952	68	
	1953–55	67	
350 scrambles	1952	68	
	1953–55	66	
	1956–62	67	
350 racing	1952	69	
	1953–55	68	
	1956–57	67	
350 Clubmans	1952	70	
	1953–55	68	
	1956–63	67	
500 tourer	1952	70	
	1953–56	68	
500 trials	1952	70	
	1953–55	69	
500 ISDT	1953–54	68	
500 scrambles	1952	69	
	1953–63	67	

Model	Year	Links
500 racing	1952	70
	1953–57	69
500 Clubmans	1952	71
	1953–57	69
	1958–63	70
M20	1945–55	69
M20 sidecar	1945–55	68
M21	1946–47	69
	1948–63	70
M21 sidecar	1946–63	68
M33	1948–57	70
M33 sidecar	1948–57	69
C15, SS80	1959–67	70
C15 Sportsman	1966	70
C15T, C15S	1959–61	70
	1962–63	68
	1964–65	70
B40, SS90	1961–65	70
B44GP, B44VE	1965–67	75
C25, B25	1967–71	70
B44VR	1967	75
B44SS, B44VS	1968–70	72
B50	1971–73	72

Final drive

D range	1949–71	0.50 × 0.335 × 0.205 in. with 116–128 links
C range	1949–55	0.50 × 0.335 × 0.305 in. with 104–107 links
C12	1956–58	0.50 × 0.335 × 0.305 in. with 114 links
C10L	1956–57	0.50 × 0.335 × 0.205 in. with 110 links
B range	1945–57	0.625 × 0.40 × 0.255 in. with 90–98 links
	1958–60	0.625 × 0.40 × 0.380 in. with 97–98 links
Gold Star	1949–57	0.625 × 0.40 × 0.255 in. with 91–98 links
	1958–63	0.625 × 0.40 × 0.380 in. with 98 links
M range	1945–63	0.625 × 0.40 × 0.255 in. with 94–98 links
Unit models	1959–66	0.50 × 0.335 × 0.305 in. with 112–127 links
C15, B44GP	1967	0.50 × 0.335 × 0.305 in. with 112–127 links
Unit models	1967–73	0.625 × 0.40 × 0.255 in. with 100–108 links

Model	Year	Links
D1	1949–55	116
D1 plunger	1950–63	117
D1 comp	1950–55	122
D1 comp, pl	1950–54	123
D3 plunger	1954–55	117
D3 comp	1954–55	122
D3 comp, pl	1954	123
D3 s/a, D5	1956–58	121
D7	1959–66	120
D10, D14, D175	1967–71	120
D10B	1967	122
D14B	1968	126
D175B	1969–70	128
C10, C11, C11G	1945–54	104
C plunger	1951–55	107
C10L	1954–57	110
C12	1956–58	114
B31	1945–46	90
	1947–48	91
	1949–51	92
	1952–54	93
B31 plunger	1949–55	96
B31 s/a	1954–59	98
B31 sidecar	1958–59	97
B32	1946–48	90
	1949–51	91
	1952–53	92
	1954–55	91
B32 plunger	1949–53	95
B32 s/a	1956–57	97
B33	1947–48	91
	1949–53	92
	1954	93
B33 plunger	1949–55	96
B33 s/a	1954–60	98
B34	1947	90
	1948–51	91
	1952–53	92
	1954–55	91
B34 plunger	1949	96
	1950–53	95
B34 s/a	1956–57	97

Gold Star

Model	Year	Links	Gearbox sprocket
B32GS	1949	95	
B34GS	1949	96	
B32GS, B34GS	1950–51	91	16, rigid
	1950–51	92	19, rigid
	1950–51	95	16, plunger
	1950	98	19, plunger
	1951	96	19, plunger
	1952–54	92	rigid frame
350 tourer	1952	96	
	1953–55	97	
	1956	98	

Model	Year	Links
350 trials	1952	95
	1953–55	96
350 ISDT	1953–54	97
350 scrambles	1952	95
	1953–62	98
350 racing	1952	96
	1953–55	97
	1956–57	98
350 Clubmans	1952	96
	1953–55	97
	1956–62	98
500 tourer	1952	96
	1953–55	97
	1956	98
500 trials	1952	95
	1953–55	96
500 ISDT	1953–54	97
500 scrambles	1952	95
	1953–63	98
500 racing	1952	96
	1953–55	97
	1956–57	98
500 Clubmans	1952	96
	1953–55	97
	1956–57	98
	1958–63	99

M20	1945–55	95
M20 plunger	1951–55	97
M21	1946–58	95
M21 plunger	1951–63	97
M21 s/c, pl	1959–63	98
M33	1948	94
	1949–55	95
M33 plunger	1951–57	97
C15	1959	113
	1960–67	112
C15T	1959–61	123
	1962	122
	1963	120
	1964–65	122
C15S	1959–63	120
	1964–65	122
SS80	1961–65	112
C15 Sportsman	1966	112
B40	1961–65	116
B40 sidecar	1965	114
SS90	1962–65	115
B44GP	1965–67	127
B44VE	1966	121
	1967	100
C25, B25	1967–70	100
B25 Fleetstar	1969	101
B25	1971	108
B44VR, B44SS	1967–70	100
B44VS	1968–70	100
B50SS	1971	108
	1972	105
B50T	1971–72	107
B50MX	1971	107
	1972–73	106

15 Wheels, brakes, tyres

Brake diameters

Model	Year	Front (in.)	Rear (in.)
D1	1949–63	$5 \times \frac{5}{8}$	$5 \times \frac{5}{8}$
D1 comp	1950–53	$5 \times \frac{5}{8}$	$5 \times \frac{5}{8}$
	1954–55	$5\frac{1}{2} \times 1$	$5 \times \frac{5}{8}$
D3	1954–57	$5 \times \frac{5}{8}$	$5 \times \frac{5}{8}$
D3 comp	1954–55	$5\frac{1}{2} \times 1$	$5 \times \frac{5}{8}$
D5	1958	$5 \times \frac{7}{8}$	$5 \times \frac{7}{8}$
D7	1959–66	$5\frac{1}{2} \times 1$	$5\frac{1}{2} \times 1$
D7 Trail	1963–65	$5 \times \frac{5}{8}$	$5\frac{1}{2} \times 1$
D7 Pastoral	1963–65	$5\frac{1}{2} \times 1$	$5\frac{1}{2} \times 1$
D10, D14, D175	1967–71	$5\frac{1}{2} \times 1$	$5\frac{1}{2} \times 1$
C10, C11	1946–53	$5\frac{1}{2} \times 1$	$5\frac{1}{2} \times 1$
C10L	1954–57	$5\frac{1}{2} \times 1$	$5 \times \frac{5}{8}$
C11G	1954	$5\frac{1}{2} \times 1$	$5\frac{1}{2} \times 1$
	1955	$7 \times 1\frac{1}{8}$	$5\frac{1}{2} \times 1$
C12	1956–58	$7 \times 1\frac{1}{8}$	$5\frac{1}{2} \times 1$
B31	1946–55	$7 \times 1\frac{1}{8}$	$7 \times 1\frac{1}{8}$
	1956–57	$7 \times 1\frac{1}{2}$	$7 \times 1\frac{1}{2}$
	1958–59	$7 \times 1\frac{1}{8}$	$7 \times 1\frac{1}{8}$
B32	1946–57	$7 \times 1\frac{1}{8}$	$7 \times 1\frac{1}{8}$
B33	1947–52	$7 \times 1\frac{1}{8}$	$7 \times 1\frac{1}{8}$
	1953–55	$8 \times 1\frac{3}{8}$	$7 \times 1\frac{1}{8}$
	1956–57	$7 \times 1\frac{1}{2}$	$7 \times 1\frac{1}{2}$
	1958–60	$7 \times 1\frac{1}{8}$	$7 \times 1\frac{1}{8}$
B34	1947–57	$7 \times 1\frac{1}{8}$	$7 \times 1\frac{1}{8}$
Gold Star	1949	$7 \times 1\frac{1}{8}$	$7 \times 1\frac{1}{8}$
	1950–63	$8 \times 1\frac{3}{8}$	$7 \times 1\frac{1}{8}$ road, race, Clubmans
	1950–63	$7 \times 1\frac{1}{8}$	$7 \times 1\frac{1}{8}$ trials, scrambles
	1956–63	190 mm × 2	$7 \times 1\frac{1}{8}$ Clubmans
M20	1946–55	$7 \times 1\frac{1}{8}$	$7 \times 1\frac{3}{8}$
M20 plunger	1951–55	$7 \times 1\frac{1}{8}$	$7 \times 1\frac{1}{8}$
M21	1946–55	$7 \times 1\frac{1}{8}$	$7 \times 1\frac{3}{8}$
M21 plunger	1951–55	$7 \times 1\frac{1}{8}$	$7 \times 1\frac{1}{8}$
	1956–63	$8 \times 1\frac{3}{8}$	$7 \times 1\frac{1}{8}$
M33	1948–55	$7 \times 1\frac{1}{8}$	$7 \times 1\frac{3}{8}$
M33 plunger	1951–55	$7 \times 1\frac{1}{8}$	$7 \times 1\frac{1}{8}$
	1956–57	$8 \times 1\frac{3}{8}$	$7 \times 1\frac{1}{8}$
C15	1959–67	$6 \times \frac{7}{8}$	$6 \times \frac{7}{8}$
C15T	1959–61	$6 \times \frac{7}{8}$	$6 \times \frac{7}{8}$
	1962–65	$7 \times 1\frac{1}{8}$	$6 \times \frac{7}{8}$
C15S	1959–61	$6 \times \frac{7}{8}$	$6 \times \frac{7}{8}$
	1962–65	$7 \times 1\frac{1}{8}$	$6 \times \frac{7}{8}$
SS80	1961–65	$6 \times \frac{7}{8}$	$6 \times \frac{7}{8}$
C15 Sports	1966–67	$6 \times \frac{7}{8}$	$6 \times \frac{7}{8}$
C25, B25	1967–68	$7 \times 1\frac{1}{8}$	$7 \times 1\frac{1}{8}$
B25	1969–70	$7 \times 1\frac{9}{16}$ 2LS front	$7 \times 1\frac{1}{8}$
B25SS	1971	$8 \times 1\frac{1}{2}$	$7 \times 1\frac{1}{8}$
B25SS export	1971	$6 \times \frac{7}{8}$	$7 \times 1\frac{1}{8}$
B25T	1971	$6 \times \frac{7}{8}$	$7 \times 1\frac{1}{8}$
B40	1961–65	$7 \times 1\frac{1}{8}$	$6 \times \frac{7}{8}$
SS90	1962–65	$7 \times 1\frac{1}{8}$	$6 \times \frac{7}{8}$
B44GP	1965–66	$7 \times 1\frac{1}{8}$	$6 \times \frac{7}{8}$
	1967	$7 \times 1\frac{1}{8}$	$7 \times 1\frac{1}{8}$
B44VE	1966	$7 \times 1\frac{1}{8}$	$6 \times \frac{7}{8}$
	1967	$7 \times 1\frac{1}{8}$	$7 \times 1\frac{1}{8}$
B44VR	1967	$7 \times 1\frac{1}{8}$	$7 \times 1\frac{1}{8}$
B44SS	1968	$8 \times 1\frac{5}{8}$	$7 \times 1\frac{1}{8}$
	1969–70	$7 \times 1\frac{9}{16}$ 2LS front	$7 \times 1\frac{1}{8}$
B44VS	1967	$7 \times 1\frac{1}{8}$	$7 \times 1\frac{1}{8}$
	1968–70	$8 \times 1\frac{5}{8}$	$7 \times 1\frac{1}{8}$
B50SS	1971–72	$8 \times 1\frac{1}{2}$	$7 \times 1\frac{1}{8}$
B50T	1971–72	$6 \times \frac{7}{8}$	$7 \times 1\frac{1}{8}$
B50MX	1971–73	$6 \times \frac{7}{8}$	$7 \times 1\frac{1}{8}$

Tyre sizes

Model	Year	Front (in.)	Rear (in.)
D1	1949–63	2.75 × 19	2.75 × 19
D1 comp	1950–55	2.75 × 19	3.25 × 19
D3	1954–57	2.75 × 19	2.75 × 19
D3 comp	1954–55	2.75 × 19	3.25 × 19
D5	1958	3.00 × 18	3.00 × 18
D7	1959–66	3.00 × 18	3.00 × 18
D10, D14, D175	1967–71	3.00 × 18	3.00 × 18
D10B, D14B	1967–68	3.00 × 19	3.00 × 19
D175B	1969–70	3.00 × 19	3.25 × 18
C10	1946–53	3.00 × 19	3.00 × 19
C11	1946–51	3.00 × 20	3.00 × 20
	1952–53	3.00 × 19	3.00 × 19
C10L	1954–57	2.75 × 19	2.75 × 19
C11G	1954–55	3.00 × 19	3.00 × 19
C12	1956–58	3.00 × 19	3.00 × 19
C12 option	1957–58	3.00 × 19	3.25 × 19 to order

Model	Year	Front (in.)	Rear (in.)
B31	1946–59	3.25 × 19	3.25 × 19
B32	1946–57	2.75 × 21	4.00 × 19
B33	1947–60	3.25 × 19	3.50 × 19
B34	1947–57	2.75 × 21	4.00 × 19
Gold Star	1949–51	2.75 × 21	4.00 × 19 plus options
350 cc	1952–55	3.00 × 21	3.25 × 19 road use
350 cc	1956	3.00 × 19	3.25 × 19 road use
500 cc	1952–55	3.00 × 21	3.50 × 19 road use
500 cc	1956	3.00 × 19	3.50 × 19 road use
trials	1952–53	3.00 × 21	4.00 × 19
trials	1954–55	2.75 × 21	4.00 × 19
ISDT	1952–55	3.00 × 21	4.00 × 19
scrambles	1952–53	2.75 × 21	4.00 × 19
scrambles	1954–63	3.00 × 21	4.00 × 19
350 Cl/race	1952–55	3.00 × 21 option 3.00 × 19	3.25 × 19
350 Cl/race	1956–57	3.00 × 19	3.25 × 19
500 Cl/race	1952–55	3.00 × 21 option 3.00 × 19	3.50 × 19
500 Cl/race	1956–57	3.00 × 19	3.50 × 19
500 Clubmans	1958–63	3.00 × 19 option 3.00 × 21	3.50 × 19
500 MX USA	1958–63	3.00 × 21	3.50 × 19
M20	1946–55	3.25 × 19	3.25 × 19
M21	1946–63	3.25 × 19	3.50 × 19
M33	1948–57	3.25 × 19	3.50 × 19
C15	1959–67	3.25 × 17	3.25 × 17
C15T	1959–65	3.00 × 20	4.00 × 18
C15S	1959–61	3.00 × 20	3.50 × 19
	1962–65	3.00 × 20	4.00 × 18
SS80	1961–65	3.25 × 17	3.25 × 17
C15 Sports	1966–67	3.25 × 17	3.25 × 17
C25, B25	1967–71	3.25 × 18	3.50 × 18
B25T	1971	3.00 × 20	4.00 × 18
B40	1961–65	3.25 × 18	3.50 × 18
SS90	1962–65	3.25 × 18	3.50 × 18
B44GP	1965–67	3.00 × 20	4.00 × 18
B44VE	1966–67	3.25 × 19	4.00 × 18
B44VR, B44SS	1967–70	3.25 × 18	3.50 × 18
B44VS	1967–70	3.25 × 19	4.00 × 18
B50	1971–72	3.25 × 18	3.50 × 18
B50T	1971–72	3.00 × 20	4.00 × 18
B50MX	1971–73	3.00 × 20	4.00 × 18

Rim part numbers

Model	Year	Front	Rear
D1	1949–52	90-5504/18	90-5504/18
	1953–57	90-5504/3	90-5504/3
	1958–63	90-5504/3	90-6159/3
D1 comp	1950–52	90-5505/18	90-5505/18
	1953–55	90-5505/3	90-5505/3
D3	1954–55	90-5504/3	90-5504/3
D3 comp	1954–55	90-5505/3	90-5505/3
D3 s/a	1956–57	90-5504/3	90-5504/3
D5	1958	90-5674	90-6180
D7	1959–66	90-6203	90-6203
D7 Pastoral	1963–65	90-6203	90-6237
D7 Pastoral (Brit. Guiana)		90-6203	90-6247
D7 Trail	1963–65	90-5505	42-5866 D1 forks
	1963–65	90-5684	42-5866 D7 forks
D7 GPO	1967	90-6203	90-6271
D10, D10S	1967	90-6203	90-6271
D10B	1967	90-5684	90-6288
D14/4 & /4S	1968	90-6203	90-6271
D14/4B	1968	90-5684	90-6288
D175	1969–71	90-6203	90-6271
D175B	1969–70	90-5684	90-6271
C10 girder	1946	29-5553	29-5553
C10	1946–53	29-5776	29-5776
C11 girder	1946	29-5554	29-5554
C11	1946–51	29-5777	29-5777
	1952–53	29-5776	29-5776
C11 d/l	1948–51	29-5777/14	29-5777/14
C10L	1954–55	90-5504/3	90-5504/3
	1956–57	29-5776/3	90-6155/3
C11G	1954	29-5776/3	29-5776/3
	1955	29-5959	29-5776/3
C12	1956–58	29-5991	29-5991
B31, B33	1946–48	65-5871	65-6263
	1949–54	67-5543	65-6263
B31, B33 pl	1949–55	67-5543	67-6005
B31, B33 s/a	1954–55	67-5543	67-6005
	1956–57	42-5637	42-5637
	1958–60	42-5810	42-5810
B32, B34	1946–48	65-5916	65-6267
	1949–53	65-5916	65-6263
	1954–55	65-5916	42-6002
B32, B34 pl	1949–53	65-5916	65-6298
B32, B34 s/a	1954–57	65-5916	42-6002

Gold Star

Model	Year	Front	Rear
Gold Star	1949	65-5916	65-6298
Clubmans	1949–52	65-5927	65-6306
	1949–52	65-5936	65-6306
	1953	42-5509	65-6306
	1954	42-5509	42-6306
	1955–57	42-5509	65-6306
	1958–63	42-5509	42-6306
	1953–63	42-5510	65-6308
	1954–57	65-5927	42-6008
	1954–57	65-5936	42-6010
	1956–63	42-5550	42-6306
	1956–63	42-5551	65-6308
	1956–63	42-5588	42-6008
	1956–63	42-5589	42-6010
trials	1953–55	65-5916	42-6002
scrambles	1953	65-5916	42-6002
	1954–63	42-5523	42-6002
M20, M21	1946–48	66-5482	66-6054
M33	1948	66-5482	66-6054
M20, M21, M33	1949	65-5871	66-6054
	1950–55	67-5543	66-6054
	1956	67-5543	66-6077
M20, M21, M33 pl	1951–63	67-5543	67-6005
C15	1959–67	40-5507	40-5507
SS80	1961–65	40-5507	40-5507
C15S	1959–64	40-5538	40-6047
	1965	40-5544	40-6044
C15T	1959–64	40-5538	40-6044
	1965	40-5544	40-6044
C15 USA	1962	40-5542	40-6044
	1962	40-5542	40-6067
	1962	40-6044	40-6044
	1965	67-5599	40-6044
C25	1967	40-5552	40-6080
B25	1968–70	37-1373	40-6080
B25SS home	1971	37-3785	37-3785
B25SS	1971	37-3892	37-3785
B25T	1971	37-3795	37-3784
B40	1961–65	41-6006	41-6006
SS90	1962–65	41-6006	41-6006
B40E	1964–65	67-5599	40-6044
B40 Rough Rider	1969	37-2093	42-6372
B40 Military	1967	37-2093	42-6372
B44GP	1965–67	41-5535	42-6371
B44VE	1966	67-5599	40-6044
	1967	67-5599	42-6371
B44VR	1967	40-5552	40-6080
B44VS	1967	67-5599	42-6371
	1968–70	68-5556	42-6371
B44SS	1968	37-1374	40-6080
	1969–70	37-1373	40-6080
B50SS	1971–72	37-3785	37-3785
B50T	1971–72	37-3795	37-3784
B50MX	1971–72	37-3795	37-3784
	1973	37-4151	37-3784

Rims—sizes

Part no.	Size	Spokes	Used
29-5553	WM1-19	40	1946
29-5554	WM1-20	40	1946
29-5776	WM1-19	40	1946–57
29-5777	WM1-20	40	1946–52
29 5959	WM1-19	40	1955
29-5991	WM1-19	40	1956–58
37-1373	WM2-18	40	1968–70
37-1374	WM2-18	40	1968
37-2093	WM2-18	40	1967, 1969
37-3784	WM3-18	40	1971–73
37-3785	WM2-18	40	1971–72
37-3795	WM1-20	40	1971–72
37-3892	WM2-18	40	1971
37-4151	WM1-21	40	1973
40-5507	WM2-17	40	1959–67
40-5538	WM1-20	40	1959–64
40-5542	WM2-19	40	1962
40-5544	WM1-20	40	1962, 1965
40-5552	WM2-18	40	1967
40-6044	WM3-18	40	1959–66
40-6047	WM1-19	40	1959–64
40-6067		40	1962
40-6080	WM2-18	40	1967–70
41-5535	WM1-20	40	1965–67
41-6006	WM2-18	40	1961–65
42-5509	WM1-19	40	1953–63
42-5510	WM1-19 LA	40	1953–63
42-5523	WM1-21	40	1954–63
42-5550	WM1-19	40	1956–63
42-5551	WM1-19 LA	40	1956–63
42 5588	WM2-19	40	1956–63
42-5589	WM2-19 LA	40	1956–63
42-5637	WM2-19	40	1956–57
42-5810	WM2-19	40	1958–60
42-5866	WM2-19	40	1963–65
42-6002	WM3-19	40	1953–63
42-6008	WM2-18	40	1954–63
42-6010	WM2-18 LA	40	1954–63
42-6306	WM2-19	40	1954, 1956–63
42-6371	WM3-18	40	1965–70
42-6372	WM3-18	40	1967, 1969
65-5871	WM2-19	40	1946–49
65-5916	WM1-21	40	1946–55
65-5927	WM1-21	40	1949–52, 1954–57
65-5936	WM1-21 LA	40	1949–52, 1954–57
65-6263	WM2-19	40	1946–55
65-6267	WM2-19	40	1946–48
65-6298	WM2-19	40	1949–53
65-6306	WM2-19	40	1949–53, 1955–57
65-6308	WM2-19 LA	40	1953–63
66-5482	WM3-19	40	1946–48
66-6054	WM3-19	40	1946–63
66-6077	WM3-19	40	1956
67-5543	WM2-19	40	1949–63
67-5599	WM2-19	40	1964–67
67-6005	WM2-19	40	1949–63
68-5556	WM2-19	40	1968–70
90-5504	WM1-19	36	1949–63
90-5505	WM1-19	36	1949–55, 1963–65
90-5674	WM1-18	36	1958

Part no.	Size	Spokes	Used
90-5684	WM1-19	40	1963–65, 1967–70
90-6155	WM1-19	36	1956–57
90-6159	WM1-19	36	1958–63
90-6180	WM1-18	36	1958
90-6203	WM1-18	40	1959–71
90-6237	WM1-18	40	1963–65
90-6247	WM2-18	40	
90-6271	WM1-18	40	1967–71
90-6288	WM1-19	40	1967–68

Tyre equivalents

Section Original	Low profile	Metric
2.75	3.10	80/90
3.00	3.60	90/90
3.25	3.60	90/90
3.50	4.10	100/90
4.00	4.25/85	110/90

Revolutions per mile

3.25 × 17	865
3.00 × 18	853
3.25 × 18	831
3.50 × 18	812
4.00 × 18	787
2.75 × 19	850
3.00 × 19	831
3.25 × 19	794
3.50 × 19	777
4.10 × 19	816
3.00 × 20	782
2.75 × 21	791
3.50 × 19 s/c	803

Data from Avon Tyres Ltd.
Sidecar tyre included for reference.

K. Ratcliffe in the 1953 Senior Manx GP on his 348 cc Gold Star

16 Headlamp, ammeter and switches

These varied and moved about over the years, and while much of the data given below is also to be found in the main text, this summary may be useful. The headlamp may have a separate shell or be fitted with a cowl or to a nacelle. The lights and ignition switches could be separate or combined into one assembly.

Bantam

D1	1949–51	Separate shell with cable-operated switch mounted on bars.
	1950–53	Lucas-equipped models with separate shell with switch and ammeter in top.
	1952–53	Wipac-equipped models with switch in shell top.
D1, D3, D5	1954–58	As 1952 with cowl added.
D1	1959–63	As 1954.
D7	1959–63	Nacelle with switch.
	1964–66	Nacelle with two switches.
D10, D14	1967–68	Silver and Supreme with nacelle, two switches and optional main-beam warning light.
D10S, D14S	1967–68	Separate shell with two switches and optional main-beam warning light in centre.
D10B	1967	Bushman as D10S. Pastoral with separate shell with one central switch.
D14/4B	1968	As D10B Pastoral.
D175	1969–71	Separate shell with two switches.
D175B	1969–70	As D10B Pastoral.

C range

C10, C11	1945–52	Separate shell with small panel carrying combined ignition and light switch and ammeter.
	1953	As 1952 plus ignition warning light between switch and ammeter.
C10L, C11G	1954–55	Cowled shell with combined switch for lights and ignition.
C10L	1956–57	Cowled shell with two switches.
C12	1956–58	Combined lights and ignition switch on right side panel and ammeter in headlamp shell.

B range	1945–52	Separate shell with small panel carrying light switch and ammeter.
	1953–57	Cowl with light switch on left and ammeter on right for road models; competition models continued as before when supplied with lights.
	1958–60	Nacelle with combined lights and ignition switch on right and ammeter on left.
Gold Star	1949–63	Separate shell with small panel carrying light switch and ammeter.
M range	1945–52	Separate shell with small panel carrying light switch and ammeter.
	1953–57	Cowl with light switch on left and ammeter on right.
	1958–63	No cowl so as 1952.
C15	1959–61	Nacelle with ammeter on left and light switch on right. Ignition switch on centre panel, facing forward and to right side.
	1962–67	Ignition switch with key, otherwise as 1959.
C15T	1959–65	Shell with both on/off and dip-switches mounted in it.
B40, SS80	1961	As C15.
	1962–65	As C15.
SS90	1962–65	As C15.
SS90 USA	1965	Separate shell with ammeter right and light switch left.

C15 Sp	1966	Separate shell with ammeter on right and light switch on left.
B40E	1965	As C15T.
C25, B25	1967	Separate shell with ammeter in centre and light switch behind it. Ignition switch on left side under seat nose. Red main-beam warning light on left of light switch.
B25	1968–69	As 1967 except toggle switch for lights.
	1970	As 1968 but with red and green warning lights for oil pressure and main beam.
	1971	Separate shell with central turn switch for lights and warning lights in red for oil pressure, green for main beam and amber for indicators. Ignition switch in left side of electrics box.
B44VE	1966–67	As C15T.
B44VS	1967	As C15T.
	1968	Separate shell with toggle light switch, dip-switch and warning light in it. Ignition switch on left side under seat nose.
	1969–70	As 1968 but with red and green warning lights.
B44VR	1967	As C25.
B44SS	1968–70	As B25 with toggle switch for lights.
B50	1971–72	As B25 except no red warning light, so only green and amber ones.

Bantam-tuner George Todd (on the right) discusses the 1967 D10 Supreme during the time he worked at the BSA factory

17 Seating

This could be either a saddle, or dualseat option in place of this, or a dualseat as standard. Below are listed the standard and optional fitments for the various models.

Model	Year	Standard	Optional	For years
D1	1949–63	Saddle	Dualseat	1953–63
D3	1954–55	Saddle	Dualseat	1954–55
D3 s/a	1956–57	Dualseat	Saddle	1956–57
D5	1958	Dualseat	Saddle	1958
D7	1959–66	Dualseat	Short seat	1962–66
D7 Pastoral		Short seat British Guiana model		
D7 GPO	1967	Short seat		
D10, D14	1967–68	Dualseat		
D10S, D14S	1967–68	Dualseat with rear hump		
D10B, D14B	1967–68	Dualseat		
D10B	1967	Short seat Pastoral model		
D175	1969–71	Dualseat		
C10, C11	1945–53	Saddle	Dualseat	1953
C10L	1954–57	Saddle	Dualseat	1954–57
C11G	1954–55	Saddle	Dualseat	1954–55
C12	1956–58	Dualseat	Saddle	1956–58
B31, B33	1945–55	Saddle	Dualseat	1952–55
B31, B33 s/a	1954–60	Dualseat	Saddle	1954–60
B32, B34	1946–57	Saddle	Dualseat	1952–57
Gold Star	1949–52	Saddle	Dualseat	1952
	1953–63	Dualseat	Saddle	1953–63
	1953–55	Saddle for some versions		
			Feridax racing	1956–63
	Scrambles		Short dualseat	1956–63
M range	1945–63	Saddle	Dualseat	1952–63
C15	1959–67	Dualseat		
C15T	1959–65	Short dualseat		
C15S	1959–65	Short dualseat		
SS80, B40	1961–65	Dualseat		
C15 Sp	1966–67	Dualseat with rear hump		
SS90	1962–65	Dualseat		
B40E	1964–65	Short seat		
B44GP	1965–67	Short seat		
B44VE	1966	Short seat		
	1967	Dualseat with rear hump		
C25, B25	1967–70	Dualseat with rear hump		
B44VR	1967	Dualseat with rear hump		
B44SS	1968–70	Dualseat with rear hump		
B44VS	1967–70	Dualseat with rear hump		
B25	1971	Dualseat		
B50	1971–72	Dualseat		
B50MX	1971–73	Short seat		

Picture indexes

These are compiled in date order, by machine and by item to give the maximum benefit. Owing to restrictions on space, it is not possible to have a picture of each side of every model for every year, but by using these indexes it is often possible to find a picture that helps. This is because the cycle parts were often common for several models in any one year, so any picture from that year will help. Thus one of a C15 will help with a B40, while a D7 can assist a D14.

So look for your model and year but also check other models of the same year. It can also be worth looking at the same model in the years before and after, as the feature you are checking may not have changed. Some of the references are for detail parts only, so check the index, list the relevant pages and have a look at each to see if it helps.

Picture index by year

Picture index by model

Component picture index

Index

Eddie Dow negotiating the Devil's Staircase during the 1953 Scottish Six Days Trial, riding a B32 Gold Star

Bob Currie testing a 1962 D1 Bantam which was still much as when introduced but was soon to be dropped from the range

Books scheduled in this series are
BSA Singles Restoration
BSA Twin Restoration
Matchless & AJS Restoration
Norton Twin Restoration
Triumph Twin Restoration

Other hardback books from Niton Publishing are
AJS & Matchless – the postwar models
Ariel – the postwar models
BMW Motorcycles
BSA Gold Star & Other Singles
BSA Twins & Triples
Honda – the early classic motorcycles
Kawasaki – Sunrise to Z1
Kawasaki – Z1 to Ninja
Norton Singles
Norton Twins
Royal Enfield – the postwar models
Suzuki Two – Strokes
Triumph Singles
Triumph Twins & Triples
Velocette Flat Twins
Villiers Singles & Twins

Illustrated Buyer's Guides by Roy Bacon
BSA – the postwar models
Norton – the postwar models
Triumph – the postwar models

Motorcycle Monographs by Roy Bacon
AJS & Matchless Singles 1945–1969
AJS & Matchless Twins 1948–1969
Ariel Leader & Arrow 1958–1965
BMW Postwar Models 1949–1969
BSA Bantam 1948–1971
BSA A7/A10 Twins 1946–1963
BSA A50/A65 Twins 1962–1972
BSA Pre-Unit Singles 1937–1963
BSA Rocket 3 & Triumph Trident 1968–1976
BSA Unit Singles 1958–1973
Ducati V-Twins, bevel drive 1971–1986
Norton Commando 1968–1977
Norton Dominator Twins 1949–1970
Norton Singles, OHV & SV 1931–1966
Triumph T90 & T100 Unit Twins 1960–1974
Triumph T100 & T110 1939–1961
Triumph T120 1959–1974
Triumph T140 1973–1988
Triumph Touring Twins 1938–1966
Velocette Viper, Venom & Thruxton 1956–1970

For a full list of titles contact Niton Publishing,
P. O. Box 3, Ventnor, Isle of Wight, PO38 2AS